Tourist Experiences

ASPECTS OF TOURISM

Series Editors: **Chris Cooper** (*Leeds Beckett University, UK*), **C. Michael Hall** (*University of Canterbury, New Zealand*) and **Dallen J. Timothy** (*Arizona State University, USA*)

Aspects of Tourism is an innovative, multifaceted series, which comprises authoritative reference handbooks on global tourism regions, research volumes, texts and monographs. It is designed to provide readers with the latest thinking on tourism worldwide and in so doing will push back the frontiers of tourism knowledge. The series also introduces a new generation of international tourism authors writing on leading edge topics.

The volumes are authoritative, readable and user-friendly, providing accessible sources for further research. Books in the series are commissioned to probe the relationship between tourism and cognate subject areas such as strategy, development, retailing, sport and environmental studies. The publisher and series editors welcome proposals from writers with projects on the above topics.

All books in this series are externally peer-reviewed.

Full details of all the books in this series and of all our other publications can be found on https://www.channelviewpublications.com, or by writing to Channel View Publications, St Nicholas House, 31-34 High Street, Bristol, BS1 2AW, UK.

ASPECTS OF TOURISM: 98

Tourist Experiences

Insights from Psychology

**Chris Ryan and
Xiaoyu (Nancy) Zhang**

CHANNEL VIEW PUBLICATIONS
Bristol • Jackson

DOI https://doi.org/10.21832/RYAN9240
Library of Congress Cataloging in Publication Data
A catalog record for this book is available from the Library of Congress.
Names: Ryan, Chris, author. | Zhang, Xiaoyu, author.
Title: Tourist Experiences: Insights from psychology / Chris Ryan and Xiaoyu (Nancy) Zhang.
Description: Bristol, UK; Jackson, TN: Channel View Publications, [2024] | Series: Aspects of Tourism: 98 | Includes bibliographical references and index. | Summary: "This book explores the application of psychological theories to tourist behaviour and experience. It offers new insights and provides final year and postgraduate students with an understanding of core psychological perspectives and an accessible resource within one volume for those researching tourist behaviour and consumer experiences"—Provided by publisher.
Identifiers: LCCN 2023038107 (print) | LCCN 2023038108 (ebook) | ISBN 9781845419233 (paperback) | ISBN 9781845419240 (hardback) | ISBN 9781845419257 (pdf) | ISBN 9781845419264 (epub)
Subjects: LCSH: Tourism—Psychological aspects.
Classification: LCC G156.5.P79 R93 2024 (print) | LCC G156.5.P79 (ebook) | DDC 910/.019—dc23/eng/20231016
LC record available at https://lccn.loc.gov/2023038107
LC ebook record available at https://lccn.loc.gov/2023038108

British Library Cataloguing in Publication Data
A catalogue entry for this book is available from the British Library.

ISBN-13: 978-1-84541-924-0 (hbk)
ISBN-13: 978-1-84541-923-3 (pbk)

Channel View Publications
UK: St Nicholas House, 31-34 High Street, Bristol, BS1 2AW, UK.
USA: Ingram, Jackson, TN, USA.

Website: https://www.channelviewpublications.com
Twitter/X: Channel_View
Facebook: https://www.facebook.com/channelviewpublications
Blog: https://www.channelviewpublications.wordpress.com

The policy of Channel View Publications is to use papers that are natural, renewable and recyclable products, made from wood grown in sustainable forests. In the manufacturing process of our books, and to further support our policy, preference is given to printers that have FSC and PEFC Chain of Custody certification. The FSC and/or PEFC logos will appear on those books where full certification has been granted to the printer concerned.

Typeset by Deanta Global Publishing Services, Chennai, India.

Contents

Tables and Figures

Preface

First Author's Note

This book was motivated by several factors, including (a) a desire to acknowledge a debt to past teachers and friends, (b) to provide a text that showed the linkages between past and present research in the application of psychological theories to tourist behaviour and (c) to provide that text within one volume that could be accessible to students and those commencing research into the nature of visitor experiences.

So, from the perspective of the first author, the book is dedicated to Charles Perkins, the only teacher that really kindled in me a sense of curiosity when I was a schoolboy, to Emeritus Professor Eric Hall of Nottingham University who introduced me to humanistic psychology when I studied for my MEd (Psychology) and to my dear friend, the late Philip Pearce, who like me had a qualification in psychology. Phil so sadly passed away far too soon, and I have fond memories of him, whether teaching clapping songs to one of my doctoral students, or of an extremely pleasant afternoon we spent on a drive to Hobbiton in New Zealand, along with many other occasions. He was a delight and of course, a challenge as we compared our different perspectives. As I finish this book, yet another fond colleague has also passed away, and that was Keith Hollinshead. With Phil, I drank wine and with Keith, beer. Both left an indefinable but definite mark on my memory and work.

The book was also motivated by a comment made by a review of my teaching curriculum for a second-year undergraduate degree course, namely, why are so few of the papers being cited in journals like *Tourism Management* being drawn from earlier years? My answer was long-winded and probably did not satisfy the questioner, but it did make me wonder if the seminal works from researchers such as Erik Cohen, Peter Murphy, Dick Butler, Doug Pearce, Keith Hollinshead, Mike Hall and of course Phil Pearce, were wholly known by a current group of researchers who are seemingly entranced by statistical methods but are unfamiliar with the evolutionary patterns of conceptual development that was being initiated more than 60 years ago. Equally, it is suspected that many tourism scholars are unaware of the nuances that exist in a tradition of psychology stretching back to the early 20th century that still inform the scales and psychometrics being used today.

Equally, as a past editor of *Tourism Management*, I also wonder to what degree undergraduates and first-year master's degree students would be able to understand many of the papers now appearing in that, and other journals. The contemporary rubric of publishing that limits word lengths of articles, and the continued emphasis on publishing a 'new' concept or finding (possibly more an aspiration rather than a reality) means that few authors can spend the time establishing historic links across several decades of research publications, and thus students may not develop a sense of continuity in tourism research, particularly with reference to the 'visitor experience'. In addition, writing in 2023 when two or three years of undergraduate study have been disrupted by the Covid pandemic, and being mindful that for the next couple of years university entrants will also have experienced many lost months of school education, it seemed to us that a single volume that contained a history and outline of developing psychological theories applied to tourism would be of service for students and new teaching staff. This is what Phil did initially several decades ago (Pearce, 1982), and I hope he would appreciate this updating of those ideas.

Finally, Nancy as second author puts me to shame with her very generous assessment of my past teaching, and I can only confirm that she has a steady hand in making sure that my references are correct, that the choice of topics is appropriate, and is of course a guide in ensuring the text can be understood by students.

The Second Author's Perspective

I must start by saying what a pleasure it has been to work on this book with the first author, Professor Chris Ryan. It is now more than a decade since I was a master's student at the University of Waikato; Chris gave my methodology lectures, where he would talk for hours without notes, discussing topics ranging from tourism to philosophy. Every one of his lectures was like a spiritual journey for me, in which I could immerse myself. (I recall one of his Management School colleagues describing him as 'a book that can speak'!) It was Chris's lectures that attracted me to tourism studies, opening the door to a larger world where I could appreciate the length, breadth and depth of this fascinating academic discipline. His discussions of the applicability of psychological and philosophical theories to tourism scholarship influenced my own research in this field. (I remember one of the examiners of my PhD thesis, Professor Geoffrey Wall, being very pleased with my discussion of the psychoanalytic theory of Jacques Lacan, praising it as a pearl in my thesis). Hence, it was an honour to be able to collaborate with Chris on a textbook. It is my hope that both current and future generations of tourism students and researchers will benefit from Chris's insights and wisdom.

Like Chris, I believe that by reviewing the history of the development of psychological and philosophical theories in tourism studies, the student of tourism will acquire some important foundational knowledge that will better equip them to engage with their university coursework and the body of literature on this fascinating topic. I further believe that readers outside of the classroom will profit from our discussion of the topics covered in this book. Our treatment of the theories of tourists' motivations and behaviours will be of interest to tourism providers wanting to understand their customers better. Tourists too will gain insights into their own behaviour from reading this book. For example, enthusiasts of adventure tourism will find our discussion of Flow Theory particularly interesting, as the theory offers an explanation of the psychological state these tourists can enter into when engaging in their favourite leisure pursuits.

Finally, it has been said that a person is the sum of places they have visited and the 'places' to which their thoughts have taken them. Hence, tourism, as I have discovered, can be an important component of a happy and fulfilling life, making it a subject worthy of study.

Structure of the Book

The book contains 10 chapters. The first serves as an introduction to the themes of the book after initially discussing definitions of the tourist and tourism. It highlights the role of holidays in the creation of memories, and it is those memories that provide benefits for the tourist long after the holiday is concluded. Holidaying is an act of consumption where the purchaser is not buying a tangible item, and at best, they are buying a right to use. A right to buy an airline seat, a hotel room, the knowledge of a guide or the presumed right to take photographs of place, self or others. It is a presumed right, and that presumption might not always be correct. In an age when images become important, so too are the rights over images, and it is argued that each individual has a right to their own image, especially in an era of social media. There are contrary rights. For example, as individuals we have the expectation that the State will protect its citizens, and the State will, at times, argue that it needs surveillance to protect the community and hence will wish to, at the very least, have records of individuals who travel, and that can also mean a right to your photographs and facial image. This is not discussed in detail in Chapter 1, but Chapter 1 does pose a model of holiday events – each of which has unique experiences associated with it, including the scripted occasions of hotel or airline check-ins.

Chapter 2 discusses the motivations for holiday taking, commencing with a standard discussion of 'push' and 'pull'. That is, the relationship between the desire for a holiday and the attributes of a destination that can meet those desires is a standard feature of tourism psychology. Equally though, desire is a reflection of personality and how people respond to the patterns of work life and the stresses of that work life. Coping behaviours are in part determined by personality, and hence the chapter considers both personality and societal work patterns that create the demand for holidays.

Chapter 3 suggests that gaps may exist between (a) the expectations derived from past holiday experiences and the images that are consumed from people's use of media and the images promoted on websites and (b) the actual destination and accommodation and encounters at the destination. For this chapter, conventional gap analysis is used based on earlier work by Oliver (1977, 1981) and the various papers by Parasuraman *et al.* (1994a, 1994b) in which they explain the ServQual model and subsequent applications of the concept applied to tourism such as HOLSAT (Tribe & Snaith, 1998).

In Chapter 4, reference is again made to humanistic psychology commencing with the sense of flow (Csikszentmihalyi, 1975, 1990a, 1990b) and how the holidaymaker becomes involved with place and activities. Such involvement leads to satisfaction and the benefits derived from that satisfaction. From this perspective, it was argued by Phil Pearce that as tourists build up experiences of holidaying it becomes possible to develop a travel career. As is stated in Chapter 5, at an intuitive level this makes much sense. However, initial papers using this theory began to find that the evidence did not support the original thesis based on Maslow's (1968, 1970) hierarchy of needs. Consequently, Pearce generated an approach that was more dynamic than the original linear progression through the hierarchical stages.

In Chapter 6, one of the aspects that create a more complex environment is examined. Drawing on the paper by Yiannakis and Gibson (1992) and subsequent research, the chapter analyses the ways in which tourists adhere to or change roles as they age and progress through life stages. The chapter also links to the work of Beard and Ragheb (1980, 1983) and the Leisure Motivation Scale because as people gain both travel experience and age, so the motivations behind travel change. Society also changes over time and increasingly the industry is adjusting to a perceived demand for 'authentic' experiences. It has also been argued that such a demand has been intensified by the lockdowns experienced globally due to Covid. Such periods meant that the ability to interact with others and to explore beyond the confines of home were severely restricted, and various commentators suggested that when taking into account environmental degradation, there would be an opportunity to reset tourism based on principles of sustainability. It is too soon to assess whether this 'regeneration' will occur, and from the viewpoint of these authors there seems little likelihood of those hopes being immediately realised. Much will depend on the rapidity of technological change that will permit more sustainable travel combined with better demand management based on advanced booking systems.

Chapter 7 uses long-debated questions: how authentic is the tourist experience, and how strong is the desire for an authentic historical and cultural truth? Is the tourist truly seeking 'authenticity', especially in an age when individuals can identify 'truths' from the sources they select in social media? What are the implications of such debates for the design of tourist experiences?

Chapter 8 considers one of the phenomena that has encouraged more travel, namely the ownership of holiday homes and the formation of place attachment. In many developed countries that have experienced economic growth for decades, and in a period when an aging population is seeking second homes in desirable places, partly with a longer-term intention relating to retirement, the phenomenon of second home ownership has become more common. That trend has been reinforced through such homes becoming an asset that supplements income through peer-to-peer web-based services such as Airbnb. The consequences of this movement are significant for health provision services, and property development and prices. Place attachment is thought to have entered the domain of tourism research through the seminal work of Coppock (1977) on holiday homes, but more recently research has absorbed the concepts of place attachment into residents' reactions to tourism-induced change. It is suggested that the pendulum may yet swing back to tourist demand in societies where an affluent baby boomer generation begins to look for desirable retirement locations.

Chapter 9 examines an area in which Phil Pearce was establishing an interest in his papers on the perceptions of time and indeed an escape from the continuous demands of the internet (Pearce, 2020). In short, why do holidays often seem to pass so quickly? The chapter examines the nature of experienced time and delves back into Roman times when it is found that how we measure timekeeping has had significant social implications. It is suggested that holidays are periods when people are free from the tyranny of the clock. The final chapter seeks to identify and draw together the implications of the previous chapters with an emphasis on lessons that might be learnt for the design of tourism experiences.

While there is a logical sequence to the chapters, the authors are well aware that the reader may well not pick up the book to commence reading from the first to the final page. Therefore, there are cross-references within the chapters to other chapters. Equally, while discussing and comparing research results, the reader will note critical comments are made of various studies and techniques. The motive behind such critical comments is not to necessarily imply significant faults in the studies, and indeed the critiques made will often reflect the original authors' own awareness of the problems they have encountered in their studies. Rather, the criticisms are made to prompt the reader to read more critically and not to accept statements as beyond contestation. Additionally, from time to time, in drawing comparisons between concepts one finds (or at least the present authors felt) a repetition of findings that are hidden behind the semantics. A study might be held out as making a new contribution to the literature, but perhaps that contribution is one of new terminology, perhaps because the author was unaware of an earlier literature.

Finally, we would wish to thank the staff at Channel View for their help and support – as always a lovely group of people with whom to work. Additionally, we would wish to thank Heather Gibson for permitting us to replicate the original diagram from her paper with Andrew Yiannakis on the roles that tourists play.

1 Introduction

This chapter includes:

(a) Definitions of the tourist and tourism.
(b) Conceptual and practical differences between tourism, recreation, leisure, tourists and visitors.
(c) The societal and personal roles of holidays.
(d) Holidays as periods of difference.
(e) The temporal construct of holidays.

Introduction

The purpose of this chapter is to introduce several themes to provide a holistic overview of the succeeding chapters. A holistic viewpoint is thought important because it provides a framework for which the succeeding chapters will complete the details. It also provides a signpost for the reader in that it helps to assess how the following chapters contribute to the whole. In several senses, the heart of this chapter is to be found in Figures 1.1 and 1.2, which adopt a chronological sequence from the initial search for information about a potential tourist destination, through the journey of reaching the destination and experiencing the place, to the final return home. Each stage produces its own experiences, but not all stages are of equal importance. Yet, each stage possesses opportunities that may make or mar the holiday. It is also further suggested that the return home is not the end of the holiday, but rather subsequent memories may well reconstruct the holiday into new sets of meanings as one reflects on what has happened in the light of subsequent life. But, to begin at the beginning, how is a tourist defined?

Defining the Tourist and Visitor

At the heart of tourism lies the experience of the tourist. If that experience is a satisfying one, the tourist may be motivated to return to the destination or attraction or may be motivated to repeat the process of travel or holidaymaking, or indeed recommend an activity or place to a friend. Two titles for this book presented themselves – 'Tourist Experiences' and 'Visitor Experiences'. Which is thought best lies in definitions and pragmatism! Often a tourist is defined as someone who requires overnight accommodation when away from home. This definition is taken from the World Tourism Organization and was primarily derived from a need to record statistical data. It is a common definition accepted globally. But, as a definition, it is silent about the purpose of the trip and the activity that gives rise to the demand for accommodation. It is also a definition about a process of travel – put simply, one is away from home. Yet, for many people, tourism is not merely about travel, it is about holidaying. And thus, one immediately starts to make distinctions, for obviously not all travel is about holidaying. People may travel to spectate or participate in sporting events, travel for conferences or to conduct business, and often travel involves more than one function.

While the terms 'visitor' and 'tourist' are often used interchangeably, there are, as indicated distinctions. Indeed, if someone visits family or friends, and the visit includes overnight accommodation, going out for a meal, attending a sporting event or going to a tourist attraction, then the group comprising family and/or friends being entertained at the different venues comprises both local and non-local persons. Thus, if one adopts a pragmatic viewpoint, from the perspective of the restaurateur, the sports stadium or the tourist attraction, all visitors are important, and the objective of the business is to generate satisfactory experiences for all clients, whether local people, those visiting local people or indeed visitors from overseas.

The 2014 Eurostat Report commented on this situation by observing that:

> The statistical definition of tourism is broader than the common definition employed on an everyday basis, as it encompasses not only private trips but also business trips. This is primarily because tourism is viewed from an economic perspective, whereby private visitors on holiday and visitors making business trips have broadly similar consumption patterns (transport, accommodation, and restaurant/catering services). *As such, it may be of secondary interest to providers of tourism services whether their customers are private tourists on holiday or visitors on a business trip.* (Eurostat, 2014: 188, emphasis in original)

For his part, taking a more holistic view Ryan defines tourism as 'The demand for, and supply of, accommodation and supportive services for those staying away from home and the resultant patterns of (a) expenditure, income creation and employment that are created, (b) the social, cultural and environmental consequences that flow from visitation and (c) the psychological changes that result for both visitor and host' (Ryan, 2003b: 26). This definition adopts the wider perspectives of tourism as being more than just an economic activity. That economic imperative initially tended to dominate earlier literatures as tourism academics sought to stress the importance of their subject by justifying tourism university degrees by appeals to the economic impacts of the industry, especially in countries such as the UK and subsequently Australia and New Zealand. Ryan's definition sought to broaden the basis of study by locating tourism squarely with environmental and sustainability concerns and he went further to note the impact of psychological changes for both tourists and host communities as did Pearce. Where such initial attempts might be criticised is that the use of careful wording of 'consequences' and 'changes' failed to make explicit that such consequences may be positive or negative, or indeed potentially both as, for example, economic change may be positive but create social disruption. In short, the analysis was particularised rather than systemised into broader harmonic systems that became more evident by 2020.

One implication is that a tourism business could be catering for both local people and tourists and generally will be attempting to provide both with the best possible experience. Hence, tourism studies are allied closely to studies of recreation and leisure, and these disciplines tend to draw upon a common set of theories derived from sociology and psychology when treating subjects such as perceptions, motivations and intentions when applied to predicting behaviour. Equally, when seeking to explain behaviour, similar theories are again applied. From the marketing perspective, all the activities associated with tourism, recreation and leisure pursuits tend to draw from concepts derived from marketing, psychology and sociology such as the use of values, attitudes and lifestyle scales.

Tourism, however, does differ from leisure and recreation in the importance it attributes to places as destinations. Perceptions of places are important for many reasons. Those perceptions and the images of place held by the potential visitor gain importance because first, in order to attract a potential tourist, the tourist must be aware of the existence of the place and the facilities it offers. In the language of marketing, the destination must reside within an awareness set in the mind of the tourist. This is often referred to as a cognitive function – that is, the tourist holds a set of facts held to be true about the place. These represent the visitor's knowledge of the destination. Second, the facts are evaluated by the potential tourist, and hence the destination marketeer seeks to persuade the holidaymaker that a place is attractive. The judgements made by the holidaymaker are affective in nature – that is, the holidaymaker assesses a place as attractive, to be worth visiting, or decides on a contrary view. If the contrary view is held, then a destination possesses an inept value – that is, the potential visitor knows of the destination (the cognitive) but has decided not to visit because it is thought to be unattractive (an emotional, affective judgement). Before proceeding further, it can be noted that a potential visitor can be mistaken as to their 'alleged knowledge' of place – something to be analysed later in this book.

In standard psychological theory, an attitude is defined by three characteristics – the cognitive and the affective that together create the third, known as the conative (Pearce, 2013). This is the predisposition to action, or alternatively the formation of an intention to act in a given way. However, the psychology literature is replete with studies that indicate that linkages between the formation of an intention and actual behaviour are far from certain, as discussed later in the book commencing with Chapter 2. In addition to the uncertainty about intention not being acted upon, tourism possesses several other features that weaken the linkage. People often talk about a 'once in a lifetime experience' or having 'a bucket list' – that is, of having a list of places to visit and things they wish to do before they die. In fast-moving consumer goods marketing theory, a commonplace is that it is easier to get the consumer to repeat a purchase than to attract a new consumer. So, the 'loyal consumer' is one who buys the same brand each time when visiting the supermarket. By the same token, destination marketeers would like to create a destination loyal clientele who return each year to the same place (Bianchi & Pike, 2011; Kim & Brown, 2012; Yoon & Uysal, 2005). This is contrary to the logic of the 'once in a lifetime experience' and especially if the 'once in a lifetime destination' is far from the visitor's home or is expensive to reach. Hence, geography and economics have a role to play in shaping the visitor's intention to visit a tourist destination, and in these considerations, tourism again differs from leisure and recreation.

McKercher and Chan (2005) also pointed out another truism about tourism, which is that people may not be loyal to a place but may be loyal to an activity. From this perspective, the tourist may have a particular hobby and interest, and so chooses locations that enable him or her to engage in an activity. For example, someone interested in water sports, such as sailing, or wind or kite surfing, might take a holiday in known windy destinations in the Mediterranean, Caribbean or Pacific Islands in different years. The activity is constant, but the destination varies. If, however, one destination is found to be more attractive, then repeat visits may follow and eventually place attachment might result.

The concept of place attachment was originally derived from environmental psychology (Guiliani, 1991; Hidalgo & Hernandez, 2001; Korpela, 1989; Lalli, 1992; Twigger-Ross & Uzzell, 1996) and human geography (Lewicka, 2011; Relph, 1976) and has come to play an important role in tourism literature. Initial studies in tourism seem to have emerged from studies of those who purchased holiday homes and date from the 1970s and 1980s (Brown & Raymond, 2007; Brown et al., 2002). At that time, which obviously predates the internet and services such as Airbnb or Tujia, people generally purchased a coastal or mountain home primarily for holiday purposes and would visit such a place as frequently as possible. In countries such as New Zealand, the coastal 'bach' – and in Canada, the lakeside cabins or cottages – became

family-based accommodation lacking refinements but creating intergenerational memories of care-free holidays based on one's escape to nature
and ignorance of the clock (Kearns & Collins, 2006; Keen & Hall, 2004;
Selwood, 2006; Svenson, 2004). Place attachment is thus associated with
frequent visits to a loved place that permits the development of nostalgic feelings (Scannell & Gifford, 2010). One problem facing destination
marketeers in the 2020s is that, unlike the period from the 1930s to the
1990s when such basic holiday places were popular, these destinations
tend to change much more rapidly than in the past. The place of holiday
escape becomes developed, the humble cottages become more sophisticated, the spread of internet and smartphones denies isolation and by
the same token many holiday homes become a commercial service due
to peer-to-peer services offering holiday rentals over the internet.

Yet concepts of place attachment remain important in the tourism literature because the impacts of tourism-induced change are far from neutral. Residents see their homes changing. There are many studies of the
changes induced by services like Airbnb (Suess, Woosman & Erul, 2020;
Suess *et al.*, 2020). Infrastructure changes, retail services develop and
indeed several countries, including notably China, specifically use tourism as an economic driver of change to alleviate the problems of poverty
in previously economically marginalised areas. While residents of tourist
destinations are not the primary focus of this book, nonetheless the issue
of place attachment from this perspective has a role to play in this text.
Holidaymakers loyal to a destination to the point of investing in a second
home can be perceived as a 'temporary resident' and they too have their
own experiences of place change. These issues are also explored later in
the book in Chapter 8.

The Tourist Attraction and Hoteliers' Dilemma

Consequently, to write about tourist experiences is a complex matter.
The tourist experience is determined to a large degree by the quality of
service offered by the attractions, services and accommodation found at
the destination. But, from the viewpoint of an attraction manager or a
hotelier, this means that they are providing a place or set of facilities that
are relatively constant for a period of time for a far from homogeneous
clientele. The implications of this for the tourist attraction business, or
for a hotelier, can be easily shown with just a few minutes of thought. For
example, the total number of guests within a hotel or users of a tourist
attraction might well be comprised of any one or more of the following:

• International holidaying tourists.
• International business travellers.
• International visitors visiting friends and relatives.
• Domestic holidaying tourists.

- Domestic business travellers.
- Domestic visitors visiting friends and relatives.
- Day trippers.

Then, in addition, one can go on to distinguish guests on the basis of the duration of their trip, visit and motives for being present.

In short, each of the above classifications of clients may have different motivations. In addition to the classifications listed above, one can also note that people may be at different stages of their trip. Consequently, again different scenarios exist, including:

- Some may be at the start of their stay – and may still be fresh and looking to explore the area where they are staying.
- Some may be in the middle of their stay – still interested in the location but perhaps beginning to anticipate returning home.
- Some may be coming to the end of their stay – possibly tired of travel and wanting or not wanting to return home.

Additionally, people have used different modes of transport to arrive at their destination and thus:

- Cars are convenient – but on arrival at the destination some may be tired from a long drive.
- Others may be airline travellers – so was it a short flight or an overnight flight. It is possible that perhaps due to overnight flights, an inability to sleep on the aircraft and potentially disturbed diurnal patterns of night and day, these travellers may feel tired upon arrival and not immediately ready to start a holiday.

Such considerations lead to the conclusion that the antecedents of the visit can impact on the quality of the visit experience.

The above text indicates that many contextual issues help to shape the experience of the visitor both before and during their trip, but the anticipation of, and the experience at the time of activity or consumption of the tourism offer are linked in the mind of the tourist. When the tourist is deciding where to go for a holiday, the decision is influenced by the images found on the internet through the webpages of online travel agents (OTAs), such as Expedia.com, Tripadvisor, Ctrip and many others, and through videos seen on YouTube, TikTok and numerous other services. In addition to these are other internet-based sources of information seen through networks of online friends including Meta (Facebook), WeChat and Weibo, plus blogs that may be maintained by others. In addition, personal offline contacts from family and friends still retain importance (Misui & Kamata, 2015; Prayag & Ryan, 2011). If a booking is made through a travel agency, then the conversation with the travel agent may help shape any final decision. Throughout this process of information acquisition there is also the creation of images in the mind of the tourist leading to expectations of the place to be visited and the activities in which to be engaged (Francken & Van Raaij, 1979; Gartner, 1989, 1994; Mansfeld, 1992).

Consequently, upon arrival the tourist possesses a set of expectations as to what will happen, and these expectations possess importance because they establish criteria by which the trip will be judged. If the photographs shown on a hotel's webpage portray a swimming pool, might the tourist be disappointed if the swimming pool is not as large as was imagined? Then again if the adventure activity is not sufficiently challenging, might that engender disappointment? These questions imply that the advertiser must retain a truth in their advertising, and in today's internet-based information system a failure not to present a truthful situation will quickly be commented upon by the traveller responding to the OTA's requests for assessments of the hotel, location or activity. In short, a reinforcing network of peer-interaction on the internet helps to establish an image and expectation that the advertised place will satisfy the tourist expectation. Given this, it is not surprising that a significant stream of tourism research is into the relationships between image creation, the internet and expectation formation (Frías *et al.*, 2008; Kaosiri *et al.*, 2017; Narangajavana *et al.*, 2017).

The evaluation of the holiday does not cease upon the return home. The holiday becomes a memory – but the memory is selective in highlighting more memorable parts of the recent experience. These may be based upon unexpected occurrences that have been labelled as critical incidents (Petrick *et al.*, 2006; Pritchard & Havitz, 2006; Wang *et al.*, 2000) that may have enhanced an experience. These unexpected occurrences may also be negative experiences – for example, a bout of traveller's stomach upsets or missed connections. Yet even such negative experiences, once the traveller is home, can become stories of difficulties overcome and are weaved into a memory that lends satisfaction during any process of recall of the holiday.

It therefore seems that the total holiday experience is not confined to the period of the holiday alone. The construction of experience commences with the anticipation of a place before the holiday commences. Indeed, that anticipation is informed by recall of past holidays, perhaps even by recall of past visits to the same destination. In short, there is a halo effect from the past that informs the present (Han, 1989; Richard *et al.*, 2019, 2021). The holiday becomes a subject of future recall and may be a comfort of remembering past good times as the tourist ages and times change. It can be said there is a temporal component to the holiday experience that takes the form of a sequence: anticipation – involvement – recall; and in this process each holiday helps shape expectations for future holidays.

Holidays – Source of Personal and Social Change

Holidays can stand out in the memory of any individual's lifespan. For many people work is characterised by patterns of routine. The same patterns of work are repeated time and time again for many weeks, months, perhaps even years. The holiday is a break from that pattern of repetition and is an escape from routine. In that sense the holiday is truly an 'extra-ordinary' period because it represents an escape from the ordinary. If our personalities are shaped by our social interactions, then arguably the holiday is important for the formation of an individual's character because each escape from routine represents opportunities for relaxation, for challenge, for finding oneself, for being momentarily different. Inherent in each holiday period is a challenge for each holiday might demonstrate that our daily life could be different.

It is not for nothing that past research has shown that specific seasonal patterns can exist when people access counselling services (McCarthy & Saks, 2019). It is suggested that holidays may be periods when adults, who, because of work commitments, have fallen into routines that leave little time for their families to be together in emotionally meaningful ways, will often use the holiday to better promote family bonding (Jepson et al., 2019). Alternatively, as noted by Backer and Schänzel (2013), the holiday is an 'obli-cation' and one that may bring into the open dysfunctioning between partners. There is also a linkage between the demand for sexual counselling in post-holiday periods (Wellings et al., 1999) and sexually transmitted disease testing that indicates holiday periods may even be periods of irresponsibility.

It has been observed that escape and relaxation can involve play, but adults do not play as children do (Gram, 2005; Nickerson & Jurowski, 2001). The play of children is often characterised by imagination, learning and frivolity yet adults appear to be more constrained (Barnett, 2011; Podilchak, 1991). But if holidays are periods of escape, should they not also be periods of fun? Podilchak (1991) identified three components of fun, namely (a) doing things on the surface – being silly, laughing, not serious, (b) escaping from activity and being purposeless and (c) being exciting, exhilarating – unique, and not an everyday, experiences. It is suggested that this is akin to Maslow's (1968, 1970) concepts of self-fulfilment and personality maturation in that the self-actualised person retains senses of wonderment as well as self-independence. As developments in technology begin to free people from being a 'cog in the machine' as demonstrated by Charlie Chaplin in his film *Modern Times* (a Marxian analysis one might observe), the role of holidays begins to be of importance for social well-being (Krippendorf, 1999). Krippendorf tended to Durkheim's (1984/1893) concepts of an anomic society, arguing that an anomic society created a functionally oriented modern holiday industry where people are holiday takers rather than holidaymakers.

Today, technology has skewed the situation from the former to the latter – people are increasingly organisers of their own holidays, can seek like-minded people and thus create a much wider diversity of holiday experiences. The retreat from top-down modernity is found in many countries demonstrated by holidays based in meditative Asian belief systems (Jiang *et al.*, 2018; Song & Yan, 2020) or the utilisation of virtual reality gaming as a holiday product (Merkx & Nawijn, 2021).

It would seem that over time (notwithstanding the impact of Covid for much of 2020 and 2021) holidays are changing in form and in terms of the experiences they offer to a growing number of holidaymakers. In doing so the opportunity for holidays to be cathartic is growing. Holidays can be literally life changing as the first author saw while being a windsurfing instructor for a holiday company in the last decades of the 20th century as past clients came back to the location as instructors or to set up a new business, thereby changing their lifestyles. This potential catharsis was caught by Willy Russell in his 1988 play 'Shirley Valentine'. This concept of cathartic change has certainly been noted by several female researchers such as Eugenia Wickens in a series of publications (Alexander *et al.*, 2010; Wickens, 2000, 2002, 2006; Wickens & Harrison, 1996; Wickens & Sönmez, 2007), while additionally several writers have spoken of western female sex tourists picking up male lovers in the Caribbean beach resorts (Taylor, 2001) or in Kenya (Kisia-Omondi & Ryan, 2023).

Consequently, on closer examination it can be seen that holidays involve far more than simply assessing whether the tourist enjoys him or herself. Their very structure reflects the nature of our society. Indeed, it can be questioned whether a society structured in such a way that makes holidays such a necessity for so many people is itself a successful society. That so many people need an 'escape' from their daily routines is, in itself, a critique of the nature of those routines. The above commentary introduces the notion that holidays might be life changing, that the holiday experience is shaped by expectations gained from images derived increasingly from the internet and social media, and furthermore in the recall of past holidays, people may be engaged in a restructuring of past experiences to shape yet future holiday behaviours.

Two further complexities can be introduced at this stage, and they form the subject of the next two sections of this chapter. Thus far, the holiday has been defined as an 'escape', thereby implying that it is a search for something different. But in a world tied together by access to the internet and media such as television and films, many of the images people consume become increasingly familiar. Hence, the question about the motivation for holiday taking can be reversed. Rather than a search for difference, is the real reason for holidaying a search for something made familiar to the tourist and which is attractive to the holidaymaker? For example, a symbol of Paris is the Eiffel Tower, and for many people a trip to Paris is not complete unless they see the Tower. Equally, in the prior discussion, many of the comments made about the nature of holidaying are premised in a belief that the 'holiday experience' is a holistic experience, but it is possible to develop an alternative view. This is the contention that a holiday is a series of sequential experiences, being sequentially linked but each for the most part standing alone. These two topics comprise the subject of the next two sections of this introductory chapter.

The Holiday Experience – A Search for the Familiar? Or the Unfamiliar?

For much of the time the analyses of holidays have assumed that holidays are periods away from the ordinary routines of life as noted above. Among those who endorsed but equally critically examined this view was the late Graham Dann. In his book, *The Language of Tourism: A Sociolinguistic Perspective* (Dann, 1996), he used the concept of *différance* drawing upon the work of French social commentators such as Jacques Derrida. The word *différance* was used by Derrida as a hybrid based on 'difference' and 'deferment' and applies to situations where a word signifies a 'difference', but the meaning is 'deferred' so that meaning is only glimpsed as a vague concept subject to possible erasure. Dann attributed such characteristics to tourism. In his earlier work, Dann (1981), commentating on MacCannell's (1973) theory that recreational travel was the result of an intrinsic desire, suggested that holidays were the outcome of what came to be termed 'push' and 'pull' factors. The push factor was both a socially and psychologically determined factor that motivates a need to travel and to go somewhere else, while the pull factors were the attributes of place that permitted the tourist to meet those needs. For example, a need to escape a city could be met by a place offering beautiful rural landscapes.

When examining the literature of the early 1970s and 1980s one finds that often the search to seek somewhere different was based on a concept of an anomic society, that is, a society containing flaws that denied individual self-fulfilment (Dann, 1977; Krippendorf, 1987). Consequently, the analysis was generally articulated by references to an escape from a place. These concepts are discussed in much more detail in Chapter 2.

Richard Prentice (again sadly deceased) posed an alternative viewpoint. Writing at the dawn of the internet age, Prentice (2004) suggested that the marketing of tourism was premised on creating familiarity because this was a key to attracting repeat purchasing. He identified five forms of familiarity, namely FAM1: informational; FAM2: experiential; FAM3: proximate; FAM4: self-described; and FAM5: educational (Prentice, 2004: 927). He suggested that tourists had come to know places through the imagery created by the marketing of destinations and activities, and in this process of learning had become familiar with the roles they had to play. For example, when an adventure tourist went white water rafting for the first time, they 'knew' what they had to do and the nature of the experience they were embarking on. They chose the activity because it was one they had seen and wished to replicate for themselves, and in selecting this activity it reinforced their own self-image as being adventurous. In these sentiments one can see the precursors of a later literature of the roles that tourists play as described by Andrew Yiannakis and Heather Gibson (Gibson & Yiannakis, 2002; Yiannakis & Gibson, 1992).

This perspective raises the notion that the terminology of 'escape' has at least two perspectives. It is either or both an escape *from* a situation and an escape *to* a place or activity. This concept is also explored in more detail in Chapter 2.

'Escape' as a word represents a dynamic of change, and change can be stressful and require procedures of change. The role of stress in the holiday experience has also been the subject of examination. One of the foundational texts examining stress generally is the work of Gray (1987). Gray notes that stress can either be a facilitating or debilitating force. As an example of the former, many athletes have noted the anticipation of competition as a stress that motivates (Mellalieu *et al.*, 2021), while the latter is exemplified when someone is unable to cope with stress and thus is unable to fulfil their potential (Tuten & Neidermeyer, 2004). Gray (1987) therefore notes that determinants of stress generally involve four determining factors, namely, *intensity* – the demands of the task and self-assessment of ability to cope with those demands, *social interaction* – the relationships incurred in being part of a group, *novelty* – the creation of concern by being in a new and unfamiliar environment, and *specific situations* – the development of perceived threat within a specific set of circumstances.

There are components of the holiday situation where stress might occur, for example, being in a foreign country where one lacks language skills, although today technology can offer immediate translation on a handheld device or smartphone. Equally, again, the same technologies provide maps to help tourists find their way through an unfamiliar city, but nonetheless evidence does show examples of stress occurring. One such example cited in the literature is the concern expressed by females in unfamiliar circumstances (Valentine, 1989; Wilson & Little, 2008).

Pearce (2019) in his chapter entitled 'Behaving Badly', also comments on irresponsible behaviours that represent forms of 'escape'. Travel to destinations where one is unknown bestows a form of anonymity on the tourist that can lead to forms of indulgent behaviour that would not normally be undertaken. These behaviours can range from theft of items from hotels to excessive use of alcohol and sex with strangers. Holidays are associated with images of hedonism and thus an escape from senses of responsibility. Citing Eldridge and Roberts' (2008: 24) descriptions of hen parties as 'drunken excess and embarrassing misdemeanours [of women] … adopting the very worse qualities of "masculine" behaviour … and boisterous (sexually suggestive or inviting) behaviour', Pearce notes the 'strong sense of empowerment by these groups of women who can use their solidarity to reclaim a place in the night entertainment scene' (Pearce, 2019: 290). One can note that hen and stag parties have been a characteristic form of British holidays to places such as Estonia, Prague and Tenerife (Carlisle & Ritchie, 2021) accompanied by the old sporting phrase, 'what happens on the field stays on the field'. Such has been the concerns expressed that, as Pearce (2019) notes, some locations have been trying to ban such party holidays. Yet, returning to the classification of stress generated by Gray (1987) it can be noted that social relationship, novelty of place (and anonymity), specific circumstances and intensity (a strong drive towards hedonism) all play a role as not stressful but as facilitating factors determining a mode of holiday behaviour.

In the final chapter of *Tourism Behaviour: An Essential Companion*, Fesenmaier and Pearce (2019) note that holiday experiences possess importance because they represent searches for meaning. While the current authors concur with this sentiment and would add that holidays are also often a search for self, and who one is, such viewpoints raise a question – is the holiday a holistic experience or a series of possibly unconnected experiences?

Holiday Experiences – A Total Experience or a Series of Unconnected Experiences

DeCrop (2006) and Hergesell *et al.* (2019) enumerate the decisions that are made when considering holidays. They list the items shown in Table 1.1.

Table 1.1 A typology of holiday-taking decisions

Subject of decision	Definition
Accommodation	Types of accommodation range from hotels to campsites via homestays and boutique hotels, and a mixed type of accommodation may be used
Travelling companion	Family members, friends and business partners
Activities	The activities undertaken range from sunbathing to adventure
Attractions	Types of activities from hiking to theme parks
Budget and expenditure	Budget available and use of budget across various headings
Destination	Places visited categorised by types, cultures and number
Duration	Ranging from short to long stays
Catering and food	From fast foods to special cuisines, and types of food outlets from street stalls to speciality restaurants
Organisation	From self-booking to organised tours, or any mix of both
Season	Summer, autumn, winter or spring – each has its own characteristics
Purchases	Shopping for souvenirs, duty free, planned or spontaneous
Route	From flights to within destination travel determines sightseeing
Mode of transport	From aircraft to hiking via driving and cycling

If one adds a temporal component to this framework, it becomes more evident that any holiday requires a sequence of events from the initial decision to take a holiday to the eventual return home. Summarising the earlier discussion on the formation of place image, one can formulate the initial stages as shown in Figure 1.1. First, there needs to be an awareness of a destination as capable of meeting the holidaymaker's needs, both functional and emotional, thus, second, leading to the conative by actually selecting and booking a holiday.

However, the choice marks only the completion of the first stage of the model. The second part relates to the actual experiences resulting from that choice, and begins with the travel to the destination, and the nature of the experiences gained by viewing attractions and interacting with others at the destination. These stages are shown in Figure 1.2. The process of holiday enjoyment can be perceived as being a sequence of stage evaluations. The trip to the destination is associated with factors such as the ease of the journey (e.g. car parking at the airport, the check-in process), comfort (the quality of the flight and service provided) and an absence of delays and the final approach to the accommodation that is to be used. Each of these stages represents opportunities for 'critical incidents' (Bitner *et al.*, 1990; Edvardsson & Roos, 2001). These incidents are said to possess the characteristic of being an unexpected occurrence that 'makes or breaks' the total experience. If arrival at the required destination occurs without undue negative elements, then it is unlikely that, in most cases, the flight, car drive or coach ride is going to adversely impact the final assessment of the total holiday. As Ryan (1994) observed, one can think of this stage of the holiday as being akin to Herzberg's hygiene factors. That is, the occurrence of a good flight, or a trouble-free car ride will not in themselves generate high levels of holiday satisfaction, but

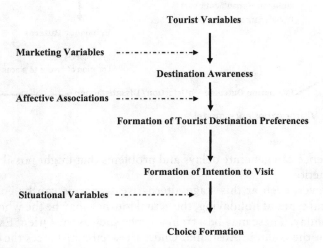

Figure 1.1 A process of choice formation

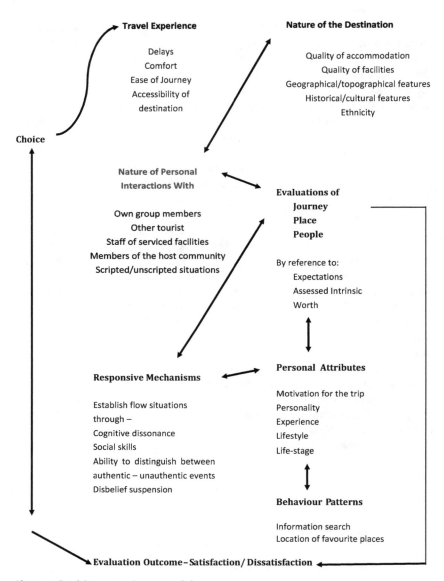

Figure 1.2 Visitor experience model

their absence can generate delays and problems that might possibly cause dissatisfaction.

However, even at this stage alternative scenarios can be envisaged. For several types of holidaying, the actual journey may be the whole point of the holiday. These may be a train journey such as the Orient Express in Europe or the Ghan in Australia. Under these circumstances the comfort of the trip becomes an expected component of the total experience, and again given the reputation of these two products, a negative experience may indeed 'spoil' the holiday. For more adventurous hiking holidays that involve camping, the actual journey may again be the purpose of the holiday and acceptable levels of discomfort might actually enhance satisfaction as the hiker expects some discomfort when camping, but such problems overcome add to the experience and the hiker may take pride in overcoming any obstacles that arose within the holiday. Both the journeys in these forms of holidaying consist of a series of events, and each event may have its own ways of generating 'highs' and 'lows'. In short, intrinsic aspects of the holiday do not possess constant values but are continually evaluated and re-evaluated by reference to the traveller's own needs, expectations and experiences. Hence, in Neil Leiper's theory of tourism systems (Leiper, 1989, 1990) as comprising three zones, namely the tourist origin zone, the tourist receiving zone and the intervening zone of travel, this last zone may have more than a passing importance. Indeed, it is the zone of travel and its changing nature that captured the interest of several of the earlier commentators on tourism, such as Daniel Boorstin and his critique of the 'pseudo-event' in his influential book *The Image: A Guide to Pseudo-events in America* (Boorstin, 1961/1964a). Boorstin argued that the very experience of travel had changed because the advent of jet aircraft now meant that thousands of miles could be traversed in a matter of hours rather than days or even months when previously the passenger experienced changes in scenery, weather and differences in locales (Boorstin, 1964: 85). Similarly, Paul Fussell (1980) offered a more nuanced take on the 'pseudo-event' even when complaining there was no travel, only tourism, suggesting that both tourist and traveller possessed similar motives, but the former was more caught up in irony. For many commentators of this period, it was the process of travel, its meanings and symbolism that captured their interest at a time when the writing of the French philosophical traditions of post-modernism were becoming accessible to the English-speaking world. Hence Dean MacCannell's *The Tourist: A New Theory of the Leisure Class* (1976) both shadows and parallels the works of Jacques Derrida and his use of deconstruction as analytical method and Jean Baudrillard's analysis of imagery in marketing and advertising. Essentially these commentators noted the manner in which commercialisation and technology combine to change the patterns of experiences and the expectations of those experiences.

These factors can be seen at work in the next stages of Figure 1.2. Conventionally the tourist literature referred to the importance of destination attributes as 'pull' factors as discussed in the next chapter (and see Cohen, 1972, 1974 and Plog, 1974, 1977 for early examples). Although Gyte (1988) and Ryan (1991) suggested that attributes need to be more closely aligned with changing tourist behaviour within a tourist zone using concepts derived from Cooper's (1981) study of tourists' physical exploration of destinations, it cannot be denied that the inherent features of the tourist destination are important determinants of visitor experiences and satisfaction. Yet, as noted by Ryan, 'A destination may possess the right type of attributes, but still not generate a satisfactory holiday experience. This can arise for at least two reasons. The first is that the holidaymaker perceives the destination as lacking in quality. A mass tourist might view a zone as possessing hotels, bars, clubs, beaches etc., but also perceive them as being "tacky," or over-priced, or otherwise not delivering "value for money"' (Ryan, 1995: 300). His second reason was that 'dissatisfaction might lie in the nature of the interactions between tourist and significant others. For example, the "explorer" might find a destination to be "authentically ethnic," but is unable, in McCannell's (1976) terms, to penetrate the "back room"' (Ryan, 1995: 300).

For some holidaymakers the lack of 'authentic' experiences or the failure to establish contact with local people may leave them frustrated, disappointed and potentially dissatisfied. Equally, what Cohen (1972) termed the mass organised tourist who uses the services of travel agents, goes on packaged holidays and uses hotels of a type familiar to them might still have a less than satisfactory experience because they disapprove of the behaviour of their fellow tourists. Also, over the duration of a summer season at popular package holiday resorts, hotel staff, guides and other service providers may begin to suffer some fatigue and service quality might fail. Consequently, many tour operators will switch their staff between locations at times during the season to ensure that staff will be energised by new surroundings. Both the issue of the journey exploring the destination and interactions with others are shown in Figure 1.2 under the heading 'Evaluations of journey, place and people'.

However, this model, thus far, seems to imply that satisfaction will be generated by a congruence of expectation and perceived reality at the time of the initial meeting of tourist and destination. This is by no means certain. It is suggested that after the initial arrival a process of information acquisition and evaluation commences, and in that process the initial expectations, evaluations and anticipated behaviour may be modified. For example, if the 'explorer' feels that the destination is more commercialised than expected, a number of behaviour choices might arise. One alternative is to accept the destination on its own terms, and so have a 'relaxing' holiday by the swimming pool before returning home in a relaxed frame of mind. A second choice is to take advantage of the comfort afforded by the facilities, but to use it as a 'home base' from which to explore the surrounding regions thought to be less commercialised and more 'authentic'. A third option may be to cut their losses and leave the area altogether. Alternatively, they may complain to the representatives of the travel agent and/or tour operator to seek some form of compensation – a mode of behaviour that some may leave to their arrival back home as to engage in a bitter dispute seems one way *not* to enjoy a holiday.

Under the heading 'Responsive mechanisms' the framework adds a process of re-evaluation of the destination by suggesting such evaluations, the ability to suspend previous expectations and adapt to new realities and/or search for alternatives, and potentially better means of securing initial holiday goals all exist. This framework implies that the tourist is not a holiday taker but rather is a holidaymaker, that is, one who is goal-seeking and an active participant, either making or setting internalised motivational adjustments leading to external behaviour changes when their initial expectations are not met.

These considerations reflect early modelling of operant performance within complex and open social settings involving contingency management. Contingency management may be defined as 'programmes of behavior modification based on the negotiation and implementation of a contract that specifies rewards and punishments contingent upon the performance of particular behaviors' (Lowe *et al.*, 1987). Holidaymaking is associated with various goals, whether of acquiring new skills, relaxing or exploring. Additionally, given the current ease of access to the internet, the goal setting is within an at least moderately high informational context. Foxall (1990: 140) proposes a behavioural perspective model that 'stresses the situational factors that are systematically related to such behaviors'. Table 1.2 (derived from Foxall, 1990) postulates opposites between open and closed settings, and between high and low hedonic and informational reinforcements. In terms of holidaymaking, an open environment is one that contrasts to the resort or hotel complex which provides a fully packaged environment for the tourist. This latter may be termed a closed system offering a limited range of options to the holiday taker. Given that the subject

Table 1.2 Contingency categories, response patterns and reinforcement schedules

		Contingency category	
Setting	**Reinforcement**	**Typical response**	**Reinforcement schedule**
Open	High Hedonic	EPS/new task	High VI/VR
Closed	High Informational	Gambling	High VR
Open	Low Hedonic	Popular entertainment	Low VR
Closed	High Informational	Primary escape	Low VI
Open	High Hedonic	LPS/modified rebuy	Low VI
Closed	Low Informational	Mandatory consumption	FI
Open	Low Hedonic	RRB/straight rebuy	Low FI/VI
Closed	Low Informational	Secondary escape	Low FI

Source: Foxall, 1990: 140.
EPS: extended problem solving; LPS: limited problem solving; RRB: routine response behaviour; VI: variable interval; VR: variable ratio; FI: fixed interval

is holidaying one might expect high hedonic goals of enjoyment, pleasure and leisure seeking whereas low hedonic components emerge in
the fields of discovery, self-testing and skill acquisition. Informational
needs may be high or low depending on degrees of previous experience,
levels of knowledge and personality traits such as being risk averse or
risk accepting.

Alternatively, one can reconsider the nature of 'Pleasure'. Generally,
Foxall and others tend to see the hedonic as relating to pleasures resulting from sensual arousal and social interaction, and distinctions are made
between the intellectual and the sensual. An alternative perspective is that
there is pleasure to be gained from intellectual, cognitive pursuits and
many such pursuits are commonly found. There is pleasure gained from
the completion of a cryptic crossword, a sudoku puzzle or completing a
wordle game – all of which are common and often completed without
social interaction. In the holidaying situation the two sources of pleasure
may be combined by having the time to complete such puzzles while
slowly sipping a morning coffee at a favoured café gazing over a beautiful landscape or enjoying the warmth of an early morning summer sun.
Classifications used in analysis are themselves concepts porous boundaries once they are examined more closely.

Other commentators argue that the informational aspect may be
important in holidaying decisions. Wearden (1988) reviewed literature
relating to experimental reinforcement schedules and concluded that the
informational tends to be a 'reinforcement agent' whereby people are
better able to assess the accuracy of data or performance and the degree
to which it is satisfactory or unsatisfactory. Consequently, in situations
of open systems with high hedonic needs, extended problem solving
and searches result. Reverting to classical conditional theories associated with psychologists such as Skinner (1933, 1953) and Krouska et al.
(2018), it becomes possible to build schedules of behaviour reinforcement shown in the last column of Table 1.2 for each of the conditions
of open and closed systems and degrees of hedonic and informational
needs.

Two apparent caveats to this approach might be mentioned. The first
is, to what degree does extended problem solving actually take place in
many holidays, and second, are behavioural approaches entirely valid
given the development of holidaymaking takes place over long periods of
time and psychological maturation according to Pearce's (1988) concept
of the travel career that is premised on Maslow's (1968, 1970) theories?
Pearce (2012) and Pearce and Packer (2013) have also suggested that
at least parts of the holiday are characterised by 'mindlessness' and by
scripted occasions. For example, it can be contended that frequently
repeated actions become routinised, and hence are characterised by a
lack of distinguishing features. It therefore becomes difficult for respondents to differentiate between the same action carried out on different

occasions. Here the concept of the 'critical incident' as developed by Bitner *et al.* (1990) may be significant. It can be suggested that the scripted
occasion is one which meets a set of low expectations–arousal levels,
and the tourist goes with the 'flow' in a low arousal challenge–low skill
situation. On the other hand, if the occasion becomes marked by a critical incident where performance either exceeds or is significantly below
expectation, the situation ceases to be a scripted occasion.

If one characteristic of scripted occasions is their routine nature
(Edwards, 1994; Michaels, 2020), then, by definition, it is unlikely to
occur in the early stages of a holiday when a tourist is learning about
the destination zone. Again, caveats need to be mentioned. The scripted
occasion may occur early in a holiday if it is a situation where the tourist has repeatedly returned to the destination (e.g. at a 'holiday home').
Indeed, the return to a familiar location and routine associated with
pleasant memories is often one of the attractions of the holiday place.
However, assuming that in most cases tourists are exploring new situations, it can be hypothesised that scripted occasions tend to occur only in
the latter part of the holiday period as the holidaymaker develops enjoyable routines or finds favourite locations, or where the tourist has significant levels of past experience of a given situation. In short, the scripted
occasion occurs through familiarity and often organisational routines,
and, from the context of information theory, not at points of discontinu-
ity. Such an analysis is from the perspective of the tourist. From the viewpoint of the service provider, what to the tourist is a new situation may in
fact be a very familiar one, and the skill of the service provider is shown
by their ability to 'persuade' the customer of the 'novelty' of the tourist
experience. Essentially a situation perceived by the tourist as a 'scripted,
mindless' experience possesses the potential for simply meeting an expectation or generating dissatisfaction. It might be said to be 'satisfaction-
neutral'. It simply is what is expected – nothing more – nothing less. On
the other hand, a series of scripted encounters might generate satisfaction
if the motivation for the holiday is primarily one of relaxation and escape
from daily pressures of family and work life. The 'mindless' occasion
requires little decision taking or mental exertion, it poses little challenge
and thus might be entirely appropriate as a relaxing holiday experience.
These considerations are explored further in Chapter 8 when examining
Yiannakis and Gibson's (1992) concepts of the roles that tourists play.

Despite this discussion, questions remain as to the degree to which
the above model can fully explain holiday satisfaction. It is a deduc-
tive model based on observation, and like many behaviourist models,
it can only make inferences about cognitive mediation. The question is
important because the motivational models which are reviewed above,
and which give rise to the items used in the Beard and Ragheb (1980)
leisure satisfaction scale, were based on concepts of autonomy and cognition associated with authors such as Maslow (1968, 1970). But can

the aforementioned critical incidents be incorporated into a model of determinants of tourist satisfaction, and is it legitimate to incorporate concepts derived from humanistic psychology into a seemingly deterministic model? Skinnerian thought can be described as the proposition that observable behaviour can be explained in terms of contingent environmental stimuli and rates of response are simply determined by consequent stimuli (reinforcers and punishments). From the viewpoint of Skinnerian theory, the model has not indicated the nature of reinforcement schedules and is relativistic in its approach. It incorporates a plurality of paradigms. For example, while arguing that the holiday experience uniquely meets a series of needs (e.g. escape and fulfilment needs) and primarily consists of extended learning behaviours as discussed above, it does include routinised procedures where Skinnerian approaches are apt descriptors. These procedures include flight check-in, the reception greeting, the hotel buffet – and these are operations being explored by hotel chains for potential robotic provision (Choi *et al.*, 2020). Perversely, given that robots such as IBM's Watson have a novelty value, the scripted hotel reception desk procedures become 'mindful' until such time that familiarity, as the old proverb states, 'breeds contempt'.

The initial steps of the model on the other hand attribute importance to cognitive internalised processes as motivators for holidays. Cognition and adaptation through processes of cognitive dissonance are also thought important as means of adjustment to initially less than satisfactory scenarios and such adaptation means the holidaymaker can subsequently derive satisfaction from the holiday. One example might be that while a hotel disappoints in its catering, the discovery of a local restaurant may more than compensate. These internalised processes of being open-minded and exploratory are important because they mean that similar motivations and similar holiday settings are not sufficient to predict either behaviour or the final level of satisfaction experienced. Given that modelling is motivated by a wish to generalise findings to the future, factors such as critical incidents and cognitive dissonance leading to changed behaviours limit the usefulness of such models.

Finally, it must be noted that the model is, at best, only a partial model. The outcome with which it is concerned is a measure of satisfaction, not behaviour. The link between satisfaction and behaviour is viewed as a reiterative process. That is, where performance meets or exceeds expectations, cognitive and affective processes are called into play as evaluating degrees of satisfaction. When performance is inferior to expectation, then the gap analysis popularised by Parasuraman, Ziethaml and Berry (1985, 1988) defines this as a situation of low service quality. They distinguish service quality from satisfaction, but for the most part one would expect that low service quality for many would be a necessary if not sufficient condition for creating dissatisfaction.

If expectations are not met, from a pragmatic perspective the holidaymaker may decide that since holiday time is generally short and alternative activities and options exist, and assuming the motive to have an enjoyable holiday is high, several other behavioural modes of holidaying can exist. Where it is not possible to achieve initial wants, alternative wants are substituted, behaviour changes and again the goal is the satisfaction of those alternative wants. But this viewpoint ignores a temporal component, and in the diagrammatic framework shown in Figure 1.2, the relationship between current and future behaviour is linked through evaluation and future information search. Hence there is an implicit assumption that the link between satisfaction with a given type of holiday and repeat visitation is, in fact, weak. Several reasons can account for this weakness, including the desire to visit new places and engage in new activities.

Generally, and in part determined by life stage (see Chapter 8), holidaymakers use different types of holidays to meet different types of needs. Equally, evaluation of a holiday as satisfactory is no guarantee of a repeat purchase. Future repeat purchases may be a function of a changing prioritisation of the needs that motivate holidays, or the ability of a holiday type to meet different needs. Those needs are primarily determined not by the nature of past holiday experiences, but by other socioeconomic factors such as lifestyle, life stage and the interpretation of the resultant experiences through the psychological network formulated by personality and learning abilities.

The model also lends credence to the theories of Plog (1974, 1977) in that specific destinations will be selected by tourists because those destinations possess the attributes that permit the fulfilment of primary leisure motivations. Plog's theories are covered in more detail when considering the relationships between types of destination and visitor experiences in Chapter 2.

Discussion of the Model

The proposed model provides an overview of holiday experiences and reinforces the temporal components of holidaymaking in addition to the geographical aspects of travel. It suggests that the holiday possesses antecedents and repercussions that commence and end far beyond the actual dates of the holiday itself. The holiday commences when a trip is being considered and includes the time taken in information collection. This period is important in terms of expectations being formulated that will come to be used as criteria by which to establish the success of the holiday. The time taken in travelling to the main holiday destination has implications for the nature and time budget being allocated for the holiday. In car driving, cycling and hiking holidays the mode of travel and the sights seen and places experienced emphasise the travel component of the holiday, but even in cases of flights to a resort and the return journey home, the time taken in travel remains part of the trip experience and inherent within such travel lies the potential for a critical incident that may make or mar the whole holiday experience (Bitner *et al.*, 1990).

The framework indicated in Figure 1.2 also notes the importance of processes of familiarisation with the holiday destination. This topic has been described by studies that have asked respondents to draw maps of places visited or places of importance to them. Some of the earlier work in this field was undertaken by Walmsley and Jenkins (1992), Jenkins and Walmsley (1993) and Walmsley and Young (1998), who asked tourists to Coffs Harbour in Australia to draw maps and used construct theory to understand the functions of personal mapping of places by tourists. Among their findings was that tourists new to Coffs Harbour tended to draw more detailed maps when those returning to the destination offered less detailed maps, but their content featured the places they most frequented. In short, tourists initially explored a location, but once they found the places they most liked, the need to explore diminished. Similar findings were also being established independently by Cooper (1995) in the Channel Islands at much the same time.

With the advent of social media and the ease of finding alternative accommodation, online accommodation providers such as Airbnb and Tujia have offered visitors opportunities to live as temporary residents in what are marketed as 'authentic non-tourist locations'. Wildish and Spierings (2019) explored this in their work entitled 'Living like a local: Amsterdam Airbnb users and the blurring of boundaries between "tourists" and "residents" in residential neighbourhoods'. They suggest a new form of tourism is emerging from 'sightseeing' to one of 'life-seeing' as tourists wish to join the life of the residents of a place and not simply to see the attractions featured in marketing campaigns as places to see. Being part of a community means not being seen to refer to maps, but the widespread use of smartphones now means use of a phone-based map is simply yet another person using their phone in public. So widespread is this behaviour, the use of a phone for map reading no longer marks one as being a stranger or non-resident. The spatial and temporal uses of spaces indicated by the model thus have implications for the nature of the tourist space in the age of the internet. Increasingly these tourist spaces are less dominated by 'attractions' but becoming instead locales of encounters and boundary blurring. To support these arguments, Wildish and Spierings (2019) also used mental mapping based on maps drawn by visitors, this time visitors to Amsterdam. Of interest in their study are the distinctions drawn between public, semi-public and personal spaces, and the ability of Airbnb accommodation to provide a personal space wherein one resides continuing one's own personal habits which also enforces a sense of residency. This is arguably different from the notion of staying in a hotel. These processes highlight the psychological adaptation noted in the framework but reduce the need for adjustment to a strange place. In such ways tourists blur the differences between the new and the familiar (Stors *et al.*, 2019).

From another perspective the framework indicates the high levels of interdependence that exist within the tourism industry and the long service chains that exist. For example, from parking a car at an airport, to flight check-in, airport experience, in-flight service, baggage retrieval, transport to the destination/hotel, reception and room experience even before actually venturing into the destination illustrates the complexity of service provision. Each service is often being carried out by independent organisations, yet the performance of each link in the chain may have consequences for other service providers who follow. The consequence of a delayed flight may mean a subsequent connecting flight is missed, a non-arrival at a hotel and a need to reschedule bookings. It is at stages such as these that having access to a trusted travel agent, or the expense of having booked a business flight comes to the fore in that help is more easily accessible for the passenger that has used such services as distinct from simply buying from an OTA. Cheaper prices can also have their penalties should arrangements go awry.

This interdependence means that any one service failure may carry over into subsequent appraisals of later stages of the travel experience – and shape assessments of the total trip. Thus, no matter how good a subsequent performance is, an initial failure may still determine a negative assessment of the holiday experience. This interdependence also means that each business has a limited control over the visitor's perception of a 'holiday service'. Hence, each separate business in the chain seeks to establish strong brand images and service provision. It also follows that for many organisations in the travel industry their marketing arrangements are far from simple. In one sense, the final consumer, the holiday-maker, is the target market. Every accommodation provider, attraction owner and airline wishes to attract the final consumer, but equally the same business is selling and marketing itself to others in the supply chain. The hotels and airlines wish to create packages where each dovetails into the other's services to create a better, seamless product for the tourist. They seek space on the websites of each other and the OTAs such as Expedia.com. All wish to be in the minds of travel agents who are used by the traveller. Travel agents are offered 'famils' by destination marketing organisations so that travel agents are better informed about what it is that they offer to their clientele.

In all of this marketing, no single person or organisation is a passive consumer of the services of the other. Business organisation in their dealings with each link in the service chain will generally seek to settle on prices that are mutually acceptable, but from the viewpoint of assessing experiences the holidaymaker occupies an interesting space. From a psychological viewpoint, that space has long been recognised in the tourism literature. Arnoud and Price (1993: 41) described a river rafting experience for tourists as 'the opportunity to participate, in rites of intensification and integration and to return to an everyday world "transformed"', while Van Gennep (1960) alluded to rituals and a transition from everyday life to a non-normal state, after which tourists pass back to their daily reality again. Other authors have likened tourist experiences to a stage that possesses not only the performance area but also a backstage. Based on Goffman's initial concept of life being a series of watched performances conducted in a public arena, behind which there lies a backstage of more private and different behaviours (Goffman, 1959), Dean MacCannell (1973, 1976) suggested that many tourists sought authenticity by intruding on the backstage. Of interest, and to be explored later in Chapter 7, is the situation where the site being explored represents a fantasy but one familiar to many from several years of emotional investment. Such is the example of the Granada Studio tours in Manchester where the decades-long television serial *Coronation Street* is filmed (Couldry, 1998).

In such circumstances the tourist brings to his or her holiday a neural network generated by interpretations of a lifetime's experience. It was not for nothing that in the much-cited work *The Experience Economy: Work Is Theatre & Every Business a Stage*, Pine and Gilmore (1999) not only used the same dramatology but chose several examples drawn from tourism and hospitality to illustrate their thesis that the new emergent economy was based on demands for experiences. The tourism literature had long attributed an active role to the tourist as a co-creator of their own experience. Prior to 1999, Holbrook and Hirschman (1982) and Arnould and Price (1993) had noted the ability of tourists to enter into role play to enhance their own experiences. Ryan (1997) had anticipated Prentice's (2004) concepts of tourist familiarity derived from their use of media when describing the ability of tourists to slip into adventurous roles when white water rafting, having been informed by previously viewing internet images of the activity. In short, the tourist can play within roles, seek to deny their role, modify responses and so work with tourism operators in co-creative acts that formulate their own experience.

Within the framework proposed in Figure 1.2, these adaptive behaviours and the ability to suspend disbelief are important psychological skills that help determine the tourist's experience. Finally, as again illustrated in Figure 1.2, the visitor assesses their holiday experience against criteria established by their initial expectations to determine whether their holiday has been a success. But the holiday does not end at that point. Sometimes tourists can restructure their past holiday through the telling of stories where disappointments are overcome to become successes, where memories are formed, shaped and possibly reformed to become assets by which future holidays can be assessed and judged.

Hence, the holiday experience is simultaneously simple (for it is about fun, relaxation and difference) and complex because holidays can challenge and it these experiences that help shape our own beliefs about ourselves and others.

This chapter has sought to establish a framework within which it becomes possible to create a gestalt perspective of holidaying and tourism. In the next chapter the motives for holidaying are examined more closely.

2 Motivations – 'Push and Pull'

The chapter includes:

(a) An introduction to the motives that lead to holiday taking and holidaymaking.
(b) Links between personality and motivation.
(c) The relationship between 'pull' and 'push' motives.
(d) Arousal and physio-psychological measures and neuroscience.
(e) Image creation and escape.
(f) Holidays and dysfunctional society.

Introduction

The motivations for holidaying taking and making are many. They range from just simply relaxing to the challenging, such as hiking along a mountainous trail. Over a lifetime, holiday motives may change. The holiday needs of individuals with young children to care for are different from those of a teenager escaping from family bonds for the first time, or from a more elderly couple possibly visiting places with a sense of nostalgia. This chapter introduces an initial exploration of holiday motives by reference to two well-established theories. The first is what is termed 'wanderlust'. Gray (1970) was among the first contemporary economists to recognise the role of tourism in international trade. Writing in 1982, he defined wanderlust as 'the visit to a different place. Here the intent is not to do what could be done less efficiently at home but to do something different from the range of activities available at home' (Gray, 1982: 109). It is perceived as an inherent need to travel to different places, something that is intrinsic to many people. Writing from a northern hemisphere perspective, many of these commentators linked a wanderlust to a 'sun lust' (Gray, 1970), noting the then emergent package holiday industry when Canadians, Northern Europeans and those living in the northern United States would seek winter holidays in more southern latitudes to ensure a warm summer stay. With the emergence of better data, many economists began modelling tourism demand with early work being undertaken by Stephen Witt and colleagues establishing some of the early methodologies (e.g. Kulendran & Wilson, 2000; Lim, 1997; Witt & Witt, 1995) and publishing in the then new journal, *Tourism Economics*. Such modelling quickly established that holiday tourism was but one form of tourism, and events, conferences, business meetings, and so on, were also important determinants of travel. However, many implicitly recognised that the desire to be 'away from the office' was still a motive, and many cited Gray's initial work.

Parallel to much of this work was the research based more on sociology and psychology and notably the work of the late Graham Dann alongside that of Eric Cohen and Seppo Iso-Ahola. Citing Johnston (1970), Dann (1977: 185) commenced his piece by writing, 'The greatest reason for travel can be summed up in one word, "Escape": escape from the dull, daily routine; escape from the familiar, the commonplace, the ordinary; escape from the job, the boss, the customer, the commuting, the house, the lawn, the leaky faucets', arguing that while intrinsically attractive as a notion, there was no real evidence behind the statement. Dann continued to suggest that there was a need for a sounder theoretical framework capable of generating empirical evidence. He suggested that much of the then existing literature was based upon a 'push-pull' process. This observation has since been adopted by many and has initiated significant research among those studying tourism.

Push and Pull – A Description

The push motivation can be described as intrinsic motives relating to desires or felt needs. They lead to behaviours that engage in a search for information, seeking activities or places that they think will satisfy those desires or needs. If one adopts the language of Gray (1970, 1982) then a wanderlust and a sun lust are intrinsic to the human condition, but it is evident that this is not necessarily the case, and deeper psychological and sociological conditions need to be examined. The 'push' is a motive to leave home, but equally powerful factors may lead a person to stay at home. A fear of the unknown may deter travel; for example, the fear of long-term health consequences from Covid in its various mutations led to risk-adverse behaviours.

Equally, there may be several different forms of push. Among these are:

- the wish to relax – where relaxation implies moments of escape from normal activities;
- the wish to escape from stress;
- the simple wish to do something different;
- the want to fulfil wishes or dreams;
- by doing these things, the seeking of personal or social enhancement;

- in turn, this implies the seeking of prestige – an enhancement of personal image to others;
- in turn, this implies the potential of mental and spiritual enhancement;
- in turn this implies a seeking of new knowledge – of self or places;
- for many, these activities involve social interaction with others;
- these others may be family – so family bonding is a motive;
-               or friends – so social interaction is a motive;
-               or meeting new people can be a motive;
- if you travel overseas – then meeting people of different cultures;
- while visiting places of different histories and heritages may meet your needs.

All of these scenarios have been examined in the research literature. Mohsin (2005, 2008) in conjunction with others has used the Beard and Ragheb (1980, 1983) Leisure Motivation Scale to examine holiday motivations in a number of different settings when assessing the importance of relaxation and escape needs as against sociodemographic variables (e.g. for Chinese travellers, Mohsin, 2008, and for Malaysians in Australia, Mohsin, 2005). The Leisure Motivation Scale is built upon four prime motivators, namely (a) social needs, (b) relaxation, the (c) acquisition of knowledge and (d) competency needs in terms of acquiring new skills (Beard & Ragheb, 1980). Stress relief is particularly associated with relaxation (Smith, 2007), and Steen Jacobsen *et al.* (2023) specifically alluded to stress relief as a motive for holidaying after the periods of lockdown that many countries experienced in 2020 and 2021 in the attempts to reduce the numbers of deaths from the Covid-19 pandemic.

In assessing the above list of motives, Dann (1996) summarised many of them as a search for difference, but that in turn raises a question – what is the difference being sought? Arguably the difference must represent some state that is positive when compared to that which is conceived as 'ordinary'. In that sense, being stress free can be concluded as being better than being stressed, although as noted in Chapter 1, stress can also be a facilitating factor when seeking to achieve a goal. Knowledge acquisition may also be better than ignorance, although it is said that 'ignorance is bliss'. In Chapter 1, Figure 1.2 highlighted the personality of the tourist and their ability to adapt to changes encountered when on holiday. Hence personality is of significance when examining intrinsic drives that motivate.

Personality and Holiday Motives

Personality has been described through the use of many scales. Motivation is closely linked to personality, for motivation integrates a person's behaviour and activity with individual needs (Yoon & Uysal, 2005) to achieve a desired end (Callebaut *et al.*, 1999).

Motivation has been referred to as psychological/biological needs and wants, including integral forces that arouse, direct and integrate a person's behaviour and activity (Yoon & Uysal, 2005). According to Callebaut *et al.* (1999), motives represent desirable end-states that people seek to attain through consumption. Motivation in a destination context has been operationalised as a process of compliance with the strength of belief in social norms, that is, the degree of importance attached to a selected social norm helps to determine behaviour. In this approach, motivation is a socio-psychological determinant and can be measured by scales seeking agreement with items relating not simply to psychological attributes but also to a willingness to conform with the norms of a social group thought important (Meng & Han, 2018). An invaluable source for tourism scholars as the scale available for measuring motivation is the *Handbook of Scales in Tourism and Hospitality Research*, edited by Gursoy *et al.* (2014).

What is noticeable about many of these scales is their contextual nature. One such example is the Rural Tourists' Travel Motivation Scale used by Xie *et al.* (2008), which measures 21 items using a five-point scale. The items were derived from prior research pertaining to rural tourism activities and include 14 items specific to rural activities and a motivation scale initially assessed using factor analysis. The scale comprised general items such as enjoying the rural area and the local culture and meeting people. In short, the scale was primarily about perceptions of rural activities and a predisposition to join them. The scale was used to test for gender differences. What, arguably, it does not do is measure aspects of the tourists' personality and thereby possibly inhibits the generalisability of the scale in terms of developing a personality type, although potentially it does measure a preference for rural-based activities.

On the other hand, some scales are better located within the framework of psychological theory. The Sensation Seeking Scale Form V (Zuckerman *et al.*, 1978) has been used in a number of studies that relate to adventure tourism. Examples include Gilchrist *et al.* (1995), who used it on a small sample (n=47) of British holidaymakers, with a further control of 46 British holidaymakers to measure the personality characteristics of those going on an adventure holiday. Eachus (2004) then used a revised brief version of the scale for 300 adventure holiday tourists, while among others who have also used the scale are Pizam *et al.* (2001), Lepp and Gibson (2008) and Yildirim and Çakici (2020). This specific scale is well embedded in the psychological literature and has been used in many different scenarios including driving behaviour (de Winter *et al.*, 2018), sexual behaviour (Ballester-Arnal *et al.*, 2018) and delinquency (Pechorro *et al.*, 2018).

The scale is based on the earlier psychometric work of Hans Eysenck, an influential British psychologist working in the mid-part of the 20th century. Much of his work was related to the dimensions of neuroticism, introversion and extraversion and was devised from psychiatric measures of the sensitivity of the hypothalamus in the brain and its response to stimuli. In 1978, his wife (Sybil) and colleague Martin Zuckerman published a paper noting the similarities between his Eysenck Personality Inventory (EPI) Scale and the Sensation Scale, to conclude that sensation seeking fell between neuroticism and psychoticism (Eysenck & Zuckerman, 1978) but that sensation seeking was also associated with a measure of lying. Hence, they surmised that American female students displayed less permissive tendencies towards sex than males, though having an equal amount of sexual experience, implying a higher score on lying. It could be observed that an alternative explanation might relate to expectations about social norms, as noted by Meng and Han (2018).

These scales have been subject to significant testing and examination. An examination of Hans Eysenck's citations using Google My Citations showed over 129,000 citations with variants of the EPI accounting for approximately half of them, and also indicating that his work continues to be referenced. In the tourism literature, one study of interest is that of Eachus (2004), who combined the EPI with Plog's theories of the allocentric and psychocentric. Stanley Plog died at the age of 80 years in 2011 and was significant for the consultancy and advisory services he provided to the US tourism industry through his company 'Plog Research'. Prior to entering consultancy, Plog was the academic director of the Social Psychiatry Training Program at the University of California, Los Angeles. His impact on both the tourism industry and academia was established when, in 1974, he published a paper in the *Cornell Hotel and Restaurant Administration Quarterly* in which he described how destinations fitted on a destination life cycle and the nature of the tourists who visited such locations (Plog, 1974). He proposed that a distribution of tourist types existed with a conventional bell-shaped curve, with the extremities marked by two different psychographic groupings. The first were the more adventuresome in their choice of holiday destinations and were motivated by educational and cultural reasons. These he initially labelled the 'allocentrics'. At the opposite end of the continuum were the 'psychocentrics', who tended to visit familiar locations that offered cultural contexts with a milieu within which they were comfortable. These tourists, Plog suggested, were motivated in part by social status and wanting comfort, rather than the psychological challenge of facing the unfamiliar. Between these two extremes existed the 'near-allocentric', 'mid-centric' and 'near-psychocentric', and Plog, from a north American perspective, indicated the destination to which they would travel.

Ryan (2020a) provides a reasonably detailed description of the impact of Plog's work on tourism research in which he notes the criticisms of the model made by academics such as Stephen Smith (1990a, 1990b) and Steven Litvin (2006). Possibly as a response to these criticisms, Plog (2002, 2006) revised his model and replaced the terms 'allocentric' and 'psychocentric' with the labels 'venturers' and 'dependables' while providing more insights into the nature of the tourists being examined. As Ryan wrote, 'Plog (2006) argued that – yes – personality is a very important determinant of destination choice, and – second – his model is meant to be a generic model applied to aggregate holiday patterns, and not used as a means of indicating each individual's next holiday choice' (Ryan, 2020: 65). From this perspective, and to these authors, the work undertaken by Eachus (2004) is totally consistent with this viewpoint, for by combining the Plog model with the Eysenck-derived Sensation Seeking Scale (Zuckerman *et al.*, 1978), a model of tourist motivation results that links 'push' motives with destination types. Eachus (2004) concedes that he was not the first to examine this concept, and is indeed dependent on the work of Jackson *et al.* (2001) who proposed a four-cell model derived from the Eysenck Scale as previously indicated in Jackson *et al.* (1999). The cells of this model were derived from the continua of the allocentric and psychocentric dimensions of the Plog Scale (1974) with the introversion-extraversion scales of the Eysenck and Eysenck (1970) EPI Scale. The model proposed by Jackson *et al.* (2001) is indicated in Figure 2.1.

Subjecting the model to empirical testing, Jackson *et al.* (2001) note a number of problems, including the role of age and a lack of true independence between the variables implying the presence of an orthogonal relationships existing, that is, the variables are not correlated with each other, but an independent variable continues to affect a dependent variable. Eachus reports similar results with reference to the Sensation

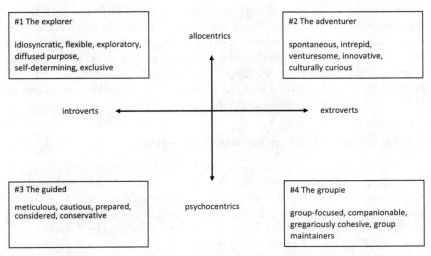

Figure 2.1 Proposed personality indicators for independent/interdependent personality types

Seeking Scale and summarises the debate by stating that studies indicate 'a significant relationship between the personality trait of sensation seeking and expressed holiday preferences. People with a high need for sensation will tend to prefer the type of holiday that can meet that need and vice versa' (Eachus, 2004: 153). He concludes 'that sensation seeking may play an important part in the complex of motivations that ultimately lead to holiday choice' (Eachus, 2004: 153).

After his death, Plog's model continued to attract attention. Litvin and Smith (2016) noted that distinctions existed between a person's actual tourist destination, which tended to the psychometric or dependable destination, and the individual tourist's 'ideal destination', which tended to echo Plog's distribution across the whole psychometric/dependable-allocentric/venturer dimension. Many reasons can be provided as to why this may be the case. Life stage, marital status and financial circumstances can explain this, while research on holiday decisions has indicated the importance of constrained choice due to senses of responsibility to significant others – a factor particularly true of females' holiday choices. As Bronner and de Hoog (2008: 967) comment, there has been a democratisation of family holidaymaking decisions and a movement away from male-oriented towards more participative holidaymaking. This trend may be further emphasised in a trend towards more intergenerational holidays (Hermans et al., 2020), although it has been noted that for several females this can mean added responsibilities for aged parents or children (Backer & Schänzel, 2013; Gram et al., 2019; Heimtun, 2019) and the formation of temporal desires and planning. The position is further compounded when considering the growth of 'blended families', that is, families comprising differing arrangements due to divorce, remarriage and the care of children resulting from different marriages. As Cross (2004) comments, under these circumstances holiday plans may well require significant negotiations and juggling between sets of parents and the nature of relationships between past and present spouses. A cross-relationship between this discussion and the concepts advanced of the roles that tourists adopt, as proposed by Yiannakis and Gibson (1992), can be noted, and is discussed in Chapter 6.

Pull Factors and Relationship with Push Factors

The push factors discussed above arise from differing wants and also different personalities, as shown by reference to psychometric scales. The degree of open-mindedness is a further dimension that can be noted. Some studies have indicated that 'open-minded' personalities are more likely to want to engage in adventure (Fieger et al., 2019; Schneider & Vogt, 2012) and meditation (Jiang et al., 2018) and enjoy self-awareness-style holidays away from cellphones (Altinay et al., 2021). They wish to meet new people (Fomo & Garibaldi, 2015) and engage with different cultures (Shaheer *et al.*, 2021), while others who are more conservative may value more physical relaxation, or possibly wish to engage in much-loved tasks and seek photography, cookery or similar holiday-based activities (Chang *et al.*, 2020).

Be this as it may, a key requirement of the holiday destination is that it possesses the capabilities to meet these requirements. In short, the holiday destination comprises attractions, accommodations, facilities and services that meet the demands of the tourist (Ryan, 2020). These, following the nomenclature of Dann (1981), are known as the 'pull' factors. These are the place attributes that the holidaymaker looks for when considering a destination. Therefore, it follows from this logic that optimal holiday experiences should occur when congruency exists between the holidaymaker's wants and the attributes of place. It then becomes possible to develop a template that indicates how certain types of pull factors equate with given patterns of demand. These are shown in Table 2.1.

Table 2.1 is premised on a list of holiday motives presented by commentators such as Horner and Swarbrooke (2016). Thus, for example, a relaxing holiday for many would include a degree of personal pampering that could well include meals being prepared for the holidaymaker and the opportunity for massage and spas. These last facilities are much appreciated by many Asians, especially those living in geo-thermal areas where spas are almost part of the culture in terms of daily living (Barendregt, 2011; Panchal, 2013). Similarly, New Zealand and Scotland have developed a global reputation as destinations for adventure holidays (Fieger *et al.*, 2019; Page *et al.*, 2005) as both have relatively benign summer climates while also offering opportunities for winter sports. Both countries have excellent hiking trails, fast-flowing rivers, limestone terrain with caves and an infrastructure that supports sky diving and other similar pursuits. Page *et al.* (2005) also draw attention to the role of trained guides who need to go through processes of certification prior to being able to take guided tours. Ryan (2003) provides a framework derived from flow theory (Csikszentmihaly, 2000) that indicates that well-trained adventure sports guides are able to effectively uplift the skills of often inexperienced tourists to better enable them to cope with the risks inherent in many of these sports, and so create a sense of flow where their skills are congruent with the level of challenge they face. He has suggested that this facet of adventure tourism is very important when dealing with new markets where concepts of 'face' are important but where there is not the same historical tradition of engaging in outdoor, challenging, physical abilities as found in many western cultures (Ryan, 2003). Whilst this may have contained some truth when, for example, the Chinese market began to emerge, it may be less valid now as Chinese millennials and generation Y tend to emulate the patterns of their western counterparts. However, Gardiner and Kwek (2017) found in their research that Chinese youth still retain a sense of filial responsibility

Table 2.1 Indicative relationships between pull factors and push motives

Push	Pull
Relax	Comfortable hotels with appropriate facilities Beautiful landscapes Appropriate levels of service
Escape	To be different in ways required by the holidaymaker: - attractions - services - friendly culture
Not be stressed	All the above plus possibly: spa and massage services entertainment supportive specialist staff
New knowledge	Places possessing unfamiliar features that motivate search behaviour Places permitting access to new information
Social interaction	Places conducive to interactions Create groups of people with shared interests and undertaking common activities – e.g. sailing holidays, class-based holidays, age-based groups, common features (e.g. single people, divorced people)
Family bonding	Places meet the needs of family groups – e.g. offer facilities appropriate to age groups (children) with care facilities permitting free parental time Impacts on choice of inclusive resort complexes/hotels/camp sites
Meeting new people	Places offering high interaction opportunities: camp sites inclusive resort complexes coach tours cruises Supported by entertainment and appropriate catering facilities
Different cultures	Possesses a different culture that is accessible
Different histories and heritage	Possesses interpretation sites, museums, temples, sources of explanation
Seeking adventure	Provides appropriate sites – e.g. mountains, wilderness Provides support in terms of qualified instructors, safety procedures, etc.
Achieving competency	Qualified instruction, mentoring, facilities, etc.
To something different	Not being home Freed from the normalities of everyday life But how different? Depends on personality and wants
Fulfil wishes or dreams	The provision of fantasy? Presence of theme parks Presence of themed/luxury hotels Presence of attributes pertinent to the 'dream/wish'
Social enhancement	Places possessing prestige/positive images/high status
Mental/spiritual needs	Places of meditation Peaceful surroundings/landscape Skilled mentors

towards their parents, suggesting therefore that many retain a sense of concern that adventure sports should be 'safe'.

While the concepts of 'push-pull' provide a much-cited framework to explain the relationship between holiday motivations and the actual choice of holidays made, it was noted by Litvin and Smith (2016) that actual choice often deviates from a desired holiday. This highlights the role of other determinants of holiday choice, and also, in the views of many, the societal context within which holiday decisions are made (Krippendorf, 1987).

In terms of the former point, a simple modelling is indicated in Figure 2.2, which shows that the desire for a holiday is followed by an action (taking the holiday) that leads to an evaluation of the holiday.

However Figure 2.2 is too simplistic for a number of reasons. First, as has been indicated by many researchers, prior to taking the holiday, a person will conduct a search for information about the destination and possibly accommodation, the potential weather, airlines and so on. Hence, to the above model can be added the search for information to create Figure 2.3. When searching for information, increasingly this is undertaken by reference to sites available on the internet. This has led a number of researchers to create and test what is termed the technology adoption model (TAM). This model was devised by Davis (1986) using the theory of reasoned action (Ajzen & Fishbein, 1980; Fishbein & Ajzen, 1975) and supported by empirical evidence (Davis, 1986; Davis *et al.*, 1989). It suggests that the acceptance and use of technology such as the internet is based on ease of use, the usefulness of the information and the general attitude of the user towards computer-based technologies. Consequently, we can add the search for information into Figure 2.3, while noting, of course, that there are several sources of information open to the potential tourist including past experience, word of mouth recommendations, press and television and also films. These last have led to the phenomenon of film tourism where tourists visit film sites (Zhang *et al.*, 2021) to better understand a film or television series, or the novels on which they are based.

In searching for information, often a key question in the mind of the potential tourist is the financial cost that might be involved. Other costs may also come to mind, including the cost of transport (Lin *et al.*, 2018), time and possible loss of income (e.g. of being away from work, Kuriyama *et al.*, 2020), and possibly potential risks to health and safety as demonstrated during the Covid-19 pandemic (Immordino *et al.*, 2021). Equally, there is also the question of the duration of the holiday and the

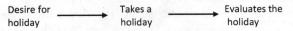

Figure 2.2 A simple push-behaviour-evaluation model

Figure 2.3 Push-seeking information-behaviour-evaluation sequential model

A slightly complex model (Introducing moderating variables)

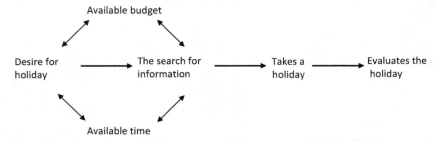

Figure 2.4 Push-information seeking-behaviour-evaluation factors with moderating variables

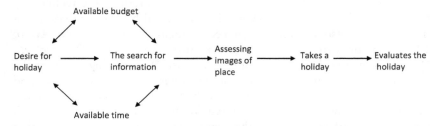

Figure 2.5 The model incorporating image creation as an intervening variable

time budget of the potential traveller. These types of factors can be added to the diagrams, as shown in Figure 2.4.

Any information that is gained also has to be evaluated before any decision is made, and this is where the pull factors of the attractiveness of the destination and the activities it offers are taken into consideration. To summarise this point, we can sum these factors under the heading 'Image and Assessment of Image' and insert this as an intervening variable in the model of holiday taking that is being constructed. This is shown in Figure 2.5. The earlier point made about the internet can again be emphasised at this point because the internet does more than simply reproduce text. It also provides visual information through photographs and videos, while for online travel agencies (OTAs), some of the text provided comes from reviews from previous tourists to the destination. Research has indicated that many users of the internet regard such reviews as being independent of the marketing and promotional bodies associated with an airline, accommodation provider or destination, and hence attribute trustfulness to the accuracy of what is being sold (Lee *et al.*, 2011). In their research into opinion leaders among reviewers on sites such as Tripadvisor.com, Lee *et al.* (2011) also note that the potential tourist is making assessments of more than just the destination. They are also assessing the value of the reviews and by implication the expertise of those making the comments. They identify, among other factors, the disclosure of age and gender of the informant as being of importance, but also they raise questions about privacy. The numbers of postings, trips made and details within the text are also matters that have been assessed by researchers (Hou *et al.*, 2019; Taecharungro & Mathayomchan, 2019).

Image Creation and Push and Pull

From the perspective of 'post-modernism', much of contemporary consumer behaviour is about the consumption of images (Baudrillard, 1970/2016; Daniel Jr *et al.*, 2018; Schroeder, 2002). Post-modernity draws much of its inspiration from the changes in consumer behaviour that occurred at some point in the 1960s. The 1960s witnessed the emergence of supermarket retailing, the mass ownership of television sets and a growth of visual imagery. These were outcomes of a growth in incomes and technology. Right up to the early 1950s, grocery purchases could be quite generic. One purchased vegetables, and even basics like flour, and walked home with them, or took the bus. The introduction of supermarkets created competition for shelf space and brand names sought the 'eye level – buy level' space. The desire for sales led to advertising on the new commercial television channels. As the end of the decade approached, supermarkets needed large car parks as car ownership grew, again based on not only the growth of incomes but the appeals made through advertising, often on the new colour television sets. According to the post-modernist thinkers such as Baudrillard (1970/2016), consumers were being swayed by imagery, and the image creator sought to align and shape personal self-images. The consumer purchased goods based on brands through which the shopper could project some part of their own image. Fashion became a key component of group identification based on pop culture and was evidenced in 1960s as the 'mods' and the 'rockers' took inspiration from popular films and magazines.

By the second decade of the 21st century the arrival of social media and ease of access to the internet via smartphones, allied to the advent of hyper-reality goggles, delivered a situation where video games were being considered as a sport that could qualify for the Olympic Games (Bowman & Cranmer, 2019; Rogers, 2019) and additionally promised a future where video and video games would morph into new fantasy hyper-realities with the player immersed in a pattern of holograms (Zikas *et al.*, 2016).

Images appeal to humans by their very vividness, and as conscious social animals, humans are able to respond to self-image as evidenced by the role of influencers on social media (Jan *et al.*, 2017). The tourism industry has long been a pioneer in the use of advertising and marketing, and of the technologies that promote it. This is evidenced, for example, by the early theme parks of Coney Island in New York State in the late 19th century, where its carnival of switchback rides and night-time glowing light-scape of thousands of light bulbs created a fairy land at a time when many households still depended on gas lights to illuminate the darkness of night (Ryan & Gu, 2007; Stein, 1998). Given this history, it is unsurprising that the tourism industry quickly adopted the use of the internet in promoting destinations. Attractions large and small quickly adopted web pages and a presence on apps such as Facebook, Twitter/X, Weibo and WeChat that provided both advertisements and booking and purchasing opportunities. It also created a disjuncture in the supply chain of the industry through the establishment of OTAs such as Ctrip, Expedia.com and others, and created a whole new means by which private homeowners entered the tourism industry through Airbnb, Bookabach and others to compete with the bed and breakfast associations as well as the hotel and motel serviced accommodation sector.

In all of this advertising and promotion, the 'push and pull' factors associated with the tourism industry were being reinforced and made more appealing as incomes and industries changed. Ryan (1991) had presented an analysis of the trade-off between income and leisure but had also referred to the fuzziness of borders between work and leisure as the growth of the tertiary sector of the economy had become apparent. Picking up themes from the seminal work of Toffler (1970), Ryan noted the social characteristics of work and its role in personal lives. In western societies, it has become a commonplace for self-identification by referencing one's occupation, whereas in other societies a person will often self-reference a family grouping as, for example, is the case of Māori and other indigenous peoples. Business travel became a habitual part of the work lives of many prior to Covid-19, and with travel came experiences of new places and sources of conversation by which one identified one's own self-image. Taken together, the images of place presented via internet and through personal experience motivated a want for further travel (i.e. the 'push') even whilst destinations responded to demand with better hotels, more exciting attractions and easier access to information, both formal and non-formal (i.e. the 'pull').

Gartner (1986, 1989) and Tasci et al. (2007) had also recognised the changing patterns and the increased promotion and advertising of tourism and spoke of the 'induced' and 'organic' nature of destination marketing and image creation. The 'induced' image is that created by the tourism marketing organisations themselves through the material that they place on the web and through press and television advertising, brochures and other media. The 'organic' image is that derived from non-formal sources such as word-of-mouth recommendations and personal experiences. The presence of the internet, social media and OTAs effectively creates something of a fusion between these two forms of image creation. While, as noted above, the reviews posted on the internet are seen as a form of electronic word-of-mouth (e-Wom) recommendation that is independent of formal destination marketing organisations, it is a mediated form of communication. As many will know, if a person has booked a holiday through an OTA, after the holiday the traveller will receive an invitation to provide a comment. If taking up the option, the traveller is then taken through a menu of options and scoring modes, so whilst the text is that of the traveller, the structure is determined by the owner of the web page. There are potential advantages and disadvantages of this process. The advantage of the standardisation is that data can be aggregated and an overall score created, often in terms of a star rating on a one-to-five-star basis with five being the highest score. This may be broken down into separate ratings of value for money, comfort and so on. The possible disadvantage is that the responder is being led through a structure not of their own making which implicitly imputes criteria that the responder may not have voluntarily chosen if left unprompted.

Whatever the situation, the importance of image creation remains at least two-fold. First, the destination seeks to create an image that moves the place into the awareness set held by the potential traveller. Second, it then seeks to move that awareness into a positive frame whereby it is attractive to the potential tourist. Should that occur, the image has induced action on the part of the tourist as it shapes the final decision and hence action to book the hotel or motel, to book a car or buy a ticket for the attraction. The tourist does so on the perception that the service will meet a need, and thus expectations are set. One can then relate again to the arguments of Oliver (1977, 1981) and Parasuraman et al. (1985, 1988) that the expectations are essentially criteria by which the quality of the service is judged by the tourist. This gap between expectation and performance is examined in more detail in the next chapter, but for the moment it can be concluded that image creation has importance because it establishes a set of criteria by which the tourist will examine the visit experience.

Escape To or Escape From

If holidays are motivated by escape, as noted by Dann (1977), then one can ask what motivates and shapes the nature of the escape. Durmus (2019) has presented one of the more detailed analyses of escape, and much of this section rests heavily on her work. One can pose a number of questions about escape in the holidaying context, and these include:

- What motivates a need to escape?
- What are the thoughts and opinions associated in the idea of 'escape'?
- What are the characteristics desired in an escape place?
- Which is the most desired escape place?

- How does one evaluate the escape place?
- How does one readjust on returning home from the escape place?
- For how long does one escape?
- What is it that one escapes from – what is it that the escape place omits?
- What is it that inhibits escape?
- Finally, is it an escape from or an escape to a place?

This last question is directed at the very idea of escape. An escape *from* a situation implies that the person feels themselves to be disadvantaged, or to be in a position that is felt to be negative, and which inhibits freedom in some way. One of Durmus's respondents notes that 'in this case, changing the immediate physical environment as the most convenient move comforts the individual. It is because the idea that the negative energy source will not reach him/her makes one feel safe. Under the circumstances, I think that escapism functions as a defense mechanism' (Durmus, 2019: 2). Alternatively, it might be said that one is wishing to escape *to* a situation. Under the circumstances, the emphasis is generally on seeking for a more positive stance. This is illustrated by another of Durmus's respondents who stated, 'The concept of escapism evokes a break and discharge. One should be able to overcome the stress and worries of modern life … Escaping for me, in the most general sense, suggests the desire to attain mental tranquillity. The human by nature is a social being and should not break away from the nature' (Durmus, 2019: 2). While the informant notes a desire to escape *from* stress, it is phrased more positively in terms of a challenge that can be overcome to 'attain mental tranquillity'.

Durmus (2019) identifies a number of sentiments associated with the concept of escapism, and these include a need for a change of place, seeking senses of sincerity, being alone and being free as positive aspects, as against more negative components such as escaping from work or family problems, being unhappy or stress. A summary of the distinction between 'escape from' and 'escape to' is provided in Table 2.2.

These distinctions between 'escape from' and 'escape to' can be combined with the psychometrics previously discussed, because reference can be made to degrees of the neurotic, open-mindedness and risk aversion that

Table 2.2 Distinctions between 'escape from' and 'escape to'

Escape from	Escape to
• Work pressure	• Rest and relaxation
• Stress	• Integrating with nature
• Urban environment	• Discovering new places
• Ordinariness	• Having fun
• Lack of peace	• Meeting new people
• Being with others	• More temperate climate
• Family priorities	• Finding oneself or rediscovering oneself
• Lack of happiness or contentment	• Acquiring new skills and knowledge

are implicit in the discussion generated by Durmus (2019). Partly derived from Eysenck's work, in a small-scale study with students, Ryan used the five temperaments framework to identify links between personality and holiday preference. The five temperaments are held to be relatively stable dispositions of character and have a relatively long history in psychology derived from the work of Galen of Pergamon, a physician believed to have lived from 129 to 216 AD. His original four temperaments were the sanguine, the phlegmatic, the choleric and the melancholic. In the 20th century, as personality theory developed, additional conceptualisations arose. Mehrabian (1996a, 1996b) was one who offered more formalised psychometric analysis, and the four factors increasingly came to number five as in Mehrabian's Power-Arousal-Dominance (P-A-D) model. These alternative dimensions were designated Extraversion, Agreeableness, Conscientiousness, Emotional Stability and Sophistication. The PAD model has been used in tourism studies by Li *et al.* (2015) and White (2005). The former identify the potential usages of P-A-D with psycho-physical responses, while White (2005) reviews past literature to suggest that emotions may have an important role in moderating the relationship between motivation and actual behaviour.

Personality Traits

The previous paragraph implies a long history of linking personality with motivation. Personality research is closely associated with the concept of traits and trait theories. Kleiber defines traits as 'emotional, motivational, cognitive, and behavioral tendencies that constitute underlying dimensions of personality on which individuals vary' (Mannell & Kleiber, 1997: 186). It is the differences between traits that help define personalities and permit distinctions to be made between people (John & Srivastava, 1999). Equally, however, individuals possess different dependencies on these traits – differences that the neurosciences are, after almost a century of research, only just beginning to ascertain to add new dimensions of understanding the nature of humans (Panksepp *et al.*, 1978).

The work of Panksepp (2010) on animal emotions and their implications for human behaviour has clearly shown how stimulation of parts of the brain can create sadness and fear for neurotics or less negative emotions for extraverted individuals (Lin *et al.*, 2014). Panksepp writes, 'It is among the inherited subcortical primary-process instinctual tools for living that the foundations of human emotional lives reside, and neurochemical imbalances there can lead to persistent affective imbalances of psychiatric significance' (Panksepp, 2010: 533). In various studies, Panksepp advances the notion of three important cortical structures or processes. The *primary process* relates to instinctive unconditioned emotional brain systems that generate intentions to act at a basic instinctive level. These processes have been shown to occur from the midbrain periaqueductal grey (PAG) regions to medial diencephalon to various basal ganglia nuclei (amygdala, bed nucleus of the stria terminalis, nucleus accumbens, etc.) that interact with paleocortical brain functions including the medial- and orbitofrontal cortices. The second tier is that of *secondary emotional processes* that arise from simple emotional learning, such as classical and operant conditioning. Panksepp (2010), in particular, attributes importance to fear conditioning. Finally, there is the *tertiary-process* emotions that are the intrapsychic ruminations and thoughts about one's lot in life, and these can be triggered by stimulation in the medial-frontal regions.

These findings link to the Big-Five trait theories of extraversion, agreeableness, conscientiousness, neuroticism and openness to experience (Goldberg, 1990) because direct cortical stimulation (Panksepp, 2010) and indirect external stimulation have shown these traits trigger different emotional responses to stimuli (Jani *et al.*, 2014; Lin *et al.*, 2014) to generate what Panksepp (2010) lists as the seven primary or basic emotional states. These are seeking, rage, fear, lust, care, grief (formerly panic) and play. There exist linkages between these neurological studies and the personality traits that indicate implications for visitor experiences and the evaluation of experience. Taking the Big-Five traits in turn, extraversion as described in this book was closely associated with the work of Eysenck and his colleagues and is among the more extensively discussed traits. It is generally associated with qualities such as being outgoing, active, sociable, assertive and unrestricted (De Raad, 2000; Kuo *et al.*, 2016). On the other hand, introverted individuals are less likely to express their thoughts and tend to conceal their emotions (De Raad, 2000). Extraversion is also linked to a high level of arousal, and in stimulating environments the differences between the more and less extraverted are likely to come to the fore (Mehrabian & Russell, 1974). Extraversion is also more closely associated with hedonic values when compared to other personality traits, and equally extraverts have been shown to be more adaptable than others in the face of challenges (De Raad, 2000).

Those whose personalities are inclined to agreeableness tend to be accommodating, amicable and kind. They are also inclined towards the search for information, not only as an objective but also as a means towards being able to help others (De Raad, 2000). This implies that such people would make effective guides and providers of information and services relating to the needs of visitors.

As the classification title implies, those who possess conscientiousness tend to be reliable, responsible and probably conform to mainstream norms (Roberts *et al.*, 2005; Tracey *et al.*, 2007) Equally, they prefer to plan ahead, indicating if not totally risk-averse at least they prefer to have a sense of control. Hence they tend to make many plans and organise things before making decisions, which makes them much more risk-averse than other personality types (Lee & Tseng, 2015), which might help explain Duckworth *et al.*'s (2012) finding that longitudinal studies indicate the trait of conscentiousness is more often associated with success than other traits. Eisenberg *et al.* (2014) point to childhood factors being important in reinforcing conscientiousness. Extreme conscientiousness, however, can create obsessiveness (Carter *et al.*, 2016).

Not surprisingly, therefore, extreme conscientiousness can be linked with measures of neuroticism. Generally, the trait of neuroticism is linked to feelings of anxiety but also depression and anger (Meyers *et al.*, 2010), with the link to conscientiousness being hypothesised when considering the behaviour of procrastination. Indeed, some have even implied that procrastination could be a further trait (Lee *et al.*, 2006). Certainly, the combination of neuroticism and extreme conscientiousness has been linked to ill-health and generally such tendencies lead people to find more negative emotions when assessing measures of satisfaction (Diener & Seligman, 2002, 2004).

The final trait is openness to experience, which is often described as the trait associated with creativity, curiosity, being imaginative and even unconventional, and indeed being intelligent and insightful (Myers *et al.*, 2010). The ability to be open to new experiences is also shown to be associated with self-assessment, as discussed in other sections of this book. Consequently, those seeking new experiences, especially if linked to greater tolerance of psychological if not physical risk, can often obtain better understanding or appreciation of the new cultural and historic locations they may be visiting as tourists and potentially gain benefits that shape their subjective well-being (De Neve & Cooper, 1998).

With the advent of improvements in easily accessible statistical routines, tourism researchers have adopted several of the scales measuring the traits in psychometric studies of tourism. For example, Kvasavo (2015), using structural equation modelling (SEM) with a small sample of 227 foreign visitors to Cyprus, concluded that four of the traits were associated with adopting eco-friendly behaviours – the odd one out being open-mindedness. However, while researching the literature and finding studies that link the traits to such aspects as visitor emotions (Lin *et al.*, 2014), internet usage (Jani *et al.*, 2014) and satisfaction (Lin & Worthley, 2012), when adopting a critical stance it was felt that many of the papers tended to be statistical exercises and not always transparent, or the number of items allegedly measuring traits seemed to be few in number or the sample was small. Also, several omitted many of the standard tests for reassurance as to reliability of the data. There were, however, others that were transparent as to shortcomings. For example, Gao *et al.* (2017) report a study of 1445 respondents based on random sampling in Xi'an, China. Scales were constructed to measure subjective well-being (including life satisfaction/evaluation, domain satisfaction and eudaimonic well-being), personality traits, moods and trip satisfaction and other variables including life satisfaction. The purpose was to examine how trip satisfaction might enhance life satisfaction; a relationship often claimed to be one of the benefits of tourism as is shown by various studies reviewed in this book. However, Gao *et al.* (2017) report, 'The empirical results of this study show that travel satisfaction does not significantly influence life evaluation, but life evaluation strongly influences travel satisfaction. This may be a disappointing result in the sense it suggests daily travel is less influential for subjective well-being than other domains such as work, health, and personal relationships. On the other hand, we would be surprised if a different result would have been obtained' (Gao *et al.*, 2017: 121).

Indeed, we tend to agree with a comment made by Bujisic *et al.* who cited even earlier work when writing, 'The effect of personality traits and personality types on tourism preferences and satisfaction in hospitality environment has not received significant academic attention in the past (Tran & Ralston, 2006)' (Bujisic *et al.*, 2015: 28). Using a sample of 252 respondents, they examined a model of visitor experience shaping satisfaction and then intentions to return. The results were congruent with other studies of what is quite a standard model in tourism, but from the perspective of the present concern, the model fits were found to improve once measures of personality based on the five traits were used as moderating variables. They specifically found this to be the case when noting 'esthetic experiences lead to higher satisfaction for people with higher levels of openness to experience when compared to people with lower openness to experience, based on the path coefficient results. In addition, entertainment experience led to higher satisfaction for participants with lower-level openness to experience compared to the ones with higher' (Bujisic *et al.*, 2015: 32/33).

The theoretical structure suggested in Chapter 1 attributes importance to personality in several ways. It notes that personality may shape demand for types of holidays, and this is also a factor in the model proposed by Stanley Plog (2002) and indeed the tourist types described by Philip Pearce (1982) and in the role model suggested by Yiannakis and Gibson (1992) – all of which are described in subsequent chapters in this book). Second, the role of personality is referenced by comments about the need to adapt to situations found at the holiday destination. As seen, aversion to risk, approaches to planning, open-mindedness, abilities to adapt, being prone to anxiety – all are aspects of personality traits that help shape the 'push' towards holidays, and also how the 'pull' attributes may be evaluated.

Stimulus-Organism-Response Theories

One commonly used approach to analysing the links between motivation and responses to theories is stimulus-organism-response

(S-O-R) models. In many respects they are akin to the models shown in Figures 2.2 to 2.5. The stimulus may be internally or externally induced whereupon a cognitive action occurs leading to a behaviour that is an observable reaction. While simple in concept, they can be described as a 'black box' model in that in several cases an externally induced stimulus can be observed as can the final pattern of behaviour, but basically little is actually known about what is actually going on in the middle within the 'organism'. Several commentators are now suggesting that the neuro-physical sciences are beginning to reveal answers. One of the more notable scholars in tourism who is advocating this approach is Noel Scott (2020) who along with other colleagues began his studies by tracing eye movements and psycho-physical responses in response to videos and advertisements for holidaying.

However, the work of Scott (2020) and Skavronskaya *et al.* (2020) evolved as a response to deficiencies perceived in earlier research, especially as indicated above, to S-O-R concepts and studies (Mehrabian & Russell, 1974). SOR theory has been widely used in many different disciplines and fields, including not only tourism but also related fields in marketing such as consumer services (Sherman *et al.*, 1997), servicescapes (Bitner, 1992) and retailing (Baker *et al.*, 1994). Bitner's 1992 paper emphasised both the environment within which a service took place and particularly the role of employees and customers' cognitive processes. In tourism research, the environmental stimuli in S-O-R theory may refer to restaurant-specific stimuli (Jang & Namkung, 2009), co-creation experiences (Wang *et al.*, 2022), hotel ambience (Jani & Han, 2015) or indeed senses of authenticity and enjoyment (Kim *et al.*, 2020).

As noted previously, one specific aspect of S-O-R theory that has often been used by tourism researchers is the pleasure-arousal-dominance (P-A-D) theory proposed by Mehrabian and Russell (1974). One possible reason for its use is that sought to emphasise the role of emotion rather than assuming a linear, logical and rational pattern of stimuli-response linkages that was often associated with the S-O-R approach, even if the outcome of 'satisfaction' might itself be described as an affective or emotional outcome. The use of statistical metrics as forms of measurement might have been said to have echoed earlier classical economists' concepts of utility and an adherence to a law of diminishing returns (Martinoia, 2003). In the three dimensions of the P-A-D model, the first is that of 'Pleasure' – the degree to which one feels happy, joyful, satisfied, and may be considered as having a temporal component as taking pleasure in the moment, or having a good quality of life or contributing to quality of life where one is content. In many tourism studies it is the former meaning that is generally considered, but quality of life studies is becoming more common. The second dimension – 'Arousal' – refers to the extent to which a person is stimulated, ready for action, excited or nervous. It has long antecedents in the psychological and psychiatric literature and is related to fear (flight or fight tensions), to athletic performance and required levels of optimal arousal prior to performance. One early assessment of arousal was found in the Yerkes-Dodson Law (1908). The third dimension – 'Dominance' – perhaps should read 'Domination' as it is generally understood to be the degree to which a person feels 'dominated' and hence constrained with restrictions on their feelings of autonomy. The continuum may therefore be understood as ranging from being dominated to feeling free, but that begs the question whether one is free to dominate others. Tourism researchers generally ignore this latter consideration, and thus in tourism the continuum is generally one from being restricted to being free to make one's own decision with the context of holidaying.

Examples of the use of the model are provided by, for example, Bigné *et al.* (2005) who used pleasure as a potential determinant of satisfaction and loyalty. Given the presence of airline loyalty schemes, Xu *et al.* (2019) looked at how potential and actual airline passengers reacted when examining airline reviews. Xu (2023) used P-A-D theory to examine the differences in emotional responses to experiences of six different types of theme parks found in Xi'an, China. He suggested there were generic aspects to all theme parks, but equally each style of theme park generated different patterns of emotional response. His sample included amusement parks, cultural parks, an animal park, a film set and a water park, and he summarised the different outcomes as shown in Table 2.3.

Reverting to the Dann 'push and pull' approach, Li *et al.* (2018) linked the viewing of advertisements to emotional pleasurable responses via psycho-physiological measures of motion. These means of measuring

Table 2.3 Summary of theme park visitors' emotional combinations based on PAD theory

	High-Pleasure	Low-Pleasure
High-Arousal, High-Dominance	High-Pleasure, High-Arousal, High-Dominance (+P+A+D)	Low-Pleasure, High-Arousal, High-Dominance (-P+A+D)
	Excitement, joy, or elation	*Anger, frustration, or irritation*
High-Arousal, Low-Dominance	High-Pleasure, High-Arousal, Low-Dominance (+P+A-D)	Low-Pleasure, High-Arousal, Low-Dominance (-P+A-D)
	Excitement, enthusiasm, or awe	*Anxiety, nervousness, or apprehension*
Low-Arousal, High-Dominance	High-Pleasure, Low-Arousal, High-Dominance (+P-A+D)	Low-Pleasure, Low-Arousal, High-Dominance (-P-A+D)
	Confidence, pride, or feeling in control	*Calm, collected, or in charge*
Low-Dominance, Low-Arousal	High-Pleasure, Low-Arousal, Low-Dominance (+P-A-D)	Low-Pleasure, Low-Arousal, Low-Dominance (-P-A-D)
	Relaxation, contentment, or tranquility	*Sadness, depression, or boredom*

Source: Xu (2023)

emotional responses have become popular among some researchers and are discussed later in this book.

Arousal and Neuroscience Research

One reason for their use is tied to the concept of arousal. It has long been recognised that high levels of arousal are associated with observable psychophysical responses such as increased heart rates measured by beats per minute, while stress is associated with increased blood pressure (Schachter & Singer, 1962). Other signs include increased rates of perspiration. Consequently, informants are asked to respond to videos or other stimuli and these physical responses are measured against oral answers to questions (Li *et al.*, 2018). Li *et al.* pose three reasons for their approach. First, they suggest that emotions exist in both the unconscious as well as the conscious mind. Second, self-reporting, especially if using survey materials, tends to the rationale while being dependent upon recall of past events. In addition, as Ryan (1994) has noted, even if the questioning involves direct face-to-face interaction, there remains the researcher's preference for the articulate respondent over the less articulate, while conversations include non-verbal as well as verbal clues. The third reason is that conventional methods of data collection by interviews and surveys cannot capture the moment-by-moment reactions to stimuli in real time, and thus again potentially important information is being lost or simply not considered. A potential fourth reason lies in the sensitivity of the equipment used to collect measures. Tassinary *et al.* (2000) note that facial muscle contractions are detected even when there are very weak affective stimuli, and no visible facial muscular changes are noticeable to the human eye. Similarly, they report zygomatic muscles are activated when smiling and positive emotions are being reported, while corrugator supercilii muscle movement is associated with frowning and negative emotions.

In their study Li *et al.* (2018) used facial electromyography (EMG) which measures electrical signals involved in subtle facial muscle movements, including those not usually noted by humans, and skin conductance (SC) that measures arousal through changes in the sweat glands (Grabe *et al.*, 2000, reported that even watching stimulating news programmes in television could trigger the sweat glands). In Li *et al.*'s study, a sample of 33 university staff and students were shown three advertisements – one each for Adelaide and Hamilton Island in Australia, and another for Switzerland. The adverts were videos of approximately 90 seconds in duration. After each video was viewed, the respondents were asked a series of questions about their emotional responses to the promotional material. In total, the exercise took approximately an hour. It was found that the self-reports and physiological responses correlated with each other, but the authors argue that the physiological responses were superior in detecting differences between the cases that elicited similar emotional content in the self-reporting. Equally, the physiological responses were better at differentiating between the affective response and levels of arousal, whereas self-reporting was less able to distinguish between the two. Similarly, the physiological responses caught a better temporal record of changes in response.

Similar studies have been conducted by Hadinejad *et al.* (2019a, 2019b). The former examined responses to the use of music in promotional videos and the latter introduced a video on skiing in Iran with facial responses being caught by FaceReader™. Results similar to those reported in the previous paragraph were found. While much of the above-cited work has been done by colleagues of Noel Scott, their findings have been replicated by others. For example, Beck and Egger (2018) examined the differences in responses to promotional materials based on two-dimensional and three-dimensional presentations, the latter involving the use of virtual reality (VR). Again, within a laboratory context, physiological responses were captured including heart rate and electrodermal measures of sweat glands. In this case, control groups were used. To briefly summarise the results, again a correlation occurred between self-reporting of emotions and those of the physiological measures, no statistical difference was found between control and experimental groups, but the use of VR found higher levels of arousal and excitement.

The studies show that in laboratory conditions, physiological responses do possess some advantages, most certainly in capturing temporal patterns in responses in real time. However, Beck and Egger (2018) are far more guarded in terms of reporting the implications of physiological measures. Recognising that emotional responses are operating at the unconscious level, they note that past experiences and differing degrees of motivation are not being measured, but these are important aspects of emotion creation and interpretation. Equally, one other aspect is whether the laboratory conditions themselves have an impact on the data being collected. The obvious question to ask is that of whether a causal linkage can be found between cognitive and affective reactions and the physiophysical and psychophysical changes being found in the human body. This is not a new debate. In 1964, for example, Lazarus and Alfert used measures of skin conductance and heart rate to assess to what extent the use of introductory statements could relieve stress after exposure to a silent film showing a primitive ritual involving subincision that involves slitting the urethra in male genitalia. In two cases, an introduction was provided, one being an 'intellectual' comment and the second a denial of harm statement. A sample of 69 male students were randomly divided into three experimental groups. Mood statements and physical reactions were measured along with personality measures. Distinct differences in stress and anxiety were found at statistically significant levels but the findings were complex, and the researchers found relationships contrary to prior work and could only speculate at times why 'low deniers' did not benefit from denial statements, while on other measures no differences were found between high and low deniers. They end their paper by commenting that, 'Of course, whether the process by which the commentary reduces stress reaction is the same or different from that involved in the effects of the orientation is not clear at this point. Nor do we know how much preparedness independent of content contributes to the effectiveness of the orientation' (Lazarus & Alfert, 1964: 205). It seems to the present authors that tourism scholars using these techniques are equally in a position of being unclear as to what the patterns of physiological changes in the brain, heart or sweat glands actually mean for conceptual development.

However, this is not to say that these physical measurements are not without practical use. The use of eye-tracking measurements has proved to be of use from a practical perspective even if the relationships between eye tracking, reported statements and brain activity remain unclear. Savin *et al.* (2022) provide a review of more than 70 studies of eye tracking in the context of tourism. They comment that most studies refer to restaurant and teahouse menus, website usability for businesses in the field of hospitality and tourism, advertising photography, exhibitions and museums, and sustainability in tourism, with an emphasis being on static materials. They write, 'We noticed a lack of studies directly focused on assessing attention level of viewers while being exposed to dynamic stimuli, none of the reviewed articles choosing to use videos as stimuli' (Savin *et al.*, 2022: 296). Many of the results have proved of practical value in capturing data on usage rates and duration of viewing, spatial aspects as to where viewing is being directed and the extent to which parts of the visual images are being revisited. They conclude, for example, that websites are being used primarily for informational purposes than actual purchasing behaviours. They also observe that issues of sustainability attract little attention and recommend that there remains a need for printed material.

The observation that few studies occur in a dynamic environment and tend to be conducted in a laboratory might be due to the review being primarily of studies that were conducted when the technology tended to be less sophisticated than that now available. That situation has changed significantly in the recent past with wearable eye-tracking equipment. Nonetheless, even recently Scott *et al.* (2020) were reporting laboratory-bound results of people's assessments of the beauty of the Great Barrier Reef based on photographs in a laboratory situation. On the other hand, Huang *et al.* (2022) reported results from the Shandong Museum using *in situ* data derived from information collected by respondents as they toured the museum viewing exhibits. The study compared learning experiences derived from self-tours and guided tours with eye-scanning spectacles recording paths taken and duration of viewing of exhibits followed by self-recall of activities and answering questions about the subject of the exhibition. Apart from differences in learning patterns, the authors suggest several practical outcomes in terms of potential management gains that could lead to an enhanced visitor experience. These lessons included better spatial and temporal planning of guided tours that avoided duplication of trails and an avoidance of other groups. It also highlighted which were the more popular exhibits and also made possible experimentation in terms of different guides telling stories geared towards different visitor segments based on degrees of knowledge and interest of the visitors.

Several confounding issues exist in trying to elicit clear answers. The first is that the correlation between verbal reports and psycho-physical changes is often weak (Beck & Egger, 2018). That, however, may simply reference the nuanced nature of the linkages. The second is that apart from the aforementioned prior antecedents of past experiences and evaluations, there are also external factors that can affect both cognitive and physical functioning. Taggart *et al.* (2023) investigated cognitive, manual dexterity and psycho-physiological responses in outdoor fly-in fly-out (FIFO) mining workers over the course of a work shift during summer and winter months. They found no difference in manual dexterity and fatigue during the two periods, but in the summer memory scores were lower. Dehydration and increased temperature are thought to account for poorer cognitive performance in the summer. Diurnal differences were also found in performance and circadian rhythms also had an influence. Obviously, there are differences between miners and holidaymakers, but the same issues appear in the tourism reports.

In at least two studies, those of Michael *et al.* (2019) and Bastiaansen *et al.* (2018), electro-encephalography (EEG) readings have been used as part of a number of other tests to examine responses to destination marketing. The latter study involved 30 participants who were shown 40 pictures divided into four sets, one set being of Bruges. Respondents were divided into groups, one of which saw a clip from the start of the film *In Bruges*, while a second viewed a clip of approximately the same length of another film, *Bay Rum*.

The results indicated neurological activities being stimulated more when the group who had seen the film *In Bruges* were shown photographs of the city, and these activities correlated with higher appraisals of the city. Hence, this study, like that of Beck and Egger (2018), reinforces the view that prior arousal and positive affective responses are likely to lead to higher appraisals in a proxy for a post-visit event. The authors also conclude that EEG readings are an effective means of studying whether visual images do elicit specific responses in parts of the brain. They do identify a series of limitations in the study. It is not known for how long the positive responses last. Nor did they examine consequent behaviour or intention. However, in their penultimate paragraph they conclude that it could be possible to 'establish linkages between these three variables (marketing material, reactions in the brain, purchase behaviour) and determine whether observe brain activity signatures can be observed that reliably predict not only that a subject feels triggered by certain marketing materials but is likely to buy the marketed (destination) product' (Bastiaansen *et al.*, 2018: 82). This is wholly consistent with the original S-O-R theory, and it places an emphasis on the initial motives of the tourist and the abilities of the destination marketing organisations to initially capture attention in a competitive marketplace and stimulate a search for information on the part of the tourist. While it can be argued that this in effect is simply reinforcing what is already known, it partially advances a reason as to why that happens and the mechanisms behind it – namely, that neurological patterns are consistent with the experience. However, we may be naïve, but it still seems to us that the argument remains at the stage of correlations rather than causality, and that in one respect both the formation of intention and evaluation, and the associated physical and neurological activities associated with those judgements are reactive and not determining variables.

The Theories of Societal Dysfunction and Holiday Taking

It was noted that Dann (1977) emphasised the nature of escape when considering motivations for holidaying. The above analysis has indicated that common motives are the need to escape from stress, but Dann went further to analyse what it was about our patterns of living that created such stress. He wrote 'anomie refers to a society whose norms governing interaction have lost their integrative force and where lawlessness and meaninglessness prevail. Its derivative, anomia, however, applies to the individual, who clearly is affected by the social situation in which he finds himself' (Dann, 1977: 186). In short, such societies are dysfunctional for they fail to provide for well-being, both psychologically and materially. These forms of analysis are often associated with the initial work of the sociologist Émile Durkheim (1858–1917). In one of his works on suicide, Durkheim analysed the differing rates of suicide between Catholics and Protestants, women and men, married and unmarried, those with and without children, and those serving in the military and civilians. The differences were significant, and Durkheim (1897) attributed this to the presence or absence of senses of connection to wider society and the nature of that society. An anomic society is a society that is structured in such a way that it disconnects people from each other, partly by the imposition of patterns of work or hegemonic structures where those at the bottom of hierarchical structures are disadvantaged by lack of opportunity. It has been suggested that anomic societies and a loss of communal values threaten to divide societies even further based on inequalities of income and wealth to the point of creating social unrest (Picketty, 2020; Rashbrooke, 2021).

Durkheim was writing at a time of significant economic change as the industrial revolution created new forms of production and organisation. The phrase, 'dark satanic mills', as used by William Blake (1757–1827) in his poem 'Jerusalem', came to be associated with harsh working conditions, long hours and deprivation as clearly shown in the United Kingdom in its Poor Law Reform Reports and the novels of Kingsley and Dickens and the autobiography of James Myles (1850). It was the conditions of the industrial revolution that led Karl Marx (1818–1883) and Frederick Engels (1820–1895) to write the *Communist Manifesto* (1848) and subsequently to describe the dehumanising aspects of factory work where the human becomes a cog in the machine (Marx, 1867). This notion was used to effect in the 1936 film *Modern Times* directed by Charlie Chaplin, when he is sucked off the production line into the cogs of the machine.

Another who examined the same topic was Jost Krippendorf, most notably in his book *The Holidaymakers: Understanding the Impact of Leisure and Travel* (1987). Krippendorf adopted Durkheim's concept of an anomic society to suggest that the package holidays that emerged in the immediate aftermath of the Second World War encapsulated a factory-like production of low-cost holidaymaking that indeed packaged the tourist into a series of rituals with relatively little scope for individual decision-taking. He also noted the need for environmental care and pleaded for more humane ways of holidaying. Growing incomes and a growing demand for individualised attention have possibly mitigated some of the more negative aspects of his analysis, alongside a growing awareness of the need for environmental care.

His analysis is based on three domains of human life, namely work, habitat and leisure, which he suggests comprise the ordinary features of daily life. He suggests that travel represents the polar opposite of the 'ordinary' and is thus the 'non-ordinary'. This is illustrated in Figure 2.6 that also places both the 'ordinary' and 'non-ordinary' within a wider social, political, economic and environmental context.

The 'ordinary' life is in itself a cause that motivates a need to travel because its dysfunctional components fail to satisfy any sense of self-completeness. That sense of 'completeness' is most likely achieved through leisure pursuits, and hence he terms the holiday as an occasion of 'mobile leisure', thereby linking the geographical components of tourism with the wider field of leisure and relaxation research. It is the interactions that visitors have with the society of the visited or host community that therefore generate a 'counter everyday life experience'. For writers like Krippendorf, holidays are times of renewal through the 'newness' of place, while those places may also be 'different' by the nature of their

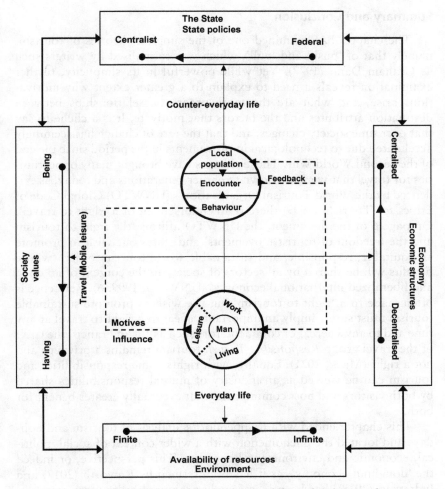

The model of life in industrial society: work-home-free time-travel

Figure 2.6 Work and leisure in an industrial society. Source: The Holidaymakers, Krippendorf (1987)

own social, political, economic and environmental contexts. It is this approach towards tourism that highlights the concerns of many tourism researchers with the authenticity of the visitor experience. They suggest that without 'authenticity' it would seem that the holidaymaker is simply consigned to a life constrained by the barriers erected by a dysfunctional society that permits people to be solely a factor of production (labour in the classical economic category of factors of production) and a consumer shaped by the images of advertising. For many commentators, people will only be themselves if they can access 'authentic' experiences. This is further explored in Chapter 4.

Summary and Conclusion

The chapter has examined one of the simplest theories of tourism, namely that of 'push' and 'pull', which was formalised by writers such as Graham Dann (1977). Yet while powerful in its simplicity, further examination reveals a need to explain to a greater extent why motivations arise, and what are the more pragmatic relationships between destination attributes and the factors that motivate. It is a cliché to say that over time society changes, and that the rate of change has seemingly accelerated due to technological improvements in the period since the end of the Second World War. Those changes have brought many opportunities for travel that were unknown to earlier generations and today, as evidenced by the World Tourism Organization's (UNWTO) Global Code of Ethics for Tourism (1999) there is an endorsement of a 'right to travel'. On page 6 of the document, the UNWTO affirms 'the right to tourism and the freedom of tourist movements' and states our wish to promote an equitable, responsible, and sustainable world tourism order, 'whose benefits will be shared by all sectors of society in the context of an open and liberalized international economy' (UNWTO, 1999: 6). Reference is often made to a 'right to tourism' but the wish to promote sustainable tourism must surely imply an important caveat to a right to travel at any time and to anywhere. For commentators such as Justin Francis, the CEO of the travel group *Responsible Travel*, tourism remains a privilege and not a right (Mack, 2021). Equally, with rights come responsibilities and tourism can be viewed as an industry of mutual responsibilities shared by both visitors and host communities that eventually creates benefit for both.

This chapter ended with Krippendorf's analysis of tourism and holidays and located the phenomenon with a wider context of social, political, economic and environmental contexts. This perspective, or indeed the 'doughnut economy', as it has been termed by Raworth (2017) and Indrawan (2018), has been increasingly promoted by tourism researchers. Indeed, Ryan (2020) has commented on how New Zealand's tourism policies, enunciated by the Ardern government, have effectively reversed the objectives of tourism as an industry by stressing not only economic objectives but rather the social and environmental benefits of tourism, if not as primary objectives then as important complementary goals.

The first two chapters of this book have looked at the context within which demands for tourism are shaped, and it has been argued that those demands shape expectations based on the images generated by social media and induced advertising. The next chapter will look at the relationship between expectation, perception of performance and the gaps that might exist in this relationship.

3 Expectations and Gap Analysis

The chapter includes:

(a) The importance of expectations.
(b) The relationship between expectations and satisfaction.
(c) Gap analysis between expectation and performance.
(d) The gaps that explain expectation and performance gaps.

Introduction

Hoorens defines expectation as a '*belief about events or behaviors that **will** occur* or that will be revealed in the future' (Hoorens, 2012: 142). Expectation is an attitude and thus comprises three dimensions, namely the cognitive, emotive and conative. The cognitive is what we believe to be factually true and thus, according to Hoorens, would appear to lie at the core of expectation, but in tourism studies, researchers often go beyond that to consider the inference or implications of belief. The emotive represents how we react to the believed truth. Do we perceive it to be a positive or negative influence, and also in part, how important do we believe it to be to us as individuals, and to those we hold dear? Valence theory in chemistry is about the nature of bonding in coordination compounds. Similarly in social science studies expectancy-valence theories are about an aggregation of expectancy and the emotional response to expectancy that strengthens a potential behaviour or valence.

The theory is associated with Vroom's (1964) framework of analysis and can be represented as Valence = Cognition × Emotion. This is, however, an overly simple representation of Vroom's original work, and tourism scholars have long recognised this when applying the concept to destination images. Thus Kaye Chon (1989, 1990), using the earlier work of Clawson and Knetch (1966) and Gunn (1989), highlighted the stage of anticipation when applying the concept of expectations derived from images of a destination that were held by a potential visitor. It might be said that the Valence = Expectation × Anticipation × Emotion.

The third element of an attitude is the conative, which is the formation of a predisposition to action. The strength of the conative is in part an outcome of cognition and emotion, but it may be a bounded dimension. As Ryan (1994) noted, the predisposition to action may be constrained by the anticipated consequences of that action, and thus in developing any theory of the relationship between perceived images of place and the likelihood of visitation, and the subsequent evaluation of a holiday and the benefits to be gained from it, one can sense that any such relationship is complex. The link between image and formation of evaluation is therefore filtered through cognition, emotion, conation, anticipated consequence and yet more.

One aspect of this approach is to what extent are the sub-sectors of attitude, namely the cognitive, emotive, consideration of consequences and conation multiplicative in nature, and are they of equal weighting? Is there a difference between perception and attitude? The two are closely linked and one distinction commonly noted is the observation that attitudes are relatively constant over at least intermediate periods of time. In which case, they may also be interpreted as being a personality trait. As such, they help shape perceptions which are responses to stimuli by which a people 'interpret and organize sensation to produce a meaningful experience of the world' (Pickens, 2005: 52) in a reasonably consistent way. The complexity of attitude construction and measurement is well evidenced from the earliest empirical research. Thurstone (1928) is said to have observed that trying to attribute a number to indicate the strength of an attitude is akin to describing a kitchen table with 'a single numerical index' (Fabrigar *et al.*, 2005: 79).

The adoption of attitude measurement as being multiplicative and each component being of equal weighting is obviously a simplifying notion, and one that lends itself easily to statistical manipulation. It can easily be criticised, and even in the tourism literature, commentators have distinguished between core and peripheral aspects of attitude. For example, Su *et al.* (2020) examined attitudes of potential Chinese tourists to South Korea at a time of tension over the deployment of the Terminal High Altitude Area Defense (THAAD) system in South Korea on 6 March 2017. The authors used a faction's algorithm to distinguish between core and peripheral components of images of South Korea in attempts to find patterns of association in attitude formation. Among their conclusions, the authors found that peripheral attitudes could be used to offset negative images within the core attitude. That study is pertinent to this discussion because it indicated the complexity of measurement and secondly the ability to measure differences across a relatively large sample (here, some 531 respondents) that is made possible by current statistical algorithms combined with computing power. Yet, one needs to remember that whether using simple or complex measures, the attempts to build models that permit generalisation remain (at least for the present) an abstraction from reality. Given that it is normally stated that 'good' theory is parsimonious (Polansky, 1986; Runco, 2009), simpler models with high effective predictive abilities may be more time and cost effective than better but more expensive complex models. Yet having stated this, technological and analytical progression continually changes the ratio between simplicity and complexity. Today's cutting-edge technique can quickly become tomorrow's commonplace as is illustrated by the contents of leading journals like *Tourism Management* and the *Journal of Travel Research*, although there remains a need to communicate with the non-expert and lay public – an issue that was writ large in the political life of several countries during the period of Covid.

These issues form the subject matter of this chapter. There are primarily three sections to the chapter. The first examines expectations and how they are formed. The second will be based on gap theories relating to expectation and performance and will include an analysis of the measures of service quality. These measures are strongly related to the pioneering work of Parasuraman, Zeithaml and Berry that commenced with their ServQual (Service Quality) Theory and which they have subsequently revisited several times since the initial statement in 1988. The final section will briefly review some alternative approaches to the measurement of service quality that has been found in the literature.

Expectation

Olson and Dover suggest that 'customer expectations are *pretrial beliefs about a product*' (Olson & Dover, 1979: 181) that serve as standards or reference points against which product performance is judged. It is further suggested that in the general marketing literature, expectations are viewed as *predictions* made by customers about what is likely to happen during an impending transaction or exchange. In a similar approach Oliver wrote that 'It is generally agreed that expectations are consumer-defined probabilities of the occurrence of positive and negative events if the consumer engages in some behavior' (Oliver, 1981: 33). These early works helped to establish an agenda of research that came to dominate much of the subsequent work in retailing, marketing and financial services as well as tourism, as quantitative work became more accessible with the advent of personal computers capable of supporting software such as the Statistical Package for the Social Sciences (SPSS). Certainly, tourism researchers have sustained similar approaches in their studies. For example, Huh *et al.* (2006) applied what has come to be known as the confirmation-disconfirmation approach in a quantitative study of visitors to Virginia Historical Triangle. They concluded that 'Cultural/Heritage Attraction, General Tour Attraction, Shopping Attraction, and Information Factors had significant relationships with overall Satisfaction ... [and] Cultural/Heritage Attraction appeared to be a more important factor that influences overall satisfaction than General Tour Attraction, Shopping Attraction, and Information Factors' (Huh *et al.*, 2006: 96).

Such research has tended to a consensus that tourists have expectations after selecting a destination for a holiday and that their satisfaction levels during and after their holiday period are indeed functions of their expectations (Huh *et al.*, 2006; Yoon & Uysal, 2005). Consequently, research supports the viewpoint adopted by many tourism marketing organisations that an understanding of tourists' expectations provides important clues when considering proposals that seek to invest in projects designed to improve the attractiveness of a destination and improve tourist goods and services (Aksu *et al.*, 2010). However, these arguments presuppose that tourists possess clear images of the destination prior to departure, and this supposition has not really been tested. It is known that tourists gain their information from several different sources, and research has been undertaken to assess the effectiveness of these sources. Among the more important sources are word-of-mouth recommendations, both directly from friends and relatives and, at least equally important, electronic word of mouth (e-Wom) derived from social media including the web pages of the online travel agencies (OTAs) as well as influencers and bloggers, and vlogs by travellers (Gretzel, 2018; Peralta, 2019). All such sources are then filtered through the past experiences of the tourist, and in that sense, it might be argued that past personal experience is perhaps the most important source of image creation and hence expectation.

However, such a comment may have more relevance for someone who has travelled extensively and is probably less relevant for a person commencing their first overseas trip. Such a person will be more dependent upon the experience of others, and hence again the role of social media and the comments left on OTA sites such as Expedia.com, Trip. com and similar websites have importance. Pinto and Castro (2019) analysed results derived from a convenience sample of 397 holidaymakers and concluded that ease of use, price and online reviews were the primary considerations, particularly when supplemented by special promotions. It was found that more than 90% of the sample's bookings were through an OTA, of which Booking.com was by far the most used site. Bernardo *et al.* (2012) reinforced web page usage of photographs when finding that a key supplementary component for many holidaymakers is hedonism. They concluded that 'Although both *functional quality* and *hedonics* had a positive impact on perceived value, the two paths were not equivalent. It is apparent that functional quality had a greater impact on perceived value than did hedonics' (Bernardo *et al.*, 2012: 345). However, the presence of both, particularly if of a 'playful quality', does create loyalty and repeat purchasing through the online agency website.

Nonetheless, it is argued that physical travel agencies retain importance. Two features support this. First, OTAs are easy to use if the trip is essentially one where the holidaymaker travels to one destination airport and then returns home. On the other hand, trips requiring multiple destinations may be easier and indeed cheaper to organise through a competent travel agency.

Again, while the use of multiple accommodations within a trip can be arranged through an on line travel agency (OTA), the conventional travel agency may be better able to develop a 'deal' for the client. A second feature, as previously noted, is that should travel arrangements go awry, one phone call or text message to a travel agent seeking help may be much more successful than trying to arrange matters over an online service whose first response is to direct the client to a talk-bot.

One lesson that has emerged from the arrival of OTAs is that tourists' expectations continue to change. Many holidaymakers believe that OTAs offer lower prices than conventional travel agencies, and many have come to expect that deals will be on offer. The increasing availability of alternatives does lead to expectations about pricing, but it can be observed that lower prices can involve costs in terms of after-sales support, the quality of rooms on offer in hotels and even the location of seats on flights. The cheapest seat on the flight just might be the one nearest the toilets. These service costs permit hotels and airlines to counter the lower prices offered on OTAs by offering specific rooms and/or seats on flights and differential pricing so that clients can manage their own value-for-money options on the providers' websites.

The above discussion indicates that expectations shape images of a destination and what a destination has to offer. The presence of OTAs also shapes expectations of the price to be paid, and the expectation of alternatives being offered in both terms of price and possible quality of service. Expectations are also the formation of criteria of evaluations, but as shown in Chapter 1, expectations can be modified by experience and newly acquired information. This process of expectation formation continues until the trip commences, after which adjustment of visitors' expectations is reassessed by experience. Equally, during the trip, the visitor absorbs and stores new information and assesses interactions with the service providers, which processes serve to adjust expectations for the rest of the trip. Finally, at the end of the trip, expectations still function as criteria for assessing experiences and setting expectations for future trips.

It was quickly realised by both those in the industry and academic researchers that the processes just described are multifaceted and complex. Pocock (1992) was one who appreciated that gaps may exist between reality and image. In a paper examining a region of north-east England around Tyneside named 'Catherine Cookson Country' by local tourism authorities to capitalise upon the historical novels by the popular fiction writer, Catherine Cookson, Pocock noted the importance of expectations through the phrase 'the reality of Cookson Country originates in the fact that the majority bring with them eyes already prepared to see' (Pocock, 1992: 240). In his sample, the majority were extremely familiar with the novels of Tyneside life from about 1850 to the early 1930s. For these visitors, the novel was by far the primary factor establishing expectations of the tours. Pocock refers to 'An eye oblivious to the extensive demolition and redevelopment' since the period Cookson describes, and how the finale of the tour – a visit to a local museum is the 'ultimate confirmation of the pilgrims' experience' (Pocock, 1992: 241) despite the primary history displayed being that of the redevelopment of Tyneside. Pocock (1992) suggests that being in the company of fellow enthusiasts, the interchange of stories and the guide's expertise created a willing suspension of disbelief. The comments of visitors that he provides in his paper are arguably an example of synchronic behaviour. Synchronic behaviour is the emergence of simultaneous behaviours among participants, with such studies initiated originally by observations of birds wheeling in the skies at dusk. Human synchronic behaviour is exemplified by patterns of rhythms in applause or the apparently spontaneous chanting found at many football grounds on a Saturday in the UK. It is a process of unintentional patterns of behavioural symmetry emerging from initial differences (Manu, 2016).

Gap Analysis

The suspension of disbelief arises due to a gap between, on the one hand, the image of place, or the expectation of place, and on the other hand, the reality of that place. As noted in Chapter 1, responses to this gap can vary, and processes of adaptation whereby the tourist responds either positively or negatively to the gap have informed thinking about the tourist experience. In addition to the use of past experience, and the images portrayed by media, the tourist effectively, prior to consumption of the holiday, is acting on beliefs generated by the implicit or explicit promise generated by those creating the images of attractiveness. Yen *et al.* suggest that situations where expectations are not met need to be analysed from three perspectives, namely 'locus (who caused the failure), stability (is the failure likely to happen again?) and controllability (could the failure have been prevented?)' (Yen *et al.*, 2004: 7–8).

This approach raises a number of interesting questions. Among them is the role of the tourist as a co-producer of the experience, the implied promise of the delivered image and the explicit promise of the physical surroundings – all of which have a role in either minimising or extending any possible gaps between the imagined place and the reality of that place. Sundaram and Webster (2000) suggest that the non-verbal behaviour of service staff can be as important as the spoken attributes that convey friendliness, courtesy, empathy and integrity. These non-verbal behaviours they list as kinesics, paralanguage, proxemics and physical appearance. Kinesics includes body language, eye contact, smiling and handshakes. Paralanguage revolves around the delivery of speech, not the specific content of the words, but rather the pitch of tone, the softness or loudness of speech and the pauses and fluency of speech – all of which add warmth or indifference, inclusiveness or exclusion to what is being stated. Proxemics refers to the physical distance between the individuals while physical appearance refers to physical attractiveness, dress code and indeed the colours of clothes being worn. Shades of red have long been held to imply warmth and friendliness, while darker suits are thought to imply authority. These elements, it is thought, may also have importance not only for the *in* situ relationships between provider and holidaymaker but also in their representations on video.

The more one looks into the possibility of gaps between the expected and the desired, the more complex appears the relationships. The services marketing literature offers several nuances of what it is that the customer expects. Thus, commentators have distinguished between the *desired service*, which reflects what customers want, and which represents the normative standard and/or the level of service customers hope to receive. Then there is the *predicted service*, the level of service that is likely to occur, and third, there is the *adequate service*, the standards customers are willing to accept, the minimum tolerable expectation or the bottom level of performance acceptable (Miller, 1977). Each of these different approaches still retains the notion that assessments of customer satisfaction result from a comparison between predicted service and perceived service.

Much of the current literature relating to these gaps between expectation and performance originated with the work of Oliver (1977) and his confirmation-disconfirmation model of expectations. In his 1977 paper, Richard Oliver does cite earlier work, including that of Anderson (1973) and Festinger (1957), both of whom suggested that 'post-exposure ratings are primarily a function of the expectation level because the task of recognizing disconfirmation is believed to be psychologically uncomfortable' (Oliver, 1977: 480). However, Oliver noted that despite this earlier literature he could only identify five prior studies with empirical data, and it is suggested that the influence of Oliver's work on later generations of researchers arose from the rigour of his own experimentation. In his 1977 paper, Oliver used a sample of 243 undergraduate students in a $2 \times 3 \times 2$ unequal n factorial design consisting of expectation (low, high), disconfirmation (negative, zero, positive) and nature of exposure (drive and inspection, or inspection only) matrix to permit comparisons to be made between groups of students' expectations and assessments of cars using seven-point scales of paired opposites. Given the subsequent criticisms of the ServQual scales discussed below, it is interesting to note that Oliver found no correlation between the expectation scales and the level of disconfirmation, but this he attributed to a common regression effect when measures of change exist. He concluded that 'The results have shown that the disconfirmation effect implicit in the expectation theories of consumer satisfaction can be a significant predictor of post-exposure affect and intention to buy and may be viewed independently of product performance expectations' and 'all results show that perceived performance is a positive function of expectation and disconfirmation when other factors are held constant' (Oliver, 1977: 485).

It is also possible that the influence of Oliver's work was also aided by developments in computing. In 1981, IBM introduced its first personal computer and it is from approximately this time that researchers had easier access to statistical programs that permitted increasingly sophisticated means of calculation. This was evident by the mid-1980s when Parasuraman *et al.* (1985) published their first paper on the ServQual model. Whereas Oliver wrote of the gap between expectation and perceived performance as a measure of consumer satisfaction, Parasuraman *et al.* suggested that it was actually a measure of service quality rather than satisfaction *per se*. This distinction continues to this day, but it seems often that the distinction is blurred in some of the tourism research literature. For the purposes of this discussion, two key points exist. The first is that the ServQual concept for a considerable time seemed to dominate the services marketing literature. A search on Scopus using the search term 'ServQual' indicates more than 2500 papers while Google Scholar notes more than 105,000 publications of various kinds on its database using gap analysis. However, Google trends indicate a decay in the popularity of ServQual as a topic since 2004, and that might be due to the criticisms that have been made of the model. One of the first criticisms was made by Carman (1990) who was unable to reproduce the five dimensions identified by the initial authors. Then, in a series of different papers, Cronin demonstrated that much of the variation in gap scores was due not to the expectation scale by rather to the evaluation or performance scale. It was suggested by Cronin and Taylor (1992), Taylor and Cronin (1994) and Brady *et al.* (2002) that the expectation scale tended to be consistent. In was also noted that in many examples of gap studies the researcher was in effect asking participants to recall their expectations as few studies were conducted in sequentially separate pre-purchase and post-purchase situations.

In the field of tourism, tourism and hospitality scholars were reaching similar conclusions. Saleh and Ryan (1991a, 1991b), Ryan and Cliff (1996, 1997) and Ryan (1999) provided empirical data that confirmed the findings of Carman (1990) and Cronin and Taylor (1992), and in 1999 Ryan also questioned the usefulness of the gap scores. He questioned the value of gap scores when, for example, a gap of one, on an expectation and performance or evaluation scale, possessed the same numeric value when considering the different situations shown in Table 3.1. He argued that while the gap remained at '1', each case represented very different sets of situations from both psychological and managerial implication perspectives.

Table 3.1 Differences between expectation and evaluation/performance scores

Expectation score	Evaluation/performance score	Gap
2	1	−1
6	7	+1
4	5	+1
3	4	+1

In response to these criticisms Parasuraman *et al.* over a series of subsequent papers maintained that for all of these flaws the scores represented useful data for management, but in doing so they made a series of suggestions to improve the scale. These suggestions included the use of nine-point scales and a reassignment of items to the five dimensions thought to underlie service quality (Parasuraman *et al.*, 1994a, 1994b; Parasuraman *et al.*, 2002). Initially there were five dimensions, namely tangibles (the physical attributes of quality such as appearance of facilities and staff), reliability (consistency of service), empathy (understanding the consumer's perspective), responsiveness (time taken to respond to customer requests) and assurance (integrity of response), but in Parasuraman *et al.* (1994b) the final three attributes were collapsed into one attribute to leave three dimensions. However, by this time, the original simplicity of the scale had become more complex with the 22 items of the scale now being asked to measure desired and minimum expectations as well as perceived performance, while the gap between desired and minimum expectations was stated to represent a zone of client tolerance. The questionnaire was therefore increased from 44 to 66 items in addition to questions about past purchase experiences and socio-demographic details. These additions run the risk of increased respondent fatigue.

These distinctions have been noted by tourism scholars, but in many instances the attention of tourism scholars has been directed to more recent constructs thought important, such as more nuanced understandings of place attachment. Indeed, using the category 'travel' with the term 'ServQual' on Google trends indicates a lack of comparative lack of contemporary (i.e. 2022) interest. An analysis using Scopus and Google Scholar also showed declining interest since about 2010, even when assessing its use in the hospitality industry. Indeed, even by 2000, Caruana *et al.* concluded that despite its earlier importance, 'findings question the usefulness of the expectations side of SERVQUAL and indicate that the addition of minimum expectations appears to have added little that is of incremental value to the measurement of service quality' (Caruana *et al.*, 2000: 63). They additionally note that it is possible that consumers have few clear-cut definitions of what it is that they expect, and indeed are often passive in their expectations. In earlier work, Saleh and Ryan (1991b) suggested that the process of expectations and evaluations was far from uniform in its formation and that extraneous factors created series of trigger points that brought the notion of evaluation into play.

This implies that the holidaymaker may indeed be broadly accepting of their holiday experiences given that basic demands of difference and key motives such as relaxation are met. Indeed, being in a different environment in itself is sufficient to create satisfaction. However, a negative or possible positive critical incident (Bitner *et al.*, 1990) will initiate as a trigger point subsequent evaluations of performance against expectations.

Where Gaps Occur

One feature that is often lost in the debate over gaps is another facet of Parasuraman *et al.*'s initial work, which was the identification of how gaps in areas other than expectation-performance can exist. These gaps are illustrated in Figure 3.1 and are seven in number. These are:

Gap 1 – The first knowledge gap

The gap between management understanding of tourist knowledge and tourist knowledge itself

This is the gap between the holidaymakers' information and the management's perception of what it is that the holidaymaker knows about a product, service or destination. As can be assessed from the literature

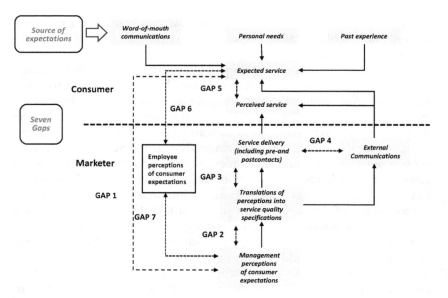

Figure 3.1 The gaps in service

review above, much of the conceptualisation and debate preceded the common usage of the internet and the development of OTA services. It is a commonplace statement that today many customers are better informed than in the past and are able to make price and quality comparisons quite easily. From the perspective of the distinction made between the induced and organic image development as described by Gartner (1986, 1989), today it must be recognised that the e-Wom sites accessed by the holidaymaker are shaped by the management of hotels, products and services. The initial images shown on sites like Booking.c om are influenced by management, and often where critical comments are made by a hotel the management can re-shape or modify holiday-maker reactions by the responses made by management. For example, Chen *et al.* (2019), Xie *et al.* (2014) and Xie *et al.* (2016) find that managerial responses can enhance the reliability of comments found on OTA sites, but the evidence does not appear conclusive because Xu *et al.* (2020) suggest that the process of verification of comments coming solely from those who use a service can determine degrees of trust in the integrity of the OTA, and equally, managerial responses are often credited as being less trustworthy. Whether the pandemic associated with Covid-19 has shaped attitudes towards the responses of hotel managers remains untested in early 2022.

Gap 2 – The standards gap

Translation of perceptions into service quality specifications vs Management perceptions *of consumer* expectations

This gap is about how management responds to their perceptions of the level of service desired by their clientele. Ideally, management can correctly identify what their customers want and are able to design facilities and service that deliver the required standard wanted by hotel guests and holidaymakers. The gap emerges from management not being able to identify what its clientele wants and/or being constrained by a lack of knowledge or resources. The former gap is being closed due to the development of the internet. Not only is there feedback on services provided by OTAs, Facebook and other social media, but improvements in software design and artificial intelligence (AI) means that data are increasingly subjected to sophisticated analysis. Credit card transactions can provide a wealth of information by looking at the combinations of services being purchased, although such usage patterns are subject to legal protection of privacy. However, even when individual names remain concealed, analysis of, for example, restaurant sales can reveal combinations and volumes of different menu items to the point where predictive purchasing may inform purchases of key ingredients. As an aside, should clients be concerned about privacy issues they may, in some instances, be able to avoid such searches by making payments in crypto currencies when such payment is permitted.

The same processes of purchase pattern identification can help the latter problem of resource constraint. If purchase patterns, staff rostering, opening times, use of discounted offers and differential pricing can all be analysed to produce efficiencies of supplies, then that in turn begins to alleviate any possible resource constraint. Even if the overall impact is marginal in terms of reducing volumes of wasted food, cleaning material and so on, each marginal improvement adds to profit.

Many companies seek to combine both better knowledge about clients and improved efficiencies in resource supply through the creation of loyalty schemes. This is quite common in the tourism industry. Airlines offer frequent traveller points that provide possible upgrades or enhanced choice of seats, and similarly hotel chains offer equivalent services such as room upgrades, executive floors that offer some improved service to guests or rooms with better views. It is quite common for small cafes and restaurants to have schemes that offer a free coffee with every ten coffees purchased in order to create a more loyal pattern of repeat purchasing. Each repeat purchase also offers an opportunity for an extra impulse purchase such a scone or similar add-on 'goodie'. Skilled wait staff might also generate additional sales through the simple enquiry as to whether the customer might like something else.

Gap 3 – The delivery gap

> Service delivery (including pre- and post-contacts) vs translation of perceptions into service *quality specifications*

This gap highlights the need for management to continually monitor the quality of service being provided to guests and visitors. The provision of standard specifications such as details of food purchases in restaurants and hotels, the handbooks on staff-customer relationships and the attempts to create means by which to be good corporate citizens will not achieve the desired results if management fails to monitor actual service provision. However, such service monitoring needs to avoid any situation where staff begin to feel that they are being checked 'from on high' and have little ability to respond to any potential perceived failing on their part. This represents a key aspect of successful employer-employee relationships. There is a delicate balance to be achieved between, on the one hand, a collaborative team approach whereby management and staff are joint partners in developing and providing good experiences for visitors, and on the other hand, the negation of management responsibility to actually manage. In an ideal world, management and staff act as one in providing the resources and quality of service desired by visitors, but the reality is that individuals can have off-days, that supplies may be delayed, that guests themselves are unrealistic in their expectations or may arrive only after flight delays, having experienced less than ideal travel conditions and hence being tired and intolerant of perceived service failures.

An added challenge that the hospitality and tourism industry will face as the third decade of the 21st century unfolds, is how to manage the great use of service robotics. The use of robots has been seen as one way of overcoming staff shortages, and a review of current practice can find examples of robots being used in cooking processes (Kolodny, 2017) and the Hilton hotel chain's experimentation with Connie – a robotic concierge (Pinillos, 2016). While there has been some use of robotics, it does seem that thus far many serve as an intriguing aside or gimmick, but Xu *et al.* (2020) note the rapidity of development of robotics in hotels, to which one can add the development of emotional and verbal reasoning and facial responses demonstrated by Sophia and her various colleagues. Almost certainly Sophia has attracted much attention as the first robot to be granted citizenship of a country (Saudi Arabia) and a series of questions as to the extent of her intelligence and the political choreography of Hanson Robotics (Parviainen & Coeckelbergh, 2021) have been discussed. There is little doubt that Sophia and her colleagues will have a future role in the tourism industry due to their ability to entertain. Incidentally, at the commencement of the second decade of the 21st century, Yeoman and Mars (2012) asked whether sex robots might be the future of Amsterdam's sex tourism. It is possibly notable that a decade later the answer remains negative.

For their part Xu *et al.* (2020), possibly more realistically, identify a number of managerial responses to the introduction of robotics in hotels, including the removal of menial and boring jobs, creating cultures that embrace change and excitement about the role of new technologies, but equally identify some disquiet about the impact of robotics, including the extent to which staff are involved in investment decisions.

While much of what is being currently written about the use of robotics in tourism remains speculative and is premised in scenario building rather than precise forecasting, the tourism industry has long been regarded as an early adopter of innovative technologies. The use of robotics in theme parks has improved upon the previous generation of animatronics – a development that long ago commenced with Disney being an early adopter. Milman *et al.* (2020) report that theme park visitors respond positively to the introduction of robots, and one might conclude that the 2020s represent the cusp of a new era in terms of robotic and holographic entertainment even before fundamental questions relating to the implications for employment and human grasp upon reality have been fully identified, much less answered. But this has always been the case with each technological advance as the human mind subsequently embraces such challenges.

Gap 4 – The communication gap

> Service delivery (including pre- and post-contact) vs external communications to customers

This represents a well-researched topic within marketing, namely the gap between what is advertised and what is the reality of the brand, product or service. It has been suggested that consumers expected some component of 'salesman's puff' or exaggeration, a viewpoint derived from the 19th century when 'snake oil' salesmanship was not uncommon with miraculous cures for fevers and illnesses being sold to the gullible (Pope, 1983). However, as the 20th century dawned, and modernity beckoned, manufacturers realised that professional advertising and the establishment of brands required a consistency between claims and actual product or service provision. As Elliot (1972) suggested, the latter stages of the industrial revolution gave rise not just to managerial classes but also senses of professionalism as evidenced by the introduction of examinations and professional and trade training as additions to the older concepts of university education.

Today it is a cliché that brand authenticity is a prerequisite to build brand trust (Portal et al., 2019) that leads to a choice between competing brands (Phung et al., 2019). Tourism scholars have made significant contributions to this area of research. The issue of destination image, as previously stated in this text, has been a core subject for tourism research from the outset (Ryan, 2020), and current work continues regarding the influence of the internet, social media and emergent trends due to 5G links and the promise of the IoT (the internet of things). For example, Chen et al. (2020) review the literature to test a model whereby brand authenticity induces revisit intention, congruency between holidaymaker self-image and destination image, engagement with the destination and post-visit recommendation to others. Using an online sample of 521 respondents, they found 'that destination brand authenticity and destination brand self-congruence are key drivers of destination brand engagement, revisit intention, and recommendation intention' (Chen et al., 2020: 7). They continue to suggest that destination brand engagement plays a complete mediating role in 'the relationship between destination brand authenticity and revisit intention, as well as the relationship between brand destination self- congruence and recommendation intention' (Chen et al., 2020: 7).

Like many such findings, the study is not immune to criticism. Being based on an online survey conducted in China, the sample is skewed towards the young, but it can be countered that this age group has been a key driving force of contemporary Chinese tourism and thus represents a significant tourist segment (Khoo-Lattimore & Yang, 2018a). More tellingly, it is possible that the factors identified in the path analysis tend towards a tautological analysis that tests possibly more the consistency of response than the presence of the factor in people's decision taking. For example, brand continuity is tested by it being timeless, persisting through time and persisting through trends. It is not therefore surprising that correlations exist between such items, but the average variance extracted is 0.54, exceeding the usual criterion of 0.5, but possibly by relatively little. To be fair to the authors, they discuss in detail such issues as to the symbolism of brands and meanings for self, but in such research, respondents can only respond to the questions set, and these may not be questions that they would normally consider in their choice-making. It might be noted that the criticism of tautology can be generalised to many exploratory factor analysis (EFA) studies.

Fortunately, and especially with reference to cultural and historic-based tourism experiences, a rich literature exists with reference to at least the objective authenticity of the tourist place, and it is a literature that incorporates qualitative open-ended questioning. Such questioning might be the primary, sole source of data, or alternatively, it may be part of a mixed method study. In one such study, Shi *et al.* (2019) examined home-sharing lodging. Among their conclusions, intellectual intimacy with the hosts adds significantly to the authenticity of the stay and cultural awareness and learning. In short, the promise of authenticity implied by the product of home sharing when fulfilled enhances the experience. A congruency of promise and offer generates satisfaction. Similarly, in two different studies, one of the Fuxi Mausoleum in Zhoukou administrative region in Henan, China, and one of Daguanyuan in Beijing, Zhang *et al.* (2021, 2022) note that the presence of pilgrimage rites and traditional practices also generates senses of an authentic experience among visitors. In such cases of pilgrimage tourism shared values, culture combined with an ambience of antiquity was thought to create a convergence between tourist types that meant high levels of satisfaction across different groupings of tourists.

The hospitality literature is also replete with image and branding concepts, especially with the emergence of competing social media products and the disruption caused by the internet, as exemplified by companies such as Airbnb. In addition, hotel chains have reacted positively to challenges required by concepts of good corporate citizenship as employers and providers of services that historically have high consumption of natural resources. The large hotel chains such as Accor are also known for careful appraisal of market segmentation by brand name as evidenced by the Ibis, Novotel, Mercure, Sofitel and Pullman brands, to mention just 5 of the 52 brands the company was operating at the commencement of 2022. Each brand of hotel is targeted at a different market segment ranging from the Ibis 3-star hotels offering convenient location and services for the more budget-oriented or short-stay visitor to the upmarket Pullman brand offering luxury facilities that would appeal to longer stay or above average income clientele. Hotels are distinguished by size, room types, location service style and so on. It has been suggested that hotel guests seek authenticity that reflects the culture of the local vicinity but to do so with the comforts of home. Adopting this perspective has led some commentators to suggest that, for hotels, brand integrity combines both the objective differences offered by chains like Accor with the guests' own social construction of what represents 'authenticity' (Mody et al., 2019; Wang, 2007). Mody et al. comment that brand authenticity 'speaks to the genuineness and originality of the service provider's brand, existential authenticity, which refers to the authenticity of relationships formed with the people and objects encountered on the trip, and intrapersonal authenticity, which refers to the way in which the travel experience affects the creation and maintenance of the traveller's identity' (Mody et al., 2019: 67). Their study examines the notion that the latter two components are important to the creation of senses of well-being and memorable experiences, with the former facet of an objectively based brand image creating brand dependency. Taken together, it is possible to build 'brand loyalty' – certainly at least in terms of recommendations to others.

Amatulli et al. (2021) consider the contribution made to brand assessment by considering the environmental policies adopted by hotel management. They test the notion that while hotel guests may respond favourably to a hotel's sustainability policies, in reality they remain more committed to the services being offered. They adopt a process of experimentation with a sample of 198 respondents randomly allocated to one of two experimental conditions, and compared the results derived from confirmatory factor analysis. They conclude that an emphasis on sustainability policies does drive a willingness to subsequently check on services offered, especially among guests more inclined to pro-environmental policies. They suggest that anecdotal evidence that indicates a preference of services may be mistaken, and the real driver for hotel choice is a perceived brand integrity based on sustainability. It might be argued that a halo effect exists whereby a hotel that provides evidence of sustainable practices is thought to be more likely to deliver on service promise than one which does not emphasise environmentally friendly policies.

Gap 5 – The service gap

The expected service vs the perceived service

As evidenced by the initial discussion on the gap between expected and perceived service, this was the gap that attracted much of the early attention to the ServQual model. A number of factors might explain this. It built upon earlier commentaries such as that of Oliver (1977), whose literature provided a conceptual base for the development of the model. Second, the 1970s and 1980s saw a significant change in economic activity that drove the services sector to attain a dominant role in the economy of several countries. For example, Ley and Hutton (1987) examined the emergence of the service sector in Vancouver in the preceding period. Banking, insurance and other financial services were more apparent, the mass media of television emerged and more administrative posts were being established in education, health, marketing and human resource management as economies reduced their dependency on the primary and secondary sectors of the economy. It was also a time when mass tourism was being established. Commentators sought to explain differences in the marketing of services as distinct from the sale of goods, noting, for example, the inability to store the service. Services were said to be intangible, that is, they could not be tested prior to purchase. The provisions of a service meant consumption and production were not separated and client and service provider were in close proximity (it was a pre-internet world at that time!). There could be a lack of consistency in performance, and hence services were heterogeneous in nature. Additionally, there was often a lack of ownership. The purchaser possessed a temporary right of usage, for example an aircraft seat or hotel room, but not a right of ownership (Lovelock, 1980). Finally, it opened up another concept – namely that the consumer was an actor in the process of establishing service quality, that is, they were a prosumer or co-consumer dependent on the commentator (Pine & Gilmore, 1999).

The ServQual model promised a means of analysing the intangible nature of services and offered a means of analysing situations for management across the dimensions of service quality. Perhaps in this initial adoption of the model, the concentration of effort on the service quality gap may have detracted attention from the other gaps discussed here. The view taken in this text is that while the gap between expectation and perceived service has been shown to be problematic when examined in detail, the wider analysis of the seven gaps retains value as an indicator to management as to how and why problems can arise in service delivery. Further they point to a systems approach to service quality management of holiday experience design wherein each part of the system interacts with other parts, so highlighting the need for more holistic approaches to management.

Gap 6 – The second knowledge gap

Employee perceptions vs consumer expectations

The first knowledge gap related to the manager's understanding of the market demand for their services, but a second gap can also exist. This second gap arises from the attitudes and knowledge possessed by the front-line staff, namely the waiters in restaurants, the reception staff in hotels, the adventure guides in adventure tourism, the interpreters on cultural tours and all the others in daily contact with the holidaymakers.

This gap has been generally under-researched, but areas of interest have attracted academic attention. One comparatively rich area of research was that on tour guides, especially those relating to Chinese tourism. Entering the term 'Chinese tour guides' into Google Scholar indicated over 96,000 items, but the more restricted search criteria used by Scopus revealed just 70 entries. The discrepancy between the two data sources probably reflects the often-heated debate about the practices adopted by Chinese tour guides that occasionally led to public debate following physical assaults on or by tour guides. This had been a running sore in Hong Kong for several years prior to Covid. In 2014, a tour guide was beaten after asking a tourist to stop smoking in Hong Kong (Kilpatrick, 2014). In October 2015, the BBC (2015) reported a tourist was killed after trying to intervene in a dispute when a tour passenger refused to shop at a tourist shop. In 2018, with the opening of the Macau bridge, journeys were disrupted when Hong Kong police conducted spot checks to ensure that unlicensed tour guides were not operating contrary to legal regulations.

Much of the issue prior to Covid arose from commission only or low-cost tours. The problem was not unique to Hong Kong because when Chinese travel commenced with the introduction of the ADS (Approved Destination Status) scheme, several tourists took, for the first time, a trip to see the world outside of Chinese mainland. However, Hong Kong in particular attracted many such tours being Cantonese, if not Mandarin speaking, and having a reputation as a shopping centre offering genuine branded goods. However, to make the trips affordable, costs were cut, and revenue was gained from tour guides taking shoppers to selected shops. These shops often had an arrangement with the tour guide, who received a commission from the retailer on the sales gained.

Deceit was often involved. The tour guide would frequently show tourists pictures of popular items with good prices – but effectively these were loss leaders, and the other items would be sold at prices that gave the retailer a good margin. In many instances, stores would only open for Asian tourists and would open up just prior to the coach arriving. In New Zealand, examples of fraud were known to go further with false descriptions and posting of false accreditations such as Qualmark being used (New Zealand Commerce Commission, 2013). The 2014 Chinese Tourism Law sought to correct this by enforcing the advertised tour schedules – prior to that a common instance would be where the tour guide would change the advertised itinerary. Shopping was only part of the scam. Tourists would be taken to public parks in Rotorua, New Zealand, to view a geothermal area rather than the better, but privately operated parks, and often accommodation arrangements might be changed if the tour guide could gain an advantage. In addition to the Chinese authorities clamping down on such practices, New Zealand's Commerce Commission instituted legal proceedings. However, the main deterrent that emerged was the introduction of cheaper roaming sim cards and making them available at the duty-free sales areas of airports prior to customs and passport control. Chinese tourists were then immediately able to undertake price comparisons, and it reduced their dependency on the tour guide (New Zealand Commerce Commission, 2013). In addition, such tourists increasingly acquired more experience of foreign travel, and combined with a growth of incomes within the People's Republic of China, the incidence of scams based on souvenir sales is significantly less than before.

However, whilst this illustrates deliberate fraud by the service provider, it should not be read that such scams are commonplace. There are other instances of course. It is believed that taxi drivers may take a longer than necessary route from the airport to the hotel (but again an obvious use of mapping software informs the tourist), and Li and Pearce (2016) found examples of false weights being used while Ouyang *et al.* (2020) report on public shaming through social media that has halted hotel scams of unjustified charging. Ouyang *et al.* (2020) also cite the use of STOP (Situational Theory of Problem Solving) suggested by Kim and Grunig (2011) as a means of analysing such situations based on degrees of perception of risk.

Any one of a number of situations can account for why front-line staff may fail to meet holidaymakers' expectations. These include (a) a failure to properly train front-line staff, (b) such staff failing to apply their training through ill-intention, tiredness or lack of resources, (c) confusion over instructions from supervisory staff, or poor instruction from unprepared supervisors and (d) a lack of or failure of staff support systems. The literature on staff empowerment considers many of these types of issues. In a study of perceived important competencies in the hotel industry, Marneros *et al.* (2021) questioned a total of 450 managerial staff employed by 158 Cypriot hotels and separately a further 30 researchers working in hotel schools and universities. The questionnaire was developed after a literature examination of gap-related studies in the hospitality industry. Out of the 40 competencies identified using a five-point scale, 28 scored more than 4.0.

When subjected to factor analysis, the most important managerial competency was leadership and critical analytical skills, followed by IT and financial analytical skills, then human relations and interpersonal skills including an ability to interact meaningfully with people of differing cultures. The final factors of importance were human resource management and professional competency, but each of these factors 'explained' less than 4% of variance in the scale. The authors then looked at gaps between importance and perceived competencies of management, and as is common in several such studies, the difference in scores was statistically significant at levels of $p<0.01$ with the means score for importance exceeding that of perceived competency.

In many respects, this study was congruent with earlier studies. Management tends to emphasise the importance of soft skills of empathy, understanding, leadership and problem solving above the professional skills of financial analysis and operational management, and one suspects that this is because the training in techniques and operations is easier to assess and for the most part is assumed to be present among staff. Some studies exist which indicate that hotel managers may initially be critical of the functional skills possessed by young staff after completion of university or college training (Goethals, 2016), but Goh and Okumus (2020) suggest that Generation Z holds positive attitudes about hotel occupations, perceiving it as 'fun'-filled, but while suggesting means of gamification that can meet the needs of Gen Z they also suggest a need for managers to be upfront about the unsocial working hours required of workers by the hospitality industry. They further suggest that the industry cannot continue with practices of low pay given the demographic trends in many countries that are characterised by aging populations.

Gap 7 – The second communication gap

> Employee perceptions of consumer expectations vs Management perceptions of consumer expectations

This last gap points to the need for congruency between how management perceive guest and holidaymaker expectations and how front-line staff perceive those clients' needs. It follows from the above discussion that management must be realistic about their customers' wants, because any failure in that perception means that front-line staff are not being properly prepared for the tasks they are being asked to perform. Similarly, there is a need for front-line staff to be able to inform management of where and when they encounter problems. This requires trust in the management's ability to see that, in most if not all instances, the problems are systematic and not those of the individual employee. A poorly trained employee represents a failure on the part of recruitment or supportive training provision. It should be noted that it is possible that staff are careless, or indeed badly intentioned, but a search of the literature indicates that such situations are far from common. For example, in their book offering advice to management when handling problematic employees, Delpo and Guerin (2021) specifically make the point that such cases tend to be exceptional rather than the norm. However, one issue of significance that has come to the fore of many people's attention since about 2017 is the emergence of a 'Post-Truth World' as characterised by the disputes surrounding the outcome of the 2020 US Presidential elections. The events of 6 January 2021, at the US Congress Buildings in Washington, and subsequent enquiries serve to demonstrate the extent to which people can go when convinced of 'the truth', even when evidence exists that the 'truth' is solely misinformation. Equally, demonstrations by those believing that various Covid vaccines are unsafe, or indeed those not believing in the reality of Covid, are further extreme examples of people acting in ways many see as being anti-social, yet such behaviour is based on a belief that their actions are for the benefit of society.

These are extreme examples of circumstances where people act on partial or total misinformation. Issues can arise within the communication gap because employees or management believe that a given set of circumstances exists, and where they do not accept evidence that points to an alternative viewpoint. Bago *et al.* (2020) illustrate just how important is the opportunity for consultation and deliberation as a means of correcting initial intuitive reactions to a headline or news content. From this perspective, a conflict between management and employees' beliefs as to what tourists, hotel guests and others want needs to be viewed as a difference of opinion arising from a common concern. Both parties wish to benefit the consumer but differ on how this might be done. One can begin with common ground, namely, how to better meet the needs of the consumer. This approach switches the onus to discussing consumer wants and away from implications of personal failure.

Tripathy (2018) suggests that the way forward is to engender common approaches to creative thinking, while for her part, Raines (2019) argues that a key to success is creating a workplace where everyone feels their opinion is valued, and where advice is not followed, then reasons are provided to illustrate that the opinions offered were taken seriously and considered in reaching decisions. In short, workplaces need to avoid situations where people talk past each other and not to each other.

The gaps – a synopsis

It was earlier suggested that the emphasis on the gap between a customer's expectation and eventual evaluation of a visit experience has distracted attention from the other gaps inherent in the wider ServQual model. The basic fact is that the expectation-evaluation gap is far more nuanced and complicated than initially thought with the result that despite much effort going into enhancements of the model, the model no longer enjoys its past pre-eminence in the service quality and marketing literature. Expectations have been shown to be relatively constant over moderate periods of time and equally often poorly detailed (Sachdev & Verma, 2002). Sachdev and Verma suggest that over time, expectations tend to rise because of technological advances, but they indicate differences exist between what respondents think is *likely* to happen, and what *should* be happening. The former tends to be closer to reality and also tends to be more consistent given rigidities in supply systems. However, in many ways the expectation-evaluation gap can be envisaged as an outcome of the processes that are involved in the six other gaps, and in a perfect world congruency in the remaining gaps would mean management and employees correctly read customer wants, have the resources to meet those wants, and both managers and employees are fully conversant with the technicalities of operations and possess the human skills to communicate openly and clearly with each other and with the customer. When considering the totality of meeting holidaymaker needs, a possible reaction is to exclaim, 'how is it that employees and managers manage to get it right as often as they do?'

It is also pertinent to recap Chapter 1, at least partially at this point. Tourism is comprised of a number of services; the numbers and types of such services are myriad, including as it does travel agencies, airlines, hoteliers and attractions. Following theories of co-consumption, it is also notable that the tourist plays a role in creating their own satisfaction in the consuming experience (Ryan, 1997b). There also remains the question as to whether a holiday is experienced and assessed as a holistic experience, or as a sequence of experiences. Each explanation has its own implications for individual management. If it is the former, then each business is part of a network of various other businesses and experiences, and if the latter, if anything does go awry, it is easier to identify the business at fault. From a third perspective, the answer probably lies in a mixture of both gestalt and aggregated individual experiences, but that still implies key roles for the separate parts of the tourism industry.

What is known is that holiday taking includes significant emotional involvement on the part of the tourist. This, in turn, predisposes the holidaymaker to possess a strong motivation for achieving successful and satisfactory outcomes. As discussed in Chapters 4 and 8, the roles adopted by tourists represent one way of understanding the factors that contribute to enjoyable holidays. These are often contextual, and a significantly long period of interaction between the tourist on the one hand and, on the other, the place and people in the holiday destination provides both a spatial and temporal context. The longer the stay, and the more diverse the place in its attractions and facilities, the higher is the opportunity for the tourist to manipulate his or her activities to achieve the desired outcomes. Such opportunities present ways of avoiding impediments to a satisfactory holiday, thereby meaning the tourist can bypass possible confrontation with agencies, hotels, restaurants and other stakeholders, including other tourists.

The Alternatives to ServQual

The criticisms made of the ServQual model led to a search for alternative ways of assessing difference between expectations and eventual holiday or service appraisal. As previously noted, the scale arose from an attempt to measure service quality in a way that was generic to all forms of services. Parasuraman *et al.* (1985, 1988) implied that similarities exist between financial and banking services, retailing and restaurant, accommodation and car rental services, and the similarities may be greater than the differences (Gawer, 2009). This viewpoint is contestable as noted below. Second, it was questioned why the scale measures service quality and not customer satisfaction (Lee *et al.*, 2000). Third, the final variant of the ServQual extended the scale used and the total number of items to the point where respondent fatigue could occur. It was suggested that a closer look at the psychometric literature could offer an easier means of measurement (Teas, 1994). Among early critics of ServQual, Mangold and Babakus (1991), Cronin and Taylor (1992) and Richard and Allaway (1993) emphasised the technicalities of service operations. Mangold and Babakus (1991) argued that clients were aware of the front stage of operations and in most cases possessed relatively little idea of the backstage, which was the prerogative of staff. Each therefore had different experiences and sets of expectations.

For their part, Cronin and Taylor (1992) suggested that while a greater emphasis on technical processes would bear fruit when examining service quality, service quality was a prerequisite for the creation of customer satisfaction, and furthermore it was customer satisfaction rather than service quality that was the better predictor of purchase intentions. Given the barrage of criticism, a series of alternative measures were constructed over subsequent years, and these are indicated in Figure 3.2.

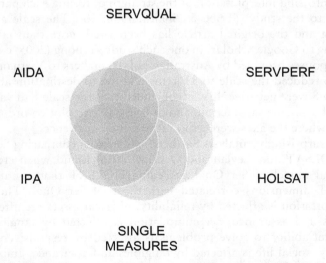

Figure 3.2 Indicative alternative measures for measuring service quality and satisfaction

SERVPERF

SERVPERF emanated from the work of Cronin and Taylor (1992) who argued that the ServQual items formed a single dimension and not the five identified by Parasuraman *et al.* (1988). They also suggested that the greater variance in the performance measure was the key determinant of evaluation, and that performance was better understood as an attitudinal measure. Adopting this approach also had the practical benefit of reducing the number of items in the scale by 50%. Their findings were in a manner consistent with the view of Teas (1993, 1994), who concluded that the 'proposed SERVQUAL mixed model is merely a restricted version of the Teas (1993) NQ [Normal Quality] model' (Teas, 1994: 132). Teas also suggested that the three qualities of desired expectation, ideal quality and performance could also be simplified into one scale.

HOLSAT

HOLSAT was introduced by Tribe and Snaith (1998). The model was specifically designed to measure satisfaction with holidays and was conceptualised as a gap between expectation and performance, but the criteria were based on (a) the physical resort and facilities, (b) ambiance, (c) restaurants, bars, shops and nightlife, (d) transfers, (e) heritage and culture and (f) accommodation. The scale of 56 items was initially tested with a small sample of 102 holidaymakers in Veradano, Cuba. Tribe and Snaith also adopted an approach where 'the mean of the sum of differences (between expectation and performance) was calculated for each respondent and for each attribute. This procedure provides a greater insight into, and interpretation of the strength of feeling each participant brought to the study' (Tribe & Snaith, 1998: 30). The scale attracted attention and the original article has been cited more than 600 times according to Google Scholar. In one such study, Truong (2005) examined 1000 responses provided by Australian holidaymakers to Vietnam and in doing so reduced the scale to 33 items relating to destination attributes of which 8 were negative. It was concluded that the scale had value as a means of assessing satisfaction, and of being able to plot co-ordinates on a graph where the axes were expectations and experience.

Not surprisingly, analysis has been undertaken comparing ServQual with HOLSAT and Ceylan and Ozcelik (2016) found when creating a sequential model of ServQual preceding HOLSAT that a number of HOLSAT dimensions correlated with those of ServQual. They note, 'Transportation is affected by reliability, physical assets are affected by tangibles and assurance, accommodation is affected by tangibles and assurance, ability to solve problems is affected by responsiveness and reliability, social life is affected by tangibles and assurance, ambiance is affected by tangibles and assurance, and heritage and culture is affected by reliability' (Ceylan & Ozcelik, 2016: 6).

The advantage of HOLSAT is its specificity to tourism and it is embedded in a literature of destination attractiveness, but in several respects, it could be argued that the model is a niche within the broader set of gap models and importance-performance and expectation-evaluation models.

Several examples of such models exist and are often presented in a grid format of four cells as shown in Figure 3.3. In both cases, whether the axes are labelled Expectation/Evaluation or Importance/Performance, the top right-hand cell is the desired cell as possessing high scores on the pairs of measures being used.

The top left-hand cell represents the most problematic case for management, as it means that where items are considered important or where expectations are high, the consumers feel the service is falling short. It is a cliché to note that while word of mouth is thought important, it is also true to note that bad news travels quickly. One aspect that commentators have noted is that in some markets the majority of disgruntled purchasers will not complain to the employees or managers but will be quick to voice their complaints to friends. Arora and Chakraborty (2020) reviewed over 226 research articles on customer-complaining behaviour and noted that several classifications had been suggested by different authors. They additionally noted that the core lay in a distinction between complaining or not complaining, but they also suggested that a third category could be added, namely the illegitimate complaint. The illegitimate claim had been generally ignored in prior research, perhaps because dissatisfaction needs to be present to initiate a complaint. Given the importance of satisfaction studies in tourism, retailing and the services marketing literature

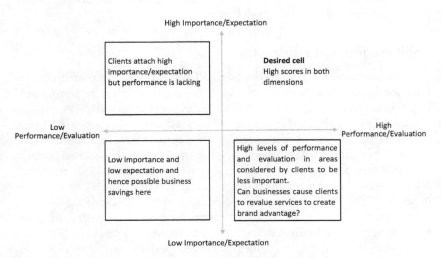

Figure 3.3 A customary modelling of holidaymaker satisfaction

as a whole, much of the discourse was premised on the absence or presence of satisfaction.

However, this means that a different stream of research had been largely ignored. The insurance industry is no stranger to false claims, and among such claims are those related to travel insurance. Within the public domain of news media reporting, a number of anecdotal stories of false insurance claims can be found, many of which fail at the first hurdle of an initial explanation. Unattended property, smartphones and handbags are not uncommonly subjects for claims. Latimer (2019) provides a summary of case law based on Australian cases and suggests that from a legal perspective most claims based on loss of unattended items would probably fail. The costs of such false claims to the travel insurance industry are not wholly known. In some instances, as in the case of claims made on the basis of bed bugs, Doggett *et al.* (2018) argue that insurance costs are but a minor loss when compared to the costs of pest control and refurbishing that such bugs induce. Dong *et al.* (2018) suggest that User Generated Content (UGC) can provide a useful means of detecting financial fraud, and in tourism UGC through OTAs and social media is a common mode of information sharing. In 2020–2021, added complications in estimating travel insurance claims existed. First, in many companies, only consolidated accounts are published in annual reports. Second, of course, due to the pandemic of late 2019 and into the following years, international travel was severely curtailed, and some insurance companies were facing claims arising from cancelled holidays and flights. To what extent illegitimate consumer behaviour of the type envisaged by Arora and Chakraborty (2020) exists, is very difficult to assess. However, in terms of reference to HOLSAT the potential for false statements about satisfaction derived from holiday experiences does open another potential subject for inclusion in modelling.

Single measures of satisfaction

This approach is akin to the SERVPERF approach in that it emphasises the immediate client, tourist or hotel-guest reaction by simply asking, 'How satisfied are you with the product/service/activity?' A copious literature exists about the nature of satisfaction and its measurement, with the majority of studies arguing that satisfaction is a multifaceted factor. Customer satisfaction has been defined as a psychological concept that involves prosperity and feelings of happiness that result from fulfilled expectations gained from the consumption of products and services (Chen & Tsai, 2007). It is a positive emotional response arising from the stimuli of action or participation in meeting a want or desire. In many ways these are tautological definitions. The emotional response is defined as satisfaction, which is an emotion! Hence, as discussed in this chapter, distinctions are then made between the desired response, the expected response, the ideal response, the tolerated response and similar semantic but distinguishable concepts. Satisfaction has also been seen as being relative and hence is contextualised, and comparisons are made between satisfied guests based on experience, age, gender and so on, and is seen as being relative (e.g. being compared with expectation).

In tourism studies, Ryan and Cessford (2003) asked a simple question, namely, does a single measure of satisfaction possess credibility? The question arose because the New Zealand Department of Conservation was creating a web-based dataset of its assets in National Parks that included visitor facilities such as viewing sites, information centres, huts and the like. The design of the database included the possibility of incorporating a satisfaction measure so that the Department could monitor responses over time and identify which sites were more or less satisfactory from the perspective of hikers and other users of park services. The research team created a series of different types of questionnaires based on the ServQual concept with varying layouts of the questionnaire using vertical and horizontal settings for the comparisons of expectations and evaluations. Correlations were found to be high with the responses to the single question 'How satisfied are you?' and the authors concluded the use of a single-item question had credibility if simply seeking a generic overview of satisfaction with a service.

Problems also exist with multi-attribute measures of satisfaction. Looking at the questions listed in Table 3.2, it can be seen that they all relate to measures of visitor satisfaction. Such items are often formatted in some form seeking degrees of agreement with the item using a five- or seven-point scale ranging from low levels of agreement to high levels of agreement.

The first item is generally found suitable if looking for an overall assessment, and evidence from both tourism and non-tourism studies indicate high correlations between single and multi-item measures of satisfaction. For example, Fonberg and Smith (2019) find correlations in excess of $r>0.65$ in measures of life satisfaction. Cheah *et al.* examine the use of single item measures in partial least squares structural equation modelling to conclude 'Overall, these results illustrate that the convergent validity assessment of formatively measured constructs can be implemented without triggering a pronounced increase in survey length

Table 3.2 Questions measuring visitor satisfaction

How satisfied are you today with your experience?
Did the experience represent value for money?
Would you recommend this experience to a friend?
How likely is it that you would return to this experience?
Did you feel the site was too congested?
Did you easily find information on the site?

by simply using a global single item to measure the criterion construct. Our results show that the single item produces sufficient levels of convergent validity and excels its multi-item counterpart in terms of out-of-sample prediction' (Cheah *et al.*, 2018: 3202) and they continue to suggest that multi-item scales might over-fit the data.

In the experience of the authors of this text, the correlations between the items shown in Table 3.2 tend to exceed 0.6 but are measuring different aspects. While a single measure of satisfaction correlates well with both 'value for money' and 'recommendation to a friend', the correlations between the two latter items tend to lower scores. Price is relative to income, and what for one tourist may be 'acceptable' may to another be 'expensive', implying a lesser value. Returning or repeat purchasing is, in retailing and brand purchases, often used as a measure of consumer loyalty. However, in tourism if the question is asked of an international tourist, elements of time, cost and distance might well reduce the likelihood of such repeat purchasing. However, the lack of repeat purchasing may not mean a lack of satisfaction.

On the other hand, the destination management, hotel general manager and others involved in tourism are often interested in more than a generic evaluation and will be wanting to analyse the performance of different aspects of the visitor experience as it relates to varying components of the product or activity. The hotel general manager will want to know about the appraisals of the bed, the choice of pillows, the standard of room cleanliness, the quality of the food in the restaurants, the interactions with staff and the ease of checking in and checking out of the hotel. For such an analysis, many turn to Importance-Performance Analysis.

IPA – Importance-Performance Analysis

As a 'technique for measuring attribute importance and performance' (Martilla & James, 1977: 77), Importance-Performance Analysis (IPA) was initially developed to evaluate automobile dealers' service. By measuring the importance and performance of the service attributes, mean gaps between them are identified, and cross-points are displayed on a two-dimensional grid akin to that shown in Figure 3.3. According to Martilla and James (1977), the IPA model not only demonstrates the areas on which a firm needs to concentrate and those areas that have over-consumed resources, it also allows the results to be easily interpreted by, and be useful for, management decisions.

The technique has been applied in many different areas, such as hospitality, health, tourism, events and marketing (Park & Noland, 2013; World Economic Forum, 2022). With reference to previous studies of tourism/event service quality and customer satisfaction, Kline *et al.* (2016) applied IPA to test how expectations influence cultural tourists' perceptions of performance while Cheng *et al.* (2016) investigated relationships of park visitors' satisfaction and service performances in Taiwan. For their part, Dwyer *et al.* (2016) evaluated the importance of tourism activities that supported the tourism industry in Serbia with a focus on industry perceptions. In a similar manner, Go and Zhang (1997) surveyed meeting planners to identify where Beijing, as an international convention destination, should concentrate its efforts and resources to increase its competitiveness. The technique continues to be used, as illustrated by Rašovská *et al.*'s (2021) analysis of spa, mountainous and wine regions of the Czech Republic. Indeed, the popularity of the approach is illustrated by Google Scholar identifying over 99,000 publications when using the Boolean search terms 'importance performance analysis' AND 'tourism'.

Despite its popularity, IPA has been criticised for both its conceptual ambiguity and the questionable reliability of its results. Oh (2001) criticised the traditional IPA model on 10 grounds. These were: (a) lack of a clear definition of the concept of importance, (b) the absence of a clear criterion variable for the IPA framework as a whole, (c) mixed uses of importance and expectation, (d) lack of research on absolute versus relative importance, (e) the implications of relationships between importance and performance and among the attributes, (f) the absence of guidelines for developing a set of attributes to be used, (g) use of unidirectional versus bi-directional measurement scales for the concept of importance, (h) use of actual means versus scale means in constructing the IPA grid, (i) potential mis-classifications of attributes on the IPA grid and (j) a philosophical issue related to strategic suggestions.

Conventionally, the IPA model is a three-step analysis, which starts with the selection of a group of attributes as service/product measurements; then surveys the participants with questions about their perceptions of the importance and performance of selected attributes; and finally, calculates the means of the two variables and plots a two-dimensional matrix. After these actions, suggestions of future managerial actions are provided according to the results and interpretations of the cells in the matrix (Lai & Hitchcock, 2015). In reviewing the use of IPA, Qiao (2019) identified three different modes to presenting results as means of overcoming some of the criticisms that had been levied by Oh (2001), Lai and Hitchcock (2015) and Arbore and Busacca (2011). In his first analysis, Qiao (2019) selected a conventional approach of defining the cross-hairs of the four-cell matrix by using the mean scale scores. In his sample of attendees at the Alibaba 2018 Hangzhou Computing Exhibition, a conventional result occurred where all items appeared in the high importance/high performance cell. The use of median scores in preference to the use of mean scores to draw the co-ordinates on the matrix produced a more scattered distribution across all four of the cells, thereby providing clearer data for management.

In a final analysis, Qiao (2019) used Z-scores to plot an IPA scattered map. Z-scores, also known as standardised scores, allow the researcher to compare the values of raw data between two different situations. Meanwhile, Z-scores not only make the data of two variables more comparable but also locate the cross-point of the X and Y axes at the centre of this coordinate system. Using the standardised values, he found that ambiguities previously associated with variables 'Opportunities for a new business partner' and 'The hotel gives me value for money' effectively disappeared, thereby permitting a more precise interpretation of his results (see Figure 3.4).

The traditional interpretations of the four quadrants are 'Keep up the good work' for Quadrant I, 'Concentrate here' for Quadrant II, 'Low priority' for Quadrant III and 'Possible overkill' for Quadrant IV (Martilla & James, 1977: 78), and many researchers continue to use those descriptions. Nonetheless, alternative modes of analysis are found in the literature. Attributes used in research have been classified into three categories: basic, performance and excitement factors (Füller & Matzler, 2008). Matzler et al. (2004) suggested that basic requirements should be fulfilled, for failure to do so would be detrimental to overall satisfaction. It is argued there is a need to improve the performance scores since the better the performance, the higher the level of satisfaction. Additionally, keeping positive performance generates more positive influences on satisfaction than the negative. These modes of thinking have led to re-evaluations of the standard IPA techniques.

One example is the three-factor theory, which suggests that fundamental factors might have less impact on generating additional positive attitudes but when they are lacking, the result is dissatisfaction on the part of attendees (Kano, 1984). While, in the IPA matrix, Quadrants III (low importance and low performance) and IV (low importance and high performance) are traditionally classified as being 'Low priority' and 'Possible overkill,' there are good reasons to question this. The attributes used to measure importance and performance are often preselected as being necessary for the research, and the unimportant attributes have been filtered out, thereby creating hidden data biases that may underestimate the importance of lower scoring items.

In tourism studies, the IPA approach has been tested by meta-analyses. Azzopardi and Nash (2013), Sever (2015) and Babu et al. (2018) pose generalised questions as to the effectiveness of the approach. In addition, a number of papers report usage of the technique for specific contexts including Taiwan's destination image (Jeng et al., 2019), Savannah's historic area (Deng & Pierskalla, 2018) and the impacts of Covid on bed and breakfast accommodation being offered in Zhejiang (Hong et al., 2020). The continued use of the technique over the decades points to the approach having sustained value. Azzopardi and Nash note that IPA is 'more practical and theoretically sounder for competitiveness analysis and measurement [for] concentrat[ing] on a particular sector such as tourism than on the economy as a whole. For example, a focus on the

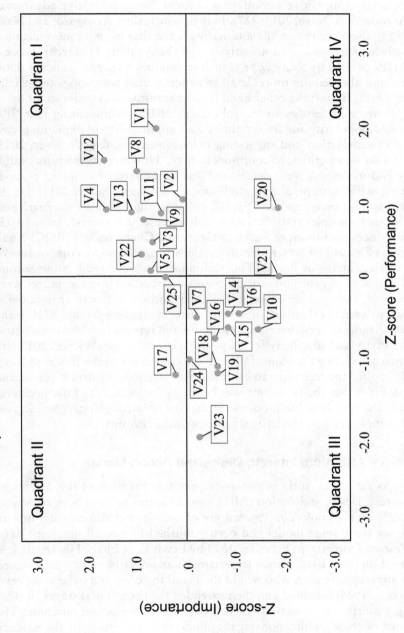

Figure 3.4 IPA matrix with Z-score coordinate system. Source: Qiao (2019: 238)

destination as a unit of tourism competitiveness analysis presents a more realistic and robust approach for assessing performance on the basis of Porterian competitive advantage and Ricardian comparative advantage' (Azzopardi & Nash, 2013: 227). In their conclusion, Azzopardi and Nash (2013) also note that while alternatives exist that promise more detailed analysis, such as conjoint analysis and the Analytic Hierarchy Process (AHP) devised by Saaty (2000), such techniques require significant data-sets and also require more detail to produce finer weightings (especially for AHP). IPA on the other hand is more intuitive and easier to model.

Sever also testifies to the robustness of IPA, commenting that 'IPA gained popularity for its simplicity and applicability in explaining cus-tomer satisfaction and suggesting management strategies' (Sever, 2015: 52). Like other critics, he continues to note, 'However, its empirical valid-ity and usefulness were questioned due to the lack of standard criteria, along with conceptual and methodological issues' (Sever, 2015: 52). In his case, however, unlike Qiao (2019) who suggested an alternative of adopting a simpler statistical approach (the use of Z-scores), Sever (2015) introduces the notion of Receiver Operating Characteristic (ROC) Anal-ysis as a means of better identifying the strong and weak components of a service, image or brand. This technique was developed in the Second World War to determine cut-off points to ascertain if radar images were credible, and rests on defining sensitivity and specificity of criteria being used to assess evaluations or performance. Sever suggests that ROC is the best diagnostic tool 'because it estimates and reports combinations of test sensitivity and specificity for all possible cut-off points' (Sever, 2015: 46) when addressing the issue of placing the cross-hairs in the IPA modelling. He applied the technique to estimations of destination attractiveness and concludes that the technique was better at distinguishing false negatives and false positives, but it does so at the cost of introducing higher degrees of complexity into the basic simplicity of the IPA method.

AIDA – Attention, Interest, Desire and Action Models

As far as the authors can assess, the first mention of the Attention, Interest, Desire and Action (AIDA) model seems to have been by Strong (1925) in his book *The Psychology of Selling and Advertising*, but an earlier three-stage model had been published in a retail magazine, *The Western Druggist*, in February 1898 by Lewis E. St Elmo. His article was based on three basic principles – namely, an advertisement was designed to attract the reader, who would then read the copy and believe the text. Strong (1925) renamed and then extended the three initial stages by add-ing a fourth stage – action – which represented the actual purchase. The dates of these publications again allude to the creation of the modern economy as previously noted, and the emergence of a middle class and their consumption patterns.

Just as Strong added to the initial three principles, so subsequent researchers have also sought to add additional stages. One of the first was the need to create loyalty and repeat purchasing, and hence 'retention' was added to the model by Fortenberry and McGoldrick (2020). Similar processes have occurred in tourism which has long been interested in the effectiveness of destination marketing. This interest was intensified with the emergence of web-based advertising and the use of social media such as Facebook as a means of attracting potential purchasers. Xu and Schrier (2019) combined the AIDA model with the TAM (Technology Adoption Model) in an analysis of online accommodation selling. The aesthetics of the website were seen as initially attracting the potential purchaser and they also noted the *billboard* affect whereby hotels and other accommodation providers used many different outlets to sell their bedspace. Their conclusions are that the sequential logic implicit in the AIDA and TAM models is consistent with their data but equally the two models work in tandem. For example, the perceived risk and the need for reassurance about safety when making an online booking is a significant variable when leading the potential client to 'action', that is, the making of a booking. It can also be noted that the importance of 'reassurance' was identified by Parasuraman *et al.* (1988) in their original ServQual model.

Perhaps one of the main contributions made to the development of the AIDA model in the field of tourism was that of Weng *et al.* (2021). They suggest a five-stage hierarchical model: Attention → Interest → Evaluation (Perceived Usefulness → Perceived Credibility) → Desire → Action. This model was developed from research conducted at the UNESCO World Heritage sites of the Longmen Grottoes and Longhushan in China. The former comprises a series of statues, primarily of Buddha, dating from 493 AD and completed in about 1127 AD. The latter site is a National Park featuring Danxia mountainous landscapes. Weng *et al.* utilised a comparison between print advertising, video advertising and virtual reality (VR), and assessed how each shaped tourists' purchasing behaviour. They measured in each case the aesthetic nature of the media, the interest it aroused, the usefulness and trustworthiness of the information and whether it led to an intention to visit the decision.

As to their conclusions, the print medium was the less effective in creating an intention to visit, but the video format was the most effective for the natural landscape region of Longhushan, while VR was the most effective form of advertising the cultural centre of Longmen. Hence, the study highlights the role of the medium in relationship to users and site. Museum studies also reinforce the role of VR techniques in explaining exhibits and enhancing the nature of the visitor experiences (Errichiello *et al.*, 2019; Jung *et al.*, 2016; Trunfio & Campana, 2020).

The importance of the AIDA method is that while not directly measuring eventual visitor satisfaction, it does effectively list the cognitive stages that lead to the purchase decision and reinforces the stages that create prior images of a destination, activity or location. As previously noted, these are important in creating the criteria by which the visitor will assess the visitation experience.

Conclusions

This chapter has taken as its theme the gap between the expectation and the actual performance experienced by the visitor. It has been shown that while the notion can be a measure of service quality or satisfaction, the analyses tend to be premised on definitions that possess degrees of ambiguity. How does one define importance? Important to whom? And for what reason? The definition of satisfaction has been suggested as being a tautology – an emotion defined by other wording for emotion. It has been suggested that often the visitors have ill-defined expectations, or reasonably passive sets of expectations, and that really expectations explain very little of the variance in eventual satisfaction.

It has also been noted that visitors are active creators of their own experiences, and it is towards this latter notion that the next two chapters turn. Chapter 4 will examine the notion of 'flow' in the visitor experience.

4 Flow Theory and Its Applications to Tourism

The chapter includes:

(a) What is flow theory?
(b) Why is it pertinent to tourism?
(c) What are the implications for tourist experience and satisfaction?
(d) What are the implications for tourist experience design (and to which types of tourist activity might it best apply)?

Introduction

Flow theory was initially expounded by Mihaly Csikszentmihalyi in his doctoral thesis that formed the basis for his subsequent book, *Beyond Boredom and Anxiety* (Csikszentmihalyi, 1975) and further explored in his later book, *FLOW: The Psychology of Optimal Experience* (Csikszentmihalyi, 1990). Csikszentmihalyi (pronounced Chicksent-mi-hee) began his studies into happiness and concepts of flow in the 1960s with his doctoral research into the working practices and motivations of male artists. He noticed that while engaged in the painting, they were totally immersed in their labour and creative processes and seemed to have little awareness of the passing of time. Yet, when they were finished, they often set the work aside, had little interest in it, and sought new tasks. In 1988, he wrote that the artists enjoyed their work, not for any extrinsic awards such as pay or fame but because it 'is the closest socially acceptable symbolic expression of the artist's true desires, which are repressed instinctual cravings' (Csikszentmihalyi, 1988: 4). This was not a wholly new observation. The 19th-century English philosopher, John Stuart Mill, had stated he 'learnt that happiness was to be found not in directly pursuing it, but in the pursuit of other ends; and learnt, also, the importance of a steady cultivation of the feelings' (Elliot, 1909: 4).

Equally, most of us when involved in a game, or looking up material on social media, will know just how quickly the time has passed, and how we spend more time than we intended on such pursuits.

The pursuit of how and why humans experience such things came to dominate not only Mihaly's own thinking but also that of his family as he came to write about the concept of flow with his wife Isabel Csikszentmihalyi (Csikszentmihalyi & Csikszentmihalyi, 1988). Indeed, Mihaly remained working and writing in his own passion of and about flow almost up to his death on 21 October 2021.

Concepts of Flow

In his various writings, Csikszentmihalyi identified a number of key dimensions that generated conditions of flow. They included the facets listed in Table 4.1.

These dimensions flow into activities other than those associated with the creative arts. Csikszentmihalyi's ideas have inspired research into the nature of recreation and leisure, and hence also into tourism. But his ideas influenced other areas of life. Thus, in parenting, the dimensions of clarity of instruction to children; centring, that is, children know their parents care for them, that children feel they have choices; challenge, that children can and do have challenges at appropriate stages of maturation; and finally, the need for trust and commitment are met – are all aspects of applications of flow theory.

As Carl (1994) indicates, the theory of flow has close links with Maslow's theories of self-actualisation (Maslow, 1970), and, equally, Carl also notes that in the 1960s and early 1970s there were few who were researching intrinsic motivation. He continues to say that the absence of such work may have accounted for the popularity of Csikszentmihalyi's concepts, for he offers five areas of potential criticism of the theory of flow based on Littlejohn's (1992) criticisms, which have now been expanded to six facets (Littlejohn, 2002; Littlejohn & Foss, 2010). The six areas are (a) theoretical scope, (b) appropriateness, (c) parsimoniousness

Table 4.1 Dimensions of flow

The activity is challenging and requires skill to complete it.
Both action and awareness merge into one entity.
Creativity requires clear goals and feedback that generate senses of achievement.
The task requires such concentration that stimuli peripheral to the activity are excluded.
A Paradox of Control Exists – the participant is NOT in control, but exercises control that is shaped by the task.
Through these processes the participant loses senses of self, and is caught in a process of thought and action.
Time is transformed – embracing the creative actions means senses of time passing are lost.
The activities are pleasurable and the participant desires to repeat them.
Deriving pleasure, the task does not feel like 'work', but equally it is more serious than play.

or Occam's Razor (Kumar, 2017), (d) validity, (e) heuristic value and (f) openness.

Carl (1994) first considers scope, that is, to what extent a theory may be generalised. He suggests that at his time of writing, the theory has not been used to inform social media and its use, but more tellingly questions whether the theory is too western, and even too male oriented for universal use. Second, he turns to appropriateness to wonder if flow theory suggests a need to create order from disorder to generate a flow, and proposes that possession of skill, even if equal to the challenge, may not be sufficient to achieve a state of flow. He provides the example of a game of tennis between two players of equal skill and observes that the potential for flow may exist but not be actualised for a number of reasons, including possibly just being 'sub-par'.

With reference to parsimony, then the core of the theory, that flow occurs within an equilibrium of challenge and skill is readily understood, and as discussed below can be readily adapted as having lessons for management applications and attempts to improve the visitor experience. Indeed, one immediate lesson for the tourism industry is to ensure that visitors are not placed into environments when their skill sets are insufficient for the challenges they face. This is easily seen in Figure 4.1.

Figure 4.1 indicates that for flow to occur, as the challenge increases, so too the amount of skill required to achieve flow also increases. It is suggested that the direction of flow is not smooth for a number of reasons. The writer or artist may feel a need to correct a mistake or come across an additional idea that requires modification of their work, or a need to revise and further enhance a concept. So, the state of flow is subject to the eddies and pools that are equated to the streams and rivers from which the notion is, in part, taken.

The next test is that of validity. Is there supporting empirical work that lends support to the theory? As will be described later, a reasonably

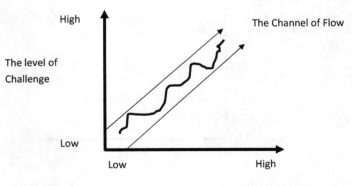

Figure 4.1 The channel of flow

substantial body of research exists, particularly in the field of adventure tourism, and more specifically in the case of white water rafting. Priest and Bunting (1993), Ryan (1997) and Jones *et al.* (2003) have linked writings that widen the concept and generate empirical data in the field of adventure sports, tourism and recreation. For example, Jones *et al.* (2003) analysed 409 recorded events experienced by 52 kayak paddlers who crossed six rapids of varying difficulty. They reminded the reader that Csikszentmihalyi has stated flow is an elusive concept to capture via statistical means, but they noted that a quantitative approach could reduce the level of elusiveness to some degree. They adopted the adventure experience paradigm used by Priest and Bunting (1993) to form the four-cell model shown in Figure 4.2.

The rationale for Figure 4.2 is that when the level of challenge exceeds the participant's skill level, the result is anxiety about being able to cope and of potential danger – whether physical or psychological. If, however, the participant is in a situation where congruence exists between skill and challenge, the participant is in a state of flow. The first author, as a former windsurfer, well remembers situations, with feet in the foot straps, of blasting across the water feeling in harmony with wind and waves and being in a state of balance with the natural forces. This was indeed a state of flow! If, however, the level of skill was faced with little wind, then the situation of skill exceeding challenge could well have induced boredom. Under these conditions, one could then try tricks like doing handstands on the board, when the first author often got wet! The situation of low levels of skill and low levels of challenge would, according to Priest and Bunting (1993), lead to a situation of apathy, or simply not caring.

Using this model, Jones *et al.* (2003: 26) concluded that the coefficients of correlation between the items used to establish the measures of challenge, skill, involvement and so on were at least of moderate

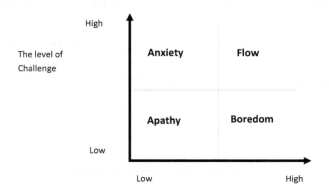

Figure 4.2 The four-cell model of flow. Source: Priest and Bunting (1993)

reliability (r>0.06 for the most part). They also found that skill and competency were generally more congruent at rapids graded I to III rather than at grade V, which is what one might intuitively expect. However, they finally concluded that the model 'explained' only small variances in the flow experience, but noted the results were better than those achieved in many previous studies. This question is again examined below when looking at more recent research studies.

In continuing to look at Littlejohn's tests of theory, two factors associated with validity are heuristics and openness. Writing in 1994, Carl commented that flow theory 'was thought of as being too ethereal, almost mystic, and lacking any hard data to support its claims. In the beginning this was accurate, but over the past twenty years, the flow theory has provided mountains of empirical support, as well as many practical applications. Also, these studies have accumulated to generate a great deal of future research, as well as provide additional theories' (Carl, 1994: 18). That continues to be the case, and examples of the research including more specific applications to holidaying are discussed in the final section of this chapter. But prior to discussing this, our gaze now turns to other aspects of Csikszentmihalyi's work that perhaps have attracted little attention in more recent years.

Concepts of Fields and Domains

Csikszentmihalyi was studying and then teaching as an academic in the United States in the 1960s and then for several decades after. Psychological research in the United States in the 1960s was influenced by and contributing to growing studies on the individual, not as a person simply responding to a series of stimuli and subjected to conditional reinforcement schedules as envisaged by B.F. Skinner but as a more creative and imaginative person. Skinner's work involved measurements of animal behaviour as a response related to schedules of reward and punishment. His findings were influential in terms of its implications in many fields including education. This was because Skinner's work showed how patterns of positive and negative reinforcement could induce learning. However, another emergent form of psychological research had commenced, partly with American psychologists of Jewish origin, who were motivated by trying to understand how people could submit to or resist or recover from the experiences of the death camps of the holocaust. Among these psychologists were Abraham Maslow, Philip Zimbardo of the Stanford prison experiment and a founder of the Heroic Imagination Project (https://www.heroicimagination.org/), Milton Rokeach, Charles Hampden-Turner, who wrote *Radical Man* in 1970, and Stanley Milgram. Taken together they ushered in a movement that has been termed humanistic psychology and which subsequently gained many adherents who share a belief in seeing people capable of independent, creative and ethical thought and behaviour. This perspective has proved influential in various fields and countries, including the work of Eric Hall in counselling at the University of Nottingham, UK; in tourism, the research of Philp Pearce in Queensland, Australia; and in studies of wellness, the seminal work of Ed Bruner in the United States.

As an aside, Hoffman notes that the United States, and in particular New York, was a veritable melting and creative pot in the late 1930s with so many German intellectuals fleeing to the United States to escape the Nazis. This was a particularly rich period for the development of psychology. Maslow himself wrote that 'New York in those days was simply fantastic. There has been nothing like it since Athens. And I knew every one of them more or less well' (Hoffman, 1988: 87). Maslow's intellectual circle included the gestalt theorists Wolfgang Kohler and Kurt Koffka, the neurologist Kurt Goldstein and among the psychoanalysts Erich Fromm, Karen Horney and Alfred Adler. It was Adler with his theories of the role of emotion and feelings of belonging, and who had broken away from his initial mentor, Sigmund Freud, who was possibly the greatest influence on the young Maslow.

Csikszentmihalyi was himself influenced by the writings of that period of New York's history, and arguably for him the notion of flow was a means to an end, and that end was human well-being. In his contribution to the book *Theories of Creativity* (Runco & Albert, 1990), Csikszentmihalyi argued that creativity is not born of the individual alone, but of the cultural and social environments and the values they espouse. This field he labelled as a *domain* – thus the domain of art, or the domain of science. The domain is nested within a cultural system that values, say, science, philosophy and the arts that informs the domain. The domain therefore comprises the knowledge, values, tools, methods and practices that characterise that domain. The domain is in turn evaluated by individuals, to which the domain imparts the existing body of knowledge, and by what he termed the *field*, which is a collective or community that may effectively operate as the gatekeepers or custodians of the knowledge transmitted by the domain. In the patterns of thinking, one can discern parallels with the earlier thinking of Thomas Kuhn and his seminal work, *The Structure of Scientific Revolutions* (Kuhn, 1962). Kuhn proposed that science did not evolve from a steady state, but understandings shifted in dynamic ways initiated by a sudden catalyst or cathartic event. The Nazi regime initiated a dynamic shift in psychology that informed Csikszentmihalyi's work combined with the advent of a post-modern society of image consumption and awareness of self. Further, Csikszentmihalyi's concepts of a domain are consistent with Kuhn's earlier definition of a paradigm as a consensual understanding among key figures.

For Csikszentmihalyi, the field and individual are each comprised of sub-divisions and parts. The individual inherits a genetic predisposition that shapes reactions to, and is shaped by the social frameworks of family, work and communities of which they are part. The field has its leading members and those who challenge the existing system. Innovation is thus an outcome of the tensions that exist within the parts of this system. On reflection, this seems to effectively predate Malcolm Gladwell's bestselling books, *Outliers: The Story of Success* (Gladwell, 2008) and *The Tipping Point* (Gladwell, 2000), in which Gladwell argues that the success that individuals achieve is not just a personal story of entrepreneurship and effort but also one of social support systems. The relationships are shown in Figure 4.3.

It can be argued that given the background and the milieu within which Csikszentmihalyi began his academic career, the concentration on systems and networks of support is not overly surprising. Indeed, Csikszentmihalyi continued working on these concepts for much of his life. He also turned to considering the importance of aging and its impacts on creativity, writing (with Nakamura) 'whereas most of us tend to remain at one end or the other of various personality continua, creative people are able to move along the full range of possibilities as the situation demands' (Nakamura & Csikszentmihalyi, 2003: 192). They emphasise the person in terms of openness and genetics, and the nature of domains

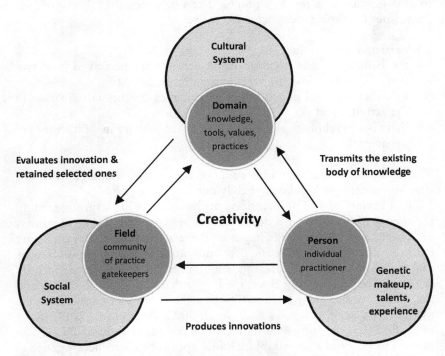

Figure 4.3 Csikszentmihalyi's system of creativity. Source: Adapted from Csikszentmihalyi M. (1999) Implications of a systems perspective for the study of creativity, in *Handbook of Creativity*, ed. Sternberg R. J. (Cambridge: Cambridge University Press), p. 315

and the field in creating *vital engagement* as the creative person ages. Indeed, in the year immediately prior to his untimely death, Csikszentmihalyi continued to publish on life spans, wellness, and creativity, and in 2020 proposed a conceptual imbalance flow model and compensatory mechanisms that permitted a continuance of creativity (Lebuda & Csikszentmihalyi, 2020; Tse *et al.*, 2020).

One of Csikszentmihalyi's critics did note that in many of Csikszentmihalyi's writings there was a high degree of self-referencing and while being stimulating and thought provoking, the empirical evidence for his notions was, at times, lacking. This prompts two questions. First, is there evidence for these theories in addition to that previously noted, and second, from the primary perspective of this book, how do these theories relate to visitor experiences?

Research and Applications with Reference to Leisure and Holidaying

Prior to discussing research that relates to notions of flow in general and their application to holidays and visitor experiences, and at this stage to also summarise a few key points, it can be noted that there are four perquisites for flow experiences. These are:

(a) participation is voluntary;
(b) the benefits of participation in an activity are perceived to derive from factors intrinsic to participation in the activity;
(c) a facilitative level of arousal is experienced during participation in the activity; and
(d) there is a psychological commitment to the activity in which they are participating.

The remainder of this chapter is based on the premise that all four conditions are present in holidaying behaviour.

In a review of 185 publications in the tourism literature regarding the theory of flow, da Silva deMatos *et al.* (2021) find that most studies are quantitative in nature. They note there are problems in measuring states of flow but conclude the preponderance of statistical analyses is due to the presence of scales questionnaires. In particular, they note the Flow State Scale (FSS) developed by Jackson and Marsh (1996) and the Dispositional Flow Scale (DFS) and the subsequent modifications of the latter scale (Jackson & Eklund, 2002; Riva *et al.*, 2017). Riva *et al.* find that despite some issues, 'The Italian version of DFS-2 has proven to be valid and reliable, and its applicability to heterogeneous samples of subjects and different situations and experiences, including but not limited to sports, has been verified' (Riva *et al.*, 2017: 13). Their sample comprised 843 respondents, and they state that while used in Italy, the items were verified translations of the English language items.

In yet another review, da Silva deMatos *et al.* (2021) examined flow theory in a number of different contexts, and they finalise their paper by reference to several propositions that they feel are implicit in the research findings. These are listed in Table 4.2, and the review finds evidence that, for the most part, supports each of the propositions.

These suppositions are also supported by a number of other studies that specifically relate to tourism. Among the studies are those of Kim and Thapa (2018), Gnoth *et al.* (2000) and Frash and Blose (2019) – the last listed noting that serious leisure is a predictor of holiday choice and experience as people are emotionally inclined to the flow associated with the activity. These papers are now described to act as a springboard for further discussion. They are selected solely for being, at the time of writing, fairly recent, while they also reflect a number of themes in the past literature.

Kim and Thapa (2018) set out to explore the dimensions of holidaying in natural environments using quantitative means. Several aspects of their study demand attention. First, it was a specific study of group holiday tourists on an eco-package holiday. The destination was Jeju Island off the southern tip of South Korea. Second, they specifically sought to identify links between flow and the quality of experience as determinants of holiday assessment through a measure of satisfaction. The correlations between flow, quality and satisfaction tended to be statistically significant ($p<0.01$) at levels greater than 0.6. They conclude that emotional values are closely associated with flow and go on to suggest that 'From a practical standpoint, in order to obtain a higher flow experience and satisfaction among tourists, DMOs [Destination Marketing Organisations]

Table 4.2 Propositions arising from empirical research using flow theory

Personality characteristics and traits, such as predisposition to flow and internalised locus of control, influence the tourists' flow process and outcomes.
In the tourism domain, the tourists' motivation to engage in tourism experiences positively influences the flow state.
The cultural background influences the tourists' flow processes and outcomes.
Flow outcomes are influenced not only by the challenges and skills match but also by the level of absorption, immersion and cognitive stimulation experienced by tourists.
The flow experience results in various positive outcomes for life satisfaction, well-being, trust and loyalty, which are relevant to assessments of tourism.
The tourists' experience of flow and non-flow performance generates negative and positive outcomes.
Technology-based methods and physiological responses may enable better measurement of tourist flow and its outcomes.

Adapted from da Silva deMatos, N. M., de Sá E. S., & de Oliveira Duarte, P. A. (2021). A review and extension of the flow experience concept. Insights and directions for tourism research. *Tourism Management Perspectives* 38, 100802, 1–17.

may need to be continuously engaged to increase the quality of eco-travel content, activities, service, and sustain the ecological system (e.g., endangered wild animals and plants) of their destination' (Kim & Thapa, 2018: 380). They urge Destination Marketing Organisations to conduct visitor surveys to better customise ecotravel products for market segments.

It is evident from much of the above that many studies in tourism have stemmed from the theme of challenge derived from the notion of flow, and consequently many studies have been oriented towards adventure holidays. White water rafting in particular seems to have attracted the attention of tourist researchers. For example, Wu and Liang (2011) conducted an examination of flow in rafting by using a questionnaire comprising 33 items covering the dimensions that included time distortion, playfulness, control, skill, challenge and attention focus. Their sample comprised 258 rafters, although initially more than 500 questionnaires were handed out. This level of non-completion illustrates one common issue in tourism research, namely that asking people to complete questionnaires after they have completed their trip or experience requires compliance on the part of participants at a time when they want to go home, get a meal or look after children's immediate post-activity wants. Hence, not everyone, despite possibly good intentions, is able to meet the researchers' requests.

After successfully testing the reliability of the scale and using structural equation modelling, they find that the influence of playfulness, skill and challenge 'on flow experience is higher than 0.6 ($R^2 = 0.65$), implying the strong prediction accuracy of the results. Playfulness was observed to be the most important influence on flow experience, followed by skill and challenge' (Wu & Liang, 2011: 323). They suggest that flow experiences are associated with positive emotions and activity satisfaction. They confirm that the participant's personality is also important and suggest that this has implications for management. They also suggest a relationship between skill and challenge is important for participants, and in doing so echo themes noted by Ryan (1997). Ryan used flow theory to emphasise the importance of qualified guides. He suggests that there are five alternative outcomes in an adventure holiday activity such as white water rafting. These are:

- **Devastation and disaster** – which is where the level of challenge is so far in excess of a participant's skill level that the potential for fatal accidents exists.
- **Misadventure** – where again the level of challenge exceeds a participant's skill, and where participants may be flung into the river, but without fatal accidents occurring.
- **Peak adventure** – where the rafter feels challenged and even endangered but comes through the experience with an 'adrenalin high' feeling that they have been fully tested and been successful.

- **Adventure** – where although not feeling endangered, a sense of excitement has been engendered.
- **Exploration and experimentation** – where participants wish to tentatively experience a sense of rafting but in comparative safety.

Adopting this framework, he then suggests the scenario indicated in Figure 4.4. Assuming the level of challenge is OX, and the tourist has a level of skill or competency of OB, then it can be seen that the tourist is at the margin of misadventure. To obtain a sense of success at the challenge level of OX the tourist needs a skill level of BC to achieve the peak adventure experience shown as YZ.

Ryan (1997a) suggests that this is achieved through the skill and guidance of the accompanying guides who know the behaviour of water through the rapids, and thus it is the guide's skill that avoids entering the zones of misadventure or indeed disaster that occur at levels of challenge above OX. In short, the presence of the experienced guide shifts the competency of the tourist from OB to OC to permit entry to peak experience zone YZ.

Two managerial implications immediately arise. First, there is a need to employ qualified and ideally highly experienced guides. In several countries, there are no training routes and established qualifications that are required of guides. For example, in New Zealand, while it is desirable that guides have qualifications from the New Zealand Outdoor Instructors Association, such a qualification is not mandatory at the time of writing. However, the industry is seeking to follow the requirements

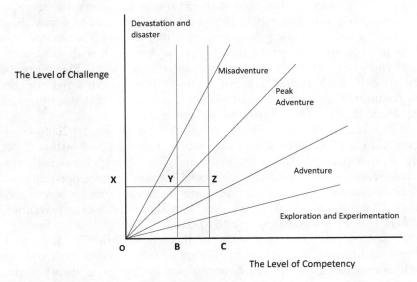

Figure 4.4 The role of the guide in white water rafting

of the International Rafting Federation certification. In the UK, canoeing and kayaking require British Canoe Union qualifications, and windsurfing/wingsurfing/dinghy/foiling instructors are generally required to have a minimum of Royal Yachting Association advanced certification for employment. Equal forms of instructor qualification are also associated with activities like hang gliding and parachute jumping. Finally, it can be noted that in China, the National Water Sport Bureau (NWB), a central government body, promotes and standardises water sports.

The next managerial implication is that of ensuring the guides have the skills to impart and gain a sense of trust from the tourist, namely that both instructor and tourist possess a sense of confidence in the skills of the guide. Personal experience of the first author can testify to the importance of this after seeing how guides permitted a young lady to overcome her initial hesitation and fear to descend a 100 metre abseil into caves in the Waikato with her boyfriend and to successfully end with a sense of peak experience, or on another occasion, seeing guides gently instructing participants at the end of a caving trip through an unexpected sump to swim out of the cave system. Such skills give a gift of enjoyment and achievement to their clients that many will remember for a long time to come. The duration of such involvement is further described below.

These skills are of importance when considering the exploration and experimentation stage in some of the new emergent markets of Asia. In societies marked by Confucian traits, many young people retain a sense of responsibility towards their parents which, for some, implies an avoidance of unnecessary risk. Another factor that has been noted is that in the often-crowded larger cities of Asia and societies where a strong motive to achieve is associated with examination success, the levels of fitness among teenagers may be lacking. This is not aided by a movement towards gaming on computers and smartphones which often result in too many hours spent sitting down. Yet the youth still wish to have fun and enjoy the status of involvement in adventure sports. This gives rise to activities such as *piaoliu ziyou*, or free drifting down a river or, not uncommonly, an artificial, controlled water channel that Buckley *et al.* (2014, 2018) describe as a form of mass tourism.

Turning to the research conducted by Gnoth *et al.* (2000), their conclusions are consistent with the theories espoused by Maslow (1968, 1970), Csikszentmihalyi (1990a) and more generally with humanistic psychology, namely 'dynamically orientated respondents are open-minded, seek challenges and strongly follow motivations to search for new experiences' (Gnoth *et al.*, 2000: 31) while those with more conservative tendencies tend to be motivated by a wish to escape. These (and other findings) they contend are consistent with the theories of flow. For their part, Frash and Blose (2019) apply the concept of flow to motorcycle tourism while associating flow to the notion of serious leisure as incorporating the elements of commitment, involvement and as a source of intrinsic motivation (Stebbins, 1992, 1997, 2001). Yet again, they demonstrate that involvement and pro-active participation create states of flow and hence satisfaction with the holiday experience. Their study is also quantitative using AMOS, a covariance-based structural equation modelling technique.

Numerous other studies testify to the reliability of the measures of challenge, skill and positive emotions aroused from situations of flow in visitor experiences. At the University of Waterloo in Canada, Mark Havitz and Roger Mannell conducted several research projects into leisure and recreation for more than a decade and have often published work relating to the importance of flow and its relationship to general senses of well-being. One ancillary question that arises is if flow can make a positive contribution to well-being, then surely it needs to be shown that flow is capable of sustaining enduring effects and by definition can sustain enduring involvement in chosen activities. One can see in such questions a linkage in the literature between the theories of Stebbins (1992, 1997, 2001) and assessments of serious leisure, those of Csikszentmihalyi and humanistic psychologists in general, and researchers into well-being. Havitz and Mannell and their colleagues at Waterloo have made a significant contribution not simply to leisure studies but also contextualising such research within a wider field of wellness and well-being. Some of their writing is embedded in Maslow's concepts which are discussed in the next chapter, and also link with the studies of Ed Diener on the importance of quality of life and lifelong well-being. However, to sustain findings from such studies requires evidence that flow experiences can be enduring in their impacts.

In one of their studies, they compared the duration of enduring involvement (EI) in non-leisure and leisure activities. In doing so, Havitz and Mannell (2005) explored the notion that over, at least, intermediate periods of time, EI was indeed a stable and consistent trait. They note that leisure tends to be described along four facets, namely 'a combination of interest in, and pleasure derived from participation; sign, which refers to the symbolism associated with participation; the risk probability associated with choosing one activity over other options; and risk consequences associated with making a poor choice' (Havitz & Mannell, 2005: 154). Any measure of duration of involvement is related to the activity selected and the situational involvement (SI) – which can be defined as the feelings aroused by being present in a given situation, although Havitz and Mannell treat SI as a cognitive component more than an affective one. They test the theory that enduring involvement directly influences feeling of flow and indirectly and additionally influences flow through situational involvement. They used an experience sampling method with 46 students requiring them to complete questionnaires at various signalled times over a one-week period. A total of 1800 responses were collected, and of the total responses 48% reflected non-leisure activities.

The next stage required comparing the two sets of data once checking the rigour of the responses using tests associated with structural equation modelling was completed. They concluded that strong and consistent relationships existed between Enduring Involvement, Situational Involvement and Flow and that, furthermore, the relationships were positive. One might ask, why does this matter? One implication is that involvement in a given situation, especially if a leisure situation, tends to create higher degrees of flow and, arguably, more enduring patterns of consistent behaviour. This has implications for studies of well-being, in that positive life outlooks and life satisfaction may be enhanced through sustaining activities that elicit in themselves sustained involvement. Turning our attention to holiday behaviour, we can first indicate that holidays meet the conditions normally associated with flow. Does that then mean that holiday experiences can have positive long-term impacts on senses of well-being?

In Chapters 1 and 2 it was stated that holidays are 'extra-ordinary times' in that the tourist is repositioned into a place (and possibly culture) that differs from their norm. Instead of the repeating patterns and rituals of the everyday, the tourist engages in new activities and hence engages in new learning. It is argued that these lessons may, because of high involvement, induce flow that has long-term effects on psychological well-being. These subjects form the matter of the next section.

Involvement, Holidays and Well-being

So, do holidays have physical and psychological benefits? Certainly, there appears to be a belief that they do. Hobson and Dietrich observed that there is an 'underlying assumption in our society that tourism is a mentally and physically healthy pursuit to follow in our leisure time' (Hobson & Dietrich, 1994: 23). For the immediate short term, the evidence is mixed. In a review of studies published under the title *Making Holidays Work*, De Bloom (2015) cites one study by Nawjin, De Bloom and Geurts (2013) that followed 96 Dutch workers prior to their holiday. It was found that health and well-being fell in the two weeks before the holiday due to reports of over-work, especially for females who had both work and home commitments. This confirmed earlier work reported by Pearce (1981), who also reported an increased frequency of minor ailments at the commencement of the holiday. These ranged from sunburn to a need to recover from travel, to stomach issues and simply tiredness. There is also evidence of a drop-off in work performance in the immediate period after a return from vacations to school (Cooper *et al.*, 1996) and work (including surgeons, Hockenberry & Helmchen, 2014).

There are, perhaps fortunately, some studies that indicate positive short-term benefits from holidaying. Hartig *et al.* (2013) examined Swedish health data for the period from 1993 to 2005 and found evidence for improved feelings of well-being. Equally, evidence exists that long stays abroad apparently generate creativity in being able to observe problems from several different perspectives leading to more nuanced solutions (Maddux & Galinsky, 2009), and some evidence also points to similar but smaller gains from short overseas stays (De Bloom *et al.*, 2014). Further evidence for the importance of weekends breaks away from work was generated by Helliwell and Wang (2014) who examined data derived from the Gallup/Healthways US daily poll data from 2 January 2008 to 30 June 2009. This large-scale poll included one question about life satisfaction and six items on emotional responses. They conclude that 'when we turn to explain the size and pattern of weekend effects, we find more positive and fewer negative emotions on weekends, with the patterns and sizes of the differences varying by gender, age, and especially the social context of life both at home and on the job. A large portion of the weekend effect is explained by differences in the amount of time spent with friends or family' (Helliwell & Wang, 2014: 403), a finding consistent with much of humanistic psychology that reinforces the roles of personality, social environments and the importance of non-work times as a proxy for leisure and relaxation (Tinsley & Tinsley, 1986). Interestingly, we would contend that the finding indirectly reinforces many of the arguments made previously when discussing the impacts of society on holidaying, as discussed by Krippendorf (1999).

One study that attempted to locate senses of well-being and holidaying in the wider domain of a respondent's daily social and work life was the study by Gilbert and Abdullah (2004). They used a sample of 355 respondents to compare the life domains and senses of well-being of those who had recently taken holidays. However, to draw conclusions they attempted to match sub-samples of holiday and non-holiday takers by sociodemographic variables such as age, gender and class. They concluded that 'The study findings indicated that holidaytaking did alter or impact on the subjective or sense of well-being of the holidaymakers: respondents experienced a higher amount of pleasant feelings after their holidays; however, the respondents feel more or less the same about their friends, family, home, and neighborhood domains before and after their holidays; and the effects of holidaytaking did not cause the respondents to feel worse after their holidays' (Gilbert & Abdullah, 2004: 117). This, they suggest, may be due to the fact that while it seems true that holidaying does increase senses of life satisfaction and well-being after holidays, that in itself is a reflection of a greater felt need for a holiday. In short, greater motivation needs are associated with higher levels of post-holiday satisfaction. This seems to imply that holidays are a socially condoned and possibly necessary source of escape in many of our societies, thereby supporting the contentions of those who link holiday taking to the nature of society.

This realisation has led some to promote the concept of social tourism. Social tourism is generally defined as 'the inclusion of groups in society who are economically weak or otherwise disadvantaged in tourism participation' (McCabe *et al.*, 2010: 762). Ryan (2002a) in a paper based on his address at the 2000 APEC Tourism Minister's meeting in Seoul, traced the use of the term back to 1956 and the work of Arthur Haulot (a former prisoner of Dachau), who initiated a movement that subsequently led to the *Bureau Internationale du Tourisme Sociale*. Ryan (2002a) also sought to link social tourism with the movement toward 'sustainability' – suggesting that 'sustainability' *per se* was an insufficient objective and should be linked more with adding value. He argued that social tourism was an important factor in generating social value to the betterment of society and urged that the World Tourism Organization's Global Ethics of Tourism meant such initiatives should be supportive of social tourism. In one sense, the current Sustainable Development Goals further reinforce such measures. However, despite anecdotal evidence and indicative initiatives, at the beginning of the 21st millennium there was relatively little empirical evidence for such a stance.

In the intervening years, some studies have emerged. One such study was the work of McCabe *et al.* (2010) who had the support of the Family Holiday Association (FHA), a UK charity that has been promoting social tourism since the 1980s. Prior to Covid, they would support about 1600 families a year, and even during the pandemic years of 2020 and 2021 managed to support over 500 families with short holidays. Given that many actual and potential respondents suffered stress, marital issues, bereavement, unemployment and other problems, the response rates were not as high as the researchers had hoped for, but they were finally able to identify various classifications that included several tens of responses. The primary motivations for applying to the charity were found to be '(1) the chance to spend quality time together, as a family; (2) the opportunity for fun and happy memories; and (3) the opportunity to spend time away from difficult and/or stressful routines or circumstances' (McCabe *et al.*, 2010: 768). They also concluded on the basis of responses to quality-of-life measures that the emotional outcomes were wholly beneficial, but given the small size of the total sample (n=21) they argued strongly for more research and the linking of tourism research into the wider agenda of health and social well-being research.

In a subsequent study undertaken again with the help of the FHA, Minnaert *et al.* (2009) chose to use focus groups in an attempt to both better define terms and to gain a larger set of respondents. They conducted two rounds of interviews; the first had 40 participants, and of these 30 attended the second round of focus groups. The first clear benefit of enjoying a holiday as a family group was the improvement of family relationships. Being able to escape the confines imposed by their daily patterns of life was an emancipating experience for several of the participants. This effect had endured by the time of the second round of focus groups that took place some six months after the actual holidays. A second effect was a broadening of social contacts with greater participation in the networks of the support agencies. However, the researchers sounded a warning note in that some parents found the process a little daunting and the authors recommend a need for further support for possibly less confident participants. Possibly one of the major observations is that 'The holiday, as a potential learning experience, had given many respondents the time to reflect on their lives, and identify areas where a change was desirable. With the help of their new social networks, the support of the social organization and by accessing new information channels, these particular respondents were able to turn motivation into positive changes to their lives' (Minnaert *et al.*, 2009: 327).

Such studies are laudable for their observations and the issue awareness they generate, but from an empirical perspective the small sample sizes make it difficult to fully assess the relationships between determining and determined variables, although, of course, the prior studies provide guidance as to how such variables might be measured. Fortunately, new technologies may be able to prise open some gateways into better understanding the relationships between social capital, personality types and quality of life, and the role holidays might have. In one example Alén *et al.* (2017) identified one way forward by targeting senior tourists and reaching out to them by telephone. They collected a sample of 358 respondents to create five clusters. These included those who travelled for health reasons, work-related reasons, leisure purposes, taking advantage of off-peak periods and for visiting friends and relatives. However, their study primarily concerned the motivations rather than emotional and well-being outcomes, but they were able to show such techniques work well for data collection.

The ageing of populations in Europe has attracted researcher interest, particularly with reference to the role of holidaying and retention of both physical and psychological health. Vega-Vázquez *et al.* (2021) examined 363 Spanish people aged over 65 years, and found clear evidence that correlations exist between holiday taking and better health and quality of life, but that does still leave a question as to directions of causality. Does travel improve health and life satisfaction? Or do the healthy and those with life satisfaction tend to take more holidays? It can be observed that holiday takers tend to average and above average incomes, and such levels of income are also associated with better health and life satisfaction outcomes. Generally, the positive correlation between income and well-being and life satisfaction is generally accepted, and Arber *et al.* (2014) have also noted the role of subjective positive health as a mediating variable that permits some lower income groups to also enjoy senses of well-being.

Equally clear is the evidence that the retention of an active lifestyle by the elderly also statistically significantly contributes to good health, and that such a lifestyle enables holiday taking to take place (Ferrer *et al.*, 2016). Thus, one enters into a 'virtuous circle' whereby activity creates health that permits holidays that in turn reinforce both physical and mental well-being. The research also changes the way that aging is defined and regarded. Instead of perceiving aging as a process of inevitable decline in faculties, it is perceived as a process of consistent negotiation with the environment, whether social, built, economic, natural or cultural. Lifestyle is therefore a key determinant of well-being, and while not necessarily making specific reference to the psychological theories outlined above, implicit references can be drawn. For example, Duedahl *et al.* (2020) reinforce the Maslovian concepts of self-actualisation and Csikszentmihalyi's concepts of fields, domains and persons when concluding their study of active and less active seniors' use of nature, despite making no reference to these concepts in their paper. They write, even if the Danish Wadden Sea National Park

> qualifies as a therapeutic landscape or an enabling place, (for some) ... the therapeutic properties of it remain dormant as they do not relate to it in ways that allow for construction of relational and emotional geographies. At the same time, research participants who see their engagements with nature as complex and dynamic, and appreciate variations of interpretation, such as changing weather conditions, seasonality, tidal waters etc., argue that being with nature makes them actively use nature more, hence contributing to more active and healthy lifestyles. When the [National Park] nature becomes a constant unfolding, it draws research participants to deepen their engagements. (Duedahl *et al.*, 2020: 15)

Combinations of open-mindedness, alertness to new experiences and a willingness to immerse self in context enriches life and health, and potentially exposure to nature can enhance quality of life.

These relationships between holiday taking, recreational activity, environment, and psychological and physical health as means of improving one's quality of life are not restricted to the old. In a study of 412 Portuguese students, Eusébio and Carneiro used the World Health Organization's Quality of Life Scale to assess the impact of holidaying on quality of life. Analysing their data through factor and cluster analysis they clearly state that 'tourism enhances the quality of life of youth tourists' (Eusébio & Carneiro, 2014: 754). Tourism was also found to positively impact on the social and psychological aspects of the quality of life, although the impact varied across four clusters of youth tourists, with 30% experiencing little or no impact – a figure akin to a finding by Dolnicar *et al.* (2013).

While the concepts of quality of life and Maslow's hierarchy of motives have close links to Csikszentmihalyi's modelling, much of the literature relating to flow has been in the fields of wellness, recreation and leisure studies than tourism *per se*. One major exception to this statement does appear to exist in the field of adventure tourism, but searching for explicit references is but part of the story. In some of the literature regarding pilgrimage and meditation holidays, there are descriptions of emotions and feelings akin to the feelings of harmony between people and the natural settings in many of the comments made by respondents in qualitative studies (e.g. Jiang *et al.*, 2018 in the case of Zen Meditation holidays).

Conclusions

The chapter began with a description of the theory of flow initiated by the Hungarian American psychologist Mihaly Csikszentmihalyi. The theory is located within an emergent school of humanistic psychology that commenced in the immediate period after the Second World War. The theory is tested by reference to various tests of validity including the scope of the theory and its wider implications and ability to ask research questions. Having attracted a significant amount of attention, early research tended to be qualitative in nature, but with easier access to statistical means and the increases of income in the period leading to more expenditure on leisure and holidaying, a growing number of empirical studies emerged.

These studies have shown that senses of flow are associated with enhanced holiday experiences, particularly with reference to adventure holidays, and relationships with life satisfaction and quality of life measures have been found. However, segmentation exercises indicate that not everyone is equally affected, but this point in itself confirms Csikszentmihalyi's wider theory of the importance of domains, fields and personality. This implies a need to ask further questions, and the next chapter takes the exploration of psychological determinants further by looking more closely at the work of Abraham Maslow and Philip Pearce's construct of the travel career ladder.

5 The Concept of the Travel Career

The chapter includes:

(a) Noting that Maslow's concept was the initial premise of the Travel Career Ladder, the stages of Maslow's hierarchy of needs are described.
(b) The issue of empirical evidence for Maslow's theory is discussed.
(c) The relationship between hierarchical needs and Pearce's concept of the travel career is discussed.

Introduction

In Chapter 4, reference was made to the humanistic psychologists and the influence of their thinking, both generally and also with reference to theories of visitor experiences, perceptions, attitudes and behaviours. In this chapter we again refer to the work of Abraham Maslow, and how it informed the thinking of the late Philip Pearce. Pearce took the notion of personal development from Maslow and argued that the motives Maslow identified were both exemplified and potentially developed in and by tourism. He suggested that this process of development led to people experiencing a travel career, what he initially called a 'travel career ladder'. Over time, with the help of some of his doctoral students, he refined the concept and in response to new findings and various criticisms, began to reduce dependency on Maslow's hierarchical notion of a hierarchical status of motivational needs to a model that recognised travellers could serially switch between meeting different needs and desires, and equally simultaneously meet such needs. His thinking also became closer to work considered later in this book, namely the concept of tourist roles that was developed by Andrew Yiannakis and Heather Gibson over a number of years, and which in turn also came to be modified in the light of findings by their own postgraduate students.

This chapter is therefore divided into two broad sections. The first introduces Maslow's concept of motivation and the much-cited hierarchical triangle of motivation. The second section examines the evolution of those notions into Pearce's travel career. The importance of Maslow to studies of tourist motivation and the evaluation of their experiences is evidenced by the numerous studies that cite his work. Indeed, Hsu and Huang state that 'Maslow's hierarchy of needs theory ... is one of the most influential motivation theories in the academic world and in the public domain' (Hsu & Huang, 2008: 14). Equally, it is not uncommon for writers to note that chapters can take on a life of their own, and that the final piece of writing differs from the original planned content. This occurred in this chapter when contrary to expectation the text veered into a consideration of the work of Michel Foucault, and particularly his *Archaeology of Knowledge* (Foucault, 1969). As described by Wright (2019, 2020), it is in this book that Foucault comes nearest to developing a structured explanation of discourse analysis. Given that Maslow's work is as much philosophical as psychological, links are drawn between the two when discussing how Maslow's concepts can and have informed research into the visitor experience.

Maslow and the Hierarchical Theory of Motivation

As noted in the previous chapter, Abraham Maslow was born in 1908, the son of first-generation Jewish migrants to the United States who had come from Ukraine. At that time, several antisemitic gangs existed in the city, and the young Maslow learnt to live in Brooklyn facing their threats, experiencing relative deprivation and having the responsibility that came as the oldest child of seven. These experiences, combined with the lessons of Nazi Germany, shaped his subsequent thinking, but possibly even more important according to Hoffman (1988) was his relationship with his mother. Hoffman records that Maslow described his mother as being selfish, not capable of love, intolerant (particularly of Afro-Americans) and consequently his early family life was one of tension.

Maslow is generally known today outside of his own field of psychology for his hierarchical model of motivation, which has been used in management (Lussier, 2019; Walsh, 2011), consumer buying in marketing (Groucutt & Hopkins, 2017) and in the area of tourist motivation (Pearce & Lee, 2005). The premise behind the theory is that there are basic needs that relate to physiological needs such as food, water and shelter. Once these needs are satisfied, the human becomes more concerned with physical and mental safety. If these two basic needs are met, then a path towards 'self-actualisation' becomes feasible. The human is both capable of, and desirous of love once the person feels healthy and safe. The higher needs are not necessarily replacing the basic needs, for these indeed are the basis of personal development, but the higher needs increasingly come to the fore. With feeling of love and a sense of belonging to a family, to a social group and possibly a place, and with the ability of being intimate with others, a sense of self-esteem is nurtured. In part, this might be associated with the sense of status that is attributed to the person by others, and such status may help create self-confidence, but for Maslow the primary issue was how people could grow to have a self-confidence based upon an honest and realistic self-appraisal with which one might be comfortable. This process is often represented by a diagram such as that shown in Figure 5.1.

The figure is usually drawn as a triangle for a number of reasons (as shown in Figure 5.1). First, it is often stated to be hierarchical with each stage being built upon the other, thereby representing a series of stages as one climbs towards the highest level of self-actualisation. Second, Maslow in his writings implies that not everyone is capable of the higher stages, a belief drawn from his own personal experience derived from his view of his own mother and being a victim of antisemitic gangs in his youth. Furthermore, he explicitly states in his own book, *Motivation and Personality*, that less than 5% of the American population display the characteristics of being 'self-actualised'.

That book is of interest for several reasons. First, in the initial pages he states that his own motivation for writing the book was a wish to correct what he thought was wrong with much of psychology up to the time of writing. He argued that psychology was directed at the problems of the mentally ill. It is relevant to note that his own life overlapped Sigmund Freud, for Freud did not die until September 1939 when Maslow was aged 31 and already teaching at Brooklyn College in New York. Maslow believed that it was not possible to 'cure' the mentally ill without a clear goal or conception of what it was to be mentally healthy. In *Towards a Psychology of Being* (Maslow, 1968) and *Motivation and Personality*

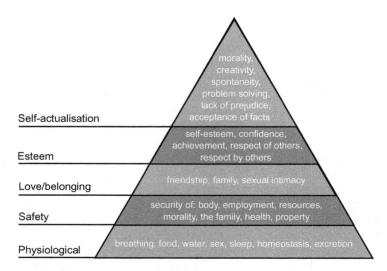

Figure 5.1 Maslow's hierarchy of needs

(Maslow, 1970), he describes the characteristics of self-actualisation. These may be characterised as an adherence to:

- Truth: honest, reality, beauty, pure, cleanliness and unadulterated completeness.
- Goodness: rightness, desirability, uprightness, benevolence, honesty.
- Wholeness: unity, integration, tendency to oneness, interconnectedness, simplicity, organisation, structure, order, not dissociated, synergy.
- Dichotomy: transcendence, acceptance, resolution, integration, polarities, opposites, contradictions.
- Aliveness: process, not-deadness, spontaneity, self-regulation, full-functioning.
- Uniqueness: idiosyncrasy, individuality, non-comparability, novelty.
- Necessity: inevitability: it must be just that way, not changed in any slightest way.
- Justice: fairness, suitability, disinterestedness, non-partiality.
- Order: lawfulness, rightness, perfectly arranged.
- Simplicity: nakedness, abstract, essential skeletal, bluntness.
- Richness: differentiation, complexity, intricacy, totality.
- Effortlessness: ease; lack of strain, striving, or difficulty.
- Playfulness: fun, joy, amusement.
- Self-sufficiency: autonomy, independence, self-determining.

In his various writings Maslow writes of a personality who still possesses a sense of wonder at the setting of the sun, who can retain a sense of fun as well as being serious, a personality that appreciates the richness and complexities of the world while seeking the simplicity of essential being. In his work *Towards a Psychology of Being*, Maslow writes of an 'intrinsic conscience' based on 'the unconscious and preconscious perception of our own nature, of our own destiny, or our own capacities, of our own "call" in life. It insists that we be true to our inner nature and that we do not deny it out of weakness or for advantages' (Maslow, 1962/2012: 4).

One point to note is that when re-reading Maslow's key works it should be realised that the famous triangular/pyramidal diagram of Maslow's motivations does not actually appear in his book, although, as in Chapter 4 of *Towards a Psychology of Being*, the staged processes of personal growth are made explicit. Bridgman *et al.* (2019) state that Maslow never drew what, to paraphrase them, might be termed the 'most iconic, but abused, pyramid in management studies'. Indeed, the earliest diagrammatic application they can find of Maslow's stages was an illustration of a staircase produced by Keith Davis in his book *Human Relations in Business* in 1957. They also note that an earlier competitor to the pyramid or triangle was in fact a ladder, to which Pearce refers in his conceptualisation of visitor motivation. It seems that the first to use the pyramid was McDermid in his 1960 paper entitled *How Money Motivates Men*. At least four observations may be made about the pyramid. First, as a concise summary of Maslow's initial work, it does represent an easily understood interpretation of at least part of his work. Second, considering he died in 1970, the diagram was being reproduced and was even used on a reprint of one of his books in 1968, and as far as it is known, he did not take exception to it. Third, it has to be noted that his own interpretation of the initial five-stage theory became less rigid and more nuanced over time, as is discussed a little further below. Finally, his own motivation for the work seemed to change over time.

From the time of being a schoolboy, Maslow kept a diary, and many of his papers, observations and the like have been retained as a collection in the Smithsonian Museum and published subsequently by his biographers (notably Edward Hoffman) and others including his wife. The diaries are of interest and include several letters with members of the Blackfoot First People's reservation in Alberta after his six-week field visit in 1938 (Feigenbaum & Smith, 2020). Blackstock (2011) suggests that Maslow derived his ideas from tribal elders and their thinking of community actualisation, and certainly Maslow's notes show he was much influenced by his experience. However, much of Maslow's work evolved considerably from 1938 and later notes indicate that one of the driving forces was as much philosophical as psychological. In 1955 he wrote, 'The only way to heal evil men is to create good men' (Maslow, 1955: 1), and, as indicated above, his theories continued to evolve. His later work suggested an eight-stage model that comprised the processes described in Table 5.1.

The needs seem now to fall into two sections, which Maslow named as the deficiency dimension (stages 1 to 4) and the being dimension (stages 5 to 8). Millard (2022) classifies the distinctions by using the diagram shown as Figure 5.2.

A distinction is thus made between the states of self-actualisation and transcendence, and Maslow identifies the distinction by writing, 'Peakers seem also to live in the realm of Being, of poetry; esthetics;

Table 5.1 An eight-stage developmental model

1. Biological and physiological needs – air, food, drink, shelter, warmth, sex, sleep, etc.
2. Safety needs – protection from elements, security, order, law, limits, stability, etc.
3. Social needs – Belongingness and Love – work group, family, affection, relationships, etc.
4. Esteem needs – self-esteem, achievement, mastery, independence, status, dominance, prestige, managerial responsibility, etc.
5. Cognitive needs – knowledge, meaning, etc.
6. Aesthetic needs – appreciation and search for beauty, balance, form, etc.
7. Self-actualisation needs – realising personal potential, self-fulfilment, seeking personal growth and peak experiences
8. Transcendence needs – helping others to achieve self-actualisation

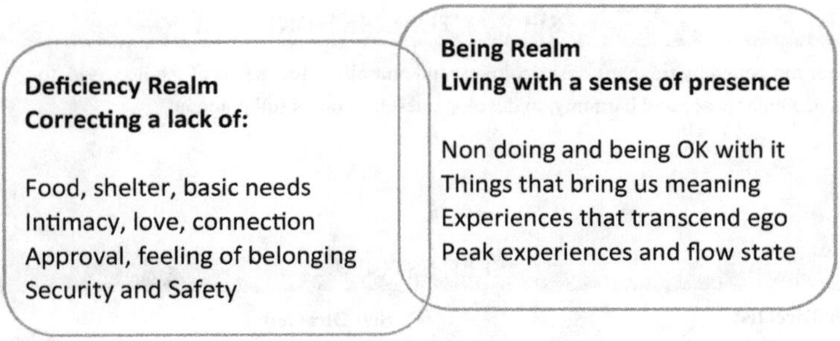

Deficiency Realm
Correcting a lack of:

Food, shelter, basic needs
Intimacy, love, connection
Approval, feeling of belonging
Security and Safety

Being Realm
Living with a sense of presence

Non doing and being OK with it
Things that bring us meaning
Experiences that transcend ego
Peak experiences and flow state

Figure 5.2 Distinction between the deficiency and being dimensions

symbols; transcendence; "religion" of the mystical, personal noninstitutional sort and of end-experiences' (Maslow, 1970: 138), while non-peaking self-actualisers are described as being 'practical, effective people, mesomorphs living in the world and doing very well in it' (Maslow, 1970: 138).

Figure 5.3 explicitly draws several links with Chapter 4. It makes direct reference to the state of flow discussed in the previous chapter and which was fundamental to the thinking of Mihaly Csikszentmihalyi who had become Professor of Psychology at the University of Chicago in 1969, just prior to Maslow's death.

Relationship between self-actualisation and tourism

So, what has Maslow's ideas contributed to our notions of tourists' and visitors' experiences? Both Maslow and Csikszentmihalyi's works are notable for the manner in which they have influenced thinking about personal development, and both were subjected to the same criticism, namely: where is the empirical proof or evidence to support their theories? One suspects that as they moved into the latter stages of their respective careers, they became less concerned about the need for proof and more concerned about further evolving their ideas. It is notable that both were creative and engaged in their work almost to the point of their death. Nonetheless, the question as to 'Where is the proof of the validity of their ideas?' is a valid question, and possibly one that tourism research may be well placed to answer.

Tourism has many features that are congruent with personal growth. As noted in prior chapters, the act of being a tourist is a role in which a person is 'extracted' from their daily life patterns. The holiday can represent an escape from normal responsibilities which at one end of a possible continuum means a hedonistic escape into pleasure, and at the other end of a possible dimension, an opportunity to question what is the daily life pattern about, what does it mean and how does it contribute to positive senses of being. While in the early 21st century pleasure

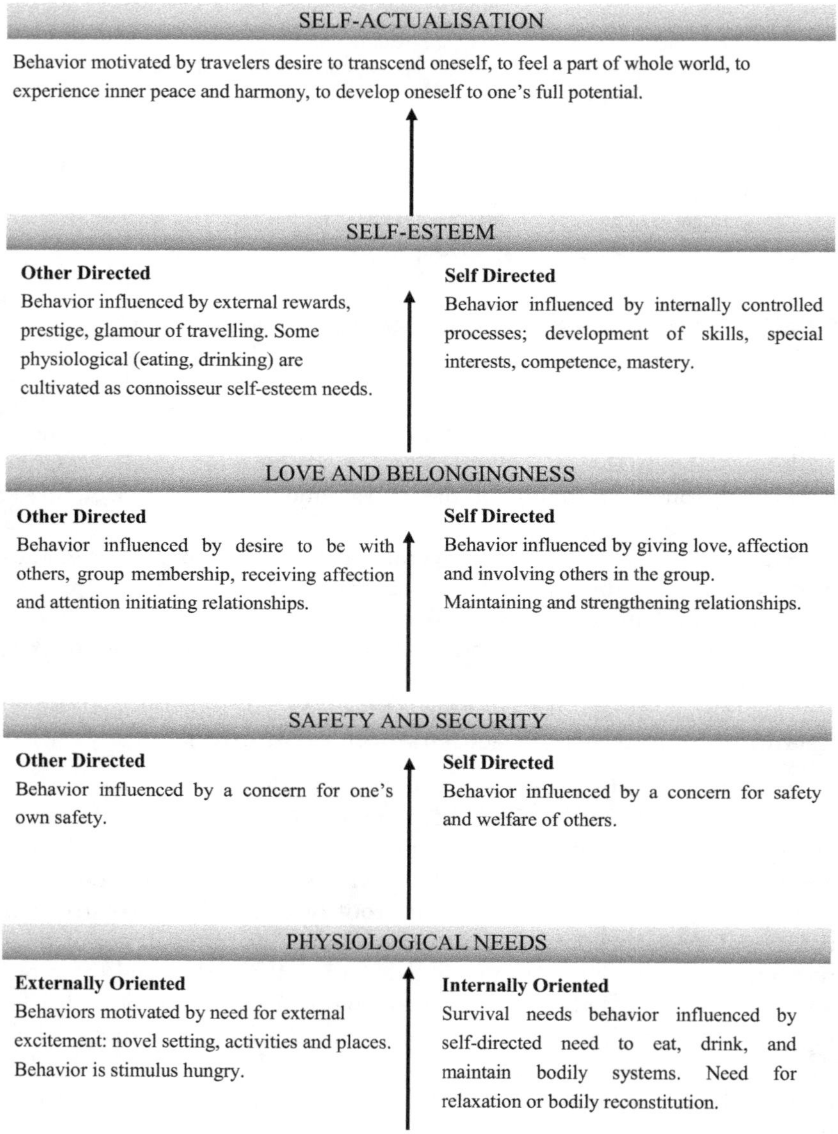

SELF-ACTUALISATION

Behavior motivated by travelers desire to transcend oneself, to feel a part of whole world, to experience inner peace and harmony, to develop oneself to one's full potential.

SELF-ESTEEM

Other Directed
Behavior influenced by external rewards, prestige, glamour of travelling. Some physiological (eating, drinking) are cultivated as connoisseur self-esteem needs.

Self Directed
Behavior influenced by internally controlled processes; development of skills, special interests, competence, mastery.

LOVE AND BELONGINGNESS

Other Directed
Behavior influenced by desire to be with others, group membership, receiving affection and attention initiating relationships.

Self Directed
Behavior influenced by giving love, affection and involving others in the group. Maintaining and strengthening relationships.

SAFETY AND SECURITY

Other Directed
Behavior influenced by a concern for one's own safety.

Self Directed
Behavior influenced by a concern for safety and welfare of others.

PHYSIOLOGICAL NEEDS

Externally Oriented
Behaviors motivated by need for external excitement: novel setting, activities and places. Behavior is stimulus hungry.

Internally Oriented
Survival needs behavior influenced by self-directed need to eat, drink, and maintain bodily systems. Need for relaxation or bodily reconstitution.

Figure 5.3 The Travel Career Ladder

is often associated with sensual if not sexual pleasure, that is a narrow perspective as has been noted from the time of Epicurus (341–270 BCE) to the philosophy (hedodynamics) expounded by Argonov in 2014. Epicurus noted 'It is impossible to live the pleasant life without also living sensibly, nobly, and justly' (Epicurus, 2012: 172). For his part, Victor Argonov (2014) argues that longer lifespans combined with technological advances including understanding of human physiology makes possible a scientific evaluation of the pleasure principle as a means of creating a better life.

Thus, hedonism is but one school of philosophy that seeks meaning in life, and hence even the most hedonistic of holidays may well lead the tourist to consider what it is that they gain from such activities. It has already been noted that many activities with holidaymaking are associated with the acquisition of knowledge – whether it be looking at historic remains, engaging with different cultures, seeking meditative environments or well-being, or to discover a sense of 'awe' which poses one's smallness against the enormity of space (Frost & Frost, 2021).

Maslow's stages of personal development are readily applicable to tourism. It was noted in Chapter 4 that the tourist is voluntarily (at least at a conscious level) engaged in the activity – even if as a response to a dysfunctional society, or a society that is structured to condone if not encourage holidaymaking. Hence the satisfied tourist requires the following from the viewpoint of Maslow's philosophical and psychological perspectives:

- Safety, to be free from violence and crime.
- To have comfortable accommodation and a good night's sleep.
- To have opportunities to gain knowledge.
- To have their interest prompted by new experiences.
- To seek more than simply escape and relaxation.
- To have opportunities for socialisation and personal reflections.
- To be respected and to show respect for others.
- To have a family and educational background that permits them to appreciate the above.

At an anecdotal level the applicability of Maslow's stages to tourism is easily shown. For many years the authors have, in their lectures, asked students to note what were the characteristics of one of their more memorable holidays, pointing out that holidays can be memorable for the things that go wrong as well as right. Almost inevitably, when recording the words used by the students, the positive words dominate, the negative words are few – and the most satisfying holidays are associated with descriptors associated with the higher 'being' needs. Interestingly, in several but not all instances, even negative words associated with a lack of comfort or poor conditions can be associated with positive post-holiday reflection. This occurs when an ability to cope and overcome the negative aspects has been displayed, so that while unedifying at the time of experiencing the problems, the ability to overcome them adds to feelings of competency and self-confidence. Such exercises have also shown that holidays memorable for going wrong are almost always associated with events connected to threats to safety, deprivation of food, comfort or sleep – that is, they are associated with the denial of the bottom components of the Maslow pyramid.

In a more structured study of backpackers and their recall of highlights, Ryan *et al.* (2003) used Maslow's hierarchy of needs to analyse what made the holiday so memorable. Many of the comments made by the informants spoke of amazing experiences that created senses of achievement, growing confidence, intimacy and a sense of awe about the natural world. Philip Pearce was one who was very conscious of Maslow, as was evidenced by the development of the concept *The Travel Career Ladder*, but equally he was concerned with rigorous analytical techniques (Fenton & Pearce, 1988) and also an awareness of overly narrow definitions. In 1985, he commented that one of the dangers of professional journals such as the *Journal of Travel Research* was 'a loss of integration [between tourism] with other problems and topic areas in the social science arena' (Pearce, 1985: 1001) which led to a poverty of definition among other ills. In one of his earlier studies, Pearce (1982) analysed some 400 cases provided by 200 tourists in Europe, the United States, Canada and Australia using the stages of the hierarchy of needs model. His findings are summarised in Table 5.2. From these findings he concluded that tourist motivation is based on an approach versus avoidance paradigm.

Pearce was much influenced by Maslow and continued to develop the theme. In 1988, in his book *The Ulysses Factor* (Pearce, 1988), Pearce began to hint at the concept of a travel career based on Maslow's concepts. The application specifically used the image of a ladder of progression and had an intuitive appeal. Initially, it might be said that at the commencement of tourism the embryonic traveller would wish to gain confidence and knowledge of travel and its rituals of bookings, check-ins, time changes and the experiences of new places. That process is made easier by travelling in environments made safe by familiarity of culture or through the use of intermediaries such as tour guides or packaged holidays. As the traveller gains confidence, independent travel might emerge, for example by hiring a car to travel away from the resort hotel. With further confidence, the tourist creates their own itinerary and modes of

Table 5.2 Maslow's stages and tourist reporting of role of the stages in their holidays

Maslow stage	% of positive experiences	% of negative experiences
Physiological needs	27	27
Safety	4	43
Love	33	17
Self-esteem	1	12
Self-actualisation	35	1

travel and seeks more unfamiliarity. They thus ascend the ladder towards more challenging encounters and through the travel career gain knowledge and proceed towards self-actualisation.

In parallel with this notion, one might also argue that there is a societal maturation of what it is that tourists as a whole wish to gain from their holidays. This has been evidenced by the debates about the nature of post-Covid tourism. For example, Spalding *et al.* (2021) identify the increasing interest in environmental issues and argue that nature is the core resource of tourism; consequently tourists will increasingly look for environmentally friendly policies when travelling. Ma *et al.* (2021) also attach importance to nature's healing powers, citing research that shows the benefit of 'forest therapy'. Moreover, they identify other trends including wellness tourism, mindfulness products and more general societal trends to conclude that 'This pandemic has forced us to review our way of life and the way we travel' (Ma *et al.*, 2021: 138). They propose that the solution is 'healing tourism' as a means of achieving mental solace.

Interpretations of tourism analytics – demanding authenticity?

For his part, Koh (2020) offers a more statistical analysis of the monies spent on Covid policies and the issues of wealth and income inequalities against a background of pre-Covid-19 situations of 'over tourism'. He suggests that the pandemic response represents a 'watershed' (Koh, 2020: 1018) that may cause governments to adopt a more assertive role in the economy. This, he argues, provides many opportunities for governments to fund new policies that focus on job creation, infrastructure development, crowding and environmental protection. Although he does not cite China as an example, he states that such policies would permit tourism to play a major role in implementing such policies. As noted by many commentators, China has for more than two decades specifically used tourism as a means of addressing rural deprivation (Ryan & Huang, 2013). Those policies have often identified rural zones around major cities and improved transport and communications structures (notably road, cell phone and internet access) while encouraging entrepreneurs to establish rural tourist activities such as farm tourism and bed and breakfast accommodation to be followed by the development of small hotels (Ryan & Huang, 2013). From approximately 2015 onwards, policies became increasingly more sophisticated including the introduction of private or state-owned larger enterprises into the rural developments under contracts often agreed with and by provincial or municipal administrations. Hence, in small villages such as the Taoist village of Qiyunshan in Anhui Province, the location was developed by the Huangshan Xiangyuan Qiyunshan Hotel Management Co., Ltd. trading as Sun River Corporation over a period from 2010, which saw the introduction of

immigrants leasing properties to establish souvenir shops, the formalisation of fortune tellers using traditional methods based on the *I Ching* and
the *yin-yang* and the use of the village for model shoots, music videos
and films. Villagers either improved their homes to host guests or leased
them to migrants in order to leave and live in other newer villages that
permitted the building of new houses or apartments that offered modern
comforts such as air conditioning or en-suite bathrooms. Such developments also took place within Qiyunshan as it is not a UNESCO world
heritage site unlike the other nearby Anhui villages of Hongcun and Xidi.
Consequently, interior developments were permitted within homes especially if they had experienced some form of damage. There is little doubt
that in several instances the more entrepreneurial members of the village
communities gained significantly, while additionally in many instances
local authorities sought to ensure that others could also gain financially
so that senior members of the village could be looked after (Li, 2013).

Such developments complement a move towards more sustainable
and societal-oriented tourism in that local communities can benefit
from tourism, while in addition such practices provide a rationale for
the protection and investment in local traditions and cultural practices.
Nonetheless, there is another side to such developments. Several commentators have suggested that in a post-Covid situation many tourists
will increasingly demand 'authenticity'. On the one hand, such a demand
can be seen as being totally consistent with a Maslowian concept of self-
actualisation. It represents a desire to experience the reality of another's
culture, to view the world through the eyes of another's gaze that is
shaped by value systems different from those of the visitor's own culture.
In his influential work, the late John Urry adopted the work of the French
philosopher and historian Michel Foucault, seizing on his notion of *The
Gaze* (Urry, 1990).

Foucault was initially attracted to existentialism and Marxism but
by the 1960s was more drawn to structuralist thinking that sought a
non-subjective assessment of societal power structures. It is difficult to
provide a short concise summary of Foucault's thinking, especially given
the evolution of his work away from studies of medicine and madness
to his later works such as *The Order of Things* (Foucault, 1966). Nonetheless, Foucault's books have significantly influenced the thoughts of
many tourism scholars, most notably John Urry and Keith Hollinshead,
but several others including Tazim Jamal, Stephen Wearing and Craig
Wight. Foucault in *The Order of Things* suggested that each period
of history possessed its own modes of discourse of truth. From the
viewpoint of tourism, many scholars adhere to the concept that a post-
modern age emerged during the 1960s that superseded a modern period
that had commenced with the industrial revolution of the 19th century.
A key distinguishing factor lay in consumer patterns with a shift towards
the consumption of experiences, symbols and images as distinct from the

consumption of things. John Urry caught this change with his book *The Tourist Gaze* in which he identified a number of ways in which a tourist gaze could be formed, captured, framed and indeed manipulated. Thus, for example, a desire for the authentic may well represent a desire not for authenticity *per se* but for a desire driven by a nostalgic gaze for a past world of certainty. The authenticity of Qiyunshan today is that the village presents a nostalgic image of the past patterns of life packaged for a touristic consumption. Many tourists seek an escape from a stressful complexity of daily life by escaping into a simpler rural lifestyle, but one that offers the comforts of 21st-century life. Hence the search for authenticity is a nostalgic drive shaped by a romantic view of past certainties of order, an order informed by Taoist philosophies that emphasise a desire for a life of internal harmony engaged by acceptance of an external world (Li *et al.*, 2012).

Keith Hollinshead is one scholar who has brought a specific perspective to tourism premised on not only Foucault's view but also a trenchant analysis of tourism. Like Urry, and indeed Krippendorf, Hollinshead proposes that Foucault's concept is one of an 'eye of power', that is, the Gaze is a means of analysing societal power structures, and tourism exists and contributes to those power structures as previously discussed. Jamal and Hollinshead (2001) go further to draw attention to the role of tourism in exploring the marginalised voices and tourist-host interactions in *performative* sites. Qiyunshan is an example of such spaces, but tourism is writ large with examples of how tourism empowers the hitherto silenced voices of the marginalised. Examples of these latter studies include work on sex workers in sex tourism (Carr & Berdychevsky, 2022; Omondi & Ryan, 2023) and indigenous peoples as subjects of observation (Yang *et al.*, 2013).

Hollinshead argues that while Urry popularised an application of Foucault's concepts to tourism, Urry's work is more than just a simple application of those ideas. Rather, Hollinshead (1999) defends Urry from a criticism that Leiper (1992) posed when stating that Urry's analysis was too simplistic an application of the French philosopher's ideas on tourism, writing that 'I now urge Leiper to reflect a little longer on Urry's appropriation of the Foucauldian *le regard* for *the Tourist Gaze* could indeed be said to contain a litany of subtle primings and gentle probings on the governmentality of things' (Hollinshead, 1999: 8). These ideas taken from Foucault's work have influenced tourism scholarship in many ways. For example, Gu and Ryan (2010) have used the concept of the tourist as a *bricoleur*, specifically when, as non-Buddhists, they attended the Wutaishan Buddhist Festival in China in company with a Buddhist monk and nun. Meeting the definition of a *bricoleur* as being part of a crowd, but not a member of the crowd, they not only analyse the festival from different viewpoints but also express their own personal reactions to it using their experience of being tourist researchers. This aspect is often present in Ryan's research, as, for example, writing of Cham culture (Trinh & Ryan, 2016). Both of these works are about visitor experiences and on reflection imply a sense of awe that is also characteristic of much psychological insight into visitor experiences. Lu *et al.* describe a sense of awe, stating 'Awe is an emotional reaction when a certain aspect of an individual's original reference frame is challenged by perceptual vast stimuli. ... As a positive emotion existing in people's daily behaviour, awe not only belongs to the basic emotion of human beings, but also is regarded as individuals' basic experience with universal culture' (Lu *et al.*, 2017: 2).

Lu *et al.* (2017) utilise a standard structural equation model to show that awe is a significant component in explaining visitor satisfaction with a visit to Mount Emei, stated to be the first location of a Buddhist temple in China. Their model 'explains' over 50% of the variance in visitor satisfaction, and measures of a sense of awe correlate with satisfaction at a value of 0.712, $p<0.01$; there is perhaps a danger that the statistical exercise begins to dominate any sense of awe, despite the fact that 'awe' is seen to be a mediating variable between religious feelings and a sense of satisfaction. Any sense of awe that visitors possessed is reflected in responses to questions set by the researchers, and the finding that 'This paper has provided evidence that the awe experience is more elicited by the perceived vastness of natural environment for secular tourists, while it is more encouraged by the perceived sanctity of religious ambience for Pilgrims' (Lu *et al.*, 2017: 12). As always, in such statistical exercises, the nature of the questions can determine outcomes, and unfortunately the article does not include a copy of the questionnaire, so one does not know the full set of measures used, but in many ways the results confirm what one might have expected. Foucault would have suggested, one suspects, that to better understand the sense of awe, a discourse analysis may have revealed more.

Wright (2019) provides an analysis of Foucault's method of discourse analysis and how it might be applied to tourism. He commences with a listing of four relatively common methods of analysis used in qualitative research, these being content analysis, thematic analysis, semiotic analysis and deconstruction. Summarising his text, it might be said that content analysis is based upon frequencies, classifications and links between what are thought to be significant within the text. Thematic analysis is concerned with cultural understanding based on coding, and increasingly with current software, measures of theme linkages found within the text. Semiotic analysis according to Wright 'examines the complex relationship between objects and representation' (Wright, 2019: 124) and he implies that it is restricted to an analysis of image, but of course it relates to the analysis of images through the use of language. Finally, deconstruction relates to an analysis of contested viewpoints and interpretations of truth, and hence within tourism this perspective is particularly applicable to issues inherent in cultural, heritage and indigenous tourism. For example, who is interpreting facets of the past, or the current impacts of minority cultures, and recently, issues of gender roles. Looking at the list, it is evident that many authors report research findings while making little reference to Foucault or indeed or any reference to discourse analysis, but rather simply refer to aspects of the technique being used. This trend seems to have been reinforced by a growing use of computer-assisted textual analysis. In the opinions of the authors, programs such as NVivo, QDA Miner and TextSmart provide graphical and statistical analysis of the coherence of themes, and an analysis of links between themes that go far beyond frequency checks and the initial clustering techniques of earlier programs such as CatPac. Equally, such programs ease comparative analysis by sociodemographics and indeed any classification imposed by the researcher while also adding mapping functions.

Consequently, in order to refine the concept of discourse analysis from a Foucaultian perspective, Wright (2019) suggests the following stages that a researcher can pursue. There are six steps, which are (a) the statement, that is, the smallest unit of analysis, (b) the archive, (c) the enunciation, (d) discursive formation, (e) knowledge and (f) surfaces of emergence. Table 5.3 provides a brief summary of each stage, and is derived from Wright's paper, which examines each in far greater detail.

Parallels can be found in the way in which Maslow describes personal development and growth and how Foucault describes societal change. Development occurs through the tension that arises from (a) a desire of harmony or homeostasis where human or societal systems are in balance wherein each component works well within a system and on the other hand (b) a desire for change, often motivated for a desire to improve personal or societal conditions, or to correct perceived deficiencies within a system. But the seemingly simple dichotomous relationship between desired stability and improvement is a temporary pattern at best. Both Maslow and Foucault, as representatives of what are broadly considered as schools of humanistic psychology and post-modernism, are all too aware of human and societal patterns being subjected to a whole range of exogenous factors. These include anything from the forces of nature that create storms and earthquakes to longer-term changes of climate and environment, to the human failure to conceive unintended consequences of past decisions, to the consequences of technological change. This is the nature of discourse, and the nature of people and societies. Whether it is the new paradigm of knowledge (Kuhn, 1962), a new discourse as noted by Foucault or a moment of transcendence, the implication of such thinking is that the future is no longer the continuance of the past, either personally or societally.

Table 5.3 Stages in Foucaultian discourse following Wright's 2019 classification

Stage	Description
The statement	The statement is the smallest unit of analysis, and in tourism may be a destination, place or activity. It is unstable for while subject to rules, such rules may be contested. One may speak of place attachment, but whose place, who is attached, what is the nature of attachment and what is its role.
The archive	The archive is a collection of statements that as it becomes more detailed may become more nuanced. The research question and context help establish the nature of the archive. The archive may be dependent on spatial and temporal context, and as the context changes so too might the rules that determine how statements change. The archive significantly shapes the analytical nature of the discourse.
The enunciation	At this point, prior analysis begins to shape not just the nature of the discourse, but rather the discourse beginning to yield results in terms of new patterns or themes.
Discursive formation	Discursive formation emerges from critiquing the emergent themes. It begins to identify how often previously unquestioned rules have shaped patterns of thought and behaviour. They lead to the next stage.
Knowledge	New knowledge is represented by the new possibilities of which the researcher is now aware. This knowledge comprises new rules, new interpretations, new representations and becomes new ways of study and definitions. They are new ways of seeing and hence of discourse.
Surfaces of emergence	With each cycle of new knowledge construction, some representations fit the model and others are deviant, challenging and challengeable. Over time new statements emerge and the discourse is not settled but remains open to new analyses.

So – where is empirical proof for such approaches?

Minca and Oakes (2014) commence their contribution to *The Wiley Blackwell Companion to Tourism* (Lew *et al.*, 2014) by noting that a decade earlier they noted the importance of the contribution made by the post-modern movement to tourism research and particularly how the subjectivity of the researcher might shape understanding of tourist behaviour. However, in 2014 they wrote 'the concept of "postmodernity" has largely evaporated from the literature' but they continue to state that it has generated a 'raft of diverse conceptual and theoretical contributions' to thinking about tourism and tourists (Minca & Oakes, 2014: 294). They suggest that one outcome is to view tourism as an *analytic* rather than a particular practice, experience or behaviour. As a rationale for this viewpoint, they note the growing lack of distinction between holiday taking and daily patterns of life. This goes to the heart of tourism, for in much of this book it has been argued that one aspect of tourism is its ability to take the tourist away from daily life into another place, culture and indeed possible behaviour. Yet at the same time in this chapter and indeed the last, much has been made of the relationship of holidaymaking to the quality of life, to personal and societal development. In short, holidays occur within a context of not simply place, time, culture and specific destination, but also in the life development of individuals and places.

Minca and Oakes (2014) argue that this represents a new turn in thinking about tourism. It is no longer a matter of applying social, economic and psychological theories to tourism but increasingly one of relearning social theory from tourism. For example, they note that much of the practice of tourism remains based on prior practice that historically links back to the days of the Grand Tour in the 17th century and more specifically to European practices in the immediate post-Second World War period. However, in the 21st century tourism is increasingly dominated by different imperatives emergent from different parts of the world. As hinted previously in this chapter, tourism has become a means of not simply travel, but also of well-being, personal identity, psychological development and increasingly requires a consideration of its consequences. In the years prior to the Covid pandemic, the language of tourism increasingly included the term 'over-tourism'. Tourism is thus a significant career social force with economic, social and environmental impacts with subsequent effects on, while being also impacted by power structures.

These arguments have been consistent with much of the text contained in this chapter, but again lead back to the question, where is the empirical evidence? This is a question that has been asked several times, and Rotfeld (2014) is critical of Maslow's work and comes close to describing it as a 'Zombie' theory because of an alleged lack of evidence. In part, one seeming problem for the current authors of this text centres on the nature of the question, was Maslow more primarily concerned with philosophical issues as hinted at in his diaries and possibly not inherently interested in the construction of empirically testable frameworks and structures?

The Travel Career Pattern

This chapter commenced with a description of the work of Abraham Maslow, and hence to complete the chapter it seems appropriate to return to Maslow as interpreted by Philip Pearce and his concept of the travel career ladder. Pearce (2014) briefly describes the work of his predecessors in terms of research into the motivation for holiday taking and subsequently distinguishes between the more general process of reasons for travel and a more specific question, namely what is it that motivates a person to travel to a specific place at a given time. There is much value in asking this question, but the question seems to imply that each destination is specifically different from any other location, and that the potential tourist has specific demands in mind. The history of the operations of the package holiday companies seems to imply that for many, holiday destinations are substitutable one for another. The European package holiday business was based on little difference between the sun, sea and sand holidays of Spanish, Greek, Italian and Turkish

Mediterranean resorts, and it was this lack of differentiation that permitted the companies to switch resorts easily in a way that enabled them to profit from the market before the chase for capacity replaced the desire for profit (Ryan, 1991). Equally, one can observe that measures of satisfaction that use repeat visitation as a proxy of satisfaction may over-rate destination loyalty because the tourist may be more loyal to an activity rather than a destination, and thus again destinations can be substituted one for another.

Despite these caveats, Pearce's concept of the travel ladder as indicated previously has importance and in citing Maslow and Csikszentmihalyi as sources, Pearce (2014) specifically acknowledges the role of well-being as an important motivator for tourism, writing 'the notion that human beings seek to build their wellbeing in ways consonant with their character represents a forward-looking approach to social motivation. ... The approach is applicable to well-being in tourism ... this involves not only immediate sensory pleasures ... but also includes attempts to achieve desired goals such as respect, status, enhanced relationships, altruism, self regulation, zest' (Pearce, 2014: 48).

The evidence for these conclusions lies partially in Pearce's later workings of the travel career ladder. The earlier model (Figure 5.3) previously discussed was significantly revised in response to criticisms (Ryan, 1998). Pearce and Lee (2005) suggest that the initial criticism was possibly distracted by the use of the term 'ladder', which reinforced an unintentional emphasis on the hierarchical components of the model. Hence, in the revised version, the nomenclature is changed to the revised model being termed *The Travel Career Pattern*. The new model had at its core a pattern of motivations. Equally, the retention of the term 'career' was to reflect that experiences built upon previous holiday experiences, while noting that careers can include a return to past activities and destinations as well as seeking new places and experiences. Each holiday possesses the potential of not simply creating relaxation but also opportunities for renewal and learning. In one of Pearce's last works on the travel career pattern, published in 2021, he provided one of his most detailed backgrounds to the theory's development. Figure 5.4 is taken from that paper, and clearly indicates both its roots in Maslow's thinking and the contribution made by Pearce in making the distinction between internally and externally created factors in motivation formation.

Based on empirical evidence gained from over 1800 tourists from both western and Asian countries, Pearce and Lee (2005) published survey results that were based on 14 dimensions revealed by factor analysis. These 14 dimensions or groups were subsequently divided into three layers or grouping of motives – the core comprising novelty, escape and relationships, a middle layer of self-development and self-actualisation representing respectively the external and internal drivers, along with

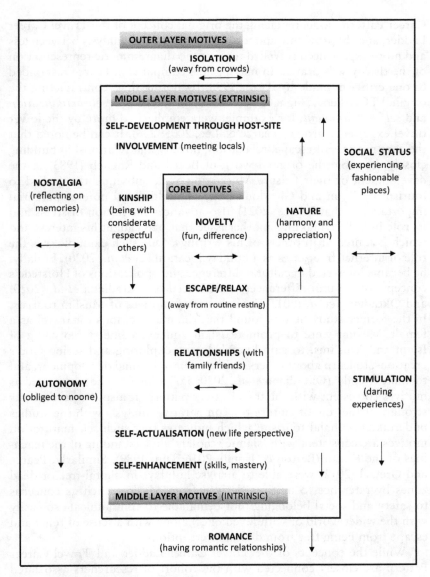

Figure 5.4 The Travel Career Pattern

a relationship with nature and respect for others, all nestling within a peripheral cluster comprising autonomy, nostalgia, social status and stimulation.

It should be noted that Figure 5.4 differs from that in the initial work by Pearce and Lee (2005). Indeed, given that the 2005 paper was concerned with (a) providing statistical support for the then new Travel

Career Pattern model replacing the original concept of the Travel Career Ladder, and (b) providing and testing a comparative analysis between less and more experienced travelled tourists, no diagrammatic representation of the theory was drawn. In making this comparison, Pearce responded to one criticism made by Ryan (1998) by noting that 'contradicting the original TCL theory, higher levels of motivation such as *self-actualization* and *self-development*, for example, were emphasised more by the lower travel experience group' (Pearce & Lee, 2005: 236). It can be noted that the core motives of escape, relaxation, novelty and relationship building closely resemble the original work of Beard and Ragheb (1983) in the development of their Leisure Motivation Scale subsequently applied to tourism by Ryan and Glendon (1998). An additional note of potential importance is that Pearce (2021) also advances the notion of stress and its role in holidaymaking, another issue that had caught his interest and which is hinted at in others of his writings. One such example was the role of internet-free zones as a holiday location (Li *et al.*, 2020). Equally, he became interested in cultural difference and applications of Hofstede's concepts of cultural difference, as evidenced by Oktadiana *et al.* (2020) and Oktadiana *et al.* (2017), into the travel motives of Muslim tourists. In the former study 'it was found that the main reasons for travel as a female Muslim were to promote Islam and overcome stereotyping of Islam and Muslims, to gain knowledge by exploring and seeing God's creations, to learn about others, achieve some personal development, and to make friends' (Oktadiana *et al.*, 2020: 557) which can be interpreted as motives consistent with the travel career pattern. It also, however, hints strongly at the role of culture for comparative analysis with the studies undertaken on halal tourism, which indicates that such self-maturation motives are consistent with Islamic scholars' understanding of the teachings of the Koran (Battou & Ismail, 2016; Din, 1989). Similarly, Pearce and Gretzel (2012) were able to analyse holidays in digital-free or dead zones by reference to motives derived from Maslow such as concerns to safety and social belonging (not being able to communicate so easily with the wider world or with loved ones) along with a sense of relief and escape from being free from digital interruptions.

While the concepts of the Travel Career Ladder and Travel Career Pattern are closely connected with the cohort of researchers associated with Phil Pearce, many others have used the concept for purposes of empirical research. For example, Paris and Teye (2010) built upon previous studies of backpackers to analyse the motivations that lead to backpacking, and to test whether the Travel Career Pattern concept could be substantiated. They found results that tended to replicate those of Pearce and Lee (2005), noting that regardless of levels of experience, the motives of cultural knowledge and relaxation appeared core to the backpacker experience. On the other hand, motives such as a desire for the experiential and personal and social growth are described as 'dynamic' factors that change with degrees of backpacking experience and tend to score higher with the less experienced. It can be suggested that this reflects a process of maturation. The less experienced have a higher awareness of uncertainty and risk as they face situations new to them, but as they find themselves able to cope with any challenge, they find higher degrees of certainty. Accordingly, self-knowledge grows, and the question of who I am becomes less important as they create better concepts of self.

In another study, Song and Bae (2018) examined the credibility of the Travel Career Pattern concept when examining the travel motivations of 585 Korean students. Akin to the study undertaken by Paris and Teye (2010), their initial concern was to test the reliability of the measures as they used a somewhat simplified version of the Pearce and Lee (2005) scale. They identified four clusters of travellers primarily based upon experience and motive, and then analysed the differences between each of the four groups with reference to their motivations. Among their conclusions, they noted 'longer travel careers of international students (e.g., Veteran) were associated with higher internally oriented motives (e.g., personal development) in the middle layer motivation and shorter travel careers with higher external motives (e.g., host-site involvement)' (Song & Bae, 2018: 142). While this is inconsistent with the findings of Paris and Teye (2010) with reference to past experience and the degrees of concern with self-development, their study confirms the statistical validity of the questions, reinforced the core role of relaxation, but more carefully analysed the differences between the layers described in Figure 5.4.

One purpose of concept creation is to motivate conceptual development, and Pearce's original notion has encouraged others to think in more nuanced ways about motivations and linkages with self-development through tourism. Filep and Greenacre (2007) and Wu et al. (2019) have sought to do this. In the former study, Filep and Greenacre establish what they feel are the criteria required for any model or concept to be considered as a sound theory of tourist motivation. These criteria are 'a specification of the role of the theory; an elaboration of the ownership and appeal of the theory; ease of communication; ability to measure travel motivation; an implementation of a multi-motive approach; employment of a dynamic approach; and an ability to consider both extrinsic and intrinsic motives' (Filep & Greenacre, 2007: 24). They comment that many studies of tourist motivation measurement and by extension, the use of motives as criteria by which to test the quality of visitor experience, fail to meet these requirements. However, they contend that the Travel Career Pattern model does meet these specifications. Their study is thus motivated by a desire to further improve the model in terms of demonstrating its generalisability and its application to empirical research.

Despite their support for the model, Filep and Greenacre suggest that initially definitions used in the Travel Career Pattern concept were at times ambiguous and, equally, experience was often measured by proxies such as the age of the respondent or similar measures (e.g. frequencies or numbers of trips) that fail to capture the qualitative nature of the experience. They thus conceive of experience as an accumulative change in an individual's self-perspective, and travel experiences are a subset of more general experiences. In other words, they adopt more consciously the psychological developmental aspects inherent in the work of the humanistic psychologists. They observed that the initial evidence from which Pearce and Lee (2005) built their model was a sequential qualitative-quantitative mixed methods approach. In their study, Filep and Greenacre (2007) used a simultaneous approach of two independent studies. The first consisted of asking 20 Australasian students (10 males and 10 females) to write pre-departure essays about an ideal day during a field study trip to Spain.

The second aspect of their study uses quantitative methods to verify the qualitative results with a sample of 172 useable responses from backpackers. As proxies of measurement of a Travel Career, they list the number of times a person has travelled, the number of different destinations travelled and the duration of the stays. They also used eight socio-demographic questions and 57 items relating to travel motives. The scales ran from -4 (unimportant) to $+4$ (important), and they conclude 'that the four most important factors are novelty ($t = 16.514$), stimulation (16.225), belonging/immersion (10.262), and self-actualisation (10.056) with a number of less important factors. Likewise, the least important factors include escape/social status (-21.602), romance/friendship (-10.895), isolation (-10.396), and nostalgia/comfort (-4.154)' (Filep & Greenacre, 2007: 34). These results are congruent with those derived from the first stage of their study. However, comparative data based on travel experience was rendered poor because only 11 respondents were classified as 'experienced', but they did conclude that age of the respondent was a poor proxy for experience.

One aspect of the Travel Career Pattern is that when it is linked to self-discovery and maturation processes, such links imply a travel *career* is correlated with age. However, psychological maturation, while often correlated with aging, is not necessarily associated with life stage, which is generally understood to stand alone as a concept and separate from age *per se*. Age is but a proxy for life stage. For example, the lives of those who have children in their late teens tend to differ from those who may wait into their thirties. If senses of well-being, emotional intelligence and empathy studies are proxies for self-actualisation, by the same token each proxy nonetheless exists as an independent variable.

Wu *et al.* (2019) sought to examine whether the Travel Career Pattern could exist independently of such proxy variables. Their data was obtained from a four-year study among 21,972 participants. The participants were visitors to Macau and had differential patterns of expenditure on various activities and also earned different levels of income being of varying ages and life stages. They find that 'Core travel motives (e.g., novelty, escape/relax and relationship) in the TCP [Travel Career Pattern] framework is affirmed to be common motivations across the different levels of the stages of TLC [Travel Life Cycle], whereas middle-layer motives (e.g., self-development) are valued by tourists who are at the early stage of TLC. Therefore, the strong link between TLC and Pearce's TCP [Travel Career Pattern] is validated' (Wu *et al.*, 2019: 275). They additionally note, 'For people between 35 and 44 years of age with middle-level incomes and with high travel experience, self-development such as acquiring experiences and knowledge is no longer as important as it used to be' (Wu *et al.*, 2019: 275).

While Wu *et al.* (2019) note several limitations with the study, it does appear that the concepts of the Travel Career Pattern in this study are not directly measured, but rather the concept is imposed on statistical factors derived from expenditure patterns to establish a conceptual component to what would otherwise be a purely descriptive analysis of sociodemographic factors and expenditure patterns. There is little consideration of the psychological aspects of self-developmental and actualisation or transcendence as understood by Maslow, and the authors suggest that differences among tourists are because of culture when explaining similarities and differences between their findings and those of Pearce and Lee (2005). Furthermore, the characteristics of the Travel Life Cycle are not fully discussed, other than to state it does not equate to the Family Life Cycle.

From the viewpoint of this discussion, while the study has interest but does possess limitations as discussed above, the point is that the application of the Travel Career Pattern to the data is, in itself, an indication of the importance being attributed to Pearce's work and its role within the visitor experience literature.

Conclusions

This chapter commenced with a description of Maslow's work on the premise that his concepts have been influential and representative of many streams of thinking in humanistic psychology. That mode of thinking has been influential in human resource management, counselling and marketing, and has given rise to several indices such as VALS (Values, Attitudes and Lifestyle) index that is used in marketing segmentation. The underlying arguments based on human striving for better knowledge of self have also been adopted in the tourism literature. That literature has particularly been impacted by two complementary facets, first, humanistic studies because holidays are periods of escape that permits self-examination, or self-discovery by engaging with new cultures, new places and new activities. The second factor has been what some have termed the post-modern turn because of the consumption of images of place. A potential third factor is the emergence of short-stay holidays wherein the tourist is often at best a temporary resident with varying degrees of attachment to place. Self-actualisation implies senses of authenticity but does a short stay permit experiences of sufficient depth that help create senses of authenticity? Authenticity is regarded as one of the features of self-actualisation or transcendence experiences in Maslow's thinking. A conundrum occurs whereby holidays offer opportunities for self-development but often in environments whereby local culture, architecture, foods and performance are increasingly divorced from the origins of place as local administrations chase tourist expenditure.

One of the key models that emanated from Maslow's work was the Travel Career Ladder that morphed into the concept of the Travel Career Pattern. But even within this model, there lie contradictions if one adopts the classic rationalisation for modelling. It is often argued that while models are abstractions from reality, or simplifications of the complexity of phenomena, they have value as generalisations that enable prediction of behaviours. But the evidence would seem to indicate that this is not the case with these models. While it is true that a basic premise of tourism is the need for safety and physiological requirements must be satisfied, the model permits much movement between the layers and associated needs associated with them. Holidays can offer exploration, relaxation, social company, new knowledge, reflection and escape, but to be a satisfactory holiday does not require that all these different needs must be meet. It can be suggested that each of these motives represents different stages on the Maslow hierarchy of needs, and consequently when one is on holiday, it is possible to move up or down the motivational hierarchy. This is not inconsistent with Maslow's original work, but the fluidity of psychological movement between these stages means one cannot use the model to make forecasts of predictions. Getz and Andersson (2020) examined 6000 athletes across five different sports when employing a derivative of the Travel Career Pattern, namely the 'event travel career trajectory'. Among their conclusions, they note 'career progression is a tendency, rather than a certainty, and as recognised in other career-related research there has to be recognition of constraints, regression at times, and eventually a termination' (Getz & Andersson, 2020: 172).

It should be noted that modelling rarely, if ever, produces prediction at the level of the individual, but does seek to identify general trends within groups of people or societies at large. In the Getz and Andersson study (2020), they note that increased involvement in sport does lead to greater activity, and to the seeking of greater challenge, but they are cautious in their conclusions. Challenge is defined within the context of sporting competition rather than self-actualisation and/or transcendence. In comparing the difference between the more active and the less active, the mean score for seeking a challenge is, for the former, 5.93 and for the latter, 5.81. The statistical difference between the two is significant at

$p=0.002$, but of more significance is that the score is high for both groups and thus highly skewed.

In a post-Covid world many commentators have spoken of a need to reset tourism to be more environmentally sensitive, more culturally aware and more self-reflective. Koh (2020) wrote of the opportunities to avoid over-tourism, Villacé-Molinero *et al.* (2021) argued that issues of risk and personal safety will dominate tourism for several years to come and Jiricka-Pürrer *et al.* (2020) wrote of the lessons learnt from the pandemic for urban-based tourism for coping with the threats of climate change. Others wrote of a need for a more radical social rethinking of tourism. Haywood (2020) wrote of taking not a road forward, but a road back, a road less travelled. Sheldon (2020) wrote of a need for tourism to transform consciousness, and of a need for greater human connectivity with each other and the natural world in a search for transcendence. Such hopes implicitly accept that human history is one of progression along the development of the human spirit, but as Haywood (2020) noted, political leadership is often lacking, and as 2022 evidenced with Putin's attack on Ukraine, for some, politics may lack a moral dimension.

In many ways a review of this literature does point to a core component of tourism that researchers continually find, and that is, tourism represents opportunities for escape and relaxation. But while emphasising this as a motivation for holiday taking, it does not specifically indicate the role adopted by tourists when on holiday. The next chapter begins to consider the roles that tourists play.

6 The Roles Tourists Play

The chapter includes:

(a) Examples of tourist typologies based on activities.
(b) Tourists change activities within and between holidays.
(c) The concepts of tourist roles that may be an alternative approach to creating typologies.
(d) The work done on roles to the dimensions of the Leisure Motivation Scale.
(e) The changes since the 1980s and the way in which technologies begin to introduce other ways of experiencing holiday places and activities.

Introduction

The last chapter explored the work of humanistic psychologists and argued that, when combined with themes derived from the work of post-modernist scholars, they pose significant insights for understanding tourist motivation, behaviour and experience. Such work certainly informed the work of many tourism scholars and also provided a theoretical basis for the theory of the Travel Career Pattern and the work of Philip Pearce and others. However, on reflection, the core motives ascribed to tourists still remain akin to those studied by Beard and Ragheb in the 1980s. In a series of articles, they suggested a four-dimensional motivational model for participation in leisure activities (Beard & Ragheb, 1983) that was based on their earlier paper on measuring leisure satisfaction (Beard & Ragheb, 1980).

These four dimensions are (a) the need for stimulus avoidance (i.e. the need to escape), (b) the need for social interaction, (c) the search for knowledge and intellectual stimulation and finally (d) to gain mastery and competency. This chapter will look at these dimensions in more detail. However, it will be shown that yet again this approach is derived from the work of Abraham Maslow. However, the questionnaire they devised will be shown to be reliable, measure consistent traits, and can be used to describe tourist types.

Tourist types, or segmentation by interest, or psychographics to use alternative terminology, have long existed in the tourism literature. Indeed, Pearce himself provided a long list of such types in his initial book *The Social Psychology of Tourist Behaviour* (Pearce, 1982) which he published after gaining his doctoral degree. Initially such typologies were based on descriptions of behaviour, but over time came to be informed by studies based on the VALS (Values, Attitudes and Lifestyles) index which will also be described later in the chapter.

It is suggested that these approaches are of interest because they again illustrate the role that humanistic psychology has played in the understanding of tourists and their experiences, especially when combined with statistical methods. They also, to some extent, confirm various nuances in the Travel Career Pattern. First, it has been noted that Pearce places at the core of tourism the need for relaxation and escape, thereby confirming the earlier conclusions of Graham Dann, and such motives are applicable to many tourist types. Second, at the end of the previous chapter, reference to the work of Getz and Andersson (2020) was made. One of their important findings among the athletes studied was the desire for social interaction among fellow competitors. Such social interaction provides a benchmark for one's own sporting prowess and provides a fellowship among like-minded people, while friendly competition is a source of challenge. The links between the Leisure Motivation Scale, Maslow's hierarchy of motives, and the Travel Career Pattern seem to revolve around various approaches that all point to similar motives being identified, but differential importance is being attributed to the motives by individuals.

Many of the differences seem to be dependent upon the context within which the tourist is found. Thus, the individual who competes in a sport enacts one given set of roles but when attending a conference endorses the role of attendee and/or speaker. As individuals, we play several different roles, partly shaped through life stage and partly through context. Consequently, a significant part of this chapter is based upon the different roles that tourists play and as described by Andrew Yiannakis and Heather Gibson. These roles also emphasise another aspect of current thought, and this is the tourist as a co-creator in their own experiences.

Describing Tourist Types

Among the earliest categorisations of tourists were descriptions based on activities. This approach provided an array of descriptions, and the classifications of tourist types provided below are drawn from Pearce's early work; several other commentators have adopted similar descriptions. While simplistic, it was nonetheless one of the first approaches to combat what Pearce noted as 'the sin of homogenisation [that] lurks within the field of tourist behaviour research' (Pearce, 2005a: 18). He then comments that each tourist is different, for each is an individual possessing their own evaluations of each of their own experiences.

Consequently, the identification of tourists by activities provides information on what tourists enjoy, and when aggregated, how many in number they are. The typologies also played a significant early role in understanding why tourists engage in any given activity, and the nomenclature remains common today. Hence academic papers exist on the 'ecotourist', 'the hedonist', the 'explorer' and many other variants. Pearce (1982) provided a full list, and the following text is simply an example of such classifications. They include (in alphabetical order):

The Action Seeker: Generally younger in age groups, the youth of the northern European cities were attracted to the discos, clubs and venues of the Spanish coastline and Balearic Islands, and particularly Ibiza. Known for being noisy, they frequented the clubs, dancing the night away to spend most of the daylight hours recovering for the next party session. A sub-set of this group was the 18 to 30 holidaymaker who frequented Mediterranean resorts where hosts of the same age conspired to create games requiring alcohol consumption and wet t-shirt competitions and were seemingly delighted in causing consternation among their older hosts by vomiting in the streets, thus bringing about the formation of tourist police to look after them as they recovered sobriety in Mediterranean jails. While a feature of the outbound British holiday scene throughout the 1980s and 1990s, and while similar holiday patterns remain as a heritage of earlier times, these activities appeared to be a little less prevalent by the 2020s, or at least, attracting less academic interest.

The Archaeologist: Interested in history and the artifacts of the past, these tourists plan their holidays around visiting the remains of primarily ancient civilisations. Being serious minded, they engage in background reading, will employ guides and will be critical of those thought to be ill-prepared.

The Drifter: Cohen (1972, 1973, 2003) described the drifters as people possessing an interest in collecting experiences of places off the beaten track and the cultures and lifestyles found there. Associated in the 1960s with hippies and backpackers, they would sustain their stays by taking generally manual labour and low-skill jobs on a transitory basis. In his 1973 paper, he describes in some detail the drifter and notes they 'have no instrumental purpose in mind, and not even a concrete goal when embarking on a trip' (Cohen, 1973: 91). However, as a distinct market segment the industry increasingly began to provide services for the backpackers, who Cohen (1973) sees as the inheritors of the drifter and 'gentlemen-adventurers' and others not generally constrained by tight time budgets. Backpackers' hostels (based partly in the concept of Youth Hostels) provided more secure accommodation, specific buses provided transport between backpacker lodges and, in close proximity to the hostels, a small service industry would grow, comprising launderettes, cafes and agencies offering car hire, jobs and sales via noticeboards that became more formal in visitor service centres. Contiki provides many organised or semi-organised backpacker holidays today on a global scale, while other companies such as Kiwi Experiences do likewise in Australasia. Today, many such holidays are associated with sustainable actions seeking to benefit previously marginal areas. Cohen (2003) and Richards and Wilson (2004) provided one of the earlier analyses of the changing trends in this market segment.

The Ecotourists: These tourists are generally defined as those wishing to holiday in ways that create little negative impact upon the planet and have been the subject of many studies (Stronza *et al.*, 2019; Wheeller, 1993, 2007). Several of these studies have at various times regarded ecotourism as a fast-growing segment (Li *et al.*, 2021) but in our view many studies fail to compare the attractiveness of the sustainable holiday when compared to other forms of holidaying. This point is discussed in more detail later. Wheeller (1993), rather famously, raised issues about their motives, asking whether they were in fact 'ego-tourists'. His terminology has been adopted by other commentators such as Munt (1994), noting its use in the *Observer*, a broadsheet newspaper published in the United Kingdom. The issue of hypocrisy still haunts the pages of both commentators and academics as evidenced by Mkono (2020). Nonetheless, there are those who identify changing trends in tourist behaviour and the growth of 'flight shame' (Becken *et al.*, 2021), although Higham and Cohen (2011) note that this may translate into a want to take a holiday where the tourist wishes to ensure that the benefits of the experience outweigh environmental loss. The less charitable might suggest that this may be a way of conducting a post-trip rationalisation or justification for the flight. Nonetheless, the impact of fast speed trains for distances of about 300 km has eroded several short-haul flights, and forthcoming electric planes may well be more available from about 2030–2035 for longer trips. A future greater use of biofuels from algae rather than prime food stuffs may be more feasible for long-haul flights by mid-century (Bradley, 2022), thereby potentially easing concerns of flight shame, but problems caused by growing numbers of tourists will still remain, albeit possibly eased by applications of smart tourism artificial intelligence (AI) and machine learning techniques. It should also be noted that several airlines and aircraft manufacturers are increasingly confident that more sustainable aircraft will be feasible by the mid-2030s, including hydrogen- and battery-powered planes for short-haul flights.

The Escapist: These holidaymakers wish to simply get away from the hustle and bustle of daily life, wanting to enjoy a more peaceful environment for purposes of relaxation. Often, they tend to stay in the same location for a period of time in a natural landscape, or alternatively may be found hiking along footpaths. They may also seek more reflective holidays to be akin to 'the seekers'.

The Explorers: Akin to the Thrill Seekers, it is not so much the adrenalin high experience that they seek, but a wanderlust that is satisfied by exploring infrequently visited terrain. They range from those buying vacations from specialist companies who support small groups to those who develop their own routes without recourse to trained guides. They are strongly motivated by a need to escape urban zones and to engage with generally untamed natural settings.

The Independent Mass Tourist: This group was identified by Cohen (1972) as a subsequent development of the Organised Mass Tourist in that they use the services of the tourist supply chain, tend to visit the same sites, but upon arrival at a destination country will tend to create their own itineraries and make their own way by car or public transport. They initially emerged from the European package holidays when people would take a cheap flight and even if using the designated hotel, would hire a car. Subsequently the charter airlines started selling flights only, picking their way through the then existing IATA regulations by providing a cheap voucher for a hotel that was rarely used by their passengers. Today, with the use of the internet, the independent mass tourist remains an important market segment searching for flights, accommodation and activities while using online travel agencies (OTAs) and social media, and not uncommonly micro-blogging their experiences.

The Jetsetters: These tourists seek to stay at the best hotels in elite world resorts supported by very high levels of service that will include helicopter transport, exclusive dining and entrée only to the best clubs and the high stakes rooms of the casinos if desired. Specialised services are provided. For example, the Burj Al Arab hotel in Dubai will make arrangements to take its guests from the airport to the hotel by helicopter or Rolls Royce to be taken care of by butlers in its suites.

The Organised Mass Tourist: Notably identified by Cohen (1972), the organised mass tourist uses the well-organised distribution chain of the tourism industry and particularly that of the packaged holiday industry. The flights, hotels and often many of the activities are purchased as an inclusive all, and the mass-organised tourist will visit the major iconic sites, partake in an organised hotel structure that will include breakfast and the evening meal (and often the lunch), take lots of photographs and buy several souvenirs but primarily stays within the confines of a tourist resort. However, over time the resorts have developed to provide much more than swimming pools beside beaches. For example, the Fosun Group from China, who took over Club Med and Thomas Cook from the original European companies, will be offering theme park style activities at its new resort in Sanya, Hainan Island, while theme park operators such as Disney have long incorporated hotels into or in proximity of their parks.

The Seekers: This group of holidaymakers seek reflection about their selves and their current life situation. While not necessarily religious, they are akin to those who would attend monasteries for retreats and are interested in the spiritual and senses of physical and psychological well-being. This group is quite diverse (as are the other groups) but have common interests in seeking guidance through reflective or meditative practices. At one extreme, one can refer to personal health issues, physical wellness and the use of spas and massage, while at the other it is primarily a search for spiritual well-being that involves periods of prayer, instruction and meditation.

The Sports Lover: Many people when younger develop sporting pursuits that become sources of serious leisure that provide enjoyment well into their later years. Consequently, many companies provide holidays associated with water sports, cycling and other sports. These holidays provide instruction to improve skills and activities shared with others having similar interests.

The Sun Lover: Motivated often by a desire to escape colder climates or to have an almost guaranteed holiday of warm summer sunshine, the sun lover is the epitome of the sun, sand and sea tourist who often visits the Mediterranean beaches during the European summer. Historically they were of importance, and have retained this, but it was they that helped the nascent tourist market to boom in the 1960s to 1980s with the advent of the package holiday market that then dominated the European marketplace. They motivated the construction of hotel chains, responded to the siren call of the package holiday companies such as Horizon, Clarksons and others, and inspired the model of low-cost, high-volume air traffic.

The Thrill Seeker: This tourist wants to experience adventure and will either purchase a selection of adventure activities such as bungy jumping, hang-gliding, canyoning or caving while independently travelling, or will sign up with guided tours that include long hiking, cycling or kayak/canoeing trips of more than a few days' duration. They are the mountain climbers, the kayakers and at the extreme, the participants of high-risk sports who solo climb precipitous cliffs or explore underground caverns.

There are many other classifications that have been used in the literature, and today commentators write of the emergence of the 'silvers' or 'senior market' (Kyriakou & Belias, 2017), sex tourists (Carr & Berdychevsky, 2022), gay tourists (Hughes & Deutsch, 2010), medical tourism (Connell, 2013) and volunteer tourism (Mensah *et al.*, 2021) among other forms. These are therefore descriptions of tourists based on observable activities and have led to a range of studies that enquire into their motives and the causes of their satisfaction. Unfortunately, too many such studies are overly specific and fail to consider wider interests. The authors have seen examples of studies of tourists which express interest in the cultures of minority peoples. However, by restricting the questions to that form of tourism without reference to competing forms of tourism, researchers

have often overstated the importance of that form of interest. It is suspected that claims about other forms of tourism suffer from the same
biases. McKercher and du Cros (2003) concluded that claims that visitors
to Hong Kong were strongly motivated by Hong Kong's history and cultural heritage were overstated by an overreliance on attendance data that
failed to question motives for the visit. Thus, in our experience, to ask
whether tourists are interested in Indigenous Culture without also asking
about interest in theme parks, theatre, cuisine, attending events and so
on, and even possibly asking them to undertake ranking exercises, will
almost inevitably overestimate the visitor's interest in minority peoples.
Yang *et al.* (2013) describe how Han tourists to the Kanas region of
China view the local minority people through a panoptic vision wherein
the motive is to perceive difference rather than understanding the cultural
norms of those people and the impacts of tourism. Similarly, McKercher
and du Cros (2003) concluded that of visitors recorded as visiting cultural
and heritage sites in Hong Kong, only 13.4% of the visitors could be
defined as 'purposeful' visitors – that is, they were specifically interested
in the history and cultural significance of the site.

Pearce (2005) notes the importance of using sociodemographic
variables as a means of distinguishing between tourists. These are the
variables of age, gender, income, level of education and potentially class.
However self-evident these criteria are, the reality is more complex
because each of the variables are not totally independent when determining their role as causes of action or as a basis of evaluating experiences.
The older white male in many western societies would be earning more
than the young female school leaver. On the other hand, the university-
qualified younger female may be earning more than the unskilled male
labourer who is a decade older than her. These variables may also reflect
class membership, but class is a difficult concept to operationalise in
empirical studies. Cohen *et al.* (2017) trace changes in the United States
using General Social Data from 1972 to 2010 and identify several features
classically associated with class including education, income, race and
occupation to assess how these influence subjective social class. They
note the growing influence of income and the diminishing role of education, and the role of race. Many factors explaining these changes can be
postulated. The spread of university education among younger people
means the possession of undergraduate degrees is no longer an automatic
progression to higher income occupations. Many occupations requiring
higher education such as teaching, several health-related posts and social
work do not generally attract many people through an expectation of
high pay, although the compensation prior to the 2020s was a better
long-term opportunity for job stability. Another factor is the growing
importance of lifestyle among many younger people for whom quality
of life is important within a more fluid society, especially if they remain
single and childless (Dalessandro, 2019). Remaining single and childless

also provides more financial rewards. Another factor is the changing nature of what were previously regarded as manual labour or blue-collar occupations. While several may be vulnerable to the increasing use of robotics and information technology, the same factors create an upskilling of many such jobs.

In 2013, Frey and Osborne analysed 702 different occupations using US data to conclude that potentially 47% of occupations were vulnerable to advances in AI, computerisation and robotics. This was a significant paper and created many further studies including an Organisation for Economic Co-operation and Development paper (Nedelkoska & Quintini, 2018) that suggested that direct job loss would be 14% with a further 32% being subject to change. Osborne and Frey (2017, 2018) subsequently analysed the differences in such calculations but generally one might share the conclusions reached by King *et al.* (2017) that adjustments will need to be made for social benefit payments, that the education curriculum will require new emphases on information technology and computerisation, and that change is inevitable. Yet, already changes are taking place as the changing demographics of an aging population are generating a scarcity of employees in several countries possessing such skills, with a consequent increase in wages among many trade occupations from car mechanics and construction workers to electricians. These factors also lead to a growing fuzziness of traditional class distinctions and a growing concern about social inequality in incomes and wealth (Moll *et al.*, 2021; Rashbrooke, 2021).

Such broader considerations identify the changing pattern of the work and social world within which the tourism of the future will exist. But if the social world changes, it does not necessarily change the underlying motivations for holiday taking and holidaymaking. Rather, it is suggested it changes the ways in which tourists may behave and the expectations that they may possess. From this perspective, there is a need to return to the basics, namely, what motivates tourists, and how might these shape patterns of behaviour that yield tourist behaviours. The next section returns to basic motives using the framework suggested by Beard and Ragheb and shows how these factors can be used to create clusters of tourist behaviours, but then pivots the earlier tourist types into tourist roles.

The Beard and Ragheb Leisure Motivation Scale

The Leisure Motivation Scale had been preceded by the Leisure Satisfaction Scale (Beard & Ragheb, 1980) in which Leisure Satisfaction had been found to be determined by six factors, namely psychological benefits, educational gains, social interaction, relaxation, physiological gains in health and finally the aesthetic. There were, however, some problems with the scale and the authors noted that the 'assumptions of orthogonality among the six subscales … were untenable' (Beard & Ragheb, 1980: 29). In addition, one might observe that satisfaction is highly dependent upon context and hence the scale was unlikely to be stable across different contexts and time. Motivations on the other hand would tend to be more stable for longer periods of time, although arguably subject to some degree of change as individual respondents gained more experience and matured through their life cycle.

Regarding motivation, Beard and Ragheb (1983) justified their research by reference to a previous report referring, in turn, to an American Academy of Science (National Academy, 1969) report and a US News & World article (1981) that even in 1980 the expenditure on recreation in the United States alone was worth US$244 billion. Economic importance alone justified research into leisure motivation. They commenced their study by identifying more than 150 possible items – each being derived from the prior literature. These were then assessed by 30 faculty and students of leisure – which assessment reduced the number of items to 106. A pilot study with 65 respondents created a possible seven factors and a further round of analysis was conducted with 174 respondents. The final stage included 48 items, 12 items for each of the four factors thought important, and the questionnaire was administered to a sample of 1205 individuals of differing ages and incomes. Finally, a shortened scale resulted as described below that achieved high reliability scores while meeting criteria of parsimony, usefulness and clarity of communication.

Beard and Ragheb (1980, 1983) suggest there are four primary motivations for participating in leisure. These are the need for stimulus avoidance, a search for intellectual stimulation or knowledge, a wish to improve competence or mastery and the need for social contact. Stimulus avoidance 'assesses the drive to escape and get away from overstimulating life situations. It is the need for some individuals to avoid social contacts, to seek solitude and calm conditions; and for others it is to seek to rest and to unwind themselves' (Ragheb & Beard, 1983: 225). In short, this is a confirmation of past and subsequent research that places the need to escape daily situations at the core of recreation, leisure and tourism. Yet it can be observed that many seek to unwind and indeed be themselves in the company of others and as previous text relating to the introversion-extraversion scale of the Eysenck Personality Scale has shown, people's predisposition to solitude can vary significantly. It is thus tempting to see this motivation as possessing the features of a continuum between high and low needs for solitude dependent upon personality predisposition. Nonetheless, one can also recognise the importance of context. It is possible that even the most extravert of people might at times wish for solitude under more extreme circumstances such as the death of a long-loved pet or indeed much-loved family members. Under these circumstances, they may need to compose themselves before turning to their friends and family. Fortunately, such circumstances are rare when on holiday, but nonetheless a continuum on the introversion-extraversion scale may exist.

The second factor is the search for knowledge or intellectual stimulation. Ragheb and Beard describe this as basically any mental activities such as exploring, learning, thinking and acts of imagination. This is a broad-brushed definition that could again be perceived as a continuum ranging from writing a poem, learning a new piece of statistical software to engaging in fantasy computer game playing when creating a strategy. The primary element of this motive is the intellectual aspect, and, in that respect, it overlaps but can be differentiated from the wish to improve competence or mastery. Derived primarily from a literature in recreation including sporting activities, Ragheb and Beard emphasise that this motive is primarily related to physical activities. Many holidays are particularly built around adventure and sporting activities such as caving, sailing, surfing, windsurfing, kitesurfing, kayaking and the like, and from personal experience as a former windsurfing instructor it was observed that holidaymakers often sought a period of skill improvement from intense periods of activity, aided by an instructor. However, it was also very noticeable that another motive was the ability to spend time with like-minded people with whom they could share experiences, tell their stories and share time. This need for social contact is also cited by Ragheb and Beard (1980, 1983).

While presented as four factors explaining 'motivation' for participating in recreation, and by extension in tourism (Ryan & Glendon, 1998), there are caveats around the use of the scale. Inasmuch as the scale is premised on personality traits, one key measure of the validity of the scale is the degree to which it is consistent over time as distinct from measures of reliability such as the Cronbach alpha metrics. A number of studies have confirmed the reliability of the scales in that the use of exploratory factor analysis by various researchers with similar or the same items has been able to achieve acceptable alpha coefficients. These studies include those of Tinsley and Tinsley (1987), Ryan and Glendon (1998), Mohsin and Ryan (2007), while Isaacs *et al.* (2021) used the scale in assessing motives for engagement in virtual reality games. In addition, other studies have sought to ensure the stability of the scale over time. One study of importance from this perspective is that of Loundsbury and Hoopes (1988) who found the measure retained stability over an interim period of five years. Loundsbury was also one of the earliest researchers who applied the concept to tourism (Loundsbury & Franz, 1990; Loundsbury & Polik, 1992).

While the scale possesses 'good provenance' on some occasions, the use of exploratory factor analysis has noted an overlap between factors. This is particularly so (in the experience of the first author) when using an abbreviated scale. Often it was found the social contact scale possesses two components, namely the desire for company, but also a desire for

Table 6.1 Leisure motivation factors as continua

Competency-mastery	Stimulus avoidance	Intellectual	Social
High	Low	Medium	High
Low	Low	High	Medium
Low	High	Medium	Low

individual prestige. If one adopts the view that each of the four factors can be viewed as a continuum between high and low scores, then it is possible to create the table shown in Table 6.1.

This approach highlights the use of the Leisure Motivation Scale with Cluster Analysis. This technique, rather than clustering individual items into factors based on correlations between those items, instead seeks to segment individual respondents into clusters based on the commonality of their response patterns. This was done several years ago with a study of hikers in New Zealand, where questions were based on the concept of push and pull, with the push questions being drawn in part from the Leisure Motivation Scale (Lawson *et al.*, 1997). The results are shown as Table 6.2 below.

Table 6.2 Illustrative segmentation of tourists – motives and profiles

Active Social Relaxers (ASR)	Less likely to be short stop visitors (< 1 hour) More likely to go with friends Mostly consisting of age groups of between 21 and 40 years of age Emphasis information about safety, parking, toilets and information centres Most satisfied with hiking time and hiking experience
Enthusiastic Visitors (EV)	Most likely to visit in the afternoons Likely to stay overnight Highest percentage of post graduate qualifications and females More likely to be managerial and professional Highly emphasise signage, campsites, trails and hiking time Highly satisfied with safety, trails and parking
Nature Isolates (NI)	Likely to go alone Tend to be between 41 and 60 years of age Care about visitor number control
Relaxers (R)	Likely to be repeat visitors Likely to come with workmates and/or family Highest number of university qualification Emphasis adequate interpretation information Most satisfied with native plants
Reluctant Visitors (RV)	Likely to be first time and short stay visitors More likely to come in the morning with a partner More likely to be aged under 20 years and over 60 years More likely to be students, unemployed or retired Highest percentage of those earning more than NZ$100,000 Emphasise picnic and emergency information Most satisfied with picnic areas

The Roles That Tourists Assume

At the commencement of this chapter, reference was made to a series of tourist 'types' and significant effort was made in the past to attempt to find evidence for the existence of these types of tourists and their characteristics. Various studies examined the sociodemographic profiles of eco-tourists. For example, Wright (1996) provided a detailed analysis of North American self-defined experienced eco-tourists, noting that they were drawn from across all age groups, but found significant differences between those she termed 'generalists' and those termed the 'experienced eco-tourist' with the latter tending to spend more and have a longer holiday, and being more willing to travel outside the main summer months. Such types of studies continue to be undertaken, especially if a given market segment is thought to be growing in number, importance or wealth. For example, Otoo *et al.* (2020) examined the growing seniors' market and their motivations for undertaking international travel. They identified eight 'domains' with a 38-item questionnaire and a usable sample of 532 respondents over the age of 55 years. These domains were seeking knowledge/learning, experiencing culture/nature, seeking self-esteem, seeking a once in a lifetime experience, achieving a sense of socialisation, escape or nostalgia and seeking time with the family. A subsequent cluster analysis found evidence for five clusters or psychographic profiles of (a) senior tourists, including those preferring upscale/luxury accommodation, (b) those desiring natural/cultural settings but not interested in nostalgia, (c) the less motivated, who tended to be male but who could be tempted by budget accommodation and (d) travel with the family, and another group (e) interested in urban setting and history.

An alternative approach that has been tried by the present authors has been to talk to operators of attractions and activities and often one finds that such operators will comment that all sorts of people are attracted to their businesses. Several adventure sports operators have found that if they are able to make some provision, several people with physical disabilities can be attracted – a fact again confirmed by empirical evidence (Devile & Moura, 2015). Indeed, it is suggested that this form of tourism is again important in creating self-esteem by providing means by which those with physical disabilities are able to achieve mastery in various sports, as is amply demonstrated in the summer and winter Paralympic Games every four years.

However, a moment's reflection about one's very own holidays would reveal that people often visit many different forms of attractions. Many of us, when travelling overseas, have visited a church, an animal sanctuary, a theme park – even perhaps all within the same holiday. But does that automatically make us a pilgrim, an eco-tourist or an escapist holidaymaker or any one of the above categories? Gibson and Yiannakis (1992) suggested that each of these various types of holidaymaking are actually roles, which people adopt as they like and equally well discard as other motives come to the fore. This notion is also totally congruent with the notion of co-consumption or the 'prosumer', that is, the holiday experience is an outcome of interaction whereby the tourist cooperates to a greater or lesser degree with the provider of an attraction or service in the creation of their own experiences. Hence, when entering a restaurant, the client may be approached by a wait person who introduces him or herself in a friendly manner and may ask if the customer wishes to know about 'today's special'. The client may respond in one of several ways. If the customer is wanting a relaxing meal and has time to spend, they might well respond in a friendly manner and commence a conversation that enhances the meal experience through friendly banter. On the other hand, if the meal-goer is simply wanting something to eat, is not too bothered about anything other than having an efficient service of a good meal delivered fairly quickly and without frills, their response may be to quickly select something from the menu. That too can create a satisfactory outcome. In short, it is the reaction of the guest themselves that co-creates the nature of the occasion. It also depends on the skill of the service provider to be able to respond correctly to the signs sent by the client in providing a satisfactory outcome. In this manner, it can be stated the satisfaction is the result of a co-production of performance between customer and server, with each responding in ways consistent with their respective roles (Pine & Gilmore, 1999).

In their study of tourist roles, Yiannakis and Gibson (1992) described how they first set about identifying tourist roles by drawing upon prior work undertaken by Philip Pearce (1982), commenting 'we found that Pearce's jetsetter, hippie (or drifter), and holidaymaker are simply subcategories of the broader tourist construct. Others, such as the anthropologist, the archaeologist, and journalist in Pearce's typology, are occupationally based and are clearly not touristic in nature' (Yiannakis & Gibson, 1992: 290). Figure 6.1 directly replicates their original diagram that illustrates the findings from their own analysis of data drawn from 521 respondents. This comprises three underlying dimensions, namely an x-axis of a continuum between the search for a familiar or unfamiliar destination, a y-axis consisting of the dimension between the stimulation and tranquillity and a z-axis of a highly structured or unstructured environment. It thus becomes possible to locate the tourist types on this framework. For example, the 'escapist' is located as being motivated by tranquil environments that are low in structure with which they tend to be familiar. On the other hand, the 'drifter' is drawn to 'novelty in relatively strange environments under conditions of minimal structure' (Yiannakis & Gibson, 1992: 294).

In their paper, Yiannakis and Gibson refer to the work of Beard and Ragheb (1983) with specific reference to the 'escapists' as being those 'who live hectic lifestyles, have stressful jobs, and generally experience

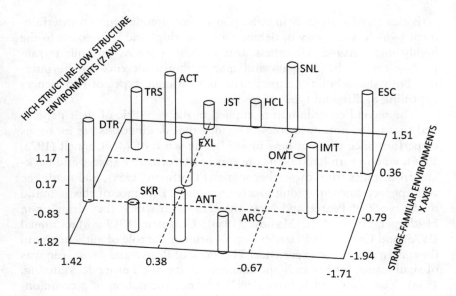

CODES: SNL = SUN LOVER, ACT = ACTION SEEKER, ANT = ANTHROPOLOGIST,

ARC = ARCHAEOLOGIST, OMT = ORGANISED MASS TOURIST,

TRS = THRILL SEEKER, EXL = EXPLORER, JST = JETSETTER,

SKR = SEEKER, IMT = INDEPENDENT MASS TOURIST,

HCT = HIGH CLASS TOURIST, DTR = DRIFTER, ESC = ESCAPIST

Figure 6.1 Motivational dimensions and tourist types. Source: Yiannakis and Gibson (1992)

stimulus overload in their life. For them, vacations serve as a form of escape from the stresses, pressures, and demands of everyday life' (Yiannakis & Gibson, 1992: 296). It is not overly difficult to fit the dimensions into the four dimensions identified by Beard and Ragheb and the theories of motivation previously discussed. The notions of escape, relaxation, social contact and a search for knowledge are writ large across many of the theories, but the work of Yiannakis and Gibson is important for at least two reasons. Firstly, they reinforce the role of both the environment of the holiday in terms of a search for an environment that is familiar or not and equally the organisational aspects of holiday packaging as to whether it is highly structured or not. The highly structured destination may be a resort complex that is designed to provide options of relaxing activities ranging from swimming pools, accommodation and entertainment (which is one way of defining a cruise ship) and is opposite to the highly unstructured wilderness area of hiking across unspoilt terrain guiding oneself by compass and map without reference to the internet. Both shape holiday experiences, but different types of experiences appealing to different types of tourists.

The second contribution is implied in the very title of their paper – and that is the notion of roles. The idea that destinations are locations of performance was not new in 1992. The work of MacCannell (1973, 1976), who in turn had taken concepts of performative spaces and back- and frontstages from the earlier work of Goffman (1959), had made the concept well known among tourism scholars. Evidence of this is found in the work of Pearce and Moscardo (1986) in which they draw upon Heidegger (1927/1962), Maslow (1954), Goffman (1959), MacCannell (1973) and Cohen (1979) to develop theories of the role of authenticity in the tourist search for experience. The work of Pearce and Moscardo was of significance for not only the ensuing debate (see Turner & Manning, 1988). Yiannakis and Gibson (1992) advance the notion in a common-sense recognition that tourists are not simply confined to one 'type' but undertake different types of holidays to meet different needs, and indeed may switch between 'types' to adopt different 'roles' within one holiday period.

This contribution is arguably within a pattern that was shaping much of social science research and its evolution. For example, when reviewing literature pertaining to the developing concept of place attachment, Williams and Miller (2020) identified seven stages dating from the 1960s. They labelled these as the modernist (in the 1960s), the humanist (the 1970s), the experiential (the 1980s), the constructionist (the 1990s), the performative (the 2000s), the systemic (2010s) and currently the nascent (2020s). As suggested in the final chapter, this sequence can be noted in much of the tourism research literature, and in one sense the work of Yiannakis and Gibson (1992) is indicative of an early transition from the constructionist period to the performative in its mix of identifying types and roles based on statistical analysis to the realisation of theory based on performances of behaviour.

The concept of roles was to be a recurring theme in the work of Yiannakis and Gibson for some time. Indeed, it had begun prior to the publication of their 1992 paper. In 1988, Yiannakis and Gibson gave a paper at that year's annual conference of the Leisure Studies Association in Brighton, UK, when they referred to a life-stage model, and in 1989 Gibson completed her master's degree with her dissertation entitled 'Tourist Roles: Stability and Change Over the Life Cycle'. In 1998, Gibson, Attle, and Yiannakis published their paper on lifespans and sorting segmentations. This line of thinking was pursued into the wider tourism terrain in 2002 with a paper published again in the *Annals of Tourism Research*.

Recognising the work done relating to tourist and leisure careers as people age, and including the concept of the travel career ladder of Pearce and the family life stages and holidaying (e.g. Bojanic, 1992), Gibson and Yiannakis (2002) related the choice of tourist roles to aspects of past experiences, age and personal preferences. They initially based their work on the studies of life stages proposed by Levinson (1996) and Levinson *et al.* (1978).

These periods of life stage were defined as early adult transition (17–22 years), entering the adult world (22–28 years), the age of transition (28–33 years), settling down and becoming one's own person (33–40 years), the mid-life transition (40–45 years), entering middle adulthood (45–50 years), the 50-year-old transition (50–55 years), the culmination of middle adulthood (55–60 years), the transition for late adulthood (65 years plus) and finally late-late adulthood commencing at approximately 80 years of age. Each stage is strongly subjected to external influences derived from an individual's sociocultural world, participation in the external world and concepts of self. The stages outlined above form primarily four periods of pre-adulthood and adolescence, early, mid- and late adulthood – each period being approximately 25 years in length, and each with its own periods of transition.

As noted above, Yiannakis and Gibson identified a number of preferred tourist roles (Gibson & Yiannakis, 2002: 365) and applied their scale to a sample of 1277 respondents of different life stages and gender to identify differing degrees of life satisfaction at their current life stage. These satisfaction ratings were then divided into two categories, namely high (Satisfaction >8) and low (Satisfaction <8) on an effective 10-point scale. Finally, for each life stage the scores for given tourist roles were subjected to a time series test in a tri-variant analysis of preferred role, life stage and life-stage satisfaction score. From this they were able to identify the stability of the preferred tourist roles. These were then classified as a declining interest in a given role, a growing interest and a varying level of interest. The driving motives for such an interest were found to be satisfied needs for home and family with a negative correlation for a need for control and health.

The roles shown as being more attractive over the life stages included the Anthropologist, the Archaeologist, the High-Class Tourist, the Organised Mass Tourist and the Educational Tourist. The intuitive explanations for such results can be based on patterns of increased income as job careers become more established, a growing interest in aspects related to the history of society and cultures, and possibly an ability to take more than one holiday as incomes increased. That might possibly explain the desire for the organised mass holiday as being one selected for relaxation purposes at reasonable prices. Females are reported to show an earlier interest in the Anthropologist role. Indeed, it emerges in the first stages of early adulthood, but by the age of about

30 years the two genders converge at over 40% expressing a preference for such a holiday activity. Over time the preference for this role continues to generally increase to as much as 70% expressing interest by an approximate age of the early 50s, albeit it tends to drop a little in the late adult transition age. For males, this role was positively correlated with a need for status and being connected with one's roots, while for females the role was associated with needs of self-actualisation, personal growth, safety and security.

The sample yielded varying results for preference for the roles of the Seeker, the Jetsetter and the Escapists, but Yiannakis and Gibson concentrate primarily on the Independent Mass Tourist for reasons of data sufficiency. Females in the early adult transition period (17–22 years) show significantly more interest in this role than their male counterparts (47% vs 38.2%); from the ages of 23 to 27 years this pattern is particularly reversed in that 62.5% of the male sample prefer this role as against 45.3% of females. There is then a slow decline in the following years for males to the mid-50% level, but after the age of 50 or so years, the expressed preference for the role significantly increases.

Gibson and Yiannakis (2002) also discuss the role of the holidays through personal life courses, noting the attraction of the more carefree-style holidays among the young and the role of gender in the attraction of more people-oriented styles of holidaying being more attractive to females. They additionally noted the emergence of more knowledge-based activities at the age of approximately 30 years when many are transitioning to more serious roles at that stage of life, while the growing attraction of mass tourism seems to coincide with the age when parenthood becomes a reality for many.

The Impact of Social and Technological Change on Holidaying Roles

In looking at several of the findings, one notes that possible explanations are dependent on conventional age and gender patterns, and one can ask if some two decades later the same results remain true. Equally, the findings arose from a North American context, and since then other countries with different intergenerational experiences have come to the fore. Among such countries, China is at the fore and yet possesses intergenerational life patterns that are more determined by the shifts in economic-political changes than is the case in several western nations. The period of opening from 1979 marked a significant change from the earlier Maoist period, thereby marking significantly different life experiences between grandparents of many of the post-millennium generation who have experienced periods of an emergent affluent consumerist urban society. This latter generation's life experience differs radically from those who experienced the turmoil of the Great Leap Forward and the Cultural Revolution. Equally, for those born since about 2012, their youth is being marked by pandemic and lockdowns, and a slowdown in economic growth, and in 2022, declines in house prices and employment. How might that influence the life pattern of their teenage years? Another significant difference between the 2020s and the earlier period of the turn of the millennium is people's experiences of information technology and its influence upon the ways people create their holidays. One could suggest that in 2000, the laptop served a function that is today served by smartphones, and needless to say the laptops of 2000 were heavier, bulkier and generally not so fast as those of 2022. The ease with which people can access information combined with an increased tendency towards individualism and generally a greater tolerance of diverse life-styles would, it is suggested, have an impact on the way tourists behave.

In 1980, when Dick Butler conceived his concept of the tourist area life cycle, the first stage of 'exploration' would generally have been understood as a period of physical exploration requiring the presence of the tourist in the actual destination. Today, exploring a destination can be taken as meaning examining the images and text of the destination via OTA sites, possibly the use of online encyclopaedias and the use of Google Review or a similar webpage. The second stage of 'involvement' would have meant a scenario experienced by one of the authors – namely, when taking a ferry from Piraeus to one of the Greek islands, one's first contact with a potential host was achieved by scanning the cardboard signs and the person holding the sign when arriving at the point of embarkation. Today that is achieved by online communications when receiving a text message containing a digital keylock code, or alternatively having but an indirect contact when picking up a key from an intermediary. The subsequent stages of development and consolidation will, in all probability, be managed through algorithms communicating through the internet of things to avoid issues of saturation and decline when doors are opening by biometric scanning (Yeoman *et al.*, 2022).

Given these trends, Urquhart not surprisingly notes that 'The rapid development of technology has revolutionised the tourism experience' (Urquhart, 2019: 120). Similar to observations made in this text, Urquhart notes how technology has changed access to information, enhancement of attractions and the role of new virtual/augmented technologies that add layers to visitor experiences. However, he notes a paradox in much of the work published thus far that the impacts on future tourist behaviours have been far from systematic and holistic in nature. Echoing some of the previous work associated with OTAs and the Technology Adoption Model (TAM), he notes that the full potential of new technologies in mediating tourism experiences will not be fulfilled if people do not know how to fully use the technology, or indeed may distrust it. He therefore envisages three possible reactions. The first is mass acceptance and customisation of experiences for the users of the new technologies.

A second is 'rewinding the clock' which is a seeking for simpler experiences that are mediated purely by people. This is akin to the work undertaken by Pearce and his co-authors on the attractions of internet-free holidays (Li *et al.*, 2018; Oktadiana & Pearce, 2020) – which work has suggested that such holidays are not simply a means to escape the stress created by continuous communication but are also means of self-discovery and restoring senses of well-being. The third of the scenarios is 'experiential convergence', which arguably is evident today not only in theme parks but also in museums and places of cultural and historic importance that are beginning to enhance the visitor experience by providing simulations of past events through the use of 3D headsets and indeed increasingly the use of holograms. Hence holograms have been used at the Dubai Museum, the Abraham Lincoln Presidential Library and Museum (Wójcik, 2017), the National Museum of Singapore and the Kennedy Space Center (Billock, 2017), to note but a few examples. Similarly, augmented virtual reality as an example of experiential convergence is becoming far less uncommon, notably in China where it may be combined with light shows and other modes of visitor experience. The spectacular shows at the Windows of the World Theme Park in Shenzhen have been using laser shows, virtual reality and light projections since the first decade of the 21st century, cementing the tradition established by New York's Coney Island for tourism being a major trendsetter in the use of new technologies.

Tourist roles are shaped by reactions to the encounters at place through the senses of sight, taste, hearing, touch and smell, and the tourism literature contains several examples of an analysis of the tourist sensescape. It has long been known that sensory sensations are a key to the quality of the visitor experience, which in turn generates reactions in terms of behaviours. In one study Buzova *et al.* (2021) sought to establish a scale suitable for establishing empirical evidence for the role of the senses in generating experience of place. After establishing criteria and then creating and testing a scale, they applied it to 717 same-day visitors to Valencia. As might be expected, the visual was a primary determinant of the visit experience but touch (the haptic input) emerged as the second most important sense in this example. This was followed by taste, smell and sound.

One interesting conundrum that faces the tourism industry in the face of developing technologies is what happens when the technology develops to a point where the senses can be fooled. Already in the field of robotics, AI and the mimicking of facial reactions is increasingly making it difficult for humans to tell that they are dealing with a non-human when communicating with robots while using internet-based modes of communication such as videoconferencing. Gittens and Garnes (2022) used Zoom and the Zenbo Social Robot to demonstrate that users of an online conversation with Zenbo recorded positive-user experiences on both pragmatic and hedonic conversations and these outscored face-to-robot interactions. However, the scores were below those required to convince users that more detailed conversations were possible, and the authors suggest that further work on accents being adopted by the robot might increase the score.

This initial and admittedly cursory discussion does indicate that the period during which Yiannakis and Gibson initially developed their work is receding into the past, and the future of tourism may require academics to reconsider carefully their notions of how the motives for relaxation, difference, search for knowledge and social bonding may need to be met. It also throws a challenge to those who believe that a core aspect of the tourist experience is that the experience is considered 'authentic'. The role of authenticity is covered in the next chapter and is also considered with regard to attachment to place.

7 Authenticity: Types and Roles

The chapter includes:

(a) The importance of senses of self.
(b) Definitions of authenticity.
(c) Stimulus-response-organism theories.
(d) Alternative theoretical approaches.
(e) Authenticity, place and holidays and senses of self.
(f) The human gaze and imputations of meaning to place and activities.
(g) Issues in measurement of authenticity.

Introduction

The Roman philosopher Seneca wrote in his *Moral Letters to Lucilius* (65 AD) that travel attracted us with false hopes. It is, he wrote 'a fool's errand. We naively believe that a change of environment will ease distress which stems from within us. But it is part of us and goes wherever we go. What we may experience is a short period of alleviation provided by the distraction of new surroundings' (Seneca, Letter XXVII, 65 AD). In short, wherever we go, we take ourselves. Consequently, if we are to be truly happy in our travels, we need to be happy in ourselves for 'Where you arrive does not matter so much as what sort of person you are when you arrive there' (Seneca, Letter XXVIII, 65 AD). Yet we travel because of a need for distraction from what we perceive as the ordinariness of daily life. In Dann's (1977, 1981) terminology, we are 'pushed' for a desire for the new, yet as Maslow (1968, 1970) argued, the fulfilled self-actualised person can find something new each day in our daily patterns of life. This tension between the secret of happiness being the contentment derived from familiarity and the love of oneself in one's place and the desire for the excitement of the new is one of the conundrums that faces the tourist.

This was well recognised by Jan Morris, who, on her death, was acclaimed in various obituaries as one of the greatest, if not the greatest of travel writers. Jan Morris was a continuous visitor to Trieste over a period of 50 years, and in one of her last books published in 2002 when she was 78 years old, she wrote that 'Trieste is not one of your iconic cities ... It offers no unforgettable landmark, no universally familiar melody, no unmistakable cuisine' (Morris, 2002: 3), but it was the capital for those she called the 'lordly ones' – those who laugh easily, are tolerant and never mean. Trieste was, in fact, 'The Capital of Nowhere' (Morris, 2002). The book, *Trieste and the Meaning of Nowhere* has been nominated by several reviewers as possibly her best travel book, but it is a book of observations of politeness, small things, a somnolent place that once, for a short time, during a phase when it was the port of the Austrian Empire enjoyed some claim to fame, but today is now so largely forgotten that, so she claims, most Italians do not even know it is in Italy. By definition, therefore, it is the best place for those who wish to escape the busyness and hassles of post-modernity in an internet age. Ironically, for a travel book, it is about staying in one place that is 'nowhere'.

From an academic perspective, there has been a changing stance about the purpose of tourism, perhaps because of the Covid pandemic or alternatively due to a trend that began before 2020. That trend recognises that tourism is truly a disrupter of social and environmental systems and while it does generate economic growth, that latter role can also be questioned. The evidence clearly shows that the current global system is unsustainable, because given current technologies, not all can aspire to a standard of living enjoyed by a majority of Europeans and North Americans. This is due to (a) resource deficiencies in the face of demands from (b) a growing global population increasingly characterised by (c) inequitable and growing income and wealth gaps. The inescapable conclusion is that a societal change is required that develops a means by which fairer distributions of wealth are achieved in ways consistent with a sustainable natural environment. It also recognises that to return the environment to a pre-industrial state of some yet to be determined date (say, 1950) requires a programme of environmental renewal. The question being asked is whether people exist for the sake of the economy, or does the economy exist to enhance the quality of life of people, and as many people as possible.

This debate is being seen in the arena of tourism, and the subject of responses to tourism-induced change has been one of the major areas of research in the period commencing about 2010, particularly in destination management (Ryan, 2020a). Inevitably, much of that research has focused on how local communities can be empowered to develop tourism businesses based on local cultures, cuisine and festivals. Equally, there has been a growth of interest in event management research from a viewpoint that urban areas should gain in infrastructure developments, enhanced housing and recreational assets and the refurbishment of areas of historical significance (Rocha & Cao, 2022; Smith, 2012). Seen from this perspective it might appear that the tourist exists as a given, meaning that the role of the tourist is simply to be a necessary catalyst for change. However, researchers have long pointed out that such a view is short-sighted, and the real need is to create a satisfied tourist who will be motivated to return in the future or at least recommend a place to friends or post positivist reviews on online travel agency (OTA) websites.

Stimulus-Organism-Response Theories

It is true that tourist satisfaction has been very closely examined in terms of defining the nature of satisfaction, and whether it is simply a short-lived temporary emotive response or does it involve cognition and conative intent, and many of the preceding chapters have analysed these relationships. Common means have included S-O-R based theories, namely Stimulus-Organism-Response. The premise is essentially simple in that behavioural responses (R) are formed by the interactions of stimuli (S) and individuals' internal states (O) (Kim & Moon, 2009). Mehrabian and Russell (1974a) pointed out that the response can be positive or negative. In the former case, the person will be drawn to the stimuli and behaviour is reinforced by feelings of pleasure, arousal and dominance. In the latter case, stimuli avoidance will take place and emotions of dislike, disgust and disassociation occur. They also argued (Mehrabian & Russell, 1974b) that positive and negative reactions could be explained by factors that exist as three bi-polar sets, namely pleasure-displeasure, arousal-non-arousal and submissiveness-dominance. In one study, they questioned 134 students about levels of anxiety and 214 students about anger and ran a regression analysis to indicate how much anxiety or anger was generated by these bi-polar sets (Russell & Mehrabain, 1974a). In the former case, the three sets 'explained' 78% of variance and in the case of anger, 87% of variance. The items used in the questionnaire were provided in their book *An Approach to Environmental Psychology* (Mehrabian & Russell, 1974a). By today's standards, the work is comparatively straightforward because in the 1970s, software such as partial equation structural modelling did not exist on an easily accessible laptop, but the nature of the items is important for two reasons. The first is that the pleasure-arousal-dominance (P-A-D) has been used in many pieces of research including tourism. For example, Lehto *et al.* (2008) used it to measure revisit intentions after natural disasters had occurred. It was found that the pleasure domain exerted the strongest pressure on revisit intention. This finding is consistent with the initial work by Mehrabian and Russell, and thus the second question asks if these findings reflect a bias within the questionnaire and what is the legitimacy of the items.

Hence, akin to earlier discussion in this book on the use of the gap analysis created by Parasuraman, Zeithaml and Berry in the ServQual model, other researchers have sought to examine the P-A-D original model. It should be noted that Russell and Mehrabian (1997) did further test the three-factor model using 151 descriptions of emotions including words such as 'sad', 'loved', 'happy', etc., and for correlations and degrees of dependency between the three dimensions in the answers provided by respondents to emotion eliciting stimuli. The adjectives used were drawn from pre-existing scales and presented in random order to the sample. It was concluded that strong evidence existed for the independence of the pleasure and arousal scales and that the submissive-dominance scale added to the reliability of the P-A-D model.

Bakker *et al.* (2014) review the model, suggesting that its use has been inhibited by different adjectives used by researchers in the intervening years, and a lack of clarity as to the role of dominance. They cite research that ranges from giving an almost equal status to the submissive-dominance set alongside those of arousal and pleasure, while other researchers chose to almost ignore it. They also identify links between arousal and pleasure with the more conventional understanding of attitudes being primarily composed of cognitive and affective dimensions. Bakker *et al.* (2014) compare the scales adopted by Russell and Mehrabian in their earlier work with the dimensions of evaluation, activity and potency used by Osgood *et al.* (1957) and Osgood (1963) in the construction of semantic differential scales, and the later interpretation of pleasure provided by Mehrabian (1996a). This brief paragraph is possibly sufficient in itself to indicate the degrees of ambiguity that relate to the P-A-D model and the extent to which it is wholly independent of other related concepts that are applied to visitor evaluations of holiday experiences.

They conclude that the P-A-D model is indeed closely related to the cognitive-affective-conative model and confirm that the submissive-dominance set is of importance. They comment that in general, psychological theory expectations are born of learnt habits, mental representations and behaviour and thus are linked to dominant patterns of response. Indeed, they refer to Plato's concept of thinking, feeling and acting, implying possibly that a lot of words have been used to describe variously quite basic reactions whereby evaluations are formed! It is suggested by Bakker *et al.* (2014) that Figure 7.1 represents the concept whereby the pleasure-non-pleasure set has a fundamental role, as does arousal-non-arousal. It is here suggested that the state of non-arousal inclines the visitor to not necessarily more critical evaluations but to degrees of indifference. The set of dominance-submission is embedded within the pleasure-arousal two-factor interpretation of tourist evaluations that are favoured by some commentators but may again be skewed towards the dominant as a reinforcement of learnt patterns of behaviour, and again, the submissive element may incline a visitor to favourable evaluations but less than those whose views are being strongly reinforced. For example, in a study of Egyptian retailing, El Sayed *et al.* state that 'Dominance as an emotional state did not have as major an impact on shoppers' behavioral intentions in this study as pleasure ... Indeed, dominance is an embedded feeling within individuals' subconscious and expressing it

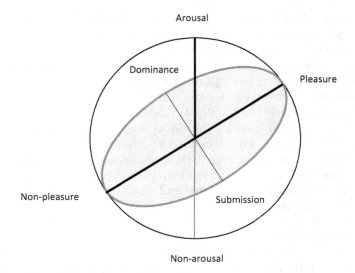

Figure 7.1 A revised P-A-D model after Bakker *et al.* (2014)

is not easy compared to expressing pleasure and arousal' (El Sayed *et al.*, 2004: 22), a result found in studies before and since that time.

The model thus seems to emphasise that much will depend on visitors' reactions to context, which reactions are reflections of expectations being met, disappointed, or totally surpassed, and also on the personality of the visitor. The P-A-D model nonetheless continues to be used in studies of tourist reactions. For example, Miniero *et al.* draw on P-A-D theory to analyse hedonic experiences at sites of cultural interest. They conclude, 'The main outcome of the model provided is the confirmation of pleasure as the main predictor and influencer of satisfaction in hedonic consumption such that pleasure generates satisfaction and, via that, recommendation ... Arousal and dominance positively and significantly affect pleasure: detracting visitors from the tedium of the visiting experience' (Miniero *et al.*, 2014: 632). Another study, that of Sihvonen and Turunen (2022) of a travel fair, has potentially interesting results for tourism experiences more generally. First, they note when comparing the point at which saturation occurs for each of the emotive stimuli, that differences exist between auditory, visual and tactile stimuli, implying responsiveness to stimuli is partly dependent on the nature of the stimuli and the context within which they exist. This was also illustrated by newspaper reports on customer reaction to the UK supermarket chain Morrisons, which in the immediate period after the death of Queen Elizabeth II in September 2022, turned off the music being played in their stores. This initiated complaints from customers that the beeping from the scanners was far too intrusive, and consequently these too had to be turned down (Tetzlaff-Deas, 2022). In short, multi-sensory stimuli are interactive and context bound.

A second finding from Sihoven and Turunen (2022) was that it is possible to create a sensory overload that, while creating an overall pleasant experience, may actually reduce pleasure due perhaps to an inhibition of arousal. This would be consistent with the theories of extraversion and introversion discussed earlier in Chapter 2. They suggest that this may result in sub-optimal experiences. In addition, they noted a distinction in responses in terms of some respondents concentrating on sensitivities at a macro-level, that is, responding to the primarily visual imagery of the Nordic Tourism Fair, while others would refer to individual stands. Generally, responses to tactile stimuli rated very low, but in the case of individual stands encounters involving tactile interactions were remembered. Again, this hints at the role of presentation and context and possibly points towards ways of creating a more memorable experience in a very competitive environment.

When comparing the importance of the sets of pleasure, arousal and dominance, pleasure prompted by visual stimuli appeared the most important, and while arousal could be increased by music, fatigue would inhibit arousal meaning that a lack of excitement was being reported by some, even if they regarded the experience of attendance relatively highly. Many of these lessons are capable of being applied within more mainstream tourism activities. The role of context was certainly found to be of importance in the case of Chinese theme parks (Xu *et al.*, 2022) as each different type of theme park elicited different responses along the P-A-D sets. It might also be true that 'less may be more' when considering the richness of visitor experiences. In the terminology of economists, each addition of utility after a certain point simply creates a diminishing marginal return until total utility begins to fall. Museums may have too many exhibits, the menu too many fine dishes, the walkway may be too long and explanations too full. One way of avoiding such problems is to pass control of such features to the tourist, and that is becoming increasingly possible with the advent of smart technologies. In these ways, the visitor experience becomes more personalised.

Finally, to conclude this discussion of the P-A-D (Pleasure-Arousal-Dominance) dimensions it would seem that, in tourism, the primary dimensions are those of pleasure and arousal. However, it is the context and environment of the location offering the tourist experiences that seems to be a key factor in determining the levels of pleasure and arousal, and equally environment may also determine the extent to which dominance may have an effect on experiences and the satisfaction gained from those experiences.

The Benefits Gained

As noted in the introduction, the identification and measurement of variables that create satisfaction as measured conventionally by items such as the willingness to revisit, make a recommendation to a friend or to rate a visit as value for money have been found incomplete. There was also often a failure to avoid tautologous findings where, for example, researchers would conclude that satisfied tourists were more likely to return, and later would suggest that those with high expectations were more likely to rate their visit more highly. Certainly, it would seem in many studies of tourist satisfaction, in effect those measures of satisfaction are skewed towards favourable responses, meaning all too often that those with low ratings are a very small proportion of any sample. This is not surprising in that very few visitors would wish to spend money on destinations and activities in which they are not interested. That outcome implies a problem for researchers of not being able to sufficiently distinguish variables that generate high and low scores due to disproportionately weighted samples towards positive outcomes.

Given these considerations, researchers are changing their perspectives and increasingly perceive satisfaction not as an outcome but as an intermediate stage in a process of either becoming or enhancing the quality of one's life. In his introductory lectures to first year students, Ryan often emphasises the psychological importance of tourism and the impacts it has on the formation of personality and senses of self. Work, he suggests (albeit slight tongue in cheek), is simply an experience that is repeated 48 times in the year because each week is like the previous week and the following week. Holidays are times of difference, and it is what one does during that time and the memories of those times that shape what people become. There are flaws in the argument, but it points the way towards asking, what is the point of satisfaction? How does being satisfied with any experience create something that benefits an individual's future?

There are a significant number of theories that relate to how benefits derived from holidaying and changes in routine can create senses of improvement in well-being, and these include:

Recovery theories including:
Effort Recovery Theory and Allostatic Load Theory
Conservation of Resources Theory
Self-determination Theory
Broaden and Build Theory

Each of these are briefly outlined below, but a number are premised on some of the psychological and psychometric theories outlined previously. They are generally derived from sports and recreation studies and are only recently being incorporated into tourism studies as it begins to study the long-term impacts of holidays and holiday behaviours more seriously (de Bloom, 2012). This is not to deny the work completed by earlier researchers such as Phil Pearce, and his interest in applying psychology to tourism was undoubtedly beginning to ask such questions, but rather seeks to complement earlier studies.

Effort Recovery Theory

Initially proposed by Meijman and Mulder (1998), the basic premise is that individuals possess a capacity to deal with and recover from stressful situations. The issues examined by the theory refer to what generates these capabilities, what happens should these capacities be exceeded and how long a recovery period might be required. The theory has been continuously used since first being published to examine issues such as staff burnout and managerial fatigue, but in the period 2020 to 2022 was also being used to examine work-home difficulties that arose from the Covid pandemic situation. The concept was developed from studies of physiological changes in the body induced by stress, and researchers examined what factors inhibited or enhanced recovery from stress. These studies were motivated by a realisation that stress would not necessarily create severe deteriorations in health, and hence there was a need to ensure fast and effective recovery strategies for those affected by stress. For example, Sonnentag and Fritz (2007) identify four key factors that expedite recovery, namely psychological detachment from work, relaxation, mastery and control. Most studies that utilise the concept are found in occupational health and similar literatures and refer to relatively quick periods of recovery and how best to manage such periods, but the work of Sonnentag and Fritz (2007) does relate to weekend breaks and an extension to longer holiday periods is inferred. Their questionnaire contains items such as the ability to relax, to undertake challenge and to determine their own schedule, and comparisons can be drawn with the Leisure Motivation Scale previously discussed in this book.

Regarding the tourism literature, applications and extensions of the theory can be found. One such example is a study reported by Chen *et al*. (2016) that adopts the concept of work effort recovery and links it to holiday and life satisfaction in a study of 777 Americans using a questionnaire that included items taken from Sonnentag and Fritz (2007). They found that holiday experiences were positively associated with both holiday and life satisfaction in conditions where respondents had reported high and low strain. They concluded that the earlier work of Sirgy (2010) was correct in arguing that holidays are indeed effective ways of overcoming work-related stress and, possibly even more importantly, in adding to life satisfaction.

Allostatic Load Theory

Allostatic Load theory is closely associated with the work of Bruce McEwan (1998, 2000) who was interested in the physiological responses of the body to stress. Somewhat akin to the earlier psychiatric theories mentioned in this book, McEwan was interested in how an individual's hippocampus within the brain responded to stress and consequent impacts on hormonal functional and the body's attempt to attain homeostasis. While recognising the individual differences of personality and the role of other factors such as the ability to retain good sleeping patterns, McEwan warned of the dangers of overloading the functioning of the body. For example, he noted the impacts of stress at an early age and how such stress might subsequently lead to early ageing of the brain.

In his examinations of the impacts of stress, he coined two terms, namely 'allostasis' and 'allostatic load'. The former represented an adaptive process dependent on the release of neuromodulators while the latter he described as 'an atrophy of neuronal processes that compromise hippocampal function' (McEwan, 1998: 36). Thus, it is evident that stress can generate long-term impacts on well-being, general health and mental capacities. Guidi et al. (2021) provide a review of past literatures that indicates the nature of such problems. Given these issues, it is self-evident that attention would turn to means of reducing 'allostatic loading', and hence yet again recourse is made to ways of improving lifestyle, diet and modes of escaping and handling stress. De Boom et al. (2014) cite earlier research that indicates that short periods of recovery from stress including evenings away from work and weekends are often far too short to permit the full recovery of allostasis. They note that more than passive recovery is required and that 'vacationing is more than stress relief. Vacations presumably enrich quality of life by offering the possibility to engage in valued, pleasant, self- chosen, non-work activities and to spend quality time with close others' (De Boom et al., 2014: 168). The key word in this statement is 'presumably' and they report findings from a comparison of four different types of holidays: long weekends (four days); midweek breaks (five days); winter sports vacations (nine days on average) and summer vacations (23 days on average).

Both good and bad news is derived from their studies. The good news is that all the holidays generated increases in health and well-being measures that included improvements in sleep patterns and positive emotional states. The 'bad news' is that the positive effects are short-lived and 'fade out within the first week after resuming work, independent from the type and duration of the holiday' (De Boom et al., 2014: 177). There was evidence, however, that longer length holidays were associated with higher senses of well-being. These results are therefore quite consistent with the earlier discussion about the nature of our society. To revert back to the work by Krippendorf (1987), a dysfunctional society reinforces personal dysfunctioning and, in his view, dysfunctional holidays that would, in McEwan's terminology, not permit full allostasis. Despite this somewhat gloomy prognosis, de Bloom and her colleagues nonetheless suggest that holidays are an important factor in aiding people to, at the very least, cope with the problems they face. Perhaps, as suggested by Hagger and Murray, only in retirement might there be hope of fully satisfactory vacations – noting that in the latter stages of life there is not a need for doctors but 'for travel agents' (Hagger & Murray, 2014: 198).

Conservation of Resources Theory

Hobfoll (1989, 2001) and Hobfoll and Shiram (2000) questioned the premise that stress was caused by situations that exceeded an individual's coping behaviours when advancing the theory of the Conservation of Resources (COR). The theory commences with an observation that often people cope admirably with stress, and that extreme cases only occur at times of breakdown. Thus, one has to look at the conditions of breakdown, and it is argued that breakdown generally involves four classifications of resources, namely (a) objects such as problems with a home or car, (b) conditions such as those that threaten a loss of a job or marital or relationship stability, (c) personal characteristics such as esteem, confidence and status and (d) energies (i.e. those factors that enable actions such as money, credit, etc.). Hobfoll and Shiram (2000) then state that breakdown occurs when there is a loss of these resources, or a threat to retaining them, or alternatively when resource investment has not achieved a desired end.

From this observation, various potential conclusions can be noted. First, mastery or competence of command over the resources is important. Second, the more resources one possesses the less is the danger of resource loss. Equally, the greater the resources one has, the greater is the opportunity of future resource gain. Consequently, the approach to resources is not a simple matter of possession, but rather one of a continuing process, and equally breakdown is also a process of resource loss and not a simple case of insufficient resource ownership as envisaged by McEwan. The major means of resource acquisition and retention is thought to be social support, and hence Hobfoll in subsequent writing often turns to issues of organisational structures and policies that can inhibit burnout and also the relationship between work and home, and hence the work-home balance (Hobfoll et al., 2018).

Past tourism research has included applications of resource conservation in the way in which it was understood by Hobfoll. For example, Zhang et al. (2021) use the theory to examine recovery from flight-induced stress. The context of their study was that of the Covid pandemic when flights were being cancelled, often because airline staff were being affected by the virus, or because of other staffing issues at airports – all of which was occurring against a background of airlines cutting services due to diminished returns. Consequently, many passengers suffered uncertainty as to flight schedules, and those on multiple destination schedules might have found that intermediary flights may have been cancelled leaving them stranded. Quantitative modelling with a sample of 1092 passengers flying in Brazil and the United States was used to test a series of hypotheses. They found an inverted U relationship between flight duration and stress towards other passengers over issues such as delays, cancellations and lost baggage, but stress levels diminished significantly if trip duration was over 21 days. It might be thought that longer trips provided a better resource of time or experience that permitted a better handling of stress. But other factors such as country (Brazil featured as creating more stress – perhaps because of a lack of familiarity for US passengers) and job status played a role. Using the resource classifications generated by Hobfoll, they found that all played a role across different flight stages other than for the dimensions of gender, cultural distance and airport status but concluded that the key factor lay in the context within which the flight took place. Moreover, from a theoretical perspective they saw a need for redefinition of resources and a need to consider temporal factors.

Generally, except for a few cases such as Li's (2021) study of star gazing, the theory has not been used intensively in tourism studies. In Li's study more of the emphasis is on aspects of 'peak experience' while even Zhang et al. (2021) refer to echoes of the cognitive, affective and conative. In a critical commentary, Lazarus (2001) critiques Hobfoll's work as a replication of previous ideas in new wording and identifies what he feels are inconsistencies with the concept (it should be noted Hobfoll (2001) replies to these and other criticisms in the same issue of the journal). What might be said is that, at least thus far, little use has been made of the theory in explaining tourist experiences.

Self-determination Theory

It was noted that Zhang et al. (2021) concluded that context had a significant role in explaining Covid-induced flight stress, and Deci and Ryan would fully concur as they write that Social Determination Theory is 'focused on the influences of social environments on attitudes, values, motivations, and behaviours both developmentally and in current situations' (Deci & Ryan, 2012: 417). They add, 'Specifically, SDT assumes that the human organism is evolved to be inherently active, intrinsically motivated, and oriented towards developing naturally through integrative processes. These qualities need not be learned; they are inherent in human nature. Still, they develop over time, play a central role in learning, and are affected by social environments' (Deci & Ryan, 2012: 417).

The work of Deci and Ryan has been widely cited across several literatures in psychology, well-being and health, and in tourism. Behind it lay several hundred papers of empirical evidence. The popularity of the theory may lie in an almost instinctive acceptance of some of its key concepts. One of its key precepts is that three key needs exist for optimal human development and effectiveness. These needs are competence, autonomy and relatedness – and it is these three factors that permit learning and adaptability. Moreover, it is important to note that these factors, while intrinsic to human behaviour, are not exclusive, and may be subject to additions, modifications and deficits dependent on the context and behaviour being examined. Consequently, these three core needs lend themselves to several different situations and modifications. For example, rewards and benefits, novelty and curiosity can be easily incorporated into the core model as being supportive of autonomy and senses of self-determination.

Self-determination theory has been extensively used in tourism, if only because as illustrated by previous chapters many of the theories of tourism motivation have been oriented towards not just discovery of new places and cultures but also discovery of self through either quiet reflection or interaction with others. Buzinde (2020) specifically draws on self-determination to examine the relationship between tourism and well-being through spiritual tourism and does so through the technique of analytical autoethnography. This technique requires explicit reflection on participation as a member engaged in group activities with a view to developing theoretical understanding, and as a technique it requires close examination of the subjective. This is both an advantage and yet a potential problem if not done well. The approach is partly justified by reference to the greater personalisation inherent in post-modern society that, states Buzinde, is due to 'scepticism regarding generalization of knowledge claims' (Buzinde, 2020: 3). One problem is that theoretical understanding is usually associated with a wish to generalise results, and from a post-positivistic platform, to permit a degree of forecasting. This nexus between the desire for richer understanding of processes of individual determination through experience and a need to generalise is not unique to autoethnography but is a problem that runs throughout much social science research. The issue is to what extent is the researcher prepared to reveal him or herself in this form of research.

Buzinde's paper provides a full description of her journey through her experience of attending an Indian Yoga Institute. Her use of self-determination theory resulted in a classification of her experiences under the headings of competence, autonomy and relatedness – that is, the theory was effectively used to impose a classification upon a wealth of experiences born of personal history, age and culture that all interacted to provide personal meanings of a spiritual holiday. Aicher and Brenner (2015) bypass the issue of strict adherence to a three-fold classification by two processes. First, they utilise an extension of self-determination theory developed by Lox *et al.* (2006) in an application to exercise-taking to make a distinction between self- and other-determined activity. They also take advantage of the theoretical modifications mentioned by Deci and Ryan (2012) and adopt the work of Vallerand *et al.* (1989). They suggest the existence of three types of intrinsic motivation, namely a motivation to accomplish, motivation to know and motivation to experience stimulation. They subsequently suggest a series of hypotheses and an embryonic regression model, but the evidence is not actually presented in the 1989 paper. Aicher, in subsequent papers, then resorts to 'push-pull' theory and conventional statistical analysis (Newland & Aicher, 2018), and again uses self-determination with the three components of the Psychological Continuum Model (pleasure, centrality and sign) with further conventional statistical analysis to motivation and evaluation of marathon participation (Aicher *et al.*, 2017).

In tourism studies, it would seem that while self-determination theory is alluded to, and indeed many papers cite the work of Deci and Ryan (2012), relatively few restrict themselves to the three dimensions of competency, autonomy and relatedness. A number of reasons might explain why. First, the concepts possess close relationships with several other concepts that are discussed in the tourism literature. Competency, as previously discussed, is a key element in the Leisure Motivation Scale (Beard & Ragheb, 1983), relatedness is associated with social bonding and building (also part of the Leisure Motivation Scale) and the search for autonomy can be likened to processes of self-discovery as explained by the humanistic psychologists. The theory evolved from earlier work by Deci and Ryan (1985) that was concerned with the relationship between intrinsic and externally imposed motivations and the consequent impact on performance. In that sense, there is a differentiation between performance and benefit gained, even while noting that high levels of performance can enhance feelings of self-esteem.

Broaden and Build Theory

Self-determination and resource conservation theories have been shown to be attempts to create meaning and structures from essentially subjective feelings. Frederickson's (2001, 2004, 2013) 'Broaden and Build' Theory tackles the distinction between performance and self-esteem. In her work, Frederickson suggests that positive emotions are motivational and related to various forms of action and behaviours. Interest and curiosity are related to exploration, contentment leads to an ability to savour and integrate within self and with others and joy leads to an ability to play. In short, positive emotions produce optimal functioning. Frederickson suggests that all too often positive emotions have been solely associated with affective states that describe functioning in generic terms of 'approach or continue' (Frederickson, 2004: 1369). She writes that she 'sensed' this approach underestimated the unique effects of positive emotions, stating 'I call this the broaden-and-build theory of positive emotions because positive emotions appear to broaden peoples' momentary thought–action repertoires and build their enduring personal resources' (Frederickson, 2004: 1369).

There is an emergent body of psychological and physiological evidence for this approach. In her own work, Frederickson cites a number of studies, but so too does Robson in his books *The Intelligence Trap: Revolutionise Your Thinking and Make Wiser Decisions* (Robson, 2019) and *The Expectation Trap* (Robson, 2022). Robson (2022) suggests that one of the main predictors of success in specifically education, but also more widely, is curiosity. He argues that success in higher education is not so much determined by intellect but by curiosity and perseverance, and evidence is provided through assessing reactions to the puzzle of Houdini's disappearing elephant trick. Two modes of presentation gave an answer to how this trick was completed in his studies. The first posed a straightforward suggestion and the second presented possible solutions in a more open-ended way. Subsequent tests of recall indicated the second mode of presentation created much higher levels of recall, and Robson suggests this is a result of prompting curiosity. Other research is reinforcing these findings. For example, Hsiung *et al.* (2022) used data from a sample of 1338 respondents to confirm that 'Curiosity encourages patience and joy in the presence of uncertainty', to cite the title of their paper.

Psychiatric measures are now providing evidence of why this may well be the case. Brain activity has been measured in a series of experiments. Gruber *et al.* (2014) found that in a set of tasks, curiosity drove activity in the dopaminergic and nucleus accumbens regions of the brain. Similarly, recall was correlated with midbrain and hippocampal activity. It was noticeable that learning was taking place, even if the participant had no prior interest in the task if curiosity was aroused. The implication is that curiosity is linked to intrinsic motivation, but Kidd and Hayden (2015) note that similar brain functions are also found when using extrinsic rewards. Equally, when reporting past work on neurological brain patterns associated with exploratory behaviour and learning, Kidd and Hayden (2015) also cite that similar brain patterns are found in other species including monkeys, pigeons and even roundworms. It would seem that the links between brain pattern activity and curiosity have become a 'hot topic' in psychiatrics in the first part of the 21st century. Zurn and Bassett (2018) suggest that curiosity has come to be regarded as an important component of personality. What this section also confirms is that while the traits of openness, conscientiousness, extraversion, neuroticism and agreeableness have long been regarded as the big five personality traits, the science of psychiatry is advancing our understanding beyond statistical tests based on descriptions of travel types and personalities (Jani, 2014). It also reinforces the notion that holidaying behaviour offers many potential benefits to people through the process of both relaxation and challenge depending on the activities in which they engage.

Curiosity is linked to senses of novelty, in that an experience or place thought novel may be a stimulant that leads to curiosity. Past psychological theory has linked novelty to the personality traits of openness to experience (Cloninger, 1986) and sensation-seeking (Zuckerman et al., 1978), albeit others have indicated that a preference for novelty may be a trait in its own right (Hirschman, 1980, 1984). Equally, novelty has been linked to the fundamentals of arousal in that novelty can initiate arousal. Some have extended this idea to suggest that this may lead to impulsive decision-taking (Zuckerman & Kuhlman, 2000). Skavronskaya et al. (2020) note the importance of novelty in both cognitive psychology and neuropsychology. They argue that cognitive psychology is primarily about how intuition and reasoning lead to thinking and evaluation in the light of stimuli, whereas neuropsychology 'considers the capacity of novelty to influence neural processes' (Skavronskaya et al., 2020: 2688). They then consider four psychological approaches, namely behavioural psychology, personality psychology, cognitive psychology and neuropsychology. Each approach brings a different perspective to an understanding of novelty. The first is said to perceive novelty as a mismatch between the expected and past experience. Personality theory perceives novelty as a personality trait that can motivate, while cognitive psychology sees novelty as a learning signal that promotes memory and shapes goal-directed behaviour. Finally, neuropsychology assesses novelty as a dimension on which the nervous system operates, so shaping both internal and external dimensions of the brain and behaviour.

Tourism research has often referenced novelty, albeit for the most part in association with other dimensions, notably as a determinant of tourist satisfaction. Nguyen et al. (2020) examined degrees of novelty seeking in a sample of 252 international tourists visiting attractions in Vietnam. They suggest that novelty comprises relaxation seeking, experience seeking, arousal seeking and boredom alleviation. Novelty was deemed to positively affect satisfaction. In an earlier study, Assaker et al. (2011) examined relationships between novelty, satisfaction and an intention to return to a destination. It was found that novelty had a positive impact on satisfaction, and satisfaction was a determinant of an intention to return. However, in cases where novelty was highly rated, they suggest that satisfaction is irrelevant as a determination of intention to return because the destination, once visited, no longer possessed the attribute of novelty. Novelty is associated with curiosity, but what happens if curiosity is satisfied?

Making the Unfamiliar Familiar – Forming Place Attachment

The role of authenticity in the tourist experience

So, does curiosity wholly explain tourism and visitor experiences? Just as the search for the novelty found in new locations has been shown to be an important motive and creator of expectations in tourism, another topic that has attracted the attention of tourism researchers in the early 21st century has been the concept of place attachment. It was noted early in Chapter 1 that place attachment was initially developed in the fields of human geography (Lewicka, 2011; Relph, 1976) and environmental psychological literature (Guiliani, 1991; Hidalgo & Hernandez, 2001; Korpela, 1989; Lalli, 1992; Twigger-Ross & Uzzell, 1996). Relph (1976) argued that space becomes important because of the meanings and connections attributed to space by humans. He identified seven classifications of space. The first is 'pragmatic' or 'primitive' space, which is the space essential for location of humans. It refers to going up or down, left or right. This leads to 'perceptual' space – that is, the space associated with intention, an intention that provides key points, senses of depth and colour and an identification of nuanced difference. In turn, these aspects of space become associated with meaning, giving rise to 'existential' space. There are various forms of existential space, including structured geographical space and sacred spaces.

As a humanistic geographer, Relph was well aware of connections between indigenous peoples and past civilisations and their natural environment, and indeed he was equally aware that cultural settings would establish meanings associated with land that would not be shared by other cultures. This has been evidenced by, for example, the differences between the Trump administration and Native American peoples about routes for oil pipelines. The meanings associated with geographical space thus lead to 'architectural and planning' spaces. As Ryan (2020) notes, the planning of destinations reflects cultural values and the establishment of priorities. Those values and priorities come to define what Relph termed 'cognitive space'. The final two classifications are those of 'abstract space' and 'inter-relationships between spaces'. In the latter half of his book, Relph explores further the implications of abstract space (i.e. a homogenous extraction of space that is featureless) and the relationships between spaces to explore both the meaning and absence of place – the latter being referred as 'placelessness'. A placelessness site can have a physical location but due to the globalisation of shopping malls, resort complexes, high-rise buildings and the like they become detached from local traditions and cultures and may be interchangeable between different locations. They represent one form of post-modernity in having features instantly recognisable anywhere and thus have little specific meaning other than possibly a pure functionality.

Arefi (1999) refers to such places as having a loss of consequence or a loss of narrative, but equally notes the emergence of the 'invented place' as a stage set. Although not alluding to theme parks, it can be noted that theme parks are a staged place, and indeed some shopping malls feature themed restaurant areas or theme park characteristics, and museums such as the Beamish Museum of Colonial Williamsburg stage settings in a street or village context.

For the tourist, acquiring a meaning of place can be said to be important in terms of meeting the needs of the holiday. At the very least, the tourist wants to acquire a 'map' of the place, that is, a knowledge of the physical location of those places having, at the most basic, a function that meets a need. These functions may be those regarding retail, banking, accommodation and the location of destinations. The advent of smartphone technologies and the internet significantly ease the problem of 'finding places'. Indeed, given that 5G and 6G will permit vehicles to plan their own route to a place in the not-too-distant future, the need for a tourist's actual knowledge of a given route may well be less than that which is currently required. If such needs are reduced, might places become yet even more 'placeless', or do tourists ascribe differing criteria of importance to generate perceptual maps of places and meanings?

The answer to such a question may lay in the rationale for the trip. Holidays motivated by relaxation needs might need little more than a taxi ride with little awareness of local geography. On the other hand, a vacation motivated by interest in local history, culture or a search for ancestors will require more detailed knowledge. Hence, yet again, we might note the importance of curiosity. This curiosity is related to a need for meaning, and that a place possesses an authentic nature capable of providing meaning. This type of place is perhaps best illustrated by pilgrims as identified in research on Marian sites such as Lourdes and Fatima (Thomas *et al.*, 2018), places of traditional Chinese faiths like the Taihao Fuxi Mausoleum (Zhang *et al.*, 2022) or places related to Zen Buddhist meditation holidays described by Jiang *et al.* (2018).

Associated with the conveyance of meaning is the concept of authenticity, especially with reference to place and the activities at that location. The role of authenticity of place has attracted attention from several scholars. Rickly (2022) provides a detailed history of at least 40 years of discussions of the concept of authenticity by tourism scholars. Certainly, it seems that by the 1990s tourism research had identified authenticity of place as a key dimension in the formation of tourism experiences. Mac-Cannell (1973) and Cohen (1979) were among that generation of scholars that saw the emergence of post-Second World War mass tourism and the social and environmental impacts associated with both tourism and globalisation. Like Boorstin's (1961/1964a) earlier work on pseudo-events, they suggested that a growing homogeneity potentially stultified individual pursuits. MacCannell wrote 'that sightseeing is a form of ritual respect for society and that tourism absorbs some of the social functions of religion in the modern world. The dimension of social life analysed in this paper is its authenticity or more exactly the search for authenticity of experience that is everywhere manifest in our society' (MacCannell, 1973: 589). It can be observed that there is a parallel between such thinking and that of Krippendorf (1987) as discussed in an earlier chapter. MacCannell's thesis of the tourist as a secular pilgrim has been adopted by many, but it should be noted that in 2008, MacCannell found himself trapped in a discourse where he self-describes his role as 'the evil castrating Lisa' (MacCannell, 2008: 334). Citing Bruner's (2005) work and experience of finding that tourists were not interested in the authenticity of a dance, but rather in the viewing of a show, MacCannell writes 'that just because I observed staged authenticity doesn't mean I believe in authenticity' (MacCannell, 2008: 335). The debate between Bruner and MacCannell was partly based on the back- and front-stage terminology generated by Goffman (1959), but for MacCannell this is no simple dichotomy for both are absorbed into tourist space dictated by a changing society. If, in the 2000s, it was possible to note changing patterns that had moved far from the distinctions of identities classified in the 1950s, that difference might now be even more so in the second decade of the 21st century.

For MacCannell there was no backstage, but a fantasy, a desire for a reality that differed from current realities that arguably give rise to some nostalgic but never real simpler past. But in critiquing Bruner's work, MacCannell suggests the search for evidence that a past simpler life might exist is arguably a search for the intimate, for relationships, but even here he concludes, 'But when everything is totalled, we will find it adds up to a particularly poignant nothingness' (MacCannell, 2008: 337). In short, authenticity from this perspective is a desired image of the past created by our ability, or rather inability to find a comfortable present. Ironically one might conclude, hearkening back to Jan Morris in Trieste, that truly that comfortable present is 'Nowhere'.

One possible problem with these somewhat philosophical debates is summed up in the opposing question – has one ever had an inauthentic experience? In many instances, the holidaymaker may want an interesting or exciting experience, or a relaxing experience, but if that fails to materialise, then what might result is an authentic boring or disappointing experience. However negative it is, the experience remains 'authentic'.

It was these definitional difficulties of authenticity that Ning Wang considered in his doctoral dissertation undertaken at Sheffield University in the late 1990s and summarised in his paper published in the *Annals of Tourism Research* (Wang, 1999). Wang argues that as the millennium drew to its close, there were three approaches towards understanding authenticity, namely those of objectivism, constructionism and the postmodern. The first of these relates to what the world art circles regard as the 'provenance' of the work in question – is there evidence of it being what it claims to be, is it genuine? It is the language of the art galleries and museums absorbed into tourism events and festivals and applied to cultural tourism. But as Wang notes, herein lies a distinction between the reality of the toured *object* and the *experience* of viewing, participating in or holding the object. It can be commented that our senses intercede between the object and our evaluation. However, the basic notion is that objective authenticity is based upon a premise of being original and genuine.

Wang then develops the notion that items also possess symbolic values and offer meanings that are not just personal but which are also shared with and among others. This is a constructed authenticity created by the ideas, images and meanings that are projected within a social setting and one that requires interactions between the promoters of meanings and the interpretations imposed on both messages and the items or locations. There might be said to be links between this perspective and that of the induced and organic images developed by Gartner (1989, 1994), but a further factor today is the role of popularising influencers on various internet platforms such as Weibo and TikTok, the reviews left on OTA sites such as Ctrip and Booking.com, and additionally the blogs and podcasts provided by individuals. This constructivist perspective implicitly emphasises the role of opinion when considering these latter means of communication. Gretzel (2018) identifies four specific types of influencers, namely (a) celebrities, (b) industry experts and thought leaders, (c) bloggers and content creators and (d) micro-influencers (defined as having fewer than 500 followers).

The role of influencers adds another complexity to the symbolism involved in selection of destinations and evaluations of experiences at such places. This is because of the role of fandom. Fans of sports stars, film stars and other celebrities may well select a location because of endorsement by the celebrity they follow and their desire to seek an experience based on the role played at that place by their favoured celebrity. They identify themselves by association with their favoured celebrity by visiting the location and probably by taking photographs and posting them to friends. Those actions enhance their experience of being at that place. The symbolism or meaning of the place is strengthened by an association with the subject of the fandom, and it is arguably a post-modern authenticity based on the consumption of images thought important.

While Wang (1999) does not consider the interaction between tourist, place and possible association with celebrity, influencer or blogger, from one perspective the relationship does not pose a new concept, and that is the question of trust. Wang writes (while citing Culler, 1981), 'The toured objects or others are experienced as authentic not because they are originals or reality, but because they are perceived as the signs or symbols of authenticity' (Wang, 1999: 356). This becomes closer to the third form of authenticity because it implies that the motive for the trip is satisfied by the consumption of signs of imputer value. That third perspective is the post-modern as noted in the previous paragraph.

Post-modernity is not in itself easy to define, and indeed there are differences in allocating time periods to the post-modern. As many commentators have pointed out, the incidence of post-modernism can be quite contextually bound. It has been suggested that tourism *per se* is the epitome of post-modernism being often associated with the consumption of signs and symbols as suggested by Wang (1999), yet its transport systems are run along the modernist lines of efficiency and purposeful clear objectives that pay little regard to sentiment. For example, the passenger fully expects to travel between tourist-originating place and final destination at given times complete with their baggage. Equally, the Masai dances noted by Bruner (2005) relate to a pre-modern society and may be performed within primarily pre-modern surroundings of African landscapes, but for the tourist may represent either entertainment or a simulacrum of earlier modes of life. Notwithstanding these observations, Wang states 'the approaches of postmodernism seem to be characterized by deconstruction of authenticity' (Wang, 1999: 346). Baudrillard (1983), somewhat famously, constructs the post-modern as being the consumption of something that possesses no original, but rather exists as a 'metaphysics of the code' (Baudrillard, 1983: 103). For him, at Disneyworld, there is a real real, real fake, fake real and fake fake. Every alternative is as legitimate as any other variant. Each, it might be said, creates an experience. Given this, if the point of holidaying is the seeking of an experience, then whether a place is authentic or not is of secondary importance.

In an earlier chapter, however, reference was made to the work of Barbara Kirshenblatt-Gimblett and the Polin Museum of Jewish History in Warsaw. At a presentation at the University of Waikato in 2019, Barbara pointed out that a museum creates a collection of artefacts from either archaeological sources or from other depositaries of the artefacts of a given culture – but how does one construct a museum when a regime deliberately and methodologically sought to destroy any evidence of a culture? Such was the case of the Nazi occupation of Warsaw, and so effective was it that even today the Jewish population of Warsaw remains quite small. In 1939, the Jewish population of about 350,000 represented about 30% of Warsaw's total population. Today, it is estimated that only 2000 of Warsaw's total population of 1.7 million people are Jews.

The Polin Museum does, of course, contain various physical items, but it is a museum of memories, statements and representations of the past (Kirshenblatt-Gimblett, 2016). As she notes, before the collection, before the building and even before there were funds, there was a story (Kirshenblatt-Gimblett, 2016: 151). She identifies the museum as a critical museum, critical for the Polish nation and arguably for the world, and it espouses a new museology predicated on exploration and learning rather than guiding and teaching. Today, many museums are moving to the use of projected images and computer-generated visuals and indeed holographic representations. Stories are indeed selected, portrayed and emphasised for many purposes (Chen & Ryan, 2020), but Kirshenblatt-Gimblett has positioned the Polin Museum as a museum of debate and challenge.

Thus, bearing these factors in mind, it seems evident that Wang's fourth conceptualisation of experience – the existential experience – follows from such a discussion. Before defining the existential experience, there remains at least one more element for consideration in assessing the classical understanding of experience. Bennett (2019) reviews theories of decline and notes that theories of cultural, national and personal decline abound throughout human history. He cites from Schopenhauer to whom Bennett (2019: 5) ascribes a whole philosophy of pessimism. In *Parerga and Paralipomena*, written in 1851, Schopenhauer describes the human situation as follows:

> We begin in the madness of carnal desire and the transport of voluptuousness; we end in the dissolution of all our parts and the musty stench of corpses. And the road from the one to the other too goes, in regard to our well-being and enjoyment of life, steadily downhill: happily dreaming childhood, exultant youth, toil-filled years of manhood, infirm and often wretched old age, the torment of the last illness and finally the throes of death - does it not look as if existence were an error the consequences of which gradually grow more and more manifest? (p. 54)

At the time of writing in 2022, there is a world full of uncertainty with a recovery from Covid, the Russian attempts at annexation of part of Ukraine, massive flooding in Pakistan, the encroachment of climate change heralded by more numerous and intensive cyclones, and human abuses. There is a youthful population not only worried about such things but also facing a realisation that possibly theirs is the first generation that will not enjoy growing standards of living, as they live longer with parents because of an inability to buy or possibly rent their own homes due to increasing pressures on house prices. Additionally, the gaps between 'haves' and 'have-nots' seem not to diminish but in fact grow. What then of the authenticity of experience when the tourist, as they grow older, sees more signs of environmental degradation, increasing congestion of airports, more frequent delays, the increased demand for establishing forward planning of itineraries as places impose quotas or bans on entry and increased surveillance diminishing privacy.

John Urry's gaze that he saw initially born of nostalgia and romance in 1990 has become increasingly less optimistic over time. In his second edition, published in 2002, he concludes that there is an end of tourism as the general economy of signs makes progress. He refers to 'countless mobilities, physical, imaginative and virtual, voluntary and coerced' set within an increasingly mediased world (Urry, 2002: 161). In the third edition, published in 2011, and co-authored with Jonas Larsen, his final chapter is entitled 'Risks and Futures'. In this chapter they ask, 'Will there still be a powerful tourist gaze by the middle of the century?' (Urry & Larsen, 2011: 233) in a world of climate change, declining supplies of fossil fuels and enormous growth of the human population. They postulate three possible scenarios and state that none are wholly desirable, and that indeed a shimmering Dubai might yet drift back into the sands from which it arose.

Against such a background, how might an existential experience be conceived and sensed? Ning Wang's book, *Tourism and Modernity* appeared at much the same time as Urry's work, and the list of the chapters reveals similar concerns about modernity, the post-modern, the consumption of signs and the lure of discourse and images. In many ways, such work might be said to be a somewhat belated response to a stream of analysis that arose in the mid-1960s with the work of Foucault and his assessments of knowledge, power and the ability to create frameworks through which the world was perceived. The same period also saw the work of American commentators such as Boorstin and Packard. As noted previously, Boorstin analysed the pseudo-event, while Packard in his books *The Hidden Persuaders* (1957) and *The Naked Society* (1964) questioned the power of corporates, their role in creating consumer-led societies and the role of marketing in a modern society. On both sides of the Atlantic, there was a recognition of a changing world and the growing influence of globalised commerciality that became summarised by Ritzer in 1993 with his book *The McDonaldization of Society*. Another key text from this period was Jean Baudrillard's *The Consumer Society* which though originally written in 1970 was not first published in English until, it is thought, 1998, by Chris Turner.

Consequently, it can be argued that the work of Urry, Wang, Cohen, Krippendorf and others was part of a zeitgeist reflecting upon the challenges of a world emerging from the World Wars and a period of economic growth prior to dismal pessimism noted by Bennett some three decades later. Given that tourism benefitted from and contributed to that economic growth premised on personal motivations, it is, with hindsight, not surprising that tourism scholars allied the sociological insights derived from examinations of post-modernity with the traditions inherited from humanistic psychology. In his chapter entitled 'Modernity and the Tourism of Authenticity', Wang initially describes the authenticities of the original, social constructionism and the post-modern. He then turns his attention to the concept of existential authenticity.

He initially cites Berger's (1973) approach to defining existential authenticity as a 'State of Being' where individuals are true to themselves. To be true to oneself implies that the tourist is no passive gazer on a scene and arguably goes beyond a search for information or knowledge to actually reflect upon meaning for self. Reflection is being proactive, but arguably such reflection is as much a cognitive motivated action even if emotionally evaluated. Wang's first example, however, recognises the role of the senses, in this case the sense of the kinaesthetic as he describes tourists participating in dance in Cuba. He uses the study by Daniel (1996) where she describes how tourists are spontaneously drawn into dance so that 'the dance becomes their entire world at that particular moment. Time and tensions are suspended' (Daniel, 1996: 789). The link with Csikszentmihalyi's concept of flow is thus obvious, as is the link with Maslow's concept of actualisation enabling the adult to enjoy moments of child-like fun. Existential experiences are creative, but as Wang points out, may have little at all to do with the original.

Wang then turns to ask, if the existential is about being true to one-self, then the epistemological question is 'how does one be false to one-self?' Wang answers this question in two ways. First, there is a silence as the concept of being false to one-self is not specifically answered. Second, is the answer that an existential authenticity is an ideal that is being sought by the tourist. Thus, the implication is that posed by MacCannell (2008) and Cohen (1985), namely that tourism is akin to a secular pilgrimage. The issue is possibly not a dichotomy between the 'true' and the 'false self' but rather a loss of 'real self' or a diminution of personal sense of being created by the dysfunctional or anomic society described by Durkheim and Krippendorf. Wang suggests that the ideal is born of romantic, nostalgic notions that rest on a desire for a simpler society. The authentic self hence exists in a space outside of the modern real world, and inasmuch as tourism helps people to discover their real self, so too tourism exists outside of the real world in a separate space. But one can question if this a realistic conclusion, especially when considering that increasingly there is a view that tourism contributes to a global environmental degradation (Becken & Hay, 2012; Scott et al., 2019). In one sense, Wang goes on to answer this question by arguing that one perspective is to conceive of the 'ideal self' as an act of resistance to a world dominated by global forces dominated by market driven forces.

This viewpoint obviously places tourism as a liminal state that intercedes between the complexities of a modern world and a desired simpler state, but how does this relate to a sense of experience of activities, seeing new things and engaging with new people in an experiential sense? For Wang, the answer lies in bodily feelings and social interaction. This is no new conclusion, and it seems that tourism scholars are forever engaged in tautological argument that is premised upon notions of relaxation, entertainment, sensual pleasures, recreation, refreshment and excitement. And we are left with vague measures of such things as illustrated by the prior discussion of the P-A-D. Questions are based on adjectives of being happy, pleased, thrilled or on Likert-type scales asking to what extent one was entertained, challenged, etc. The alternative is that one can engage in physiological measures that record an increase in heart beats per minute, or a scan that indicates increased neurological activity. And while we can catch a moment and describe it using such words, the question raised by Diener and others schooled in humanistic psychology remains – namely how long lasting is the effect, to what extent does it contribute to our quality of life, and possibly an ethical question, does it permit us to work with others to create better social and even environmental conditions?

One commentator who has sought to assess the existential moment is Elvi Whittaker. In her work entitled *Seeking the Existential Moment* (Whittaker, 2012), she too relates to a separation from the physical world and, however fleeting, a touch with an inner self illuminated by a sense of togetherness with a wider universe. She notes that when examining peak-experience, 'one of the major tenets of western philosophy, Cartesian dualism seems to disappear' (Whittaker, 2012: 80). She continues to note that time disappears, and one is overcome by a 'sense of universality'. For her, a sense of sense falls away to be replaced by a connectedness, especially with the natural. As an anthropologist, she is very aware of the perceived burden of empiricism that favours logicality over emotion, yet she concludes that perhaps this relationship should be reversed. That in fact it is emotion that defines the human being, and that it is the mystery of emotion that underlies the existential tourist experience.

Whilst sympathetic to such a view, it would seem that the concept of authenticity seems intangible, elusive and abstract. It almost appears that the old saying of 'I don't know how to define it, but I know it when I see it' is most apposite. However, Daniel's own work does suggest a key variable, which is that of context. This is hinted at throughout her article as she refers to the context of the dance or the experience of natural places. This role of the context is taken up by Knudsen and Waade (2010a) as they build on prior work by O'Dell and Billing (2005). O'Dell and Billing (2005) coined the term *experiencescapes*. Picking up the theme of the experience economy (Pine & Gilmore, 1999) and the development of theme parks, fantasy shopping malls and travel agencies that emphasise emotional components in their décor, they write, 'As sites of market production, the spaces in which experiences are staged and consumed can be likened to stylized landscapes that are strategically planned, laid out and designed. They are, in this sense, landscapes of experience – *experiencescapes*' (O'Dell & Billing, 2005: 16). Knudsen and Waade specifically pick up from this definition to state 'These economies are presented as being based on investment and exchange, not primarily of meaning and signs as in the symbolic economy but of involvement, energy and the capacity for the user to be affected' (Knudsen & Waade, 2010: 5). The experience is clearly seen as being a marketable proposition supported by an industry – and thus to return to Pine and Gilmore (1999) and the sub-title of their book – 'Work is Theatre & Every Business a Stage'.

It is a relatively easy conceptual step from such a concept of 'work as theatre' to speak of a *performative* experience, and indeed a *performative authenticity*. This takes us beyond the conceptualisation of the front- and back-stage (Goffman, 1959) by emphasising the role of the tourist as a performer, or in the terms of other scholars, a co-producer or co-consumer of the experience. Yet again, the discussion appears to be circular in that, as discussed earlier, one has to assess the willingness of the tourist to play along (pun intended) with the performance (or fantasy) and their ability to dissociate from reality. Parallels might be made with popular forms of entertainment encapsulated in the successful television series *Game of Thrones*, which was not only popular with audiences but which apparently was thought to contain history by some. A survey conducted in the UK by Sky HISTORY (Zamora, 2022) of 2000 respondents found that 5% of the respondents thought the Wars of the Roses were fought between the houses of Lannister and Stark. One can also find several papers on Google Scholar that analyse the medieval realities of that specific television series, noting therefore a blurring of the historical and fantasy. It can be objected that 5% of the sample possessed a faulty knowledge of history, and there is a distinction between a knowing acknowledgement of a fantasy and a failure to perceive a fantasy, but if the key variable is that of experiencing performance, to what extent does a failure to perceive or an acknowledgement of 'pretence' shape an experience? Again, as observed, Cohen (1972, 1979) has considered this question when asking if a failure to observe an event as originally 'authentic', or wrongly ascribing 'authenticity' to a fake performance has importance for a tourist who expresses satisfaction with a performance. As Cohen and Cohen (2012) imply – hot or cold authenticity – both possess authenticity. One is tempted to cite the Greek philosopher, Protagoras, who reputedly stated, 'Man in the measure of all things'. That is, only man can ascribe meaning, veracity or falsehood to things, statements and opinions.

Moore *et al.* (2021) seek to find a way through the contested and vague nature of 'authenticity' emphasising the active role of the tourist. They take, as a starting point, the view that '"authentication" is not just a process applied (in either "cool" or "hot" ways – Cohen & Cohen, 2012) to objects, people, culture, and places. It is also a process that each tourist (and person) applies to their ongoing experiences (we can make attempts to "authenticate" our own experiences)' (Moore *et al.*, 2021: 7). They suggest a reciprocity exists between tourist and place, and there is what some call a script within the culture of tourism where a tourist possesses a cognitive knowledge of what is seen and adopts an improved course of action. Their example is the tourist at the Eiffel Tower who takes an almost obligatory photograph, an act of varying symbolism as noted in the next paragraph.

They subsequently make the important point that there is a difference between knowing what is true and being true to one-self. It is possible to quibble and state that the knowing may be simply a belief in what *is thought to* be true, as in our discussion above about those who confuse *Game of Thrones* characters with the Lancastrian and Yorkist leaders in the Wars of the Roses (which, one admits, was seemingly one of the inspirations for George Martin's novel). Reverting to a knowledge of what is true and being true permits the distinction made by Cohen and Cohen (2012) between 'cool' and 'hot' authentication. Thus, the person viewing the Eiffel Tower may, in fact, feel slightly disappointed in that it looks just like the photographs and the replicas of the Tower found around the world in places like Las Vegas or Shenzhen. That would be an example of 'cool' authenticity in the language of Cohen and Cohen (2012), but as the tourist takes a 'selfie' and gazes at a view from Paris, that 'appreciation' of being at the Tower and relating to 'being there' as part of one's experience – then that may represent a 'hot' authentication. From this perspective, one can view 'authentication' as a process of *being at a specific site* that possesses value (or comes to be valued through a process of memory and recall). In a similar manner, Zhang and Ryan (2023) write of a convergence of visitor evaluations of place by visitors to the Fuxi Mausoleum in Zhoukou. They note differences among visitors in terms of age, education and belief in ancestor worship and other facets of Chinese belief systems, but because of the consensual perspective of importance attributed to the site because Fuxi was the 'ancestor' (or founder of a sense of being Chinese) and the evident displays of faith by pilgrims, all place a high evaluation on the experience of being at the Mausoleum. They suggest that similar 'authenticities' could be found at the Marian sites of Europe.

Matteucci (2014) adds a further variable to the process of authentication when discussing pilgrimage tourism. The study suggest that a sense of self-fulfilment is often associated with a sense of achievement in the face of a challenge. Traditionally, pilgrimage is associated with journeys on foot, as with the Camino de Santiago, and it is thus a physiological and psychological challenge. The same applies to adventure tourism. Bungy jumping is generally regarded as an example of adventure tourism, but it is a product of generally short duration with most of the time taken with the preamble to the jump and the final recapture by staff. It combines being generally physically safe with the psychological challenge of jumping into space. The outcome is a heightened sense of achievement. Laviolette (2011) cites Søren Kierkegaard in noting that in the moment of decision to jump, at a point of fear and trembling, that is the point 'when one faces his or her own God, an all-encompassing understanding from the body that exists out with rhyme or reason. Pure viscerality' (Laviolette, 2011: 1). The presence of challenge, whether of a long duration such as 'walking the way' or of a short duration, as in bungee jumping, intensifies the sense of active participation and the experience of 'doing'. It reinforces the agency of the tourist's own self in creating an 'authentic experience'. Matteucci's (2014) notion is that authenticity is an exercise of agency, of a positive sense of being involved in a process of importance to the tourist. This does seem to require significant pre-planning on the part of the tourist, and it presents a view different to the study by Ryan *et al.* (2023) of backpackers' peak experiences when it can be argued that serendipity and the unexpected can peak experiences such as viewing a cloud of meteors sweeping across a cloudless night sky.

Gardiner *et al.* (2022) return to a long-discussed issue of whether it is possible to have an authentic experience with a facsimile built at a place that possesses no relationship with the original. They comment that post-modernity has no issue with inauthenticity (Gardiner *et al.*, 2022: 3) and their work reinforces this notion with a study of a Medieval Festival being held in Australia. The medieval culture being evidenced is thus entirely divorced from reality by time and geographical location. They utilise the dimensions of degree of client participation (active or passive) and connection (absorption vs immersion derived from Pine & Gilmore, 1999), interpreting absorption as a desire to learn. This represents a slight misreading of Pine and Gilmore's statement that absorption is 'occupying a person's attention by bringing the experience into the mind' (Pine & Gilmore, 1999: 31). Equally, immersion is interpreted as a desire for escapism. According to Pine and Gilmore, the escapism represents a polar opposite to pure entertainment (and tends to represent a state of 'voyaging to' (Pine & Gilmore, 1999: 34)). Gardiner *et al.* (2022) imply that the visitor to the Medieval Fair is wishing to escape to a world different to that of the modernity. This very brief statement of concepts does imply a possibility of semantic confusion over the dimensions and quadrants of the Pine and Gilmore (1999) model, but Gardiner *et al.* are very clear in their findings that education, entertainment, escapism, aesthetics and staging are the key determinants of visitors' attitudes towards the product. In short, it seems that objective authenticity simply has no role to play, and authenticity lies in the mind of the beholder, as per Protagoras's dictum. Actually, examining the results of the study, a cluster analysis of respondents' attitudes implies that interest in the arts and culture of the medieval period tended to be higher than interest in religion, yet a historian may question how, for that period, is it possible (objectively?) to disentangle religion from general culture.

In many ways, as Gardiner *et al.* (2022) admit, the findings tend to reinforce prior results. Ryan (2007a), writing of the re-enactment of the Battle of Aicken by the American Civil War Enactment Societies, clearly describes the immersion and absorption of participants driven by senses of geographical, historical and familial linkages to the events of that War. Equally, in another chapter he describes the temporal decay of memories associated with objective realities when describing the difficulties facing conservation of the aircraft carrier *Yorktown* (Ryan, 2007b), noting that memories dim over time and undermine the connection between current and past generations. It does appear that 'connectedness' is an important component in not simply generating a 'peak experience' but also in terms of sustaining meanings extracted from such experiences so that they contribute to a sustained improvement in the quality of life and the living of that life. Yet such an observation further reinforces the notion that authenticity is increasingly being driven by the meaning imputed to the object and activity within the context of place and time by the tourist and less by an objective authenticity. Reverting back to the example of the confusion between objective data of the Wars of the Roses and the series *Game of Thrones*, we are seeing an emergent imputed meaning to places and things premised on false understandings. In this way, scholarship on tourism begins to parallel discussions in the political and wider social science fields that came to the fore after the events of 6 January 2021 and the storming of the US Capitol Building (Cooner & McMurray, 2022).

Another parallel between tourism and a wider literature is that between tourism and marketing. It cannot be denied that the marketing literature has had an impact on the thinking of several researchers who have adopted instruments and concepts derived from, in particular, research into the FMCG (Fast-Moving Consumer Goods) literature, especially that related to brands. Consequently, many studies of destinations have conceived of destinations being akin to a brand and have argued that revisiting a location is akin to the continuous purchase of, say, a brand of toothpaste. This is a notion that does not appeal to many tourism scholars, a view generally concurred with by the current authors. As has been pointed out in earlier chapters, the tourist is often one who has travelled from afar at costs of time and financial resource, and revisitation at best may be infrequent. Given gaps in time, the destination may well have changed, while previous visits also shape expectations, and hence no revisitation exactly imitates the first. However, researchers who incline to the adaptation of FMCG marketing theories have also viewed authenticity as simply another measured variable among others that shape revisitation.

One example is the work of Shi *et al.* (2022). They define brand awareness as the strength of presence in a consumer's mind, brand image as the rational and emotive evaluation of the brand and brand equity as the relative comparative strength of the brand in relation to its competitors. Brand loyalty is the consumers' attachment to the brand and comprises attitudinal and behavioural loyalties. They then conceive of brand authenticity being objective, constructive and existential. Destination brand authenticity is measured by dimensions of originality, continuity, credibility and 'being upright'. In a standard statistical approach, satisfaction is perceived as a mediating variable between destination authenticity and revisit intention, and equally satisfaction has a mediating role between brand equity and revisit intention. To further the model, destination familiarity is conceived as being a moderating role between brand equity and revisit intention.

The stage is thus set for a collection of data, and the location selected is that of Guilin in China. Thus, from the perspective of this chapter, one turns to how 'authenticity' is measured. The measures are those that 'Guilin persists through time', 'Guilin is a timeless brand', 'Guilin will not betray you', 'Guilin keeps its value promise, 'Guilin is an honest destination brand', 'Guilin has moral principles', 'Guilin is true to a set of moral values', 'Guilin cares about its consumers', 'Guilin embodies the important values that tourists care about', 'Guilin links visitors to their true selves' and 'Guilin links visitors to things that really matter for them'. They finally conclude, after analysing the data, that 'destination brand authenticity positively impacts destination brand equity and revisit intention. Hence, managers should prioritize monitoring and improving their services and provide tourists with authentic travel experiences' (Shi *et al.*, 2022: 772). Consequently, they suggest 'configuring' traditional performances for tourists and encouraging tourist participation in such activities.

It could be argued that the findings and recommendations are quite evident, and many managers would already be attempting to find ways in which they could better involve visitors, but the paper makes observations of nuanced differences that contribute to understanding how perceptions of authenticity interact with measures of tourist loyalty. Yet, there remains a caveat. The items cited above are drawn from previous research, and the only testing in the current paper is a testing of statistical reliability. Statistical programmes are primarily about the relationships between numbers and in themselves can say nothing about how respondents understand the questions, and while accepting the rationale proffered by Shi *et al.* (2022) for the measures of authenticity one is left with questions. How does a geographical location have moral principles and moral values? It might, if associated with a place of pilgrimage or association with a philosopher or philosophical stance be associated with ethics and be symbolic of a particular set of values – but as a broad geographical term, how did respondents understand the question? And is it not the experience of activities at the place that links visitors to their true selves – not a place *per se*? And, to use the researchers' own terminology, is it not the values represented by an image of place that may affect self-image – but what are the values associated with the place? Yet again we appear to be defining one set of descriptive terms by applying another set of adjectives or rather opaque patterns of terminology.

Conclusion

Authenticity and authenticity of experience are commonly thought to be of importance in tourism, but the authenticity of place and authenticity of experience are separable entities. From a very pragmatic perspective it seems that the term 'authentic experience' can be interpreted in two ways. The first is that it represents an experience of the original – in short it is the first of Wang's interpretations. It is the second sense, that is, what is the authenticity of our own experience of what we consider to be real that presents, as just discussed, the real conundrum. Humans are capable of fantasising, and of self-delusion. Equally, tourism is capable of offering facsimiles of places and events far divorced from the original – as evidenced by King Tutankhamen's tomb at the Luxor Casino in Las Vegas or the Eiffel Tower in Shenzhen. The tourist cognitively 'knows' they are false but can derive enjoyment, a playful understanding that this is not real, but to understand the joke must have the knowledge that the real is elsewhere. Yet the emotional authenticity of enjoyment remains with the tourist at the time of the activity and into the future of recall, and possibly even in a past of anticipation. Moore *et al.* summarise the role of authenticity in tourism research as being 'In theory, as a contentious, complicated and disputed construct; empirically, as a recurrent theme in accounts of tourist experiences of place and culture and as a quality of tourists' experiences' (Moore *et al.*, 2021: 1). Indeed, they provide the adjective 'mischievous' as a description of the theories of authenticity in tourism.

There is an inherent dualism in the concept, for authenticity signals an objective reality about the place that is visited, and the activity undertaken, but it is experienced through senses and understood in the light of past knowledge gained and evaluated through emotion. It has also become a troublesome concept as the world moves into a state where not only is abstract knowledge important, but images are commercialised and consumed. Yet authenticity remains at the core of tourism. This book was motivated by a belief that the core of tourism is not necessarily travel but rather the experiences gained from travel – hence one speaks of visitor experiences so that tourism and travel is related to the world of recreation and leisure. But today's world is teetering on an edge of technology that may be able to offer technologies that fool the senses. In the 19th century, Marx was said to have identified religion as the opium of the masses. In the 20th century, at least in some parts of the developed world, opiates became an opium that relieved people of pain, stress and yet caused physical and psychological distress. If tourism is justified by offering escape that permits relaxation and self-examination, while immersion in virtual reality, gaming and holographic representations become possible, are they not an equivalent to the bread and circuses of the latter days of Rome? Or alternatively, are they the 'feelies' of Huxley's *Brave New World* that become the next opium of the 21st century?

8 Making the Unfamiliar Familiar: Place Attachment

This chapter includes:

(a) The emergence of holiday and second homes.
(b) Holiday homes and place attachment.
(c) Place attachment – the determinants of place attachment.
(d) Place attachment and senses of self.
(e) Place attachment and new technologies.

Introduction

At the end of Chapter 7, one aspect of debate about 'authenticity' was that it was suggested that tourists were attracted to 'authentic' destinations and experiences. This was thought to reinforce a sense of 'destination loyalty' that was evidenced by a willingness to recommend a place to others and by a strengthening of a desire to make repeat visits. Subsequent visits to a destination initiates learning about a place and a greater familiarity with the location occurs. That familiarity includes a greater knowledge of the geography of place and possibly the creation of favourite places that come to account for a greater proportion of visits, while other places are visited less frequently. In addition to familiarity with the natural and built environments of the place, a social familiarity is developed as the repeat visitor comes to better know residents within the destination. Consequently, there are two themes to this chapter. They are place attachment and senses of tourist responsibility.

Generally, it might be said that the most likely initial source of getting to know local residents is through a repeat patronage of retail outlets and favoured restaurants, while if a routine is established that creates a local pattern of walking to those shops and restaurants at much the same time, then familiar figures appear, and eventually initially polite recognitions of a morning salutation might lead to a conversation through which a friendship might be established. Equally, repetitive patronage of a restaurant for a morning coffee leads to a recognition of other customers and over time the morning coffee may become a routine conversation with a local resident.

For this to occur, the frequency and duration of repeat visitation needs to be quite high and probably beyond that of a simple summer holiday visit. The spread of ownership of holiday homes permits such high levels of frequent visits to the 'holiday place' as it permits the possibility of a longer summer stay and also the use of holiday accommodation over various national holiday weekends. In addition, and reinforced by the experience of Covid, the development of the internet and the movement towards more service-based, customer support roles and analytically based occupations has meant that it is possible for more work to be undertaken in the home environment. For example, much of this book was completed at three locations, namely the authors' offices, their primary homes and a holiday home, while other writing has been completed in hotel rooms. Access to data, reports and an exchange of ideas has become increasingly geographically mobile while co-workers communicate online, and equally services to clients are also online. The combination of fuzzy distinctions between the workplace and home and the want and ability to own a second home in a desired place have together permitted the development of a place attachment to a location other than one's main residence for an increasing number of people. In tourism, it appears that the concept of place attachment was in fact first used when considering holiday home ownership (Coppock, 1977).

Prior to discussing the conceptual development of tourist place attachment, it should be recognised that this is yet a further example of how tourism complements social issues that arise from the inequalities of income and wealth that have become an important issue in recent decades. Indeed, the 2021 World Economic Forum Report argued that the Covid pandemic added to existing inequalities in income. It was calculated that, on a global scale, the richest 10% of the world's population received 52% of global income (World Economic Forum, 2021). Inequalities in income are measured by the Gini coefficient where the value of zero represents equality of income. The World Bank (2022) reported that the Gini coefficient was 0.382 for China in 2019, 0.49 for the United States and 0.38 for the UK. It is recognised that these are very crude estimates and the literature notes that many nuances need to be considered including age profiles, taxation policies and disposable income levels, and equally income is only one criterion. Possibly more important is the inclusion of wealth, as that includes any inheritance received from past family members. Piketty (2014) analysed income and wealth data for 20 countries for periods extending back into the 18th century and concluded that under current social and economic conditions many countries were heading back to late Victorian inequalities of income and wealth. For example, Rashbrooke (2021) calculated that in New Zealand the top 1% of the population had assets exceeding NZ$7 million per capita whilst the lowest 50% had a net worth of NZ$12,438 per capita. Rashbrooke also notes that Gini coefficients can vary considerably in response to social trends and global events such as wars and pandemics. But he too notes that since the 1980s and the adoption of trickle-down economic policies, the share of wealth taken by the top 10% of the population has increased. He notes that in New Zealand in the 1890s the top 1% of the population held about two-thirds of all the assets and tends to agree with Picketty as to general post-Covid trends that promise a potential reversion to past inequalities of wealth.

There is a lesson in this digression for tourism. What is often overlooked is that tourism is indeed a vast industry involving the international movement of more than a billion people, but these are the people who can afford to travel. As such, they represent 12% of the global population, to which can be added those who are only engaging in domestic travel. But it can be concluded that if a formation of place attachment can be achieved through the ownership of holiday homes or the ability to undertake frequent repeat visitation to a place, then it is suggested that we are probably speaking of again the world's top 10% of the population. This takes us to a second theme in this chapter which is the concept of the 'responsible tourist'.

Holiday Homes and Place Attachment

The topic of holiday homes is one useful way to enter a discussion of place attachment from the visitor's perspective, because, as far as we can discern, it was with reference to holiday homes that the concept entered the tourism literature. The antecedents of place attachment seemingly began in environmental psychology as noted in Chapter 1 with the work of Guiliani (1991), Korpela (1989), Lalli (1992) and Twigger-Ross and Uzzell (1996). Looking back at that literature, we find that in turn the concept evolved from studies of child development that examined the interaction between mothers and children (Morgan, 2010) and mother-child bonding. For example, Ainsworth (1969) notes that the term 'attachment' seems to have originated with the work of Bowlby (1958, 1969) who sought to reassess concepts of dependency upon a parent by substituting the term 'attachment' for dependency. This was to specifically direct attention to the role of emotion in the relationships between child and parent.

Place attachment from the outset has therefore incorporated 'emotion' as a key component when applying to tourism. Another early paper of importance is that of Tuan (1975). He begins by locating experiences within the senses, but also imputing different roles to those senses. Taste, smell and feel are perceived as more passive modes of receiving information, but he designates sight and hearing as more active ways of exploration. Indeed, he writes that 'seeing is thinking' (Tuan, 1975: 152). Like others, Tuan perceives places as centres of meaning, but he again distinguishes places like home from the wider world including cities, each classification possessing differing meanings. The home, he suggests, is a place of privacy. This perspective implies that the holiday home is a place of privacy, yet often it is a place of family-based and potential commercial accommodation hosting friends, guests and paying guests through apps such as Airbnb.

This early approach to structuring scales of place and attribution of meanings to distinctive private and public places paralleled the work of those adopting a phenomenological approach to concepts of place attachment. Thus, commentators such as Arronson link holiday home ownership to the concept of authenticity discussed in the previous chapter. He writes, 'vacation residence is both an expression of escape from modernity and a longing for authenticity, roots and identity in a place. ... In a more and more placeless world, vacation residence stands out as meaningful and filled with sense of place' (Arronson, 2004: 77).

Research into the use of holiday homes and their meaning has a long history in several parts of the world. From a historical perspective, there have long been holiday homes. The Roman aristocracy had their summer villas away from Rome, and throughout history rulers and their courts had places in addition to their main places of residence. With the growth of a mercantile class and then managerial class during the industrial revolution, the increasingly confident and richer middle class copied the pattern of aristocratic second home ownership. Indeed, Birch (1973) reports that among his respondents some regarded the ownership of a holiday home as a sign of 'arrival' in their career and lives – that they had 'achieved'. Early examples of participation in a holiday home for many less privileged was often made possible through charitable enterprises or individuals. For example, Von (1933) provides the example of Pastor Bion who first took 68 Zurich children to the countryside in 1876, motivated by the idea that a change of scenery and activity could literally 'recharge their vitality'. This would be an early example of social tourism through which underprivileged families who could ill afford holidays would be supported by charitable organisations or indeed business organisations in the tourism industry who would offer such holidays as a pre-season 'soft opening' to train seasonal staff (Ryan, 2002b).

Birch (1973) and Coppock (1977) identify a number of motivations and types of experiences being sought by the post-Second World War generation of an affluent middle class when buying a holiday property in Britain. Both classify a number of reasons that remain important more than a half-century later. It is the realisation of a dream through which the owner can express individuality by enjoying an 'unpressurised lifestyle' (Birch, 1973: 3), a chance to reconnect with nature so as to enjoy 'peace and quiet' (Birch, 1973: 120). Another motive lay in a number of people planning to use their second home as a potential place for retirement. Birch also noted other studies that showed quite high usage rates of holiday homes in Weardale and Denbighshire in the UK, both locations set in areas of outstanding natural beauty. The contemporary use of holiday homes has a long history and as early as the 1960s Clout (1971) was able to identify patterns of clusters of holiday home ownership among French families seeking second homes in desirable areas of that country. That raises an issue of to what extent holiday home ownership might be driven by a demand emanating from the more affluent within nearby urban cities, or whether it is driven by externally induced visitors from much further away. As an aside, it might be noted that Zoğal *et al.* (2020), noting how many second home owners travelled to their second homes during the Covid pandemic, suggested that such homes were a place of refuge, while at the same time such travel carried a risk of transmission of the virus to rural communities that possessed fewer hospital facilities if required.

In some parts of the world, second home ownership might be said to have acquired a cultural significance. In New Zealand, the 'bach' if in North Island, or the 'crib' in South Island, has an almost iconic status of being associated with long summer beach holidays where traditionally the front porches were littered with old chairs and surf boards, cold drinks were in an old beaten-up fridge and nights were spent gossiping while watching the stars (e.g. Walters, 2011, 2019). Bogardus (2013) also argues that in the period after 1945 it was another manifestation of 'Kiwi Blokeness' and inventiveness as bits of wood and metal were hammered onto the sometimes failing fabric of what were initially wooden shacks – completed as a change from a day's fishing. However, time and changing economics have wrought a transformation of the hitherto simple bach, and seaside and particularly beach properties have become well-endowed and furnished buildings attracting very high prices often well over a million dollars (Walters, 2019). In areas of Auckland, such beach properties have attracted controversy as owners now wish to access their holiday homes by helicopter. Walters (2019) suggests that a combination of commercialism and neoliberal economic policies since the 1980s are probably causal factors for such changes.

If this is the case, then one would expect to find similar changes in other parts of the globe. Several of the Scandinavian countries and additionally Canada had traditions similar to New Zealand in having generational ownership of much-loved family holiday homes – the only difference being that in such countries these homes tended to be situated by lakesides rather than the beach. Vittersø (2007) analyses changes in the Norwegian equivalent to the New Zealand 'bach' or Canadian 'cabin', which is the *hytte*. He notes a growing pattern of holiday home purchases by Norwegians, not only within their own country but also overseas. This is also accompanied by the size of the homes increasing and as found in other countries, a growing standard of facilities and comfort including holiday homes with access to internet that permit maintaining contact with work and relaxation derived from viewing streaming services like

Netflix. Like Walters (2011, 2019), he draws a distinction between the traditional holiday home with its connotations of 'back' to nature and family bonding with the more hedonistic styles of the package holidays or holidaying at resort complexes. But as holiday homes grow and become better equipped, so too, slowly, has the nature of the holiday experience changed. He notes how there is less emphasis on cabin maintenance and a greater propensity to employ others to do that work. Also, the recreational equipment becomes upgraded, something also seen in New Zealand with many bach owners having boats and jet skis. Vittersø (2007) notes that while parents may wish to emulate their past holidaying activities such as hiking or cross-country skiing, as their children grow older the latter will often prefer a more commercial activity such as downhill skiing. Nonetheless, family bonding through shared mealtimes and an emphasis on being 'outdoors' continues to be important.

For their part Nouza et al. (2018) examined holiday home ownership in Iceland and again report significant increases in such ownership. Their examination of motives for ownership reveals similarities to the research findings reported above, notably the demand for experiencing a different place and relaxation. They also observe a more recent trend noted by other researchers, which is a growing importance of the acquired property as an investment. Like all investments, there is then a desire for a rate of return, and while the 'soft returns' of having an accessible 'home away from home' are present in people's minds, so too are the opportunities for commercially renting the property to other holidaymakers through social media outlets such as Airbnb. That, in turn, has significant implications for communities as is illustrated by the work of Ryan and Ma (2021). They describe how a combination of past neoliberal economic policies, the desire for second home ownership and peer-to-peer social media has had negative impacts on tenants and tourism operators in Raglan in New Zealand. They note longer-term local tenants are displaced during the summer season in favour of higher-paying tourists and while tourism operators may want seasonal workers, they cannot offer accommodation to such employees. In short, disruptions in a local housing market occur when housing supply fails to keep up with housing demand and these become particularly evident in popular summer-time locations.

A slightly different picture emerges when considering British ownership of holiday homes since approximately the 1990s. Gallent and Tewdwr-Jones (2020) clearly indicate how ownership of holiday homes within Europe has been determined by other factors including the inheritance of homes from grandparents and also economic decline in areas marginal to the emergent mainstream of economic activity. This has meant the emergence of houses being offered in rural or seaside areas where job opportunities are scarce. Such economic conditions have led to a fall in house prices, or indeed to homes falling into a state of dereliction. This last has been particularly noted in Italy where the authorities have specifically initiated policies of cheap property purchasing to encourage home buying with conditions that will aid such areas economically (Di Figlia, 2016). Many of the British have been attracted to holiday home ownership in the South of France due to attractively priced properties being highlighted in the quality Sunday newspapers by their travel writers and the popularity of such books as those by Peter Mayles about Provence including *Encore Provence: New Adventures in the South of France* (Mayles, 2000). Additionally, prior to Brexit, a combination of easy access to the countries of the European Union in terms of travel formalities, the development of low-cost flights to secondary airports and transferable superannuation payments meant that many retirees also chose to live significant parts of the year in their holiday homes. Williams *et al.* (2000) comment that distance from family was not an overly problematic issue for many retirees, citing that the obligations of family membership and friendship are complex but distance has relatively little impact. Communication by phone or internet can be as frequent as is desired, an emotional independence generated by having separate homes can be fulfilling and indeed make family visits even more meaningful, and they found significant variation in the cases then examined.

Another aspect of holiday homes that is emerging in the literature relates to the increasing use of campervans and caravans (Hall & Müller, 2018a). Both support Urry's (2016) notion that greater mobilities are one facet of a post-modern lifestyle, and hence the holiday home is itself becoming mobile offering not only a recreational place away from the main residence but also a choice of not being fixed to a location. However, as discussed below, with that choice comes the opportunity cost of not establishing neighbourhood links as discussed below. One caveat to that observation is that evidence exists of campervan owners selecting given sites at specific times of the year because of friendly relationships being established with others who camp at the same site (Hardy, 2017). Hassell *et al.* (2015) examine camping in National Parks and refer to their respondents liking the disconnection from responsibility and the internet to strengthen existing friendships and secure new ones. Sometimes, this might outlive the initial cause of such relationships that were created by friendships established by children, particularly in cases where camping brought together families with common interests over children, including health issues (Martiniuk *et al.*, 2014; Parker & Seal, 1996). Wu and Pearce (2014) also show how the internet can be used to establish friend and familial bonding over distance in the case of Chinese campervan holidaying in Australia.

Another issue noted by Hall and Müller (2018b) is that of sustainability. The emergence of second and holiday home ownership has been premised to a large extent on relatively low costs of travel, but that assumption can be questioned when fossil fuels are subject to high price shocks induced by events such as the Russian invasion of Ukraine in

2022, while issues of peak supply continue. A second factor is a growing concern of carbon emissions resulting from land and air-based travel and the desire to address those issues. Hall and Müller (2018b) suggest that the growth of holiday home ownership contributes to greater carbon emissions. A counterargument is that if true, a longer-term solution is increasingly closer to being practical. That solution is the advent of electric vehicles, and even interim steps of hybrid and plug-in hybrid vehicles show significant diminution in fuel per kilometre travelled. While true, that answer does not assess the resources used to generate electricity and if coal-powered power stations are being used that raises a whole set of alternative questions about efficiency and also the consequent distribution of local as well as global degradation. Further questions are also noted as to the ability to recycle and recapture the rare minerals within the batteries while critics also suggest that mining practices are very far from ideal (Liu & Agusdinata, 2020).

Another aspect of holiday home ownership much discussed in the literature is that it is a means of tourism-induced change in destinations. This has been long recognised in the destination management literature with both Miossec (1976, 1977) and Young (1983) specifically referencing the changing patterns of land and home usage as places are 'discovered' by more affluent citizens seeking their holiday escapes in places to which they have become attached. Other books discuss the issues of destination management under tourism-induced change including Ryan (2020) but for the purposes of this text, it needs to be recognised that non-permanent residents can account for a significant proportion of visitors to an area. Yet, the question of the experience of non-permanent residents and their experiences of place remains a relatively under-researched subject in the tourism literature. One exception is the paper by Kelly and Hosking (2008), who analysed the responses of approximately 1000 home owners who, according to the local Shire Council of Augusta-Margaret River in Western Australia, had addresses outside of the Shire. These records are based on the demands for rates or property taxes collected by local authorities for local services such as sewage, water supply, waste collection and road maintenance.

It was notable that about 70% of the property owners recorded higher than average household incomes. Kelly and Hosking (2008) found that frequency of visitation correlated with higher levels of place attachment, as did future intentions, and plans included longer stays when retired. As might be expected from the above discussion, the appeal of a natural landscape and more relaxing lifestyle featured as causes of place attachment, and they refer to a congruity of place with senses of self-identity.

There are policy implications arising from the sense of place attachment experienced by holiday homeowners. It is suggested that the social relationships developed by such property owners contribute to not only a sense of place attachment but also to community attachment. Kelly and Hosking (2008) specifically state that such an appeal to second home purchasers may inhibit the purchasing of homes solely for investment purposes. It should, however, be noted that the paper was written prior to the widespread use of peer-to-peer services such as Airbnb or Tujia, and this innovation has increased the problems of less permanent populations that have little attachment to place while causing problems for longer-term renters described by Ryan and Ma (2021) among others.

One can question as a result of these findings if concepts such as community identification need to be more closely assessed in an age of greater mobility of information and geographical movement. Gurney *et al.* suggest that 'as human–environment interactions change with increasing mobility (both corporeal and that mediated by communication and information technology), new types of people–place relations that transcend geographic and social boundaries and do not require ongoing direct experience to form are emerging' (Gurney *et al.*, 2017: 10077). One answer they propose from a study of 5403 residents living in 12 coastal regions bordering the Great Barrier Reef off the east coast of Australia is the enhancement of community attachment rather than place attachment. In their study, they found four types of community attachment among their respondents. First were the 'Armchair Community', that is, those with little place dependency but who identified with the Reef. Second were the 'Reef Connected Community' scoring highly on all attributes of place attachment. Third were the 'Reef User Community' who scored high on direct and indirect place dependency, but low on place identity. Last were the 'Reef Disconnected Community' who scored low on items of both place dependency and identity. The challenge for encouraging policies premised on engendering community attachment is the need to change attitudes and subsequent behaviours. In the study, only about 15% of the sample scored highly on both place dependency and place identity, while 21% of the total formed the 'Reef Disconnected Community'.

Reference to work on stress that can occur within communities facing change also requires consideration of the formation of groups and tensions between groups. Visitor senses of place attachment can obviously be undermined by less than satisfactory interactions with members of the host community. In a world of 'over-tourism', it is evident that such occasions can occur (Dodds & Butler, 2019). Even in the absence of over-tourism, there is little doubt that tensions can arise within tourist destinations as incoming 'new residents' arrive within seaside destinations. This was anticipated by Lyons (1982), who considered issues associated with the arrival of seasonal workers in a UK seaside town. Among those findings, he found tensions existed between young migrant workers and local youth at bars and dance halls. In a series of papers Chen *et al.* (2021, 2022a, 2022b) have made distinctions between generational responses to tourism-induced change and also the relationship between well-established residents and those newly arrived. They also suggest that age, greater mobility, familiarity with internet-based communication and database systems, governmental policies and other factors combine to influence the intra-community tensions that arise to greater or lesser degrees when facing tourism-induced change.

When examining the impact of tourism on the ethnic minority group, the Tuva people of Xinjiang Province in China, Yang *et al.* (2014) had recourse to the sociological approach adopted by Coser (1956) who observed that dispute, contention and possibly crisis was not an aberration but rather a natural process inherent within transformations of communities. This continues to be borne out by studies of change as evidenced by the work of Li *et al.* (2023) among the Russian-speaking enclaves in northern China. Consequently, one can conclude that the economic context of the resort area, the respective ease of access to capital by local and external businesses, the degrees of open-mindedness exhibited by residents, the nature of the tourists and the patterns of shared experiences are important.

When considering such findings, the concept of place attachment comes to have a wider meaning than simply referring to repeat purchasing or the formation of an intention to revisit or recommend a place to others when considering holiday homes. The remaining part of this chapter relates to further examining the concept and role of place attachment and its relationship to visitor experiences.

Place Attachment

Nouza *et al.* (2018) found in their study of Icelandic ownership of holiday homes that those with close prior ties to the location of that home stood out as having distinctive differences from other holiday homeowners. First, relatively easy and close accessibility to the holiday home tended to be less important for the former than the latter. From our perspective, one important finding was that the distance-decay effect played a relatively minor role in the choice of location of the holiday home. Simply put, the distance-decay concept argues that that there is an inverse relationship between interaction and distance – that is, the further the distance between two locations the less is the interaction. The concept, although initially geographical, has also been applied to cultures. In short, the greater the distance between two cultures, the less the interaction. Both interpretations have relevance to tourism and visitor experiences. That the relationship is found wanting (Martin *et al.*, 2017; McKercher & Chow So-Ming, 2001) is not wholly surprising given that a core motive behind tourism is the search for difference (Dann, 1981). Yee and Ismail (2020) report a literature review of the concept and reveal many different nuances emerging from past research. They suggest variance exists between rural and urban tourism, while measures such as frequencies of visitation, duration of stay, pricing and other variables have a role to play. Additionally, McKercher (2018) reviews some of his own prior research into distance-decay relationships, notes the existence of 'Effective Tourism Exclusion Zones' due to non-participation in tourism and finds differences between short-haul and long-haul destinations and specific market segment differences. In short, for those with higher incomes it can be suggested that emotional ties to a place can overcome at least the monetary costs associated with long-haul travel.

Place attachment is certainly a concept that has attracted significant amounts of interest from scholars. A quick Google Scholar search reveals more than a quarter of a million papers that define or utilise the concept. As noted above, in the field of tourism the concept first attracted attention several decades ago, and many early papers cited the work of Coppock (1977) as being a pioneering work in its collection of studies and critiques of holiday homes. Initial studies of place attachment in tourism were much influenced by Coppock, notably the studies by Graham Brown and his colleagues. Brown initially examined the relationship between tourists and frequency of visitation and place attachment as part of his doctoral thesis at Texas A&M University. He might well be regarded as one of the foundation scholars of tourism as he helped establish tourism courses in the 1980s at what was then the Dorset Institute of Higher Education, which today is better known as the University of Bournemouth. Today, he holds a professorial position at the University of New South Wales. In his doctoral thesis, he identified that an emotional attachment to place had economic implications that included the purchase of holiday homes (Brown, 1990).

On arriving in Australia, Brown has continued his interest in place attachment and tourists as evidenced by the papers by Gross and Brown in 2006 and 2008. In 2006 they observed that a combination of the concepts of place attachment and involvement was relatively new in the field of tourism research. For that paper, they surveyed visitors in South Australia using a 35-item scale to identify the dimensions that formed place attachment as understood by tourists. Those items were drawn from prior research in marketing research and recreational studies including the concept of involvement advanced by Dimanche and Havitz (1997), as discussed in prior chapters. The context, as is often the case, has importance because South Australia is famed for the Barossa Valley and the quality of its red wines, notably from the Shiraz grape, and wine and food has become a feature of its tourism product. As a result, questions pertaining to culinary and wine tourism were also included. Therefore, and as a test of the logicality of respondents' replies, food and wine emerged as a dimension of place attachment (Gross & Brown, 2006) when using exploratory factor analysis. However, it is probably the other factors that are of more general interest.

These other factors were designated as being 'attachment', 'centrality', 'attraction' and 'expression'. The items that clustered to form the factor 'attachment' refer to identification with the place and reinforces research that locates place identity as a component congruent with place attachment. Gross and Brown note that this factor poses some issues of definition in that it includes items such as 'The distinctive lifestyle of the region is something that attracted me here'. The concept of a place supporting a sense of self identity is caught by the factor 'expression' wherein respondents agreed that the place makes a statement that they feel is consistent with whom they actually are. In short, the features of the place support aspects of self-concept. Thus, attending or participating in a given activity or being present at a specific place is symbolic of a person being adventurous, cultured or 'sexy'. 'Centrality' referred to proxies for the level of importance and interest in engaging in tourism activities such as 'If I stopped engaging in tourism experiences, I would probably lose touch with a lot of my friends'. 'Attraction' related to statements of the enjoyment being derived from being at the place and participating in activities at a generic level. One example of the items included in this factor is 'I really enjoy engaging in tourism experiences'.

In 2008, Gross and Brown returned to the topic of visitor's attachment of place again using the associated concept of involvement. In this case they utilised the technique of covariance-based structural equation modelling that had become a popular technique among many researchers. One reason for the popularity of the technique is that it not only quantifies a statistical relationship between independent and dependent variables, but it also measures the relationship between the independent variables. A second reason for the popularity of the technique was the advent of advanced programs that could run successfully on laptops allied to an ability to set up proposed relationships via a diagrammatic interface. This bypassed a need to program relationships, while some critics also suggested that such ease also bypassed a need to fully understand the process. Ryan (2020b) has also criticised the usage made of some programs because authors 'dive' into the sequence of establishing causalities without closely examining the quality of the data in terms of patterns of skew, thereby avoiding potential issues of non-normality and indeed, non-linearity of relationships. It is added that these latter comments are of a general nature and not a criticism of the article by Gross and Brown.

Taking advantage of confirmatory factor analysis that sought to assess the degree to which 'expression', 'attachment', 'attraction' and 'centrality' as measures of involvement contribute to a measure of place attachment, they concluded that 'involvement in tourism experiences was a positive predictor for both dimensions of place attachment for the involvement dimensions of centrality to lifestyle and food & wine' (Gross & Brown, 2008: 1148). They suggested that the more tourism experiences play a central role in a visitor's lifestyle, the more is the emotional attachment to place. They also found that 'attraction' was a negative predictor for place dependency and had no statistical relationship with place identity.

Taken together, one can say that these findings are congruent with much that has been found in prior studies within the field of environmental psychology, namely that distinctions can be made between place attachment, place identity and place dependency. It can be asked, why such an emphasis on these two studies? They are important because with other work by Brown and Gross and their other associates they did much to draw the attention of tourism scholars to the concepts of place attachment and they laid the groundwork for much of the work that followed in tourism research. However, after 2008 a distinction emerges in the literature. Coincidentally in the same year as Gross and Brown's second paper, Gu and Ryan (2008), in a study of Beijing's hutong, pointed out that much of the previous tourism literature using place attachment had been studied from the perspective of the tourist, but if anyone had an attachment to place it would most likely be the residents of place. They also noted that tourism-induced change was most likely to impact on the place dependency, place identity and place attachment of the residents, especially if those changes were relatively rapid and significant in size.

This observation led to a significant amount of research on residents' place attachment, particularly because the impacts of tourism on communities had long been a subject of research ever since the formalisation of frameworks for tourism research had been established by such publications as Alister Mathieson and Geoff Wall's (1982) *Tourism: Economic, Physical, and Social Impacts* and Peter Murphy's (1985) *Tourism: A Community Approach*. For many academics, these would probably be regarded as two of the seminal books in tourism literature. That baton of tourism-induced change and place attachment was then taken up and included research by many including Strzelecka *et al.* (2017), Stylidis (2018a, 2018b) and Ganji *et al.* (2021). These three examples also highlight the concern of several researchers, which was to what extent would tourism-induced change influence residents' support for tourism? Other researchers adopted an alternative but congruent perspective being more concerned about the impact on residents' quality of life (Li *et al.*, 2021; Ramkissoon, 2023). As research advanced in this topic area, so one can also discern new nuances emerging in the research. As noted above, Chen *et al.* (2021) looked at intergenerational patterns of change and how age cohorts responded differently to tourism-induced change. The existing studies on tourists' attachment to place also hint at future consequential links between residents and holiday home non-permanent residents when the latter reach the stage of retirement. There are already signs of such changes in seaside locations in New Zealand. For example, after several years of planning, the seaside town of Whitianga on the Coromandel peninsula has commenced an upgrading of existing medical facilities by attaching them to a new residential complex for seniors. In China, Pan *et al.* (2021) analysed future demand from Chinese retirees for residential homes and the preference by many for retirement in rural areas. They suggested that the development of senior care rest homes in rural areas would complement China's poverty alleviation policies in rural areas through tourism and have the extended impact of providing better community health care that could benefit others besides retirees.

Following the logic of these research initiatives, there is, naturally, something of a spillover effect when comparing the use of place attachment theory in studying residents' reactions to change caused, at least in part by tourism, and tourists' attachment to a holiday destination as a reservoir of (hopefully) good memories. While core concepts associated with place attachment are place dependence and identity, others have been added to the lexicon. For example, 'place social bonding' is suggested by Kyle *et al.* (2005). The inclusion of social bonding is justified by reference to the earlier work of Low and Altman (1992) that emphasised the role of emotion, especially in the context of person-to-person bonding. Second, clusters of people and indeed cultures attach a consensual importance to places. For example, the Beijing Palace Museum is highly regarded by several Chinese just as Mount Rushmore with its carvings of four Presidents is similarly regarded by several Americans. Equally, cultural values may change, as too might personal human relationships, and this adds another variable, namely temporal change. Given such variations, it is also possible for different people to value the same place but for varying reasons. For one person a place is associated with nostalgic memories and for another it possesses an aesthetic value. Kyle *et al.* (2005) seek to (a) assess whether social bonding has an important role in seeking to explain people's desire to associate with place and (b) devise a sufficiently rigorous scale that measures that attachment to place. They create three models and conclude that the second with three dimensions, namely place dependency, place identity and social bonding presents the best results. There are issues, as the authors correctly explain in their paper, and it can be noted that there are only four items measuring each of the three dimensions. The nature of the items leads one to expect high correlations between each of the four items forming a dimension. Assuming a logicality of response by respondents, possibly the most interesting part of the paper is that there was some question as to which of two models was the better. Nonetheless, the rationale of imputing a role to social bonding as part of place attachment has some appeal.

Another aspect of place attachment has come to be labelled 'place affect'. It is recognised that various places possess attributes that trigger place affects among those who live in or visit a place. The term 'place affect' refers to the affective relationship and the expression of sentiments that a person has with a place. Tuan (1977) uses the term 'topophilia', that is, the love of place to express much the same feeling. At an individual level, 'place affect' may be associated with personal memories, often associated with childhood or other significant affects associated with life stage such as marriage, honeymoons and the like. But it has been suggested that place affect can be aggregative and a shared response. Qu *et al.* write that 'The sentiments are influenced and amplified by social investments through ways such as sharing experiences, communicating feelings and transforming from positive social emotions ... Affectively-attached mass tourists thus may transfer the importance they assign to the place they love and value to the more abstract concept of environment, and end up with extrinsic-driven environmental activation' (Qu *et al.*, 2019: 202). Zhang and Ryan (in press) suggest that place affect can create a uniformity of response to a place across many different sociodemographic groupings of visitors. They argue that this may be found in places of pilgrimage and suggest from a study of the Taihao Mausoleum that a shared cultural sense of collectivism, the very obvious acts of devotion shown by pilgrims, and the ambience of temples and grounds associated with cultural understanding of the foundation of China combined with an active respect for ancestor worship explain why common evaluations of visit experience resulted across different visitor profiles.

For their part, Ramkissoon *et al.* (2013) would seem to concur with this viewpoint while also introducing the term 'place satisfaction' to the lexicon of definitions associated with place attachment. Like many other researchers in this field, they recognise the multivalent nature of place that creates place attachment via place identity, dependency, socially valued experiences, bonding and place affect. These dimensions potentially generate place satisfaction. Their data is drawn from a survey of 452 questionnaires completed by visitors to the Dandenong Ranges National Park in Victoria, Australia. They concluded that place identity and place affect significantly contributed to place attachment. In turn, place attachment significantly contributed to place satisfaction.

In their study, place affect was measured by three items, namely 'I am very attached to this park', 'I feel a strong sense of belonging to this National park and its settings/facilities' and 'This National Park means a lot to me'. One can observe that there is a significant overlap between these items and those listed above when discussing the work of Gross and Brown (2006). This observation does in part explain some of the problems associated with place attachment research. The core dimensions of place identity, place dependence, place attachment and extensions to concepts such as community identity and the relationships with evaluations of visit experiences often indicate that while separate concepts, the measure of these concepts involves a potential fuzziness of definition at the level at which the respondent understands the question. In part, this may arise from the emotional content of the terms being used in the questionnaire design. Hence, to ask 'I care for this place' or 'This place is important to me' might be seen as a statement of place identity, but the cause of the answer might be a social bonding dimension (because that is where my friends are) or simply a restatement of place attachment (because I am nostalgic about the place). Consequently, the dimensions found in quantitative studies are statistical relationships but still relationships that at the emotional level are less clear cut than might be thought.

The importance of the subjective is clearly shown by a study undertaken by Han *et al.* (2019) of tourist holidaying in Cheongsando in South Korea that evidences the attributes of a 'cittáslow' destination. Slow tourism was once summarised succinctly by Professor David Simmons in a conversation as being tourism based on 'slow and savour', that is delay, enjoy, do not rush, let the place dictate a slower pace of life and draw you into an observation of the quieter aspects of life. In short, the type of visitor experience exemplified by Jan Morris (2001) when writing of her stay at Trieste. In the study by Han *et al.* (2019), eight dimensions are identified – these being four aspects of place attachment (identity, dependence, affect and social bonding) and separately measures of attitude, subjective measures, behavioural intent and 'perceived behavioural control' that measures the ability to take a decision to visit a slow city destination. The sample comprised 379 respondents on a boat journeying to Cheongsando Island. It is not stated if these were visitors who had completed their visit by returning, or who were on the outward trip to the island. Given that they were passengers on the boat and no-one in the sample had not visited the island, then the variable 'perceived behavioural control' was found to correlate positively with variables of place attachment and intention to revisit. The seemingly high levels of intention to revisit 'the slow city' seem to fly against the observation made by McKercher (2018) that actual revisitation may be dependent upon distance between the original point of departure and arrival, and that often a distance-decay function exists. Frequency of visitation is also important (McKercher, 2018; Tan *et al.*, 2022). One might also ask if some passengers returning frequently might not have been workers. But these are quite 'nit-picky' points and much of tourism research faces such issues. The key thing is, what was actually found?

Han *et al.* (2019: 115) write, 'findings show that if tourists have a favourable attitude toward revisiting the Cittaslow destination … positive subjective norm of revisiting (H2), and strong perceived behavioural control over revisiting …then they are likely to have an intention to revisit the destination' (Han *et al.*, 2019: 115). It is suspected that those responsible for marketing the destination may have already known that. They also note that among the major theoretical contributions, the model extends work prior to the consideration of cittáslow destinations (Han *et al.*, 2019: 116). The true intent of the study is really the confirmation of a questionnaire to effectively measure intentions to revisit based upon concepts of place attachment, and there is no doubt that good statistical relationships are found. Yet, a key finding is that subjective and attitudinal norms are the most important determinants of the visit, and it is recommended that marketing organisations should concentrate on those factors. This highlights one truth about much of tourism behavioural research, namely, that often the best that can be done is to quantify relationships that are already known and to confirm that promotional marketing oriented towards the experiential is often important. It also highlights the importance of the affective and social bonding in experiencing places, but the nagging assessment remains – was this not already known and how can we really assess the subjective nature of experience when not actually engaging and interacting with visitors? And are we not actually creating biases in our research if we are only talking to those who choose to visit a destination, and, as in this example, have not spoken to those who chose not to visit a cittáslow destination?

It is openly admitted that these questions have been asked before. Maria Lewicka (2011) asked what progress had actually been made in our understanding of place attachment when looking at research undertaken in the prior 40 years. She asks – is place important? This is a question worth asking in the light of a literature that references 'placelessness' (Relph, 1976) and a growing mobility and arguably in the face of new technologies, a possible dislocation between the fantastical and reality as explored in the previous chapter. Yet, as noted above, a sense of place continues to be important and she concludes 'a sense of place is a natural condition of human existence' (Lewicka, 2011: 209). But what is it that we are attached to? On the one hand, place is 'home – a cosy place of stability' but on the other hand, place is a nexus of interaction and an exchange of ideas. Rarely has this paradox been explored in the tourism literature. Perhaps, as she suggests, place is a process, yet too this has been rarely examined. In the environmental psychological literature, various geographical aspects of scale have been closely examined. For example, is place attachment greater in smaller-scale communities? Basically, she concludes that over the 40 years there has been little theoretical advance despite the growing numbers of studies, particularly since 2000. Yet equally, she notes that there is no need for pessimism, for an important question remains, which is how does one need to reconcile the need for an attachment to place in an increasingly fluid and mobile world? And that, possibly, is a key question for tourism academics and researchers.

One could argue that 'Place and Placelessness' are arguably concepts fixed on a notion of fixity, that is, the place exists or does not. Alternatively, and possibly truer to the spirit of Relph (1976), it might be stated that the place has meaning, or lacks meaning. However, Cresswell postulates a third alternative, that of mobility. He defined mobility as 'a kind of blank space that stands as an alternative to place, boundedness, foundation and stability' (Creswell, 2006: 2). It differs from 'placelessness' by reason that the placeless occupies a given space, but by reasons of absence of uniqueness, meaning, proactive human interaction and a lack of memorability and the nature of what Pearce and Moscardo (2007) termed the mindless experience, its very ubiquitous nature makes any visit hard to recall. Mobility offers the potential for recall by reason of being an active transition from one location to another. However, that movement from one place to another is not simply a geographical movement for it can transverse, if not time itself, then between simulacra of time periods. As already stated, one can attend a medieval banquet, thus dislocated from time, or visit a Waterworld or Terminator show at a theme park to be dislocated in space and indeed reality.

The introduction of the internet has introduced a further dislocation in terms of reality and fantasy. Game playing takes one into a space where a person uses an imaginative space to achieve desired ends. This imaginative space is made more apparently real by feedback mechanisms. Simulated motor racing enhances the feedback mechanisms through purpose-built frameworks of seat, controls and high-definition surround providing senses of movement. The cross-over between simulation and reality is made more real by the participation of Formula One stars such as Lando Norris and George Russell in simulated Grand Prix races, while simulation is part of the procedures by which Formula One (and other categories) train potential works drivers. Such use of simulation can exist not only in a replication of real tracks and cars, but in science fantasy it takes the player into future worlds or other galaxies.

Hannam (2009) questions whether such factors may lead to an end of tourism as currently understood and proposes a new activity and theorisation, that of nomadology. Urry draws parallels between the nomad and the writer, arguing that being a nomad changes the nature between point of origination and destination, for once the journey begins, there is no return to the point of origin – it is like academic writing, for 'There is no home or fixed point from which the theorist departs and returns' (Urry, 2000: 240). Rather, the nomad (or writer) travels hopefully. Hannam (2009) also draws a distinction between the nomad and the migrant. The latter seeks a place of refuge after a displacement. The nomad is situated in a continuous process of displacement and the reality is that of constant journeying. This perspective challenges the more traditional 'push and pull' theory with which this book commenced. Rather, this introduces a different notion, that of mobilities.

The concept of mobilities has gained traction, albeit thwarted for a time with the advent of the Covid pandemic that created a new reality of immobility for many and a dependency upon individual resources, especially for those isolated from family and friends. With the easing of Covid restrictions in 2022 the resilience of tourism demand was again quickly evidenced in many parts of the world and posed problems for many in the industry. Those problems were highlighted by stories of long queues at airports, luggage being lost or delayed and hotels not being able to provide full restaurant services while cafes and restaurants needed to reduce hours of opening. Much of this was caused by a shortage of labour as employees may still have had responsibilities with family members catching the virus, and many sought alternative employment that permitted working at home. Equally as noted before, sustainability and concepts of regenerative tourism based on different modes of travel behaviour were being voiced by various commentators as the realities of environmental degradation became increasingly obvious. What then of concepts of mobile, fluid societies?

Long before Covid, Gretzel and Jamal had caught what was thought to be a new zeitgeist, writing 'In general, there is a new sense of heightened mobilities and dynamism. Every component of life—people, goods, services, labour, technologies, etc.—has become mobile to the point that all are tourists in their own cities. People travel and move more frequently; as they uproot and move to other cities, fewer have full knowledge of the cities in which they live. Long-distance commuters, who live in one city and work in another, have some local knowledge of both cities, but not enough to be considered true residents of either' (Gretzel & Jamal, 2009: 472). Commentators such as Franklin and Crang (2001) had suggested that the world was becoming but an extension of home while others advanced the notion that 'time and space' was collapsing (Hall, 2005; Urry, 2016). Such commentaries led to a call for new formulations of the tourist experience. If tourism is about a need for difference, in a fluid world when ease of access to difference ceased to be a difficulty but was a common day experience, where was there an existential difference between tourism and non-tourism?

Parallel with this form of thinking was the emergence of the creative economy. Politicians such as the former Prime Minister of New Zealand, Helen Clark, appreciated that creative performance had economic value, and that investment in the creative arts could contribute to economic growth and to the diversity of experiences in people's lives. She strongly supported (in the face of criticism) such endeavours as the World of Wearable (WoW) Arts, and in 2001 supported the WoW programme from Parliament (Parliamentary Press Release, 2001). That policy was certainly seen as being successful with the Government's support of Peter Jackson and Wētā Workshop as the film trilogy based on *The Lord of the Rings* by Tolkien gathered international recognition and secured a successful period for New Zealand's tourism industry. Gretzel and Jamal (2009) emphasised the role of the 'creative class' as a professional, highly mobile group of people who, allied with the new technologies were creating new tourism experiences that ranged from the 'Disney Main Streets' to the gaming boxes in people's lounges.

Those gaming boxes certainly provided solace to many young people when locked in their bedsits during the years of the pandemic lockdowns from 2020 to 2022, but also showed that differences did exist between human perception of physical and technologically induced travel.

Large-scale studies of loneliness that compared feelings of loneliness prior to and during the period of Covid, such as those of Bu *et al.*, concluded that those previously at risk of being lonely, namely 'young adults, people living alone, people with lower education or income, the economically inactive, women, ethnic minority groups and urban residents had a higher risk of being lonely both before and during the pandemic' (Bu *et al.*, 2020: 32). Feelings of solitude are strongly correlated with a lack of social health networks, and lower-income and isolated groups are particularly vulnerable to such feelings and are also among those less likely to afford going on holidays. The commentaries of those who study holiday taking and tourism are seemingly oblivious to divides that exist within societies, and references to a creative class might in itself be seen as divisive. From the viewpoint of education, Sharma (2020) not only highlight students as being a vulnerable group, but also that this had been trending prior to Covid, and hence one might question the sustainability of distance learning for students in the longer term.

The previous chapters suggested that the peak experience represents states where a person is able to almost escape self into a rhythm or sense of connections with other flows of being, but as yet, as shown by the problems of Mark Zuckerberg in creating a reality of the Metaverse, technology is currently unable to reproduce those connections for humans. Our bodies remain bound to physical places through our senses, and place attachment remains a key aspect of our understanding of the tourist experience.

Technology and the Responsible Tourist

In a criticism of the first edition of *The Tourist Gaze*, Ryan (2013) recalls noting the absence of the 'Gaze of Surveillance' in Urry's book. Today, that 'Gaze of Surveillance' is experienced by every traveller as they pass through the passport controls of airport departure lounges, and in some that ocular check is being done literally through biometric scanning of the eyes. This in itself measures the rapidity of change since Urry's book was first published in 1990. In a series of lectures in 2022 over the internet in China, the Philippines, Sri Lanka and South Korea, Ryan argued that the installation of smart tourism techniques would make redundant the tourist area life cycle initially described by Richard Butler. Essentially, the argument can be summarised in Figures 8.1 and 8.2.

In Figures 8.1 and 8.2, the S-curve derived from Butler's tourist area life cycle is paralleled by a curve of smart tourism development. In the original life cycle model, the exploration and involvement stages were generally times of initial personal contacts between the 'Guest' and the 'Host', to use Valene Smith's (2012) terminology, but under smart tourism the tourist replaces the 'Guest' and contact is initiated over the internet. The tourist becomes familiar to some degree with the place and establishes contact with accommodation suppliers and others via an online

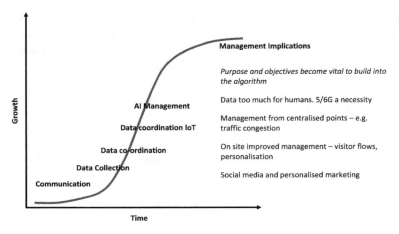

Figure 8.1 The stages of digitisation in tourism

Combining cycles – temporal patterns of change

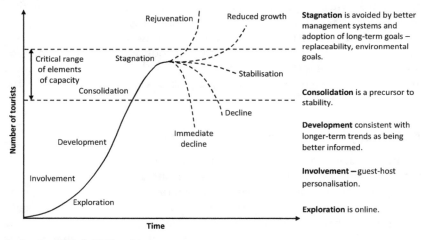

Tourism Area Life Cycle (TALC) model

Figure 8.2 Combining temporal patterns of change

travel agency or social media. Those contacts establish data records, the collection of those records and the coordination of data as tourist flows increase. These flows of data permit organisations to better plan arrivals and patterns of flow across a destination, but humans may become overwhelmed by the data flows. At this point, artificial intelligence (AI) based on real-time communications and working on algorithms based on machine learning (ML) begins to have primacy and can control usage patterns of places through means such as requiring advanced bookings, price adjustments and similar promotional means as shown in Figure 8.1.

The implications of this are shown in Figure 8.2. Given the ability to co-ordinate and act upon information, the issue of over-tourism might now be averted. Congestion is avoided by simply having assessed the location's carrying capacity, and in addition flows of visitors may be better managed through the allocation of quotas, time slots and potentially the allocation of visitors to guides. Those guides can potentially enhance the visitor experience through the provision of information, and indeed the nature of the guide might even be determined by choices made by the visitor or by algorithms working from data derived from client profiles. In time, the guide may also be able to further enhance visitor satisfaction by the use of augmented and virtual realities, perhaps aided by the use of hologram images.

Two immediate implications arise from this. The first question is how are the algorithms to be written? The second is what might be the long-term consequences of dependency on computer-based learning? Carrying capacities are not simply some fixed static number, for the sites can be designed and redesigned in the light of varying patterns of duration of stay, assignment of priorities to environmental, social and economic goals and the designation of desired tourist types. There is also the matter of what type of tourist experience is being planned by the destination managers. The nature of these problems is well described by Etzioni and Etzioni (2017) who use the examples of driverless cars to illustrate the differences between legal rules (for example, to stop at a red traffic light) and ethical decisions where harm may come to more than one person. They argue that the extreme scenarios of having to make choices between one or another fatality is likely to be rare, and the options present are in fact those that would face humans. There is, in fact, no real ethical rule for choosing between repugnant choices. Consequently, they conclude that 'When all is said and done, it seems that one need not, and most likely cannot, implant ethics into machines … Society can set legal limits on what these machines do in many cases; their users can provide them with ethical guidance in other situations, employing ethics bots to keep AI-equipped machines in line; and one can leave alone the one-in-a-million situations, without neglecting to compensate those that are harmed' (Etzioni & Etzioni, 2017: 417).

An associated problem is that evidence already exists that AI and ML pick up undesirable patterns of human thinking when crawling over data derived from messages left on the web by humans. As Zou and Schiebinger say, 'AI can be sexist and racist—it's time to make it fair' (Zou & Schiebinger, 2018: 324). As Owens and Walker (2020) and Fountain (2022) discuss, and as stated in the public media, issues abound when considering 'hate speech' and a need to limit and condemn it on the one hand, and on the other to sustain the right to free speech. That debate transfers into the considerations of AI-determined attendance quotas, and a possible danger that tourists are discriminated against (possibly unknowingly) by an algorithm banning people because of a failure to distinguish legitimacy due to a wrong classification of people's colour or gender.

Accepting the arguments of Etzioni and Etzioni (2017) does not answer the second type of problem, how might humans react to the increasingly intrusive methods of tourist management and indeed the management of their experiences? In the reset of tourism commencing in 2022, much has been written about the need for greater responsibility on the part of both tourists and the industry. At the time of writing (November 2022), it would seem that both tourists and the industry are engaging in 'revenge tourism' – that is, the demand for travel is high and flight schedules are quickly filling up, even at higher than pre-Covid prices. In many ways, this is understandable in societies that have experienced long periods of lockdown and have been denied international travel. In addition, family members may not have been able to see each other for long periods in excess of a year. But with successive Conference of the Parties (COP) summits increasingly noting the increase in carbon emissions, short-term desires seem to have priority over long-term consequences. It does seem, as previously discussed, that the major initiatives will need to come from the industry itself as previously discussed.

In the longer term, another consideration that was touched upon earlier was the extent to which impressions created by technology can meet demands for authenticity. Much, it is suspected, will rest on personality and also possibly on how one views tourism. It was Neil Leiper (2004) who staunchly defended the role of travel and the distinction between tourist-generating and -receiving countries in his model of tourism. For Neil, as for others following the United Nations World Tourism Organization (UNWTO) definition of tourism, the act of travelling is a key and unique component of the industry. The current authors recognise this but hold to the nuanced view that the claim of tourism being the world's largest industry was always false. Rather, we tend to view it as a subset of recreation and leisure and as such the core of the subject matter is the quality of experience and the contribution tourism makes to senses of well-being. The act of travel and being in settings different to those at home is driven by needs to escape from and to sets of experiences, and it is through the challenges and equally the relaxation gained from such experiences that tourism gains its value for human beings. Hence, authenticity possesses value as previously discussed, but equally so too do games and acts of imagination and fantasy and products such as Hobbiton and theme parks and resorts like Macau in China and Sentosa Island in Singapore. These sites allow people to escape into an immersive experience that appeals to our senses. In the same way, gaming may also do so. As has also been seen, tourists are capable of choosing roles, and some will happily partake in the 'fantasy' experience at times, while some may come to lose themselves in it just as some succumb to drugs and alcohol. Hence, as previously noted, some will find the technological immersive experience satisfying, and thus the analysis of the visitor experiences undertaken in this book may well apply to hyperreality.

9 Experiencing Holiday Time

This chapter includes:

(a) The quality of holiday time.
(b) Social implications of time measurement and time keeping.
(c) Holiday time, needs and space.
(d) Gender differentials in experiencing time.

Introduction

Both Pearce (2005) and Ryan (2002) were increasingly being drawn to a consideration of time and the role that it plays in the holiday experience. The latter noted that holidays are a temporal experience in at least four ways, namely (a) they are moments of freedom from constraints from a perceived or actual lack of time commonly experienced in daily life, (b) holidays possess a chronological sequence of generally pleasurable events, (c) holiday time possesses an elasticity of time that seems to pass quickly, or where one forgets the time of day and (d) holidays are anticipated and experienced, and thus extend beyond the temporal boundaries of the actual length of stay at the holiday destination (Ryan, 2002a: 202). Accepting for the moment these observations, one can observe that a distinction exists between objective time as measured in the ticking of a clock, and an experiential pattern of time where some things are remembered as meaningful, while others are mindless or meaningless (Pearce, 2012). There is hence a psychological construct of time and also a sociological construct that reflects a cultural consensus as to the parameters of time. For example, the culture of many indigenous peoples like the New Zealand Māori possess senses of personal identity associated to intergenerational linkages across time and related to time, whereas arguably modern western man talks of a pragmatic and functional aspect of time when referring to 'time management'.

This chapter examines time to suggest that our interpretations of time represent a nexus created by emotions, social context, gender identities and much else. Finally, one can observe that through photographic and visual film images we can actually revisit memories of events of a past time. In doing so, the tourist may come to not simply enrich past memories but even replace the actual events of the past with a newer sequencing that enhances and changes our memory of the past to enrich a future time. Such is the frailty of memory and the need to enhance storytelling!

Holiday Time and the Holiday Home Space

Picking up on the theme of holiday homes from the previous chapter, when writing from an architectural perspective, King (1980) drew attention to the spatial implications of buildings constructed for holiday time. He noted that the holiday home, generally being small in earlier times, numerically insignificant when set against the numbers of other buildings and often visually unappealing, had subsequently failed to attract academic attention. While true in 1980, as the previous chapter showed, there is now far more attention than was the case when King was writing. Nonetheless, even today literature on the architectural and spatial implications of holiday homes remains somewhat deficient, and rarely, if ever, associated with an experience of holiday time. As previously noted, the growing wealth of a middle class, ease of access by car and air and increased leisure time has all accounted for a growing number of holiday homes. Yet, to enjoy vacation time, the holiday home had to possess various attributes. It needed to be different from an 'artisan's cottage' (King, 1980: 113), but be picturesque, permitting good views to, ideally, natural land or seascapes whilst having sufficient bedrooms, a communal living space and room for the accoutrements of leisure such as cycles, boats, jet skis or drying rooms if at a winter destination. The architecture spoke of comfort, adaptability and less formality – a place where sand would not ruin carpets and furniture would not be worn by salty bodies fresh from swimming. Leisure time thus speaks of a less formal life structure that inclines to a more egalitarian style of building. The time spent at the holiday home thus speaks of social fabrics, and indeed it might be said to reinforce the perspective expressed by Krippendorf (1999) and other writers – that is, our holidays are structured by the nature of society.

As also noted in the previous chapter, in a neoliberal consumerist society and one oriented towards an ownership of assets, King's original notion of the modest nature of the holiday home is arguably now reverting back to an earlier time when affluence was self-evident in the development of the European seaside resorts of the 19th century. The towns of Monaca, Biarritz and St Moritz were established for an affluent class and hierarchical social system that was evident in its buildings and services (Walton, 1983). Currently, the modest cabin and camping sites are being replaced by the buildings of millionaires. Arguably the changing spatial landscape of the holiday time is being reflected in language as increasingly the nouns of 'cabins', 'huts', 'bach' and indeed 'holiday homes' are being replaced by the terminology of 'second homes', implicitly reinforcing hierarchical social structures.

Nonetheless, some truths continue – these homes are located in desired natural locations and the social hours dictated by the clock are broken by conversations late into the night, to be followed by leisurely and often communal breakfasts and a habit of strolling to places without purpose.

Measuring Time-Keeping and Social Implications

The experience of passing time thus changes. Equally, the very measurement of time has its social implications. The first means of measuring time was the use of sundials, and these were known to the ancient Babylonian and Egyptian civilisations. They may have been based on observing the changing paths of shadows created by obelisks and cast by the sun throughout the day. The Romans in turn inherited sundials from the Greeks who themselves were familiar with those of earlier civilisations. The social implications of sundials were noted by the Roman playwrights. Noting the fashion for establishing sundials by politicians to celebrate success, as evidenced by Marcus Novius Tubula who dedicated a marble sundial to the town of Interamna Lirenas to commemorate an election in about 50 BCE, Plautus noted in poem 1901:

> The gods confound the man who first found out
> How to distinguish hours! Confound him, too,
> Who in this place set up a sundial,
> To cut and hack my days so wretchedly
> Into small portions! When I was a boy,
> My belly was my sundial – one surer,
> Truer, and more exact than any of them.
> This dial told me when 'twas proper time
> To go to dinner, when I had aught to eat.
> But nowadays, why even when I have,
> I can't fall to unless the sun gives leave.
> The town's so full of these confounded dials
> The greatest part of the inhabitants,
> Shrunk up with hunger, crawl along the street.

Plautus was not alone in his deriding the social implications of the sundial imposing time constrained on daily life dictating when it was time to eat and sleep. In a fragment from the Athenian dramatist, Meander's (c.342–c.292 BCE) work *Boiotia*, it is noted, 'When I was a boy, my stomach told me when to eat; … but nowadays our lives are regimented by these infernal timekeepers' (Gratwick, 1979: 312).

However, much as dramatists may have derided the fashion of sundials and the change imposed on social life, there is significant evidence that by the 2nd century AD sundials were common, and communities organised their social functions around a consensual understanding of time. Indeed, Talbert (2017) notes that portable sundials existed and would be carried by the Roman affluent classes.

In passing, it may be noted that the measurement of time has not always been based upon the 360 degrees of a circle and its division into 60 seconds to the minute. Seemingly, early Chinese time measurement systems were based on units of 12 measures, while the rationalising tendencies of the French Revolution sought to impose a decimal system upon the measurement of time. There would be 100 seconds to a minute and 100 minutes to an hour, with a day comprising 10 hours. Similarly, there would be 10 days to a week, and three weeks to a month with 10 months to the year. The attempt to establish this mode of measurement was short-lived due to popular resistance (Rooney, 2021) and probably illogicality. One reason had been anticipated by the English astronomer, William Emerson, who had made the same suggestion in 1776. However, while making that suggestion he commented that such an idea would probably fail as 'the tyranny of custom would never let go of the old system of 60 and 60' (Gellius, 1927: 3). His prescient words proved to be true two decades later.

While the above is of historic interest, the issue of early timekeeping goes beyond being a historical curiosity. The examples indicate that human action creates social consequences that often extend beyond the original intention. The personal consequences of administrations of measured time are experienced by tourists when travelling internationally across time zones. It is not uncommon for such tourists to spend time readjusting to changing waking, sleeping and eating hours, and indeed feeling fatigue when doing so if the flights are long in duration and travelling east to west or vice versa. Equally in countries like China which are large in size but have a common time zone, variances in local custom might arise between east and west because of the different hours of light and dark. Similar 'oddities' arise in retail practices in bordering areas of Queensland and New South Wales in Australia due to varying practice in daylight saving hours between the two States.

Developing Chronogenesis

While noting these, it can be observed that in terms of time influencing behavioural patterns, the impacts tend to be more nuanced than significant at the local level. However, time possesses not only the objectivity that emerges from a measured linear pattern that proceeds from the past to the present and beyond to the future but also an elasticity in the human mind. As previously noted, several times in this book, experiences are based upon human senses, and those senses are mediated through the workings of the brain. The same relates to our interpretations and experiences of time. Sato and Valsiner (2010) neatly make a qualitative distinction in their aptly entitled paper, *Time in Life, Life in Time: Between Experiencing and Accounting*. As evidenced above, they too comment on the difference between 'clock time' and 'non-clock time' – the former being irreversible and the latter subject to variations in pace and senses of relaxation. As Csikszentmihalyi (1975) observed, when fully engaged in attention-grabbing activities, the participant enters a situation of flow when there is no sense of the passing of time. It is as if there is an extension of time, and for their part Sato and Valsiner (2010) suggest that in moments of distress it can be said that time has the capacity to converge. People involved in traffic accidents speak of a slowing down of time as they seek to control the car. Parallel to this, Maslow (1968, 1970) suggested the actualised personality is able to find the new amidst daily life and thereby give a meaning to time spent in seemingly idle pursuit. Sato and Valsiner (2010) draw on parallel concepts to ask whether it is possible to create a synthesis between clock time and non-clock time.

They suggest a concept of chronogenesis as a state of being common to all humans, as we exist within time, and would we indeed have a sense of existence if there is no time? Chronogenesis is defined as a cultural invention of time in all its forms – the repetitive, indicative, experiential and abstract. This concept involves both the formality of a measured unit and a more general sense of time having signs, symbols and a relationship with space. They thus refer to the chronotope or time-space. Equally, it can be noted that future time holds a promise of possibilities. However, after developing these themes it is concluded that chronogenesis occurs at decisive points at peaceful or mundane junctures that are associated with transitional phases in what they refer to as a trajectory and equifinality model. In short, our perceptions of time are associated with being in space and subject to processes of bifurcation where an awareness of change is present. Their ideas possess interest as seeking an integration between objective measured and irreversible time and a concept of flow that offers possibilities of change. Does it relate to the way in which we experience time when on holiday?

Events and Senses of Time

First, it has been shown that holidays are representative of a change in patterns of life – whether, in the case of the international tourist, in meeting the physiological changes of time zones or in changing patterns of work or non-work as the case may be. In that sense, it might be said there is a point of bifurcation, of transition from one state of being to another. At this point, the motive for the holiday may come into play – is it about relaxation, or is it related to securing knowledge or competencies as per the Leisure Motivation Scale? Motive plays into the clock time aspect of time as motive will dictate whether there is a need to be at a certain place. Equally, motive and purpose relate to the flow of time. The generally busy person when relaxing may be surprised how quickly time has passed as they sit chatting with family or friends, whereas time may pass so slowly if waiting for a flight to be called while sitting in a departure lounge. This last might be an example of compressed time, while chatting to friends is extended time.

But what is actually being perceived at such times? It can be suggested that it is the event that is perceived, not the actual awareness of time. In Csikszentmihalyi's model of flow, the awareness of clock time passing is almost an after-thought – along the lines of 'really, did it really take that long, it did not seem like it'. The point of flow is being caught up in the event, the doing, the immersing of self in an activity. Hancock defines time as 'perceptually malleable and so can be "designed" in terms of user experience and activity' (Hancock, 2018: 8). For Smith (2022), the terminology of 'designed' implies the existence of feedback mechanisms. However, as has been argued in this text several times, perceptions and experiences are dependent upon the senses, and Smith considers that awareness of time can be subject to delayed reaction in the absence of stimuli. He cites several studies that indicate that visual feedback delay can create significant changes in behaviour (K.U. Smith, 1962; Levine, 1953; Smith et al., 1998, 2015; Vince, 2020). Based on such physiological evidence, Smith suggests that time is not being directly perceived but a more subjective process is at work. What is known is that a part of the brain, the lateral intraparietal cortex, has a function in perceiving timed visual reproduction, and this can be inhibited. Similarly other parts of the body are associated with the maintenance of circadian rhythms that relate to night and day and more seasonal patterns.

What implications might this have when considering experiences of time when on holiday? For the most part, tourists tend to experience not a visual deficiency but if anything, the opposite. There might even be a visual saturation of new sights. Another aspect worthy of consideration is the role of the auditory senses. If one walks down an alley way strewn with posters, it is known that the experience of walking is different when (a) you have no knowledge of the language, and thus the experience is primarily dominated by the visual aesthetic and (b) you do understand the language, and then meanings become associated with the walk, especially if accompanied by auditory reinforcement from hearing conversations in the known language. It becomes evident that our experience is being moderated through the senses.

We can intensify experiential quality by the amount of attention we pay to the clock, as noted in the earlier example of chatting to friends or waiting for a flight departure. Apart from these sensed determinants of our experiences of time, there is evidence of gendered differences. One study of interest from a psychometric perspective is that of Ely and Mercurio (2011). In their study of 230 adults, they used a large questionnaire that comprised the Zimbardo Time Perspective Inventory (ZTPI) (Zimbardo & Boyd, 1999), the Big Five Inventory (BFI) (John & Srivastava, 1999) and the Autobiographical Memory Questionnaire (AMQ) (Rubin *et al.*, 2003). The ZTPI comprises (a) a 'Past Positive (PP)' orientation that encompasses warm and sentimental feelings towards the past, (b) a 'Past Negative (PN)' perspective that reflects a history of negative past life experiences and a sense of regret, (c) a 'Future (FU)' perspective associated with goal-striving, and a willingness to forgo immediate gratification for future rewards, and (d) two 'Present orientations' – the hedonistic and fatalistic (Zimbardo & Boyd, 1999). These orientations are associated with specific personality traits. The past positive is associated with extraversion and agreeableness, the past negative with negative experiences and senses of regret, and thus tends to low-esteem and depression, while future orientation is correlated with senses of conscientiousness. The present orientations are associated with hedonistic motives and more fatalistic orientations towards life and a feeling that control lives outside oneself.

Time and Gender Differences in Perceptions of Time

The gender differences are statistically significant on the ZPTI with $p<0.01$ on all the dimensions of the ZPTI. Women score higher on the PP and FU scale and men higher on the PN scale. In addition, Ely and Mercurio (2011) also found that women scored significantly higher on a nostalgia scale (Routledge *et al.*, 2011) at $p<0.001$.

The AMQ is based on work by Rubin (2005), Rubin *et al.* (2003) and Rubin and Siegler (2004) and is composed of the attributes of reliving the past, placing oneself in the past situation, remembering, seeing the past, recalling the setting, hearing and talking of the past, emotional responses, word choice, storytelling, the significance of past events, frequency of talking about the past and the sense of the past continuing to be real. Women scored higher than males on a composite AMQ score and produced longer memory reports than men. Females also tended to cite more emotive content than males, but not at statistically significant levels. Finally, on the BFI, women scored higher than men in extraversion, conscientiousness and neuroticism.

In short, there are gender differences in the ways in which males and females tend to record and interpret past events that have implications for the manner in which they may experience and recall time. However, those differences may reflect the patterns of activities, especially with reference to vacation behaviours and senses of responsibility. Maume (2006) cites earlier studies of how males and females use vacation time differently. He cites studies by Deem (1996) that showed that males may well spend some of their holiday time on work-related activities such as answering emails and completing various work-related tasks, and today one suspects that increasingly that is not simply confined to males. Indeed, it is possible that with a greater uptake of working at home during the Covid pandemic the fuzziness of divisions between home- and work-centred time is far more fluid than previously, and this pattern may be even more prevalent during holidays than prior to 2020. Yet one pattern noticed by Deem (1996, 1998, 1999) is seemingly still prevalent, and that is for families with children it is generally females who continue to undertake childcare and many of the domestic tasks of cleaning, cooking and the like.

In interviews with Chinese females, Zhang *et al.* (in press) found several comments that supported this perspective. One 26-year-old commented, 'I don't see any difference between travelling on holiday and my normal daily life, as I also take it easy at work and there is no pressure … I put my children's feelings first when I go on holiday'. One 37-year-old commented that her husband played little role in childcare and went on to state:

> Compared to my daily life, I felt the last trip was more relaxed, at least I didn't need to do housework. But it wasn't entirely relaxing because the kid will run around, and I need to keep an eye on him. One day, my kid didn't feel well, I was worried that he was sick. I seldom thought about my own feelings. I feel that taking my child on holiday has increased the pressure on me to take care of him, everything is under control at home, but outside everything is out of control … and I am under a lot of mental stress.

Nonetheless, many of their informants spoke positively about the improving status of females in contemporary Chinese society and some spoke of how their husbands were more proactive in sharing responsibilities. It can be observed that childcare does impinge on holiday enjoyment, and it implies that for some a holiday can seem longer than the objective number of days because 'things are out of control' in new environments when looking after children. Maume (2006) also notes, however, that it is females who are often concerned with family memory making, implying that holiday time will become a future memory of times past and that such memories can be richer than those of their male counterparts.

A significant point in Maume's study is his argument that while vacations may represent a continuation of the family-work nexus, in much of the feminist literature there may be insufficient consideration of the role of holidaying *per se* and its potential for disruption of the hitherto stable patterns of allocation of domestic work. He suggests that there is a need to look at commitment to an allocation of time. Drawing on large data sets, he finds that in 1992 in the United States it was males who tended to have higher levels of unused vacation time with the excuse of having work commitments. Such observations reinforce the previous discussion on social values, structures and pressures creating potentially dysfunctional human lives. It can be objected that the data sets behind much of the research cited above reflect long outdated patterns of work and family times, and hence later studies are of interest. Nonetheless, the themes noted of gender differences seem to be perpetuated, with Catherine Kelly (2022) providing an apt response in her paper on holidays in Brighton on England's southern coastline. She notes that 'the subtleties of paid versus hidden domestic labour emerged for some respondents – "I work all week, so it's nice to get down here and relax and do nothing" (dad, xi) – followed by his wife's reply (mother, xxvii): "So you think I don't work all week? I wonder who looks after the children and keeps the house going then? Or who organised this trip, packed this picnic, this sunscreen, these buckets and spades?"' Kelly proceeds to note that there is seemingly a resignation to this service role among several she interviewed, but the purpose of this role is to provide satisfaction for others, particularly children, and therein lies the satisfaction and value of the holiday.

Among other later studies are those of Catheryn Khoo and her various co-authors (Khoo-Lattimore, 2018; Khoo-Lattimore & Yang, 2018b) who also consider the gendered roles of Asian females. In one paper Pung *et al.* (2020) note there is, in fact, a significant literature that has evolved around the figure of the solo female traveller, and that much of it refers to transformative experiences created by memorable events and interactions, both positive and negative. Negative aspects do undoubtedly exist due, in the main part, to harassment by males as evidenced by stories of a female tourist from Taiwan (Su & Wu, 2022) and much earlier studies of business female travellers (Ryan & Lutz, 1993). A common theme between these two latter studies is the restrictions that such male behaviour unfairly imposes on the female travellers, something that should not be condoned. Pung *et al.* (2020) also note an asymmetric approach by researchers to the gendered experiences of solo travellers, noting that there is relatively little literature on the single male traveller, particularly away from the theme of adventure-based journeys. Pung *et al.* (2020) also distinguish between transformational learning and existential transformation, arguing that not only are they separate, but one or the other, or both may be encountered during holiday periods. The two dimensions are triggered by different stimuli. The former is triggered by encountering cultural shock and disorientation in the journey, while existential transformation is triggered by particularly meaningful experiences. Indeed, Pung *et al.* refer to 'experiencing majestic nature and different cultural contexts, by a sudden and emotionally charged peak event' (Pung *et al.*, 2020: 539). From the perspective of earlier chapters in this book, the difference appears nuanced, and Pung *et al.* state that existential transformation 'involves a major existential re-evaluation of one's existence and value-system, initiating a different life direction towards existential authenticity' (Pung *et al.*, 2020: 539). Be this as it may, there follows a quick and succinct analysis of gendered studies in the tourism literature summarising straight, gay and sex work to which one might add lesbian and trans identities. They note the differential role of emotion between the traditional muscular-oriented male experiences and the relationship-orientation found in many studies of females.

The focus of their research was to compare the experiences of male and female tourists using a duoethnographic approach, that is, to compare the 'lived-in' experiences of two young researchers of similar age and educational backgrounds travelling overseas, one being male and the second female. As is well known, such research is very limited in terms of developing theory from such a minuscule sample, and in such cases the 'creditworthiness' of the research lies in a comparison between any results with a general literature. Does the study indicate any potential future path for research and does the case possess credibility in being representative of a selected pattern of behaviour? One issue with all research is that the research questions quite naturally direct the focus of the research, and in this example the focus was to find and compare differences. This Pung *et al.* (2020) do but to the minds of the authors of this text, differences found are in part a question of semantics and semiotics as we hint at in the earlier paragraph above. What is suggested here is that the similarities might be greater than the differences. Both young people in the case experienced a stage of liminality as they sought to readjust to their new environments. Both went through processes of transformation that centred, in part, on changes of self-awareness through reflection and the nature of relationships. For the female, though, the trip reinforced needs for family relationship bonding while the male gained from being primarily solo or in temporary relationships.

A key finding is that, reading between the lines of the text, the context of their trips, that is, the countries visited, played a key role in terms of the opportunities that emerged and which shaped evaluations of those trips. A second key finding noted by the authors was that 'findings also contradicted the need for a specific peak episode to suddenly trigger existential authenticity towards the end of the trip (Kirillova *et al.*, 2016); instead supporting a "layered" tourist transformation that lasts through time and influences multiple behaviour changes' (Pung *et al.*, 2020: 553).

Age and Time

The memorability of the holiday creates long-lasting perceptual constructs within the brain and humans interpret and re-interpret past experiences as they combine with subsequent experiences. Often the chronological sequences become confused, but the experiences remain impactful and are guides for future behaviour even though the recall of the specificity of years can fade unless it is possible to take recourse to actual records. One common experience of time is associated with ageing, for it is said that as people grow older, so the years appear to pass faster. One theory is that our perception of time is related to chronological age. Thus, for example, for a 10-year-old a year can seem to take 'ages', whereas for the 70-year-old the previous year seems to have passed in a flash. It has been suggested that for the 10-year-old a period of one year represents 10% of the child's lifetime, whereas for the 70-year-old that one year is 1/70th of a lifetime. A much smaller percentage of the lifetime seems to compress the perceptions of the previous 12-month sequence.

Although quite well-established at an anecdotal level, the reasons for this relationship between age and senses of time are not wholly known. It might, for example, be associated with the neural changes noted previously, but there appears to be a growing appreciation that 'we should stop accepting chronological age as a factor in itself' (Griffiths, 1997: 208). An alternative viewpoint argues that attention should focus more on the ageing process itself, and chronological age is only, at best, a proxy for ageing. Other factors seem to account for personal attitudes towards future age. Health and sense of well-being are certainly part of the process and as people approach older age, differentials between apparent and chronological age can become quite apparent. Some seem old for their age while others retain a vitality associated with younger people. In that sense, there is a link between holidays and age, for the evidence is accruing that holidays can be beneficial for the good health that is often associated with senses of well-being that help preserve a sense of 'being young'.

Much of the evidence of psychological well-being has been discussed previously and can be found also in the edited work by Smith and Puczkó (2016). Thus far, we have found that perceptions of time can be influenced by the memorability of the occasion, one's age, health, personality, the context and social environment and gender, but issues remain. Other factors include how closely we are paying attention to things or the person, our emotional state and the degree of interest the activity or context possesses for the individual tourist. It seems that we have distinctions between objective, measured time, our own physiological time based on the beats of our hearts and perceptual patterns of time. As part of this list, we can add cultural sensitivities of time. Ryan (2002b) notes that Hopi Indians allegedly did not possess a word for time, while as noted above Māori have sense of generational identity across time. It can be observed that time in rural societies created seasonal patterns of repetition across the years associated with the changing seasons such as a harvest festival, a new moon or the end of an equinox. Chinese culture has its Spring National Holiday on dates determined by the phases of the moon, while the New Zealand Matariki National Holiday is based on a Māori celebration of mid-winter. In many countries, such times were celebrated as holidays, but modernity often either (a) requires a fixed date in the year and/or (b) commercialises the traditional celebrations, and over time meanings may change as the festival is displaced in time and decontextualised from often religious connotations. This is particularly so in tourism if an event is repeated to fit into schedules determined by coach tours or other touristic timetables.

Images and Time

The examples of tourism changing meanings of events and imposing changed time structures to meet commercial needs may be said to represent time-space boundaries that are meeting points between cultures or transitions of historical value systems compromising with current norms. As such, they are contested zones, but it should not be said that each party to the negotiation sustains a consistent perspective. Each may well make a concession to past or new portrayals of the celebration, particularly if each sees benefits in making changes or modifying requests. The tourist industry may change a schedule to market an event as being 'more authentic' and the hosts may find benefits in using new materials or technologies, or conveniences in using newer clothing. Thus, for example, the Māori kapa haka Te Matatini Festival (formerly the Māori Arts and Performing Festival) permits the use of two acoustic guitars that are often used along with traditional instruments such as the pūtātara (a horn from a couch shell) and pūkāea (a wooden trumpet up to 2.5 metres long) in addition to flutes made from wood, flax and other natural materials easily accessible to Māori. This enables Māori to embellish further their music and songs to create a more aesthetically appealing sound. Equally, it is possible that such events may be stretched or shortened in time to fit the schedules of contemporary businesses or lifestyles. One implication is that such festivals or events may lose a sense of 'authenticity' – a topic discussed in Chapter 7.

From one perspective it can be argued that cameras and smartphones can be regarded as 'containers of time' as they record events for future viewing. Additionally, such technology makes it possible to 'play with time'. Tourists may go home and edit their visual memories to create more vivid 'collections of memory'. For example, it becomes possible to change the sequencing of holiday events by pasting and editing visual material filmed at different stages of the holiday. It becomes possible to 'beautify' an image. Equally, time may be slowed down to highlight an occurrence in slow motion. And the act of recording and editing these memories is literally a 'saving of a time' – just as the tourist consumes places (Urry, 1990) so the tourist 'saves time'. Such actions create what can be termed 'Place Accessibility' for by reviewing a holiday video it enriches memory by taking us in our minds back to a place and time. In

some ways, it potentially can change our experience of the place and holiday by replacing a direct memory by a filmed memory, and it is possible
that over time the created visual memory changes our recall of the initial
sequence of events that took place in the past.

Summary

The interactions between time and holidaying are complex because
for the most part holidays are based in differences of activity between
holiday and non-holiday times. Non-holiday times are often characterised by timetables of repetition to the point where it becomes difficult
to distinguish when exactly a routine task last took place because it
is a commonplace. The commonplace of the work and domestic routines is, during a holiday, replaced by the out of the ordinary – the
extra-ordinary – and what we do on holidays can be acts of renewal
through relaxation, learning, challenge or social interaction including
family bonding. The very use of this terminology takes us back to the
1980s with the work of Beard and Ragheb (1980, 1983) and the discussions about the contention that no experience is inauthentic as we are
excited, bored or indifferent to events – each evaluation is itself an
authentic and not artificial response to holidaying. The next chapter will
seek to summarise the previous chapters to look at the implications of
psychology and its understanding of holidays for tourists and those seeking to manage holiday experiences.

10 Coda

This chapter includes:

(a) A brief review of previous chapters.
(b) Potential future directions of research.

The motive for this book was initially stated as being a desire to state, describe and trace the evolution of psychological theories and to indicate the ways in which they have been applied to the subject of the 'tourist experience'. It was suggested that holidays are of significance because they represent times outside of the normal patterns of life, and in experiencing the 'extra-ordinary' they are important for the development of our own senses of being and are formative in shaping our personalities. From this perspective, many of the theories identified as having importance are associated with significant conceptual trends over the last century. It was noted how the Jewish migration to New York to escape the Nazi regime instilled a desire by psychologists to understand how humans might conform to extreme ideologies or otherwise stand firm in seeking their true nature. The 1930s saw the birth of humanistic psychology which wove a philosophical belief about human potential into theories of self-actualisation. Holidays, it was argued, are periods when self-discovery may occur, and even at their most prosaic, holidays are periods of relaxation, of relief from stress, and in that sense contribute to well-being.

With advances in technology, income and a post-Second World War recovery, existentialism became a somewhat ill-formed but important stream of thinking with the work of Sartre, Camus and others. The existentialists are not a consistent school of thinking for there are differences between the highly religious tendencies of a Søren Kierkegaard and an atheistic Jean-Paul Sartre. Indeed, Sartre was said to have rebutted any attempt at defining existentialism and as Solomon (2001) notes, many of the writings associated with existentialism lie in novels such as *The Stranger* (Camus, 1942) or from an earlier time the novels of Dostoyevsky. There are arguable differences between those usually designated as existentialists. Some (e.g. Husserl) have been said to be concerned with the nature of knowledge and belief, while others like Hei-degger and Sartre are concerned with human practice (Soloman, 2001). Indeed, in his defence of existentialism Sartre likened it to a humanism (Sartre & Mairet, 1960).

Thus, whatever the differences between the individual thinkers, a common theme was the notion of 'being' and their work involved how senses of being existed and the responsibilities of humans to develop their full potential of being. In doing this, they tended to reverse procedures so that while modernist thought encourages the primacy of logic and rationality, the existentialists emphasise the role of passion and emotion in the 'becoming of self'. Such thinking has, at least indirectly, influenced thinking in an analysis of tourism. As shown in the previous chapters, tourism scholars have engaged in measurements of authenticity and have argued that tourist experiences contribute to fuller senses of experiencing senses of being through both physical and mental challenges when facing new interactions with others. This too is an element of existential thought – for the paradox exists that senses of being are perhaps best engaged in being with others, and possibly to know ourselves we should see ourselves as others see us. Equally, the tourist experience is born of the senses, and evaluations of those experiences are, even at the simplest level, 'good', 'bad', 'enjoyable', 'challenging', etc. In short, the evaluations are emotive and not wholly rationale at times. The young clubgoer in Ibiza may have had a 'sick' (i.e. great) time, but vomiting in the gutter was indeed being 'sick' and enjoying it in retrospect.

The development of the post-modern economies in the 1960s created new issues. Thinkers such as Foucault, Derrida and Bourdieu considered how the new marketing technologies combined with the emergence of mass media and tourism created a consumption of signs and symbols. By the first part of the 21st century, the emergent technologies of the internet and 5/6G shaped new thinking in tourism. John Urry's concept of 'The Gaze' influenced tourism through a physical framing of landscapes and built upon Cohen's notion of a Gaze directed outward from a 'tourist bubble'. An era of personalisation of services also emerged aided by the new technologies that enabled first the statistical analysis of lifestyles based on values, attitudes, life stage and lifestyle to generate psychometric profiles that continues to impel several analyses of tourist segments. But, as noted in Chapter 6 scholars have questioned the consistency of these segments suggesting instead that tourists are free to adopt and change roles within and between holidays.

This book was written in 2023, and evolving patterns of research continue to present new challenges. Reference was made earlier to the potential impact of the neurosciences to our understanding of humans and the nature of the tourism experience. The neurosciences may also contribute to an explanation of the irrationality of much of human behaviour, and indeed it may be the human ability to be irrational that may present problems in the use of the new artificial intelligence (AI) apps that began to appear such as ChatGPT in October 2022. Humans have written the algorithms and it is known that both ChatGPT and Bing possess the capacity to 'hallucinate', that is, support opinions with false references. The neurosciences have conceptualised the 'two brain' concept, one being the rational brain and the second the emotional brain (LeDoux, 1996). LeDoux comments that at the time prior to his book, the subject of emotions attracted little attention from psychologists, psychiatrists and those interested in the working of the brain. Emotions were said to be too complex, but he would 'rather learn a little about emotions than more about less interesting things' (LeDoux, 1996: 11). He added 'Skeptics be warned, we have gotten pretty far' (LeDoux, 1996: 11).

Things have progressed further since 1996. Casey *et al.* illustrate recent imagining studies of the brain that show 'a cascade of changes in limbic and cognitive control circuitry' (Casey *et al.*, 2019: 29) during adolescence and argue that the dichotomous structure of the cognitive and emotional brains is supported by neuroscience imaging of brain functions, albeit emerging studies are delving further into the sub-cortical recesses of the brain. These studies and others challenge the rationality inherent in Stimulus-Organism-Response theories. Williams (2011) wrote of this tendency and the importance of the visual image as source of cognitive learning, yet Williams (2005) also warns of the over-dependency on the 'allegedly' rational due to the animacy existing in sentence structures that implies hierarchical structures in sentence construction.

One potential implication of the argument is that human decision-making is primarily based upon emotional responses which the cognitive side then rationalises to support the decision. It follows the argument that it is possible to create a logical argument from a premise, once the premise is accepted. This would be true even if the premise is false. Social evidence to support this thesis is clearly shown in debates that surrounded the claim of President Trump after his loss in the US elections that 'the election was stolen' – a claim that several years later retained its appeal among his supporters. The neurological evidence is, of necessity, not wholly clear for several reasons. It is generally agreed that one cannot simply cut open a person's brain and sever links within the cortex simply to undertake an experiment! So, often one is citing individual cases where an operation has been undertaken under extreme cases.

Uddin *et al.* (2005) cite one such case of an individual referred to as Ng. In this case they write, 'the right and left hemispheres of this patient independently and equally possessed the ability to self-recognize, but only the right hemisphere could successfully recognize familiar others' (Uddin *et al.*, 2005: 633). Similarly, a loss of empathy has been known in cases among those suffering from a neurodegenerative disorder associated with progressive deterioration of frontal and/or temporal lobes. This is not uncommon in cases of dementia.

The presence of rationality but little empathy for others is found in psychopaths, but yet the psychopath may 'enjoy' the psychotic act.

These considerations may be far removed from considerations of tourism, but here are linkages. If tourism is truly about the nature of experience, then a tourist's expectation, experience and evaluation of an experience, and the duration of that experience are all aspects of sentience. Hence, we return to a key point made at the commencement of this book, namely that tourism experiences are psychologically important and add to the maturation of self. Past research, psychometric studies, psychology in general and the neurosciences all point to the role of arousal in creating expectations and evaluations and add to the notion that travel can improve one's quality of life.

Today, society sits at the cusp of the internet of things that will permit yet larger sets of data to be collected, but of even more importance is the greater ability to integrate and analyse such information and to interact with it in real time. Hollinshead was fascinated by the tourist gaze, which he analysed in a series of papers (Hollinshead, 1991, 1994; Hollinshead & Hou, 2013; Hollinshead & Kuon, 2013; Jamal & Hollinshead, 2001). Drawn to the work of European philosophers, Hollinshead sought to locate much of their thinking into a global setting that befitted the period that followed the opening of China in 1978. One specific example of this was his paper entitled *The 'worldmaking' prodigy of tourism: The reach and power of tourism in the dynamics of change and transformation* (Hollinshead, 2009). Hollinshead (2008: 643) defined world-making as a creative but commonly false activity projecting the interests of businesses and individuals 'to purposely (or otherwise unconsciously) privilege particular dominant/favoured representations of people/places/interests within a given or assumed region, area, or 'world', over and above other actual or potential representations of those subjects. Like Durkheim, Simmel and Krippendorf, Hollinshead (who self-described himself not as a tourism scholar, but a sociologist interested in tourism) was strongly aware of a zeitgeist or a modern movement that was shaping the world. He argued that tourism created specifically managerially condoned storylines (like Heron, 1983) but which change or are re-interpreted in the light of later power shifts, that it borrows from cultural settings to create fusions of those cultures designed to sell product to tourists and that in advantaging some it may disadvantage the original inheritors of those cultures. He suggested that tourism as a social phenomenon was understudied, not wholly appreciated for its role in shaping authorised versions of culture, and hence was also probably misunderstood. Not surprisingly therefore he saw 'authenticity' as manipulative performative exercise that may have been a pale shadow of earlier meanings.

Phil Pearce was very aware of these histories of thought and the notable twists and turns that tourism scholarship has taken over the years since Thomas Cook established the basis of tourism as it is known today back in the 19th century. In his book *Tourist Behaviour* (Pearce, 2005), Pearce concluded by proposing a structure comprising three continua. These were the regulatory-emancipatory, the interpretative-functional and the macro-micro. He proposed that all of the contributing disciplines of tourism could be encased within their borders, ranging from the anthropological to the opposing worlds of business (Pearce, 2005: 194). Along the micro-macro continuum, he placed psychology at the micro end and philosophy at the macro end. In this book, we have attempted to show that the psychological and philosophical are entwined around each other rather like the serpent tails of Fuxi and Nüwa in Chinese creation myths of the origin of China, and they stand together reflecting sociological, political and economic factors. That is part of the fascination of the study of the tourist experience for it ranges and incorporates both the simple (as in the need for a change and relaxation) and the complex (the sense of becoming, or a yearning or better understanding of self) both sequentially and simultaneously as decided by the internet-empowered individual who chooses roles to meet the momentary or long-term needs. Such a confusion of fusion, and that is why tourist experiences are so fascinating.

Does the Future Lie in a Better Understanding of Philosophy?

As a researcher, we are often told by referees that one should not introduce new material into the final section of an article, but as we wrote this book, we became increasingly aware of deficiencies that were remaining silent, and hence the remaining paragraphs are offered as thoughts on alternative ways of approaching the subject of visitor experiences that might encourage future research. As previously noted, the concept of authenticity has long been considered as essential to understanding the evaluations provided by tourists. But from a philosophical perspective it can be questioned whether the writings on authenticity are a cul-de-sac that are misleading any search for better understanding of visitor experiences. 'Who am I really?' and 'What is reality?' have been key philosophical questions – seemingly for ever. They are the questions that led to the phenomenological and existentialist approaches that have influenced tourist research as demonstrated in previous chapters even when empirical quantitative data tends to dominate. But there are alternative modes of analysis. The chapters have assumed that our perceptions lie within ourselves as we look at the world but is it possible that we are shaped by our own cultures more than we think?

If we think about how language is acquired, a few moments' thought shows it to be a complex process. If we wish to play ball with a baby, we roll a ball and say 'ball' – but how is it being understood? The ball might be a tennis ball and yellow in colour, or it is a cricket ball, red in colour. So perhaps when rolling the ball the baby understands a colour, a texture or the act of rolling. In short, the baby could associate attributes other than the ball to the word 'ball'. We learn by comparisons. So, one can roll the basketball and the cricket ball to say the word 'ball', but while excluding colour and size from the frame of understanding a 'ball' it might still refer to 'rolling' or the 'act of rolling'. This is possibly an extreme example, but behind this notion is the idea of extension – we learn by extending and comparing our sets of words, behaviours, etc., and in short it is the culture inherent in our environment that is strongly influencing how we think. It was Descartes who noted the doubtful nature of dependency on sensory data, and it was Hume who indicated the importance of interaction with others to better understand one's own sense of authenticity (Kernis & Goldman, 2006). In turn, Heidegger (1968) wrote of how we are born into a world that we did not construct with its historical and cultural setting that exists independently of us and yet presents meanings to us. By extension, meanings are presented to us as visitors and shape our constructions of an authenticity. Thus, for Sartre, being is about making choices. Hence, authenticity is not something inherent in an object or place, but rather we make choice based often upon an imperfect understanding. Yet earlier, Kant (1908/1781) had objected to a dependency upon prior experience in his analytic-synthetic diagram, distinguishing between a-priori and a-posteriori (independent of and dependent upon) experience (de Jong, 2010). Very few papers in tourism research appear to possess research paradigms other than the post-positivistic (that rarely seem to justify the paradigm used or consider alternative methods) or the phenomenological (that usually consider the advantages bestowed by rich data but rarely consider problems pertaining to generalisation and the Yin-Eisenhardt debates on implications for theory – although this is beginning to emerge).

However, tourism still seems embedded in what Cahoone (2003) refers to as foundational philosophical paradigms. With the emergence of new technologies and better understandings of physics, biology and computing, philosophy has begun to embrace these new modes of thinking. Equally, AI specialists such as Judea Pearl and Dana Mackenzie (in their book *The Question of Why*) advance concepts of causal inference through the imagination of counterfactuals – a process that is comparative, imaginative and in examining cause and effect seeks a credible 'truth' based on incomplete knowledge. Rorty rather famously declared that 'philosophy is dead' (Rorty, 2016: 61). Equally, it might be said that authenticity is dead. As places are deconstructed, they dissolve through a hybrid lens of disparate differences of meaning. In his book *Battlefield Tourism*, Ryan (2007c) provides examples of changing contested understandings of sites as previously perceived heroic deeds are challenged and history is rewritten.

The philosophers' responses are many, but one perspective is that the complexities should be welcomed as representing new questioning modes of thinking requiring, as Rorty (2016) suggests, teams of researchers engaged in multi-paradigmatic patterns of research that often require longer periods of field work than customarily found in the tourism journal. It requires also that tourism researchers think more differently espousing, as is suggested in this book, not only the philosophical and the psychological, but understandings from the science, technological, environmental, medicinal and mathematical perspectives. At the very least, there is need to embrace more writing from beyond the narrow confines of tourism journals, just as the late Phil Pearce and Keith Hollinshead did. Equally, tourism researchers might wish to embrace horizons beyond simply those of assessing destinations and satisfaction. Philosophy and the neurosciences are morphing into discussions of sentience and a state of consciousness. It is argued that many animals are capable of logical thought, but the philosopher asks, can they envisage suffering? Can they dream? Despite not knowing the answer, legislations are awarding legal protection to animals based on the notion of sentience (e.g. the 2022 Animal Welfare (Sentience) Act). Some countries have awarded the status of being a person to natural features, including Ecuador, Bolivia and New Zealand.

It is suggested that tourism researchers have long grappled with problems of self, authenticity, conservation, identity, attachment to place, the shaping of behaviours and the role of culture to name but a few problems that past research has studied. We have looked at intergenerational differences, the impacts of externally induced change on senses of community and the role of heritage shaping the physical environments within which we live. Our concerns include the relationship of humans and the natural environment. Tourism research has been criticised for being a collage of different disciplines and the particularisation of fragments of human behaviour. But in a world becoming more integrated through travel and technology, it just might be that those skills of analysis are of use when seeking to understand the position of humans in relation to self, others, communities and nature as the world progresses to a point of singularity.

References

Aicher, T.J., Brenner, J. and Aicher, T.J. (2015) Individuals' motivation to participate in sport tourism: A self-determination theory perspective. *International Journal of Sport Management, Recreation and Tourism* 18 (1), 56–81.

Aicher, T.J., Rice, J.A. and Hambrick, M.E. (2017) Understanding the relationship between motivation, sport involvement and sport event evaluation meanings as factors influencing marathon participation. *Journal of Global Sport Management* 2 (4), 217–233.

Ainsworth, M.D.S. (1969) Object relations, dependency, and attachment: A theoretical review of the infant-mother relationship. *Child Development* 40 (4), 969–1025.

Ajzen, I. and Fishbein, M. (1980) *Understanding Attitudes and Predicting Social Behavior.* Englewood Cliffs, NJ: Prentice-Hall.

Aksu, A., İçigen, T.E. and Ehtiyar, R. (2010) A comparison of tourist expectations and satisfaction: A case study from Antalya region of Turkey. *Turizam* 14 (2), 66–77.

Alén, E., Losada, N. and de Carlos, P. (2017) Profiling the segments of senior tourists throughout motivation and travel characteristics. *Current Issues in Tourism* 20 (14), 1454–1469.

Alexander, Z., Bakir, A. and Wickens, E. (2010) An investigation into the impact of vacation travel on the tourist. *International Journal of Tourism Research* 12 (5), 574–590.

Altınay Özdemir, M. and Göktaş, L.S. (2021) Research trends on digital detox holidays: A bibliometric analysis, 2012–2020. *Tourism & Management Studies* 17 (3), 21–35.

Amatulli, C., De Angelis, M. and Stoppani, A. (2021) The appeal of sustainability in luxury hospitality: An investigation on the role of perceived integrity. *Tourism Management* 83, 104228.

Anderson, R.E. (1973) Consumer dissatisfaction: The effect of disconfirmed expectancy on perceived product performance. *Journal of Marketing Research* 10 (1), 38–44.

Arber, S., Fenn, K. and Meadows, R. (2014) Subjective financial well-being, income and health inequalities in mid and later life in Britain. *Social Science & Medicine* 100, 12–20.

Arbore, A. and Busacca, B. (2011) Rejuvenating importance-performance analysis. *Journal of Service Management* 22 (3), 409–429.

Argonov, V.Yu. (2012) Neural correlate of consciousness in a single electron: Radical answer to "quantum theories ofconsciousness". *Neuroquantology* 10, 276–285.

Argonov, V.Y. (2014) The pleasure principle as a tool for scientific forecasting of human self-evolution. *Journal of Evolution and Technology* 24 (2), 63–78.

Arefi, M. (1999) Non-place and placelessness as narratives of loss: Rethinking the notion of place. *Journal of Urban Design* 4 (2), 179–193.

Argonov, V. (2014) The pleasure principle as a tool for scientific forecasting of human self-evolution. *Journal of Evolution and Technology* 24 (2), 63–78.

Arnould, E. and Price, L. (1993) River magic: Extraordinary experience and the extended service encounter. *Journal of Consumer Research* 20 (1), 24–45.

Aronsson, L. (2004) Place attachment of vacation residents: Between tourists and permanent residents. In C.M. Hall and D.K. Müller (eds) *Tourism, Mobility and Second Homes: Between Elite Landscape and Common Ground* (pp. 75–86). Clevedon: Channel View Publications.

Arora, S.D. and Chakraborty, A. (2020) Legitimate and illegitimate consumer complaining behavior: A review and taxonomy. *Journal of Services Marketing* 34 (7), 921–937.

Assaker, G., Vinzi, V.E. and O'Connor, P. (2011) Examining the effect of novelty seeking, satisfaction, and destination image on tourists' return pattern: A two factor, nonlinear latent growth model. *Tourism Management* 32 (4), 890–901.

Azzopardi, E. and Nash, R. (2013) A critical evaluation of importance–performance analysis. *Tourism Management* 35, 222–233.

Babu, D.E., Kaur, A. and Rajendran, C. (2018) Sustainability practices in tourism supply chain: Importance performance analysis. *Benchmarking: An International Journal* 25 (4), 1148–1170.

Backer, E. and Schänzel, H. (2013) Family holidays—Vacation or Obli-cation? *Tourism Recreation Research* 38 (2), 159–173.

Bago, B., Rand, D.G. and Pennycook, G. (2020) Fake news, fast and slow: Deliberation reduces belief in false (but not true) news headlines. *Journal of Experimental Psychology: General* 149 (8), 1608–1613.

Baker, J., Grewal, D. and Parasuraman, A. (1994) The influence of store environment on quality inferences and store image. *Journal of the Academy of Marketing Science* 22 (4), 328–339.

Bakker, I., Van Der Voordt, T., Vink, P. and De Boon, J. (2014) Pleasure, arousal, dominance: Mehrabian and Russell revisited. *Current Psychology* 33 (3), 405–421.

Ballester-Arnal, R., Ruiz-Palomino, E., Espada-Sánchez, J.P., Morell-Mengual, V. and Gil-Llario, M.D. (2018) Psychometric properties and validation of the sexual sensation seeking scale in Spanish adolescents: Brief screening method for use in research and clinical practice. *Personality and Individual Differences* 122, 47–54.

Barendregt, B. (2011) Tropical spa cultures, eco-chic, and the complexities of new Asianism. In K. Van Dijk and J.T. Gelma (eds) *Cleanliness and Culture: Indonesian Histories* (pp. 159–192). Leiden: KITLV Press Koninklijk Instituut voor Taal, Landen Volkenkunde (Royal Netherlands Institute of Southeast Asian and Caribbean Studies).

Barnett, L.A. (2011) How do playful people play? Gendered and racial leisure perspectives, motives, and preferences of college students. *Leisure Sciences* 33 (5), 382–401.

Bastiaansen, M., Straatman, S., Driessen, E., Mitas, O., Stekelenburg, J. and Wang, L. (2018) My destination in your brain: A novel neuromarketing approach for evaluating the effectiveness of destination marketing. *Journal of Destination Marketing & Management* 7, 76–88.

Battour, M. and Ismail, M.N. (2016) Halal tourism: Concepts, practises, challenges and future. *Tourism Management Perspectives* 19, 150–154.

Baudrillard, J. (1970/1998) *The Consumer Society: Myths and Structures*. Thousand Oaks, CA: Sage (trans Chris Turner).

Baudrillard, J. (1983) *Simulations*. New York: Smiotext(e).

Baudrillard, J. (2016) *The Consumer Society: Myths and Structures*. London: Sage.

Beard, J.G. and Ragheb, M.G. (1980) Measuring leisure satisfaction. *Journal of Leisure Research* 12 (1), 20–33.

Beard, J.G. and Ragheb, M.G. (1983) Measuring leisure motivation. *Journal of Leisure Research* 15 (3), 219–228.

Beck, J. and Egger, R. (2018) Emotionalise me: Self-reporting and arousal measurements in virtual tourism environments. In *Information and Communication Technologies in Tourism 2018: Proceedings of the International Conference in Jönköping, Sweden, January 24–26, 2018* (pp. 3–15). Cham: Springer International Publishing.

Becken, S. and Hay, J. (2012) *Climate Change and Tourism: From Policy to Practice.* New York: Routledge.

Becken, S., Friedl, H., Stantic, B., Connolly, R.M. and Chen, J. (2021) Climate crisis and flying: Social media analysis traces the rise of "flightshame". *Journal of Sustainable Tourism* 29 (9), 1450–1469.

Bennett, O. (2019) *Cultural Pessimism: Narratives of Decline in a Post-Modern World.* Edinburgh: University of Edinburgh Press.

Berger, P.L. (1973) "Sincerity" and "Authenticity" in Modern Society. *Public Interest* 31 (Spring), 81–90.

Bernardo, M., Marimon, F. and del Mar Alonso-Almeida, M. (2012) Functional quality and hedonic quality: A study of the dimensions of e-service quality in online travel agencies. *Information & Management* 49 (7–8), 342–347.

Bianchi, C. and Pike, S. (2011) Antecedents of destination brand loyalty for a long-haul market: Australia's destination loyalty among Chilean travellers. *Journal of Travel & Tourism Marketing* 28 (7), 736–750.

Bigné, J.E., Andreu, L. and Gnoth, J. (2005) The theme park experience: An analysis of pleasure, arousal and satisfaction. *Tourism Management* 26 (6), 833–844.

Billock, J. (2017) *Five Augmented Reality Experiences That Bring Museum Exhibits to Life.* June 29. Retrieved on July 29, 2023, from http://www.smithsonianmag.com/travel/expanding-exhibits-augmented-reality-180963810/

Birch, S.J. (1973) A Survey of Second Homes: Their Number, Character, Owners and Use (master's thesis, Durham University, England). Retrieved on October 7, 2022, from http://etheses.dur.ac.uk/10208/

Bitner, M.J. (1992) Servicescapes: The impact of physical surroundings on customers and employees. *Journal of Marketing* 56 (2), 57–71.

Bitner, M.J., Booms, B.H. and Tetreault, M.S. (1990) The service encounter: Diagnosing favorable and unfavorable incidents. *Journal of Marketing* 54 (1), 71–84.

Blackstock, C. (2011) The emergence of the breath of life theory. *Journal of Social Work Values and Ethics* 8 (1), 1–16.

Bogardus, R. (2013) The DIY Man: Do-It-Yourself Culture and Masculinities in Post-war New Zealand, 1945–1976 (Doctoral dissertation, The University of Auckland, New Zealand). Retrieved on October 25, 2022, from https://researchspace.auckland.ac.nz/handle/2292/21110

Bojanic, D.C. (1992) A look at modernized family life cycle and overseas travel. *Journal of Travel & Tourism Marketing* 1 (1), 61–79.

Boorstin, D.J. (1961/1964a) *The Image: A Guide to Pseudo-Events in American Society.* New York: Harper & Row.

Boorstin, D.J. (1961/1964b) From traveler to tourist: The lost art of travel. In D.J. Boorstin (ed.) *The Image: A Guide to Pseudo-Events in American* (pp. 1800–1918). New York: Harper Colophon Books.

Bowlby, J. (1958) The nature of the child's tie to his mother. *International Journal of Psycho-Analysis* 39, 350–373.

Bowlby, J. (1969) *Attachment and Loss, Vol. 1. Attachment.* London: Hogarth Press and the Institute of Psycho-analysis.

Bowman, N.D. and Cranmer, G.A. (2019) Can video games be a sport? In K.L. Adams, A.C. Billings, N. Bowman, J. Coble, G.A. Cranmer, G. Devia-Allen ... and S. Young (eds) *Understanding Esports: An Introduction to the Global Phenomenon* (pp. 15–31). Lanham, MD: Rowman & Littlefield.

Bradley, G. (2022) Air NZ imports first load of green aviation fuel. *New Zealand Herald*, 15 September, pp. 30–31.

Brady, M.K., Cronin Jr, J.J. and Brand, R.R. (2002) Performance-only measurement of service quality: A replication and extension. *Journal of Business Research* 55 (1), 17–31.

Bridgman, T., Cummings, S. and Ballard, J. (2019) Who built Maslow's pyramid? A history of the creation of management studies' most famous symbol and its implications for management education. *Academy of Management Learning & Education* 18 (1), 81–98.

British Broadcasting Corporation (BBC) (2015, October 20) Hong Kong 'forced shopping' attack sees tourist killed. Retrieved on October 7, 2022, from https://www.bbc.com/news/world-asia-34584235

Bronner, F. and De Hoog, R. (2008) Agreement and disagreement in family vacation decision-making. *Tourism Management* 29 (5), 967–979.

Brown, G.P. (1990) *Tourism and Place-Identity*. College Station: Texas A&M University.

Brown, G. and Raymond, C. (2007) The relationship between place attachment and landscape values: Toward mapping place attachment. *Applied Geography* 27 (2), 89–111.

Brown, G., Reed, P. and Harris, C. (2002) Testing a place-based theory for environmental evaluation: An Alaska case study. *Applied Geography* 22 (1), 49–77.

Bruner, E. (2005) *Culture on Tour: Ethnographies of Travel*. Chicago: University of Chicago Press.

Bu, F., Steptoe, A. and Fancourt, D. (2020) Who is lonely in lockdown? Cross-cohort analyses of predictors of loneliness before and during the COVID-19 pandemic. *Public Health* 186, 31–34.

Buckley, R., McDonald, K., Duan, L., Sun, L. and Chen, L.X. (2014) Chinese model for mass adventure tourism. *Tourism Management* 44, 5–13.

Buckley R., Winn T., Li W., Winn P. and Zhong, L. (2018) River tourism in China. In Y. Wang, A. Shakeela, A. Kwek and C. Khoo-Lattimore (eds) *Managing Asian Destinations. Perspectives on Asian Tourism* (pp. 231–240). Singapore: Springer Verlag.

Bujisic, M., Bilgihan, A. and Smith, S. (2015) Relationship between guest experience, personality characteristics, and satisfaction: Moderating effect of extraversion and openness to experience. *Tourism Analysis* 20 (1), 25–38.

Buzinde, C.N. (2020) Theoretical linkages between well-being and tourism: The case of self-determination theory and spiritual tourism. *Annals of Tourism Research* 83, 102920.

Buzova, D., Sanz-Blas, S. and Cervera-Taulet, A. (2021) "Sensing" the destination: Development of the destination sensescape index. *Tourism Management* 87, 104362.

Cahoone, L. (2003) *From Modernism to Postmodernism* (2nd edn). Cambridge: Blackwell Publishers.

Callebaut, J.M., Janssens, D., Beeck, O., Lone, D. and Hendricks, H. (1999) *Motivational Marketing Research Revisited*. Leuven: Garant.

Camus, A. (1942) *L' Étranger/The Stranger*. Paris: Gallimard.

Cappelli, G. (2006) *Sun, Sea, Sex, and the Unspoilt Countryside: How the English Language Makes Tourists Out of Readers*. Pari, Italy: Pari Publishing.

Carl III, W.J. (1994) Flow-a theory of optimal experience: History and critical evaluation. *Theories of Communication*. Retrieved on February 24, 2022, from https:citeseerx.ist.psu.edu/viewdoc/download?doi=10.1.1.93.4724&rep=rep1&type=pdf

Carlisle, S. and Ritchie, C. (2021) Permission to rebel: A critical evaluation of alcohol consumption and party tourism. *International Journal of the Sociology of Leisure* 4 (1), 25–44.

Carman, J.M. (1990) Consumer perceptions of service quality: An assessment of T. *Journal of Retailing* 66 (1), 33–55.

Carr, N. and Berdychevsky, L. (2022) *Sex in Tourism: Exploring the Light and the Dark*. Bristol: Channel View Publications.

Carter, N.T., Guan, L., Maples, J.L., Williamson, R.L. and Miller, J.D. (2016) The downsides of extreme conscientiousness for psychological well-being: The role of obsessive compulsive tendencies. *Journal of Personality* 84 (4), 510–522.

Caruana, A., Ewing, M.T. and Ramaseshan, B. (2000) Assessment of the three-column format SERVQUAL: An experimental approach. *Journal of Business Research* 49 (1), 57–65.

Casey, B.J., Heller, A.S., Gee, D.G. and Cohen, A.O. (2019) Development of the emotional brain. *Neuroscience Letters* 693, 29–34.

Ceylan, C. and Ozcelik, A.B. (2016) A circular approach to SERVQUAL and HOLSAT: An implementation suggestion. *Journal of Hotel & Business Management* 5 (1), 1–10.

Chang, J., Okumus, B., Wang, C.H. and Chiu, C.Y. (2020) Food tourism: Cooking holiday experiences in East Asia. *Tourism Review* 76 (5), 1067–1083.

Cheah, J.H., Sarstedt, M., Ringle, C.M., Ramayah, T. and Ting, H. (2018) Convergent validity assessment of formatively measured constructs in PLS-SEM: On using single-item versus multi-item measures in redundancy analyses. *International Journal of Contemporary Hospitality Management* 30 (11), 3192–3210.

Chen, C. and Tsai, D. (2007) How destination image and evaluative factors affect behavioral intentions? *Tourism Management* 28 (4), 1115–1122.

Chen, C.C., Huang, W.J. and Petrick, J.F. (2016) Holiday recovery experiences, tourism satisfaction and life satisfaction–Is there a relationship? *Tourism Management* 53, 140–147.

Chen, H. and Ryan, C. (2020) Transforming the Museum and meeting visitor requirements: The case of the Shaanxi History Museum. *Journal of Destination Marketing and Management* 18, 100483

Chen, R., Zhou, Z., Zhan, G. and Zhou, N. (2020) The impact of destination brand authenticity and destination brand self-congruence on tourist loyalty: The mediating role of destination brand engagement. *Journal of Destination Marketing & Management* 15, 100402.

Chen, W., Gu, B., Ye, Q. and Zhu, K.X. (2019) Measuring and managing the externality of managerial responses to online customer reviews. *Information Systems Research* 30 (1), 81–96.

Chen, Z., Ryan, C. and Zhang, Y. (2021) Transgenerational place attachment in a New Zealand seaside destination. *Tourism Management* 82, 104196.

Chen, Z., Ryan, C. and Zhang, Y. (2022a) Cross-generational analysis of residential place attachment to a Chinese rural destination. *Journal of Sustainable Tourism* 30 (4), 787–806.

Chen, Z., Ryan, C. and Zhang, Y. (2022b) Generational challenges of resident-destination bonding. *Annals of Tourism Research* 97, 103493.

Cheng, Q., Guo, J. and Ling, S. (2016) Fuzzy importance-performance analysis of visitor satisfaction for theme park: The case of Fantawild Adventure in Taiwan, China. *Current Issues in Tourism* 19 (9), 895–912.

Choi, Y., Choi, M., Oh, M. and Kim, S. (2020) Service robots in hotels: Understanding the service quality perceptions of human-robot interaction. *Journal of Hospitality Marketing & Management* 29 (6), 613–635.

Chon, K.S. (1989) Understanding recreational traveler's motivation, attitude and satisfaction. *The Tourist Review* 44 (1), 3–7.

Chon, K.S. (1990) The role of destination image in tourism: A review and discussion. *The Tourist Review* 45 (2), 2–9.

Clawson, M. and Knetch, J.L. (1966) *Economics of Outdoor Recreation*. Baltimore: Johns Hopkins University Press.

Cloninger, C.R. (1986) A unified biosocial theory of personality and its role in the development of anxiety states. *Psychiatric Developments* 3 (2), 167–226.

Clout, H.D. (1971) Second homes in the Auvergne. *Geographical Review* 530–553.

Cohen, E. (1972) Towards a sociology of international tourism. *Social Research* 39 (1), 164–182.

Cohen, E. (1973) Nomads from affluence: Notes on the phenomenon of drifter-tourism. *International Journal of Comparative Sociology* 14 (1/2), 89–103.

Cohen, E. (1979) Rethinking the sociology of tourism. *Annals of Tourism Research* 6 (1), 18–35.

Cohen, E. (1985) Tourism as play. *Religion* 15 (3), 291–304.

Cohen, E. (2003) Backpacking: Diversity and change. *Journal of Tourism and Cultural Change* 1 (2), 95–110.

Cohen, E. and Cohen, S. (2012) Authentication: Hot and cold. *Annals of Tourism Research* 39 (3), 1295–1314.

Cohen, D., Shin, F., Liu, X., Ondish, P. and Kraus, M.W. (2017) Defining social class across time and between groups. *Personality and Social Psychology Bulletin* 43 (11), 1530–1545.

Connell, J. (2013) Contemporary medical tourism: Conceptualisation, culture and commodification. *Tourism Management* 34, 1–13.

Conner, C.T. and MacMurray, N. (2022) The perfect storm: A subcultural analysis of the Qanon movement. *Critical Sociology* 48 (6), 1049–1071.

Coon, D. (2006) Abraham H. Maslow: Reconnaissance for eupsycia. In D.A. Dewsbury, L.T. Benjamin Jr. and M. Wertheimer (eds) *Portraits of Pioneers in Psychology* (Vol. 6., pp. 255–273). Washington DC: American Psychological Association and Lawrence Erlbaum Associates.

Cooper, C.P. (1981) Spatial and temporal patterns of tourist behaviour. *Regional Studies* 15 (5), 359–371.

Cooper, C. (1995) Strategic planning for sustainable tourism: The case of the offshore islands of the UK. *Journal of Sustainable Tourism* 3 (4), 191–209.

Cooper, H., Nye, B., Charlton, K., Lindsay, J. and Greathouse, S. (1996) The effects of summer vacation on achievement test scores: A narrative and meta-analytic review. *Review of Educational Research* 66 (3), 227–268.

Coppock, J.T. (1977) *Second Homes: Curse or Blessing?* Oxford: Pergamon.

Coser, R.L. (1956) A home away from home. *Social Problems* 4 (1), 3–17.

Couldry, N. (1998) The view from inside the 'simulacrum': Visitors' tales from the set of Coronation Street. *Leisure Studies* 17 (2), 94–107.

Creswell, T. (2006) *On the Move: Mobility in the Modern Western World*. Abingdon: Routledge.

Cronin Jr, J.J. and Taylor, S.A. (1992) Measuring service quality: A re-examination and extension. *Journal of Marketing* 56 (3), 55–68.

Cross, K.L. (2004) Staying centered during the holidays: Frazzled by the holidays? Learn how to stay calm during this frantic season. *IDEA Fitness Journal* 1 (5), 100–102.

Csikszentmihalyi, M. (1975) *Beyond Boredom and Anxiety*. San Francisco: Jossey-Bass.

Csikszentmihalyi, M. (1988) The flow experience and its significance for human psychology. In M. Csikszentmihalyi and I. Csikszentmihalyi (eds) *Optimal Experience: Psychological Studies of Flow in Consciousness* (pp. 15–35). Cambridge: Cambridge University Press.

Csikszentmihalyi, M. (1990a) *FLOW: The Psychology of Optimal Experience*. New York: HarperPerennial.

Csikszentmihalyi, M. (1990b) The domain of creativity. In M.A. Runco and R.S. Albert (eds) *Theories of Creativity* (pp. 190–212). Thousand Oaks, CA: Sage Publications.

Csikszentmihalyi, M. (1995) Plurilingualism as a catalyst for creativity in superdiverse societies: A systemic analysis. *Frontiers in Psychology* 8, 2169.

Csikszentmihalyi, M. (1997) *Creativity: Flow and the Psychology of Discovery and Invention*. New York: HarperCollins Publishers Inc. Retrieved on October13, 2022 from http://mkc.ac.in/pdf/study-material/psychology/2ndSem/UNIT-4-flow-and-creativty-AG.pdf

Csikszentmihalyi, M. (1999) Implications of a systems perspective for the study of creativity. In R.J. Sternberg (ed) *Handbook of Creativity* (pp. 313–335). Cambridge: Cambridge University Press.

Csikszentmihalyi, M. (2000) *Beyond Boredom and Anxiety. Experiencing Flow in Work and Play.* San Francisco: Jossey-Bass. (Original work published 1975).

Csikszentmihalyi, M. (2015) *The Systems Model of Creativity. The Collected Works of Mihaly Csikszentmihalyi.* Dordrecht: Springer.

Csikszentmihalyi, I. and Csikszentmihalyi, M. (1988) *Optimal Experience: Psychological Studies of Flow in Consciousness.* New York: Cambridge University Press.

Culler, J. (1981) Semiotics of tourism. *American Journal of Semiotics* 1 (1), 127–140.

da Silva deMatos, N.M., de Sá, E.S. and de Oliveira Duarte, P.A. (2021) A review and extension of the flow experience concept. Insights and directions for tourism research. *Tourism Management Perspectives* 38 (100802), 1–17.

Dalessandro, C. (2019) "It's a lifestyle": Social class, flexibility, and young adults' stories about defining adulthood. *Sociological Spectrum* 39 (4), 250–263.

Daniel, M. and Garry, C. (2018) *Video Games as Culture: Considering the Role and Importance of Video Games in Contemporary Society.* Abingdon: Routledge.

Daniel Jr, E.S., Crawford Jackson, E.C. and Westerman, D.K. (2018) The influence of social media influencers: Understanding online vaping communities and parasocial interaction through the lens of Taylor's six-segment strategy wheel. *Journal of Interactive Advertising* 18 (2), 96–109.

Daniel, Y.P. (1996) Semiotics of tourism. *American Journal of Semiotics* 1 (1–2), 127–140.

Dann, G.M. (1977) Anomie, ego-enhancement, and tourism. *Annals of Tourism Research* 4 (4), 184–194.

Dann, G.M. (1981) Tourist motivation an appraisal. *Annals of Tourism Research* 8 (2), 187–219.

Dann, G.M. (1996) *The Language of Tourism: A Sociolinguistic Perspective.* Wallingford: CAB International.

Dann, G.M. (2001) Targeting seniors through the language of tourism. *Journal of Hospitality & Leisure Marketing* 8 (3–4), 5–35.

Dann, G.M.S. (2005) Content/semiotic analysis: Applications for tourism research. In J. Aramberri and R. Butler (eds) *Tourism Development: Issues for a Vulnerable Industry* (pp. 27–43). Clevedon: Channel View Publications.

Dann, G. (2011) Take me to the Hilton: The language of tourism paradigm. *Folia Turistica* 25 (1), 23–40.

Davis, F.D. (1986) A Technology Acceptance Model for Empirically Testing New End-User Information Systems: Theory and Results (Doctoral dissertation, Sloan School of Management, Massachusetts Institute of Technology, The United States). Retrieved on October 25, 2022, from https://dspace.mit.edu/bitstream/handle/1721.1/15192/14927137-MIT.pdf

Davis, F.D., Bagozzi, R.P. and Warshaw, P.R. (1989) User acceptance of computer technology: A comparison of two theoretical models. *Management Science* 35 (8), 982–1003.

Davis, K. (1957) *Human Relations in Business.* New York: McGraw-Hill Book Company.

De Bloom, J. (2012) *How Do Vacations Affect Workers' Health and Well-Being? Vacation (After-) Effects and the Role of Vacation Activities and Experiences.* Oisterwijk, Netherlands: Uitgeverij BOXPress.

De Bloom, J. (2015) Making holidays work. *The Psychologist* 28 (8), 632–636.

De Bloom, J.D., Geurts, S. and Kompier, M. (2014) How does a vacation from work affect tourists' health and well-being? In S. Filep and P. Pearce (eds) *Tourist Experience and Fulfilment; Insights from Positive Psychology* (pp. 181–199) Abingdon: Routledge.

De Bloom, J., Ritter, S., Kühnel, J., Reinders, J. and Geurts, S. (2014) Vacation from work: A 'ticket to creativity'? The effects of recreational travel on cognitive flexibility and originality. *Tourism Management* 44, 164–171.

De Jong, W.R. (2010) The analytic-synthetic distinction and the classical model of science: Kant, Bolzano and Frege. *Synthese* 174 (2), 237–261.

De Raad, B. (2000) *The Big Five Personality Factors: The Psycholexical Approach to Personality*. Boston, MA: Hogrefe & Huber Publishers.

De Winter, J.C., Dreger, F.A., Huang, W., Miller, A., Soccolich, S., Machiani, S.G. and Engström, J. (2018) The relationship between the Driver Behavior Questionnaire, Sensation Seeking Scale, and recorded crashes: A brief comment on Martinussen et al. (2017) and new data from SHRP2. *Accident Analysis & Prevention* 118, 54–56.

Deci, E.L. and Ryan, R.M. (1985) *Intrinsic Motivation and Self-determination in Human Behavior*. New York: Plenum

Deci, E.L. and Ryan, R.M. (2012) Self-determination theory. In P.A.M. Van Lange, A.W. Kruglanski and E.T. Higgins (eds) *Handbook of Theories of Social Psychology* (pp. 416–436). London: Sage Publications.

Decrop, A. (2006) *Vacation Decision Making*. Wallingford: CABI Publishing.

Deem, R. (1996) No time for a rest? An exploration of women's work, engendered leisure and holidays. *Time & Society* 5 (1), 5–25.

Deem, R. (1998) Dangerous territories. Struggles for difference and quality in education. *The Sociological Review* 46 (3), 622–625.

Deem, R. (1999) How do we get out of the ghetto? Strategies for research on gender and leisure for the twenty-first century. *Leisure Studies* 18 (3), 161–177.

Delpo, A. and Guerin, L. (2021) *Dealing With Problem Employees: How to Manage Performance & Personal Issues in the Workplace* (11th edn). Berkeley, CA: Nolo.

DeNeve, K.M. and Cooper, H. (1998) The happy personality: A meta-analysis of 137 personality traits and subjective well-being. *Psychological Bulletin* 124 (2), 197–229.

Deng, J. and Pierskalla, C.D. (2018) Linking importance–performance analysis, satisfaction, and loyalty: A study of Savannah, GA. *Sustainability* 10 (3), 704–721.

Derrida, J. (1968) *Différance*. in Bulletin de la Societe Francaise de Philosophie LXII, Number 3, July–September, 1968, pp. 73–101. Paris.

Devile, E.L. and Moura, A. (2015) Adventure tourism for people with disabilities in Portugal: Opportunities and challenges. In R. Melo (eds) *Sport Tourism: New Challenges in a Globalized World* (pp. 9–21). Coimbra, Portugal: Coimbra College of Education.

Di Figlia, L. (2016) Turnaround: Abandoned villages, from discarded elements of modern Italian society to possible resources. *International Planning Studies* 21 (3), 278–297.

Diener, E. and Seligman, M.E. (2002) Very happy people. *Psychological Science* 13 (1), 81–84.

Diener, E. and Seligman, M.E. (2004) Beyond money: Toward an economy of well-being. *Psychological Science in the Public Interest* 5 (1), 1–31.

Din, K.H. (1989) Islam and tourism, patterns, issues and options. *Annals of Tourism Research* 16 (4), 542–563.

Dodds, R. and Butler, R. (2019) The phenomena of overtourism: A review. *International Journal of Tourism Cities* 5 (4), 519–528.

Doggett, S.L., Miller, D.M., Vail, K. and Wilson, M.S. (2018) Fiscal impacts. In *Advances in the Biology and Management of Modern Bed Bugs* (pp. 139–147). Chichester: John Wiley and Sons.

Dolnicar, S., Lazarevski, K. and Yanamandram, V. (2013) Quality of life and tourism: A conceptual framework and novel segmentation base. *Journal of Business Research* 66 (6), 724–729.

Dong, W., Liao, S. and Zhang, Z. (2018) Leveraging financial social media data for corporate fraud detection. *Journal of Management Information Systems* 35 (2), 461–487.

Duckworth, A.L., Weir, D., Tsukayama, E. and Kwok, D. (2012) Who does well in life? Conscientious adults excel in both objective and subjective success. *Frontiers in Psychology* 3, 356.

Duedahl, E., Blichfeldt, B. and Liburd, J. (2020) How engaging with nature can facilitate active healthy ageing. *Tourism Geographies,* 1–21. https://doi.org/10.1080/14616688.2020.1819398

Durkheim, É. (1979/1897) *Suicide: A Study in Sociology*. New York: The Free Press. (trans John A. Spaulding).

Durkheim, E. (1984/1893) *The Division of labor in Society*. New York: The Free Press.

Durmus, E. (2019) The Nature of Escape and Holidaying. Unpublished Working Paper. First University, Turkey.

Dwyer, L., Dragićević, V., Armenski, T., Mihalič, T. and Knežević Cvelbar, L. (2016) Achieving destination competitiveness: An importance–performance analysis of Serbia. *Current Issues in Tourism* 19 (13), 1309–1336.

Eachus, P. (2004) Using the Brief Sensation Seeking Scale (BSSS) to predict holiday preferences. *Personality and Individual Differences* 36 (1), 141–153.

Edwards, D. (1994) Script formulations: An analysis of event descriptions in conversation. *Journal of Language and Social Psychology* 13 (3), 211–247.

Edvardsson, B. and Roos, I. (2001) Critical incident techniques: Towards a framework for analysing the criticality of critical incidents. *International Journal of Service Industry Management* 12 (3), 251–268.

Eisenberg, N., Duckworth, A.L., Spinrad, T.L. and Valiente, C. (2014) Conscientiousness: Origins in childhood? *Developmental Psychology* 50 (5), 1331.

El Sayed, I.M., Farrag, D.A. and Belk, R.W. (2004) The effects of physical surroundings on Egyptian consumers' emotional states and buying intentions. *Journal of International Consumer Marketing* 16 (1), 5–27.

Eldridge, A. and Roberts, M. (2008) Hen parties: Bonding or brawling? *Drugs: Education, Prevention, and Policy* 15 (3), 323–328.

Elliot, C.W. (1909) *John Stuart Mill, Essays on Liberty*. New York: P.F. Collier and Son Company.

Elliott, P. (1972) *The Sociology of the Professions*. New York: Herder and Herder.

Ely, R. and Mercurio, A. (2011) Time perspective and autobiographical memory: Individual and gender differences in experiencing time and remembering the past. *Time & Society* 20 (3), 375–400.

Epicurus. (2012) *The Art of Happiness*. New York: Penguin Books.

Errichiello, L., Micera, R., Atzeni, M. and Del Chiappa, G. (2019) Exploring the implications of wearable virtual reality technology for museum visitors' experience: A cluster analysis. *International Journal of Tourism Research* 21 (5), 590–605.

Etzioni, A. and Etzioni, O. (2017) Incorporating ethics into artificial intelligence. *The Journal of Ethics* 21 (4), 403–418.

Eurostat (2014) Tourism. In *Eurostat Regional Yearbook 2014* (pp. 187–210). Luxembourg: Publications Office of the European Union. Retrieved from https://ec.europa.eu/eurostat/documents/3217494/5785629/KS-HA-14-001-EN.PDF

Eusébio, C. and Carneiro, M.J. (2014) The impact of tourism on quality of life: A segmentation analysis of the youth market. *Tourism Analysis* 19 (6), 741–757.

Eysenck, H.J. and Eysenck, S.G.B. (1970) *The Eysenck Personality Inventory*. San Diego: Edits.

Eysenck, S. and Zuckerman, M. (1978) The relationship between sensation-seeking and Eysenck's dimensions of personality. *British Journal of Psychology* 69 (4), 483–487.

Fabrigar, L.R., MacDonald, T.K. and Wegener, D.T. (2005) The structure of attitudes. In D. Albarracín, B.T. Johnson and M.P. Zanna (eds) *The Handbook of Attitudes* (pp. 79–125). Mahwah, NJ: Lawrence Erlbaum.

Feigenbaum, K.D. and Smith, R.A. (2020) Historical narratives: Abraham Maslow and Blackfoot interpretations. *The Humanistic Psychologist* 48 (3), 232.

Fenton, M. and Pearce, P. (1988) Multidimensional scaling and tourism research. *Annals of Tourism Research* 15 (2), 236–254.

Ferrer, J.G., Sanz, M.F., Ferrandis, E.D., McCabe, S. and García, J.S. (2016) Social tourism and healthy ageing. *International Journal of Tourism Research* 18 (4), 297–307.

Fesenmaier, D.R. and Pearce, P.L. (2019) Searching ... for what is important. In P.L. Pearce (eds) *Tourist Behaviour: The Essential Companion* (pp. 385–405). Cheltenham: Edward Elgar Publishing.

Festinger, L. (1957) *A Theory of Cognitive Dissonance.* New York: Harper & Row.

Fieger, P., Prayag, G. and Bruwer, J. (2019) 'Pull' motivation: An activity-based typology of international visitors to New Zealand. *Current Issues in Tourism* 22 (2), 173–196.

Filep, S. and Greenacre, L. (2007) Evaluating and extending the travel career patterns model. *Tourism: An International Interdisciplinary Journal* 55 (1), 23–38.

Fishbein, M. and Ajzen, I. (1975) *Belief, Attitude, Intention and Behavior: An Introduction to Theory and Research.* Reading, MA: Addison-Wesley.

Fonberg, J. and Smith, A.P. (2019) The validity of a single question about life satisfaction. *International Journal of Arts, Humanities and Social Sciences* 4, 38–44.

Forno, F. and Garibaldi, R. (2015) Sharing economy in travel and tourism: The case of home-swapping in Italy. *Journal of Quality Assurance in Hospitality & Tourism* 16 (2), 202–220.

Fortenberry, J.L. and McGoldrick, P.J. (2020) Do billboard advertisements drive customer retention? Expanding the "AIDA" model to "AIDAR". *Journal of Advertising Research* 60 (2), 135–147.

Foucault, M. (1966) *Les Mots et les choses: Une archéologie des sciences humaines.* Paris: Éditions Gallimard.

Foucault, M. (1969) *L'archéologie du savoir.* Paris: Éditions Gallimard.

Fountain, J.E. (2022) The moon, the ghetto and artificial intelligence: Reducing systemic racism in computational algorithms. *Government Information Quarterly* 39 (2), 101645.

Foxall, G. (1990) *Consumer Psychology in Behavioural Perspective.* London and New York: Routledge.

Francken, D.A. and van Raaij, W.F. (1979) Longitudinal study of vacationers' information acquisition behavior. *Papers on Economic Psychology,* 2. Rotterdam: Erasmus University.

Franklin, A. and Crang, M. (2001) The trouble with tourism and travel theory? *Tourist Studies* 1 (1), 5–22.

Frash Jr, R.E. and Blose, J.E. (2019) Serious leisure as a predictor of travel intentions and flow in motorcycle tourism. *Tourism Recreation Research* 44 (4), 516–531.

Fredrickson, B.L. (2001) The role of positive emotions in positive psychology: The broaden-and-build theory of positive emotions. *American Psychologist* 56 (3), 218.

Fredrickson, B.L. (2004) The broaden–and–build theory of positive emotions. *Philosophical Transactions of the Royal Society of London. Series B: Biological Sciences* 359 (1449), 1367–1377.

Fredrickson, B.L. (2013) Positive emotions broaden and build. In P. Devine and A. Plant (eds) *Advances in Experimental Social Psychology* (Vol. 47, pp. 1–53). Burlington: Academic Press.

Frey, C.B. and Osborne, M. (2013) *The Future of Employment.* Oxford Martin Programme on Employment and Technology Working Paper, Oxford University.

Frey, C.B. and Osborne, M.A. (2017) The future of employment: How susceptible are jobs to computerisation? *Technological Forecasting and Social Change* 114, 254–280.

Frías, D.M., Rodríguez, M.A. and Castaneda, J.A. (2008) Internet vs. travel agencies on pre-visit destination image formation: An information processing view. *Tourism Management* 29, 163–179.

Frost, J., and Frost, W. (2021) Exploring prosocial and environmental motivations of frontier tourists: Implications for sustainable space tourism. *Journal of Sustainable Tourism* 30 (9), 2254–2270.

Fussell, P. (1980) *Abroad: British Literary Traveling Between the Wars.* New York: Oxford University Press.

Füller, J. and Matzler, K. (2008) Customer delight and market segmentation: An application of the three-factor theory of customer satisfaction on life style groups. *Tourism Management* 29 (1), 116–126.

Gallent, N. and Tewdwr-Jones, M. (2020) *Rural Second Homes in Europe: Examining Housing Supply and Planning Control.* Abingdon: Routledge.

Ganji, S.F.G., Johnson, L.W. and Sadeghian, S. (2021) The effect of place image and place attachment on residents' perceived value and support for tourism development. *Current Issues in Tourism* 24 (9), 1304–1318.

Gao, Y., Rasouli, S., Timmermans, H. and Wang, Y. (2017) Understanding the relationship between travel satisfaction and subjective well-being considering the role of personality traits: A structural equation model. *Transportation Research Part F: Traffic Psychology and Behaviour* 49, 110–123.

Gardiner, A.H. (2022) *Notes on the Story of Sinuhe.* Eugene, Oregon: Wipf and Stock Publishers.

Gardiner, S., Vada, S., Yang, E.C.L., Khoo, C. and Le, T.H. (2022) Recreating history: The evolving negotiation of staged authenticity in tourism experiences. *Tourism Management* 91, 104515.

Gardiner, S. and Kwek, A. (2017) Chinese participation in adventure tourism: A study of generation Y international students' perceptions. *Journal of Travel Research* 56 (4), 496–506.

Gartner, W.C. (1986) Temporal influences on image change. *Annals of Tourism Research* 13 (4), 635–644.

Gartner, W.C. (1989) Tourism image: Attribute measurement of state tourism products using multidimensional scaling techniques. *Journal of Travel Research* 28 (2), 16–20.

Gartner, W.C. (1994) Image formation process. *Journal of Travel & Tourism Marketing* 2 (2–3), 191–216.

Gawer, A. (2009) Platform dynamics and strategies: From products to services. In A. Gawer (ed.) *Platforms, Markets and Innovation* (pp. 45–57). Cheltenham: Edward Elgar Publishing.

Gellius, A. (250BCE/1927) *Attic Nights of Aulus Gellius* (trans by J.C. Rolfe). Book 3 (3). Cambridge: Loeb Classical Library, p. 3.

Getz, D. and Andersson, T. (2020) Testing the event travel career trajectory in multiple participation sports. *Journal of Sport & Tourism* 24 (3), 155–176.

Gibson, H. and Yiannakis, A. (2002) Tourist roles: Needs and lifecourse. *Annals of Tourism Research* 29 (2), 358–383.

Gibson, H.J., Attle, S.P. and Yiannakis, A. (1998) Segmenting the active sport tourist market: A life-span perspective. *Journal of Vacation Marketing* 4 (1), 52–64.

Gilbert, D. and Abdullah, J. (2004) Holidaytaking and the sense of well-being. *Annals of Tourism Research* 31 (1), 103–121.

Gilchrist, H., Povey, R., Dickinson, A. and Povey, R. (1995) The sensation seeking scale: Its use in a study of the characteristics of people choosing 'Adventure holidays.' *Personality and Individual Differences* 19 (4), 513–516.

Gittens, C.L. and Garnes, D. (2022, January) Zenbo on zoom: Evaluating the human-robot interaction user experience in a video conferencing session. In *2022 IEEE International Conference on Consumer Electronics (ICCE)* (pp. 1–6). IEEE.

Gladwell, M. (2000) *The Tipping Point: How Little Things Can Make a Big Difference.* New York & Boston: Little, Brown and Company.

Gladwell, M. (2008) *Outliers: The Story of Success.* New York: Little, Brown and Company.

Gnoth, J., Zins, A.H., Lengmueller, R. and Boshoff, C. (2000) Emotions, mood, flow and motivations to travel. *Journal of Travel & Tourism Marketing* 9 (3), 23–34.

Go, F. and Zhang, W. (1997) Applying importance-performance analysis to Beijing as an international meeting destination. *Journal of Travel Research* 35 (4), 42–49.

Goethals, P. (2016) Multilingualism and international tourism: A content-and discourse-based approach to language-related judgments in web 2.0 hotel reviews. *Language and Intercultural Communication* 16 (2), 235–253.

Goffman, E. (1959) *The Presentation of Self in Everyday Life*. New York: Anchor Books.

Goh, E. and Okumus, F. (2020) Avoiding the hospitality workforce bubble: Strategies to attract and retain generation Z talent in the hospitality workforce. *Tourism Management Perspectives* 33, 100603.

Goldberg, L.R. (1990) An alternative "description of personality": The big-five factor structure. *Journal of Personality and Social Psychology* 59 (6), 1216–1229.

Grabe, M.E., Zhou, S.H., Lang, A. and Bolls, P.D. (2000) Packaging television news: The effectsoftabloid on information processing and evaluative responses. *Journal of Broadcasting & Electronic Media* 44 (4), 581–598.

Gram, G. (2005) Family holidays: A qualitative analysis of family holiday experiences. *Scandinavian Journal of Hospitality and Tourism* 5 (1), 2–22.

Gram, M., O'Donohoe, S., Schänzel, H., Marchant, C. and Kastarinen, A. (2019) Fun time, finite time: Temporal and emotional dimensions of grand travel experiences. *Annals of Tourism Research* 79, 102769.

Gratwick, A.S. (1979) Sundials, parasites, and girls from Boeotia. *The Classical Quarterly* 29 (2), 308–323.

Gray, H.P. (1970) *International Travel: International Trade*. Lexington, MA: Heath Lexington.

Gray, H.P. (1982) The contributions of economics to tourism. *Annals of Tourism Research* 9 (1), 105–125.

Gray, J.A. (1987) *The Psychology of Fear and Stress* (Vol. 5). Cambridge: Cambridge University Press.

Gretzel, U. (2018) Influencer marketing in travel and tourism. In M. Sigala and U. Gretzel (eds) *Advances in Social Media for Travel, Tourism and Hospitality: New Perspectives, Practice and Cases* (pp. 147–156). New York: Routledge.

Gretzel, U. and Jamal, T. (2009) Conceptualizing the creative tourist class: Technology, mobility, and tourism experiences. *Tourism Analysis* 14 (4), 471–481.

Griffiths, A. (1997) Ageing, health and productivity: A challenge for the new millennium. *Work & Stress* 11 (3), 197–214.

Gross, M.J. and Brown, G. (2006) Tourism experiences in a lifestyle destination setting: The roles of involvement and place attachment. *Journal of Business Research* 59 (6), 696–700.

Gross, M.J. and Brown, G. (2008) An empirical structural model of tourists and places: Progressing involvement and place attachment into tourism. *Tourism Management* 29 (6), 1141–1151.

Gruber, M.J., Gelman, B.D. and Ranganath, C. (2014) States of curiosity modulate hippocampus-dependent learning via the dopaminergic circuit. *Neuron* 84 (2), 486–496.

Groucutt, J. and Hopkins, C. (2017) *Marketing*. Bloomsbury Publishing.

Gu, H. and Ryan, C. (2008) Place attachment, identity and community impacts of tourism – the case of a Beijing hutong. *Tourism Management* 29 (4), 637–647.

Guidi, J., Lucente, M., Sonino, N. and Fava, G.A. (2021) Allostatic load and its impact on health: A systematic review. *Psychotherapy and Psychosomatics* 90 (1), 11–27.

Guiliani, M.V. (1991) Towards an analysis of mental representations of attachment to the home. *Journal of Architecture and Planning Research* 8 (2), 133–146.

Gunn, C.A. (1989), *Vacationscape: Designing Tourist Regions* (2nd edn). New York: Van Nostrand Reinhold Publishers.

Gurney, G.G., Blythe, J., Adams, H., Adger, W.N., Curnock, M., Faulkner, L., James, T. and Marshall, N.A. (2017) Redefining community based on place attachment in a connected world. *Proceedings of the National Academy of Sciences* 114 (38), 10077–10082.

Gursoy, D., Uysal, M., Sirakaya-Turk, E., Ekinci, Y. and Baloglu, S. (2014) *Handbook of Scales in Tourism and Hospitality Research*. Wallingford: CAB International.

Gyte, D.M. (1988) Repertory grid analysis of images of destination: British tourists in Mallorca. *Trent Working Papers in Geography*. Nottingham: Nottingham Polytecnice/ Nottingham Trent University.

Hadinejad, A., Moyle, B.D., Kralj, A. and Scott, N. (2019a) Physiological and self-report methods to the measurement of emotion in tourism. *Tourism Recreation Research* 44 (4), 466–478.

Hadinejad, A., Moyle, B.D., Scott, N. and Kralj, A. (2019b) Emotional responses to tourism advertisements: The application of FaceReader™. *Tourism Recreation Research* 44 (1), 131–135.

Hagger, C. and Murray, D. (2014) Anticipating a flourishing future with tourism experiences. In S. Filep and P. Pearce (eds) *Tourist Experience and Fulfilment; Insights from Positive Psychology* (pp. 186–201). Abingdon: Routledge.

Hall, C.M. (2005) *Tourism: Rethinking the Social Science of Mobility*. Harlow: Prentice Hall.

Hall, C.M. and Müller, H.K. (2018a) *The Routledge Handbook of Second Home Tourism And Mobilities*. New York: Routledge.

Hall, C.M. and Müller, H.K. (2018b) The future of second homes. In C.M. Hall and H.K. Müller (eds) *The Routledge Handbook of Second Home Tourism and Mobilities* (pp. 355–360). New York: Routledge.

Hampden-Turner, C. (1970) *Radical Man: The Process of Psycho-Social Development*. Cambridge: Schenkman Publishing Company.

Han, C.M. (1989) Country image: Halo or summary construct? *Journal of Marketing Research* 26 (2), 222–229.

Han, J.H., Kim, J.S., Lee, C.K. and Kim, N. (2019) Role of place attachment dimensions in tourists' decision-making process in Cittáslow. *Journal of Destination Marketing & Management* 11, 108–119.

Hancock, P.A. (2018) On the design of time. *Ergonomics in Design: The Quarterly of Human Factors Applications* 26 (2), 4–9.

Hannam, K. (2009) The end of tourism? Nomadology and the mobilities paradigm. In J. Tribe (ed.) *Philosophical Issues in Tourism* (pp. 101–113). Bristol: Channel View Publications.

Hardy, A. (2017) Community and connection: Exploring non-monetary aspects of the collaborative economy through recreation vehicle use. In D. Dredge and S. Gyimóthy (eds) *Collaborative Economy and Tourism* (pp. 255–270). Cham: Springer.

Hartig, T., Catalano, R., Ong, M. and Syme, S.L. (2013) Vacation, collective restoration, and mental health in a population. *Society and Mental Health* 3 (3), 221–236.

Hassell, S., Moore, S.A. and Macbeth, J. (2015) Exploring the motivations, experiences and meanings of camping in national parks. *Leisure Sciences* 37 (3), 269–287.

Havitz, M.E. and Dimanche, F. (1997) Leisure involvement revisited: Conceptual conundrums and measurement advances. *Journal of Leisure Research* 29 (3), 245–278.

Havitz, M.E. and Mannell, R.C. (2005) Enduring involvement, situational involvement, and flow in leisure and non-leisure activities. *Journal of Leisure Research* 37 (2), 152–177.

Haywood, K.M. (2020) A post COVID-19 future-tourism re-imagined and re-enabled. *Tourism Geographies* 22 (3), 599–609.

Heidegger, M. (1927/1962) *Being and Time*. Oxford: Basil Blackwell.

Heidegger, M. (1968) *What Is Called Thinking?* (Translated by Glen Gray, F. and Wieck, F). New York: Harper and Row.

Heimtun, B. (2019) Holidays with aging parents: Pleasures, duties and constraints. *Annals of Tourism Research* 76, 129–139.

Helliwell, J.F. and Wang, S. (2014) Weekends and subjective well-being. *Social Indicators Research* 116 (2), 389–407.

Hermans, E., Herregodts, E. and Cops, V. (2020) Intergenerational holidays. In A. Diekmann and S. McCabe (eds) *Handbook of Social Tourism* (pp. 221–231). Cheltenham: Edward Elgar Publishing.

Hergesell, A., Dwyer, L. and Edwards, D. (2019) Deciding and choosing. In P.L. Pearce (ed.) *Tourist Behaviour: The Essential Companion* (pp. 41–59). Cheltenham: Edward Elgar Publishing.

Heron, R.P. (1983) Heritage presentation for community development: A planning perspective. In *Leisure Research. Proceedings from a Workshop Meeting [European Leisure and Recreation Association, Advisory Group 3, Växjö, Sweden, May 13–15, 1983]* (pp. 283–309).

Hidalgo, M.C. and Hernandez, B. (2001) Place attachment: Conceptual and empirical questions. *Journal of Environmental Psychology* 21 (3), 273–281.

Higham, J.E. and Cohen, S.A. (2011) Canary in the coalmine: Norwegian attitudes towards climate change and extreme long-haul air travel to Aotearoa/New Zealand. *Tourism Management* 32 (1), 98–105.

Hirschman, E.C. (1980) Innovativeness, novelty seeking, and consumer creativity. *Journal of Consumer Research* 7 (3), 283–295.

Hirschman, E.C. (1984) Experience seeking: A subjectivist perspective of consumption. *Journal of Business Research* 12 (1), 115–136.

Ho, G.K. and McKercher, B. (2015) A review of life cycle models by Plog and Butler from a marketing perspective. In M. Kozak and N. Kozak (eds) *Destination Marketing: An International Perspective* (pp. 145–154). Abingdon: Routledge.

Hobfoll, S.E. (1989) Conservation of resources: A new attempt at conceptualizing stress. *American Psychologist* 44 (3), 513–524.

Hobfoll, S.E. (2001) Conservation of resources: A rejoinder to the commentaries. *Applied Psychology: An International Review* 50 (3), 419–421.

Hobfoll, S.E. and Shirom, A. (2000) Conservation of resources theory: Applications to stress and management in the workplace. In R.T. Golembiewski (ed) *Handbook of Organization Behavior* (pp. 57–80). New York: Marcel Dekker.

Hobfoll, S.E., Halbesleben, J., Neveu, J.P. and Westman, M. (2018) Conservation of resources in the organizational context: The reality of resources and their consequences. *Annual Review of Organizational Psychology and Organizational Behavior* 5, 103–128.

Hobson, J. and Dietrich, U. (1994) Tourism, health and quality of life: Challenging the responsibility of using the traditional tenets of sun, sea, sand and sex in tourism marketing. *Journal of Travel and Tourism Marketing* 3 (4), 21–38.

Hockenberry, J.M. and Helmchen, L.A. (2014) The nature of surgeon human capital depreciation. Working paper available at: Tinyurl.com/kxl6l4e.

Hoffman, E. (1988) *The Right to be Human: A Biography of Abraham Maslow*. Los Angeles: Jeremy P. Tarcher, Inc.

Hoffman, E. (1996) *Future Visions: The Unpublished Papers of Abraham Maslow*. Thousand Oaks, CA: Sage Publications.

Hoffman, E. and Compton, W.C. (2022) The Dao of Maslow: A new direction for mentorship. Journal of Humanistic Psychology, 00221678221076574.

Holbrook, M.B. and Hirschman, E.C. (1982) The experiential aspects of consumption: Consumer fantasies, feelings, and fun. *Journal of Consumer Research* 9 (2), 132–140.

Hollinshead, K. (1991) Land of promise: Aborigines and development in the East Kimberley. *Annals of Tourism Research* 18 (4), 677–681.

Hollinshead, K. (1994) The unconscious realm of tourism. *Annals of Tourism Research* 21 (2), 387–391.

Hollinshead, K. (1999) Surveillance of the worlds of tourism: Foucault and the eye-of-power. *Tourism Management* 20 (1), 7–23.

Hollinshead, K. (2008) Tourism and the social production of culture and place: Critical conceptualizations on the projection of location. *Tourism Analysis* 13 (5–6), 639–660.

Hollinshead, K. (2009) The "worldmaking" prodigy of tourism: The reach and power of tourism in the dynamics of change and transformation. *Tourism Analysis* 14 (1), 139–152.

Hollinshead, K. and Hou, C. (2013) Synthesis–the eye of power in and through tourism: The banal ubiquity of agents of naturalization. In O. Moufakkir and Y. Reisinger (eds) *The Host Gaze in Global Tourism* (pp. 235–252). Wallingford: CABI.

Hollinshead, K. and Kuon, V. (2013) The scopic drive of tourism: Foucault and eye dialectics. In O. Moufakkir and Y. Reisinger (eds) *The Host Gaze in Global Tourism* (pp. 1–18). Wallingford: CABI.

Hong, Y., Cai, G., Mo, Z., Gao, W., Xu, L., Jiang, Y. and Jiang, J. (2020) The impact of COVID-19 on tourist satisfaction with B&B in Zhejiang, China: An importance–performance analysis. *International Journal of Environmental Research and Public Health* 17 (10), 37–47.

Hoorens, V. (2012) Expectation. In V.S. Ramachandran (ed) *Encyclopedia of Human Behavior* (pp. 142–149). San Diego: Elsevier Science Publishing Co Inc.

Hou, Z., Cui, F., Meng, Y., Lian, T. and Yu, C. (2019) Opinion mining from online travel reviews: A comparative analysis of Chinese major OTAs using semantic association analysis. *Tourism Management* 74, 276–289.

Horner, S. and Swarbrooke, J. (2016) *Consumer Behaviour in Tourism*. Abingdon: Routledge.

Huang, X., Chen, M., Wang, Y., Yi, J., Song, Z. and Ryan, C. (2022) Visitors' spatial-temporal behaviour and their learning experience: A comparative study. *Tourism Management Perspectives* 42, 100951.

Hughes, H.L. and Deutsch, R. (2010) Holidays of older gay men: Age or sexual orientation as decisive factors? *Tourism Management* 31 (4), 454–463.

Huh, J., Uysal, M. and McCleary, K. (2006) Cultural/heritage destinations: Tourist satisfaction and market segmentation. *Journal of Hospitality & Leisure Marketing* 14 (3), 81–99.

Hsiung, A., Poh, J-H., Huettel, S.A. and Adcock, R.A. (2022) Curiosity encourages patience and joy in the presence of uncertainty. Retrieved on September 18, 2022, from https://www.researchgate.net/publication/361306069_Spoiler_Alert_Curiosity_encourages_patience_and_joy_in_the_presence_of_uncertainty.

Hsu, C.H.C. and Huang, S. (2008) Travel motivation: A critical review of the concept's development. In A.G. Woodside and D. Martin (eds) *Tourism Management: Analysis, Behaviour and Strategy* (pp. 14–27). Wallingford: CABI Publishing.

Immordino, G., Jappelli, T., Oliviero, T. and Zazzaro, A. (2021) *Fear of COVID-19 Contagion and Consumption: Evidence from a Survey of Italian Households*. CSEF Working Papers 601, Centre for Studies in Economics and Finance (CSEF), University of Naples, Italy.

Immordino, G., Jappelli, T., Oliviero, T. and Zazzaro, A. (2022) Fear of COVID-19 contagion and consumption: Evidence from a survey of Italian households. *Health Economics* 31 (3), 496–507.

Indrawan, I.W. (2018) Doughnut economics. *International Journal of Economics, Management and Accounting* 26 (2), 499–503.

Isaacs, L.L., Nelson, R. and Trapp, S. (2021) Recreational therapists consider leisure motivation when evaluating virtual reality games. *Therapeutic Recreation Journal* 55 (4), 399–413.

Iso-Ahola, S.E. (1983) Towards a social psychology of recreational travel. *Leisure Studies* 2 (1), 45–56.

Jackson, M., Schmierer, C. and White, G. (1999) Is there a unique tourist personality which is predictive of tourist behaviour? In J. Molloy and J. Evans (eds) *Tourism and Hospitality: Delighting the Senses* (pp. 39–47). Canberra: Bureau of Tourism Research.

Jackson, M., White, G. and White, M.G. (2001, February) Developing a tourist personality typology. Paper presented at the *Proceedings of Council for Australian University Tourism and Hospitality Education (CAUTHE) National Research Conference*, Australia. Retrieved on October 1, 2022, from https://www.researchgate.net/profile /Mervyn Jackson/publication/313646818_Developing_a_tourist_personality_typolog y/links/5de987f5299bf10bc34367af/Developing-a-tourist-personality-typology.pdf

Jackson, S.A. and Marsh, H.W. (1996) Development and validation of a scale to measure optimal experience: The flow state scale. *Journal of Sport and Exercise Psychology* 18 (1), 17–35.

Jackson, S.A. and Eklund, R.C. (2002) Assessing flow in physical activity: The flow state scale-2 and dispositional flow scale-2. *Journal of Sport and Exercise Psychology* 24 (2), 133–150.

Jackson, S.A., Ford, S.K., Kimiecik, J.C. and Marsh, H.W. (1998) Psychological correlates of flow in sport. *Journal of Sport & Exercise Psychology* 20 (4), 358–378.

Jacobsen, J.K.S., Farstad, E., Higham, J., Hopkins, D. and Landa-Mata, I. (2023) Travel discontinuities enforced holidaying-at-home and alternative leisure travel futures after COVID-19. *Tourism Geographies* 25 (2/3), 615–633.

Jamal, T. and Hollinshead, K. (2001) Tourism and the forbidden zone: The underserved power of qualitative inquiry. *Tourism Management* 22 (1), 63–82.

Jan, M., Soomro, S., Ahmad, N. (2017) Impact of social media on self-esteem. *European Scientific Journal* 13 (23), 329–341.

Jang, S.S. and Namkung, Y. (2009) Perceived quality, emotions, and behavioral intentions: Application of an extended Mehrabian-Russell model to restaurants. *Journal of Business Research* 62 (4), 451–460.

Jani, D. (2014) Relating travel personality to Big Five Factors of personality. *Tourism: An International Interdisciplinary Journal* 62 (4), 347–359.

Jani, D. and Han, H. (2015) Influence of environmental stimuli on hotel customer emotional loyalty response: Testing the moderating effect of the big five personality factors. *International Journal of Hospitality Management* 44, 48–57.

Jani, D., Jang, J.H. and Hwang, Y.H. (2014) Big five factors of personality and tourists' Internet search behavior. *Asia Pacific Journal of Tourism Research* 19 (5), 600–615.

Jeng, C.R., Snyder, A.T. and Chen, C.F. (2019) Importance–performance analysis as a strategic tool for tourism marketers: The case of Taiwan's Destination Image. *Tourism and Hospitality Research* 19 (1), 112–125.

Jenkins, J.M. and Walmsley, D.J. (1993) Mental maps of tourists: A study of Coffs Harbour, New South Wales. *GeoJournal* 29 (3), 233–241.

Jepson, A., Stadler, R. and Spencer, N. (2019) Making positive family memories together and improving quality-of-life through thick sociality and bonding at local community festivals and events. *Tourism Management* 75, 34–50.

Jiang, T., Ryan, C. and Zhang, C. (2018) The spiritual or secular tourist? The experience of Zen meditation in Chinese temples. *Tourism Management* 65, 187–199.

Jiricka-Pürrer, A., Brandenburg, C. and Pröbstl-Haider, U. (2020) City tourism pre-and post-covid-19 pandemic–messages to take home for climate change adaptation and mitigation? *Journal of Outdoor Recreation and Tourism* 31, 100329.

John, O.P. and Srivastava, S. (1999) The big five trait taxonomy: History, measurement, and theoretical perspectives. In L.A. Pervin and O.P. John (eds) *Handbook of Personality: Theory and Research* (pp. 102–138). New York: Guilford Press.

Johnston, R. (1970) Motivation in a changing environment. *Operations Bulletin*, American Hotel and Motel Association, September, 1970.

Jones, C.D., Hollenhorst, S.J. and Perna, F. (2003) An empirical comparison of the four-channel flow model and adventure experience paradigm. *Leisure Sciences* 25 (1), 17–31.

Jung, T., tom Dieck, M.C., Lee, H. and Chung, N. (2016) Effects of virtual reality and augmented reality on visitor experiences in museum. In A. Inversini and R. Schegg (eds) *Information and Communication Technologies in Tourism 2016* (pp. 621–635). Cham: Springer International Publishing.

Kano, N. (1984) Attractive quality and must-be quality. *Journal of the Japanese Society for Quality Control* 31 (4), 147–156.

Kant, I. (1781) *Critik der reinen Vernunft*. Riga: Johann Friedrich Hartknoch.

Kant, I. (1908) Critique of pure reason. 1781. *Modern Classical Philosophers*. Cambridge, MA: Houghton Mifflin.

Kaosiri, Y.N., Fiol, L.J.C., Tena, M.A., Artola, R.M.R. and Garcia, J.S. (2017) User-generated content sources in social media: A new approach to explore tourist satisfaction. *Journal of Travel Research* 58 (3), 1–13.

Kearns, R. and Collins, D. (2006) On the rocks': New Zealand's coastal bach landscape and the case of Rangitoto Island. *New Zealand Geographer* 62 (3), 227–235.

Keen, D. and Hall, C.M. (2004) Second homes in New Zealand. In C.M. Hall and D.K. Müller (eds) *Tourism, Mobility and Second Homes: Between Elite Landscape and Common Ground* (pp. 174–195). Clevedon: Channel View Publications.

Kelly, C. (2022) Beyond 'a trip to the seaside': Exploring emotions and family tourism experiences. *Tourism Geographies* 24 (2–3), 284–305.

Kelly, G. and Hosking, K. (2008) Nonpermanent residents, place attachment, and "sea change" communities. *Environment and Behavior* 40 (4), 575–594.

Kernis, M.H. and Goldman, B.M. (2006) A multicomponent conceptualization of authenticity: Theory and research. *Advances in Experimental Social Psychology* 38, 283–357.

Khoo-Lattimore, C. (2018) The effect of motherhood on tourism fieldwork with young children: An autoethnographic approach. In B.A. Porter and H.A. Schänzel (eds) *Femininities in the Field: Tourism and Transdisciplinary Research* (pp. 126–139). Bristol: Channel View Publications.

Khoo-Lattimore, C. and Yang, E.C.L. (2018a) Asian youth tourism: Contemporary trends, cases and issues. In C. Khoo-Lattimore and E.C.L. Yang (eds) *Asian Youth Travellers* (pp. 1–13). Singapore: Springer Verlag.

Khoo-Lattimore, C. and Yang, E.E.C.L. (2018b) Tourism gender studies. In C. Cooper, S. Volo, W.C. Gartner and N. Scott (eds) *The SAGE Handbook of Tourism Management: Applications of Theories and Concepts to Tourism* (Vol. 2, pp. 38–48). London: SAGE.

Kidd, C. and Hayden, B.Y. (2015) The psychology and neuroscience of curiosity. *Neuron* 88 (3), 449–460.

Kilpatrick, R. (2014) Hong Kong tour guides attacked for asking mainland tourists not to litter. Retrieved on July 1, 2022 from https://www.thatsmags.com/china/post/6385/hong-kong-tour-guides-attacked-for-asking-mainland-tourists-not-to-litter

Kim, A.K. and Brown, G. (2012) Understanding the relationships between perceived travel experiences, overall satisfaction, and destination loyalty. *An International Journal of Tourism and Hospitality Research* 23 (3), 328–347.

Kim, J.-N. and Grunig, J.E. (2011) Problem solving and communicative action: A situational theory of problem solving. *Journal of Communication* 61 (1), 120–149.

Kim, M. and Thapa, B. (2018) Perceived value and flow experience: Application in a nature-based tourism context. *Journal of Destination Marketing & Management* 8, 373–384.

Kim, M.J., Lee, C.K. and Jung, T. (2020) Exploring consumer behavior in virtual reality tourism using an extended stimulus-organism-response model. *Journal of Travel Research* 59 (1), 69–89.

Kim, W.G. and Moon, Y.J. (2009) Customers' cognitive, emotional, and actionable response to the servicescape: A test of the moderating effect of the restaurant type. *International Journal of Hospitality Management* 28 (1), 144–156.

King, A.D. (1980) A space for time and a time for space: The social production of the vacation house. In A.D. King (ed.) *Buildings and Society: Essays on the Social Development of the Built Environment* (pp. 193–227). Henley-on-Thames, Oxon: Routledge and Kegan Paul.

King, B.A., Hammond, T. and Harrington, J. (2017) Disruptive technology: Economic consequences of artificial intelligence and the robotics revolution. *Journal of Strategic Innovation and Sustainability* 12 (2), 53–67.

Kirillova, K., Lehto, X. and Cai, L. (2016) Tourism and existential transformation: An empirical investigation. *Journal of Travel Research* 56 (5), 638–650.

Kirshenblatt-Gimblett, B. (2016) Historical space and critical museologies: POLIN museum of the history of polish Jews. In K. Murawska-Muthesius and P. Piotrowski (eds) *From Museum Critique to the Critical Museum* (pp. 147–162). New York: Routledge.

Kisia-Omondi, R. and Ryan, C. (2023) *Sex Tourism on the Kenyan Coast: Romantics Safaris and Unfulfilled Dreams*. Singapore: Springer.

Kline, C., Bulla, B., Rubright, H., Green, E. and Harris, E. (2016) An exploratory study of expectation-importance-performance analysis with cultural tourists in Havana, Cuba. *Tourism and Hospitality Research* 16 (1), 19–34.

Knudsen, B.T. and Waade, A.M. (2010a) *Re-Investing Authenticity: Tourism, Place and Emotions*. Bristol: Channel View Publications.

Knudsen, B.T. and Waade, A.M. (2010b) Performative authenticity in tourism and spatial experience: Rethinking the relations between travel, place and emotion. In B.T. Knudsen and A.M. Waade (eds) *Re-Investing Authenticity: Tourism, Place and Emotions* (pp. 1–19). Bristol: Channel View Publications.

Koh, E. (2020) The end of over-tourism? Opportunities in a post-Covid-19 world. *International Journal of Tourism Cities* 6 (4), 1015–1023.

Kolodny, L. (2017) Meet flippy, a burger-grilling robot from miso robotics and CaliBurger. Retrieved on August 28, 2019, from https://techcrunch.com/2017/03/07/meet-flippy-a-burger-grilling-robot-from-miso-roboticsand-caliburger/

Korpela, K.M. (1989) Place identity as a product of environmental self-regulation. *Journal of Environmental Psychology* 9 (3), 241–256.

Kostoff, R.N., Boylan, R. and Simons, G.R. (2004) Disruptive technology roadmaps. *Technological Forecasting and Social Change* 71 (1–2), 141–159.

Krippendorf, J. (1987) *The Holidaymakers*. Oxford: Butterworth Heinemann.

Krippendorf, J. (1999) *The Holiday Makers: Understanding the Impact of Leisure and Travel*. London: Routledge.

Krouska, A., Troussas, C., Virvou, M. and Fragkakis, C.K. (2018, July) Applying Skinnerian conditioning for shaping skill performance in online tutoring of programming languages. Paper presented at *2018 9th International Conference on Information, Intelligence, Systems and Applications (IISA)* (pp. 1–5). Retrieved on October 1, 2022 from https://www.researchgate.net/publication/330876068_Applying_Skinnerian_Conditioning_for_Shaping_Skill_Performance_in_Online_Tutoring_of_Programming_Languages.

Kuhn, T. (1962) *The Structure of Scientific Revolutions*. Chicago: University of Chicago Press.

Kulendran, N. and Wilson, K. (2000) Modelling business travel. *Tourism Economics* 6 (1), 47–59.

Kumar, R. (2017) Developing a stakeholder communication strategy: The case of Indian Railways and Swachh campaign. In T. Kanti, J.N. Girl, H. Bhatia, J. Pandit and A. Gupta (eds) *Technological and Managerial Strategies for Next Generation Transformation* (pp. 311–322). New Delhi: Bloomsbury.

Kuo, N.T., Cheng, Y.S., Chiu, W.H. and Cho, S. (2016) Personalities of travel agents with strong sales records in Taiwan. *Asia Pacific Journal of Tourism Research* 21 (9), 1001–1019.

Kuriyama, K., Shoji, Y. and Tsuge, T. (2020) The value of leisure time of weekends and long holidays: The multiple discrete–continuous extreme value (MDCEV) choice model with triple constraints. *Journal of Choice Modelling* 37, 100238.

Kvasova, O. (2015) The big five personality traits as antecedents of eco-friendly tourist behavior. *Personality and Individual Differences* 83, 111–116.

Kyriakou, D. and Belias, D. (2017) Is silver economy a new way of tourism potential for Greece? In V. Katsoni, A. Upadhya and A. Stratigea (eds) *Tourism, Culture and Heritage in a Smart Economy* (pp. 425–435). Cham: Springer International Publishing.

Kyle, G., Graefe, A. and Manning, R. (2005) Testing the dimensionality of place attachment in recreational settings. *Environment and Behavior* 37 (2), 153–177.

Lai, I.K.W. and Hitchcock, M. (2015) Importance-performance analysis in tourism: A framework for researchers. *Tourism Management* 48, 242–267.

Lalli, M. (1992) Urban-related identity: Theory, measurement, and empirical findings. *Journal of Environmental Psychology* 12 (4), 285–303.

Latimer, P. (2019) Loss of property 'unattended in a public place' — Testing the good faith of the travel insurer. *Australian Bar Review* 47 (1), 49–71.

Laviolette, P. (2011) Introduction – Fearless Theorising. In P. Laviolette (ed.) *Extreme Landscapes of Leisure: Not a Hap-Hazardous Sport* (pp. 1–20). Abingdon: Routledge.

Lawson, R., Thyne, M. and Young, T. (1997) New Zealand Holidays: A Travel Lifesylles Study. The Marketing Department, University of Otago, ISBN 1-877156-18-3.

Lazarus, R.S. (2001) Conservation of Resources theory (COR): Little more than words masquerading as a new theory. *Applied Psychology: An International Review* 50 (3), 381–391.

Lazarus, R.S. and Alfert, E. (1964) Short-circuiting of threat by experimentally altering cognitive appraisal. *The Journal of Abnormal and Social Psychology* 69 (2), 195–205.

Lebuda, I. and Csikszentmihalyi, M. (2020) All you need is love: The importance of partner and family relations to highly creative individuals' well-being and success. *The Journal of Creative Behavior* 54 (1), 100–114.

LeDoux, J.E. (1996) *The Emotional Brain: The Mysterious Underpinnings of Emotional Life*. New York: Simon & Schuster.

Lee, D.G., Kelly, K.R. and Edwards, J.K. (2006) A closer look at the relationships among trait procrastination, neuroticism, and conscientiousness. *Personality and Individual Differences* 40 (1), 27–37.

Lee, H.A., Law, R. and Murphy, J. (2011) Helpful reviewers in TripAdvisor, an online travel community. *Journal of Travel & Tourism Marketing* 28 (7), 675–688.

Lee, H., Lee, Y. and Yoo, D. (2000) The determinants of perceived service quality and its relationship with satisfaction. *Journal of Services Marketing* 14 (3), 217–231.

Lee, R., Khan, H. and Bellman, S. (2021) Mere association of product image and travel destination. *Annals of Tourism Research* 86, 103062.

Lee, R., Lockshin, L., Cohen, J. and Corsi, A. (2019) A latent growth model of destination image's halo effect. *Annals of Tourism Research* 79 (1), 102767.

Lee, T.H. and Tseng, C.H. (2015) How personality and risk-taking attitude affect the behavior of adventure recreationists. *Tourism Geographies* 17 (3), 307–331.

Lehto, X., Douglas, A.C. and Park, J. (2008) Mediating the effects of natural disasters on travel intention. *Journal of Travel & Tourism Marketing* 23 (2–4), 29–43.

Leiper, N. (1989) Tourism and tourism systems (occasional paper no.1). Palmerston North, New Zealand: Department of Management Systems, Massey University.

Leiper, N. (1990) Tourism systems: An interdisciplinary perspective (occasional papers no.2). Palmerston North, New Zealand: Department of Management Systems, Massey University.

Leiper, N. (1992) The tourist gaze review. *Annals of Tourism Research* 19 (3), 604–606.

Leiper, N. (2004) *Tourism Management*. Frenchs Forest, NSW: Pearson Education Australia.

Lepp, A. and Gibson, H. (2008) Sensation seeking and tourism: Tourist role, perception of risk and destination choice. *Tourism Management* 29 (4), 740–750.

Levine, M. (1953) *Tracking Performance as a Function of Exponential Delay Between Control and Display*. Wright Air Development Center, Air Research and Development Command, United States Air Force.

Levinson, D.J. (1996) *The Seasons of a Woman's Life*. New York: Alfred Knopf.

Levinson, D.J. (2011) *The Seasons of a Woman's Life: A Fascinating Exploration of the Events, Thoughts, and Life Experiences that All Women Share*. New York: Ballantine Books.

Levinson, D., Darrow, E., Klein, N., Levinson, M. and McKee, B. (1978) *The Seasons of a Man's Life*. New York: Knopf.

Lew, A.A., Hall, C.M. and Williams, A.M. (2014) *The Wiley Blackwell Companion to Tourism*. Chichester: John Wiley & Sons.

Lewicka, M. (2011) Place attachment: How far have we come in the last 40 years? *Journal of Environmental Psychology* 31 (3), 207–230.

Lewis, E.S.E. (1899) Side talks about advertising. *The Western Druggist* 21 (2), 65–66.

Lewis, R.C. (1987) The measurement of gaps in the quality of hotel services. *International Journal of Hospitality Management* 6 (2), 83–88.

Ley, D. and Hutton, T. (1987) Vancouver's corporate complex and producer services sector: Linkages and divergence within a provincial staple economy. *Regional Studies* 21 (5), 413–424.

Li, J. and Pearce, P. (2016) Tourist scams in the city: Challenges for domestic travelers in urban China. *International Journal of Tourism Cities* 2 (4), 294–308.

Li, J., Pan, L. and Hu, Y. (2021) Cultural involvement and attitudes toward tourism: Examining serial mediation effects of residents' spiritual wellbeing and place attachment. *Journal of Destination Marketing & Management* 20, 100601.

Li, J., Pearce, P.L. and Low, D. (2018) Media representation of digital-free tourism: A critical discourse analysis. *Tourism Management* 69, 317–329.

Li, J., Pearce, P.L. and Oktadiana, H. (2020) Can digital-free tourism build character strengths? *Annals of Tourism Research* 85, 103037.

Li, P. (2013) Comparisons of Stakeholders' Perceptions and Attitudes of Tourism Impacts in Mt. Qiyun, Anhui Province, China. Doctoral Thesis, University of Waikato Management School, New Zealand.

Li, P., Wang, Q. and Ryan, C. (2012) The impacts of tourism on traditional villages: A case study of Mt Qiyun, Anhui province. *Tourism Tribune* 27 (4), 57–63.

Li, S., Scott, N. and Walters, G. (2015) Current and potential methods for measuring emotion in tourism experiences: A review. *Current Issues in Tourism* 18 (9), 805–827.

Li, S., Walters, G., Packer, J. and Scott, N. (2018) Using skin conductance and facial electromyography to measure emotional responses to tourism advertising. *Current Issues in Tourism* 21 (15), 1761–1783.

Li, T. (2021) Universal therapy: A two-stage mediation model of the effects of stargazing tourism on tourists' behavioral intentions. *Journal of Destination Marketing & Management* 20, 100572.

Li, T., Liu, F. and Soutar, G.N. (2021) Experiences and value perceptions of an ecotourism trip–an empirical study of outbound Chinese tourists. *Tourism Recreation Research* 46 (3), 333–344.

Li, Y., Shi, J., Zhang, L. and Ryan, C. (in press) Rally-around-the-destination? changes in host-guest emotional solidarity following crises. *Annals of Tourism Research*.

Li, Y., Zhang, L, Shi, J. and Ryan, C. (2023) Values in residents' experience: Impacts of perceived value on life satisfaction and value co-creation. Paper under review for *Tourism Management Perspectives*.

Lu, D., Liu, Y., Lai, I. and Yang, L. (2017) Awe: An important emotional experience in sustainable tourism. *Sustainability* 9 (12), 2189–2204.

Lim, C. (1997) An econometric classification and review of international tourism demand models. *Tourism Economics* 3 (1), 69–81.

Lin, I.Y. and Worthley, R. (2012) Servicescape moderation on personality traits, emotions, satisfaction, and behaviors. *International Journal of Hospitality Management* 31 (1), 31–42.

Lin, Y., Kerstetter, D., Nawijn, J. and Mitas, O. (2014) Changes in emotions and their interactions with personality in a vacation context. *Tourism Management* 40, 416–424. https://doi.org/10.1016/j.tourman.2013.07.013

Lin, X., Susilo, Y.O., Shao, C. and Liu, C. (2018) The implication of road toll discount for mode choice: Intercity travel during the Chinese spring festival holiday. *Sustainability* 10 (8), 2700.

Littlejohn, S.W. (1992) *Theories of Human Communication* (4th edn). Belmont: Wadswortf Publishing Company.

Littlejohn, S.W. (2002) *Theories of Human Communication* (7th edn). Belmont: Wadswortf Publishing Company.

Littlejohn, S.W. and Foss, K.A. (2010) *Theories of Human Communication* (10th edn). Long Grove, IL: Waveland press.

Litvin, S.W. (2006) Revisiting Plog's model of allocentricity and psychocentricity … one more time. *Cornell Hotel and Restaurant Administration* 47 (3), 245–253.

Litvin, S.W. and Smith, W.W. (2016) A new perspective on the Plog psychographic system. *Journal of Vacation Marketing* 22 (2), 89–97.

Litvin, S.W., Guttentag, D. and Smith, W.W. (2021) Who should you market to in a crisis? Examining Plog's model during the COVID-19 Pandemic. *Journal of Travel Research* 61 (5), 981–989.

Liu, W. and Agusdinata, D.B. (2020) Interdependencies of lithium mining and communities' sustainability in Salar de Atacama, Chile. *Journal of Cleaner Production* 260, 120838.

Lounsbury, J.W. and Franz, C.P. (1990) Vacation discrepancy: A leisure motivation approach. *Psychological Reports* 66 (2), 699–702.

Lounsbury, J.W. and Hoopes, L.L. (1988) Five-year stability of leisure activity and motivation factors. *Journal of Leisure Research* 20 (2), 118–134.

Lounsbury, J.W. and Polik, J.R. (1992) Leisure needs and vacation satisfaction. *Leisure Sciences* 14 (2), 105–119.

Lovelock, C.H. (1980) Towards a classification of services. *Theoretical Developments in Marketing* 72 (6), 72–76.

Low, S. and Altman, I. (1992) *Place Attachment*. New York: Plenum Press.

Lowe, C.F., Horne, P.J. and Higson, P.J. (1987) Operant conditioning: The hiatus between theory and practice in clinical psychology. In H.J. Eysenck and I. Martin (eds) *Theoretical Foundations of Behavior Therapy* (pp. 153–165). Boston, MA: Springer.

Lox, C.L., Martin Ginnis, K.A. and Pertruzzello, S.J. (2006) *The Psychology of Exercise: Integrating Theory and Practice*. Scottsdale, AZ: Holcomb Hathaway Publishers.

Lussier, K. (2019) Of Maslow, motives, and managers: The hierarchy of needs in American business, 1960–1985. *Journal of the History of the Behavioral Sciences* 55 (4), 319–341.

Lyons, A. (1982) Timeshare – The Decline. Unpublished thesis, Nottingham Business School, Nottingham Trent University.

Ma, S., Zhao, X., Gong, Y. and Wengel, Y. (2021) Proposing "healing tourism" as a post-COVID-19 tourism product. *Anatolia* 32 (1), 136–139.

MacCannell, D. (1973) Staged authenticity: Arrangements of social space in tourist settings. *American Journal of Sociology* 79 (3), 589–603.

MacCannell, D. (1976) *The Tourist: A New Theory of the Leisure Class*. New York: Schocken.

MacCannell, D. (2008) Why it never really was about authenticity. *Society* 45 (4), 334–337.

Mack, C. (2021) Is Travel a Right? – The concept of right, and when it's just wrong. Retrieved on October 26, 2022, from https://www.responsibletravel.com/copy/over-tourism-is-travel-a-right

Maddux, W.W. and Galinsky, A.D. (2009) Cultural borders and mental barriers: The relationship between living abroad and creativity. *Journal of Personality and Social Psychology* 96 (5), 1047.

Mangold, W.G. and Babakus, E. (1991) Service quality: The front-stage vs. the back-stage perspective. *Journal of Services Marketing* 5 (4), 59–70.

Mannell, R.C. and Kleiber, D.A. (1997) *A Social Psychology of Leisure*. Edenbridge: Venture Publishing Inc.

Manu, A. (2016) *Behavior Space: Play, Pleasure and Discovery as a Model for Business Value*. New York: Routledge.

Mansfeld, Y. (1992) From motivation to actual travel. *Annals of Tourism Research* 19 (3), 399–419.

Marneros, S., Papageorgiou, G. and Efstathiades, A. (2021) Examining the core competencies for success in the hotel industry: The case of Cyprus. *Journal of Hospitality, Leisure, Sport & Tourism Education* 28, 100303.

Martilla, J.A. and James, J.C. (1977) Importance-performance analysis. *Journal of Marketing* 41 (1), 77–79.

Martin, B.A., Jin, H.S. and Trang, N.V. (2017) The entitled tourist: The influence of psychological entitlement and cultural distance on tourist judgments in a hotel context. *Journal of Travel & Tourism Marketing* 34 (1), 99–112.

Martinoia, R. (2003) That which is desired, which pleases, and which satisfies: Utility according to Alfred Marshall. *Journal of the History of Economic Thought* 25 (3), 349–364.

Martiniuk, A., Silva, M., Amylon, M. and Barr, R. (2014) Camp programs for children with cancer and their families: Review of research progress over the past decade. *Pediatric Blood & Cancer* 61 (5), 778–787.

Marx, K. (1867/2019) *Capital: Volume One: A Critique of Political Economy (Dover Thrift Editions: Political Science)*. Courier: Dover Publications.

Marx, K. and Engels, F. (1848/2021) *The Communist Manifesto*. Phoenix Classics Ebooks.

Maslow, A. (1962/2012) *Toward a Psychology of Being*. Princeton, NJ: D. Van Nostrand Company.

Maslow, A. (1968) *Towards a Psychology of Being* (2nd edn). New York: Van Nostrand.

Maslow, A. (1970) *Motivation and Personality*. New York: Harper & Row.

Maslow, A.H. (1954) *Motivation and Personality*. New York: Harper and Row.

Maslow, A.H. (1955) Deficiency and growth motivation. In M.R. Marshall (ed) *Nebraska Symposium on Motivation* (pp. 1–30). Lincoln: University of Nebraska Press.

Matzler, K., Bailom, F., Hinterhuber, H.H., Renzl, B. and Pichler, J. (2004) The asymmetric relationship between attribute-level performance and overall customer satisfaction: A reconsideration of the importance-performance analysis. *Industrial Marketing Management* 33 (4), 271–277.

Mathieson, A. and Wall, G. (1982) *Tourism – Economic, Physical and Economic Impacts*. London & New York: Longman.

Mathieson, A. and Wall, G. (1982) *Tourism, Economic, Physical and Social Impacts*. London: Longman.

Maume, D.J. (2006) Gender differences in taking vacation time. *Work and Occupations* 33 (2), 161–190.

Mayles, P. (2000) *Encore Provence: New Adventures in the South of France*. London: Vintage.

McCabe, S., Joldersma, T. and Li, C. (2010) Understanding the benefits of social tourism: Linking participation to subjective well-being and quality of life. *International Journal of Tourism Research* 12 (6), 761–773.

McCarthy, K.S. and Saks, J.V. (2019) Postelection stress: Symptoms, relationships, and counseling service utilization in clients before and after the 2016 US national election. *Journal of Counseling Psychology* 66 (6), 726–735.

McDermid, C.D. (1960) How money motivates men. *Business Horizons* 3 (4), 93–100.

McEwen, B.S. (1998) Stress, adaptation, and disease: Allostasis and allostatic load. *Annals of the New York Academy of Sciences* 840 (1), 33–44.

McEwen, B.S. (2000) Allostasis and allostatic load: Implications for neuropsychopharmacology. *Neuropsychopharmacology* 22 (2), 108–124.

McKercher, B. (2018) The impact of distance on tourism: A tourism geography law. *Tourism Geographies* 20 (5), 905–909.

McKercher, B. and Chow So-Ming, B. (2001) Cultural distance and participation in cultural tourism. *Pacific Tourism Review* 5 (1–2), 23–32.

McKercher, B. and Du Cros, H. (2003) Testing a cultural tourism typology. *International Journal of Tourism Research* 5 (1), 45–58.

McKercher, B. and Chan, A. (2005) How special is special interest tourism? *Journal of Travel Research* 44 (1), 21–31.

Matteucci, X. (2014) Flamenco, tourism and spirituality. In S. Filep and P. Pearce (eds) *Tourist Experience and Fulfilment* (pp. 110–126). Abingdon: Routledge.

Mellalieu, S., Jones, C., Wagstaff, C., Kemp, S. and Cross, M.J. (2021) Measuring psychological load in sport. *International Journal of Sports Medicine* 42 (9), 782–788.

Mehrabian, A. (1996a) Pleasure-arousal-dominance: A general framework for describing and measuring individual differences in temperament. *Current Psychology* 14 (4), 261–292.

Mehrabian, A. (1996b) Analysis of the big-five personality factors in terms of the PAD temperament model. *Australian Journal of Psychology* 48 (2), 86–92.

Mehrabian, A. and Russell, J.A. (1974a) *An Approach to Environmental Psychology*. Cambridge, MA: MIT Press.

Mehrabian, A. and Russell, J.A. (1974b) The basic emotional impact of environments. *Perceptual and Motor Skills* 38 (1), 283–301.

Meijman, T.F. and Mulder, G. (1998) Psychological aspects of workload. In P.J.D. Drenth, H. Thierry and C.J. de Wolff (eds) *Handbook of Work and Organizational Psychology: Volume 2 Work Psychology* (pp. 5–33). Hove: Psychology Press.

Meng, B. and Han, H. (2018) Investigating individuals' decision formation in working-holiday tourism: The role of sensation-seeking and gender. *Journal of Travel & Tourism Marketing* 35 (8), 973–987.

Mensah, E.A., Agyeiwaah, E. and Otoo, F.E. (2021) Re-conceptualizing volunteer tourism organizations roles: A host perspective. *Tourism Management Perspectives* 37, 100785.

Merkx, C. and Nawijn, J. (2021) Virtual reality tourism experiences: Addiction and isolation. *Tourism Management* 87, 104394.

Michael, I., Ramsoy, T., Stephens, M. and Kotsi, F. (2019) A study of unconscious emotional and cognitive responses to tourism images using a neuroscience method. *Journal of Islamic Marketing* 10, 543–564.

Michaels, A. (2020) Performative tears: Emotions in rituals and ritualized emotions. In A.
Michaels and C. Wulf (eds) *Emotions in Rituals and Performances* (pp. 29–40). New
York: Routledge.

Millard, D.E. (2022) Strange patterns: Structure and post-structure in interactive digital
narratives. In C. Hargood, D.E. Millard, Mitchell, A. and Spierling, U. (eds) *The
Authoring Problem*. Cham: Springer.

Miller, J.A. (1977) Studying satisfaction, modifying models, eliciting expectations, posing
problems, and making meaningful measurements. In H.K. Hunt (ed.) *Conceptualization and Measurement of Consumer Satisfaction and Dissatisfaction* (pp. 72–91).
Bloomington: School of Business, Indiana University.

Milman, A., Tasci, A. and Zhang, T.C. (2020) Perceived robotic server qualities and functions explaining customer loyalty in the theme park context. *International Journal of
Contemporary Hospitality Management* 32 (12), 3895–3923.

Minca, C. and Oakes, T. (2014) Tourism after the postmodern turn. In A.A. Lew, C.M.
Hall and A.M. Williams (eds) *The Wiley Blackwell Companion to Tourism* (pp.
294–303). Chichester: John Wiley & Sons.

Miniero, G., Rurale, A. and Addis, M. (2014) Effects of arousal, dominance, and their
interaction on pleasure in a cultural environment. *Psychology & Marketing* 31 (8),
628–634.

Miossec, J.-M. (1976) *Elements pour une théorie de l'espace touristique, Les Cahiers du
Tourisme.* C-36, Centre des hautes études touristiques, Aix-en-Provence.

Miossec, J.-M. (1977) Un modèle de l'espace touristique. *L'Espace géographique* 1, 41–48.

Mkono, M. (2020) Eco-hypocrisy and inauthenticity: Criticisms and confessions of the
eco-conscious tourist/traveller. *Annals of Tourism Research* 84, 102967.

Minnaert, L., Maitland, R. and Miller, G. (2009) Tourism and social policy: The value of
social tourism. *Annals of Tourism Research* 36 (2), 316–334.

Misui, Y. and Kamata, H. (2015) Why do they choose a spa destination? The case of Japanese tourists. *Tourism Economics* 21 (2), 283–305.

Mody, M., Hanks, L. and Dogru, T. (2019) Parallel pathways to brand loyalty: Mapping
the consequences of authentic consumption experiences for hotels and Airbnb. *Tourism Management* 74, 65–80.

Mohsin, A. (2005) Tourist attitudes and destination marketing—The case of Australia's
Northern Territory and Malaysia. *Tourism Management* 26 (5), 723–732.

Mohsin, A. (2008) Analysis of Chinese travellers' attitudes toward holidaying in New Zealand: The impact of socio-demographic variables. *Journal of Hospitality & Leisure
Marketing* 16 (1–2), 21–40.

Mohsin, A. and Ryan, C. (2007) Exploring attitudes of Indian students toward holidaying
in New Zealand using the leisure motivation scale. *Asia Pacific Journal of Tourism
Research* 12 (1), 1–18.

Moll, B., Rachel, L. and Restrepo, P. (2021) *Uneven Growth: Automation's Impact on
Income and Wealth Inequality* (No. w28440). National Bureau of Economic Research.

Moore, K., Buchmann, A., Månsson, M. and Fisher, D. (2021) Authenticity in tourism
theory and experience. Practically indispensable and theoretically mischievous?
Annals of Tourism Research 89, 103208.

Morgan, P. (2010) Towards a developmental theory of place attachment. *Journal of Environmental Psychology* 30 (1), 11–22.

Munt, I. (1994) Eco-tourism or ego-tourism? *Race & Class* 36 (1), 49–60.

Murphy, P. (1985) *Tourism – A Community Approach*. New York & London: Methuen.

Morris, J. (2001) *Trieste and the Meaning of Nowhere*. London: Faber & Faber.

Morris, J. (2002) *Trieste and the Meaning of Nowhere*. Boston: Da Capo Press.

Myers, S.D., Sen, S. and Alexandrov, A. (2010) The moderating effect of personality traits on attitudes toward advertisements: A contingency framework. *Management & Marketing 5* (3), 3–20.

Myles, J. (1850) *Chapters in the Life of a Dundee Factory Boy: An Autobiography*. Edinburgh: Adam and Charles Black.

Nakamura, J. and Csikszentmihalyi, M. (2003) Creativity in later life. In R.K. Sawyer, V.J. Steiner, S. Moran, R.J. Sternberg, D.H. Feldman, J. Nakamura and M. Csikszentmihalyi (eds) *Creativity and Development* (pp. 186–216). Oxford: Oxford University Press.

Narangajavana, Y., Fiol, L.J.C., Tena, M.A.M., Artola, R.M. and Garcia, J.S. (2017) The influence of social media in creating expectations. An empirical study for a tourist destination. *Annals of Tourism Research 65*, 60–70.

National Academy of Sciences, Washington, DC. (1969) *A Program for Outdoor Recreation Research*. Peru: Printing and Publishing Office.

Nawijn, J., De Bloom, J. and Geurts, S. (2013) Pre-vacation time: Blessing or burden? *Leisure Sciences 35* (1), 33–44.

Nedelkoska, L. and Quintini, G. (2018) *Automation, Skills Use and Training*. Documents de travail de l'OCDE sur les questions sociales, l'emploi et les migrations, No. 202, Editions OCDE, Paris.

New Zealand Commerce Commission. (2013) Penalties for souvenir companies that misled tourists with untrue claims. April 13, 2013. https://comcom.govt.nz/news-and-media/media-releases/2013/penalties-for-souvenir-companies-that-misled-tourists-with-untrue-claims

Newland, B.L. and Aicher, T.J. (2018) Exploring sport participants' event and destination choices. *Journal of Sport & Tourism 22* (2), 131–149.

Nickerson, N.P. and Jurowski, C. (2001) The influence of children on vacation travel patterns, *Journal of Vacation Marketing 7* (1), 19–30.

Nguyen, Q., Nguyen, H. and Le, T. (2020) Relationships among novelty seeking, satisfaction, return intention, and willingness to recommend of foreign tourists in Vietnam. *Management Science Letters 10* (10), 2249–2258.

Nouza, M., Ólafsdóttir, R. and Sæþórsdóttir, A.D. (2018) Motives and behaviour of second home owners in Iceland reflected by place attachment. *Current Issues in Tourism 21* (2), 225–242.

O'Dell, T. and Billing, P. (2005) *Experiencescape: Tourism, Culture, and Economy*. Copenhagen: Copenhagen Business School Press.

Oh, H. (2001) Revisiting importance—Performance analysis. *Tourism Management 22* (6), 617–627.

Oktadiana, H. and Pearce, P.L. (2020) Losing touch: Uncomfortable encounters with tourism technology. *Journal of Hospitality and Tourism Management 42*, 266–276.

Oktadiana, H., Pearce, P.L. and Li, J. (2020) Let's travel: Voices from the millennial female Muslim travellers. *International Journal of Tourism Research 22* (5), 551–563.

Oktadiana, H., Pearce, P.L., Pusiran, A.K. and Manisha, A. (2017) Travel career patterns: The motivations of Indonesian and Malaysian Muslim tourists. *Tourism Culture & Communication 17* (4), 231–248.

Oliver, R.L. (1977) Effect of expectation and disconfirmation on postexposure product evaluations: An alternative interpretation. *Journal of Applied Psychology 62* (4), 480–486.

Oliver, R. (1981) Measurement and evaluation of satisfaction process in retail settings. *Journal of Retailing 57* (3), 25–48.

Olson, J.C. and Dover, P.A. (1979) Disconfirmation of consumer expectations through product trial. *Journal of Applied Psychology 64* (2), 179–189.

Omondi, R. and Ryan, C. (2022) "Romantic Entertainers" on Kenya's coastal tourism: A case of sex tourism. In L. Berdychevsky and N. Carr (eds) *Innovation and Impact of Sex as Leisure in Research and Practice* (pp. 104–120). Abingdon: Routledge.

Omondi, R. and Ryan, C. (2023) *Sex Tourism on the Kenyan Coastline - The Search for Older Tourists*. Singapore: Springer.

Osborne, M.A. and Frey, C.B. (2018) *Automation and the Future of Work–Understanding the Numbers*. News Opinion, Oxford Martin School, Oxford: Oxford Martin Programme on the Future of Work. Retrieved on October 22, 2022 from https://www.oxfordmartin.ox.ac.uk/blog/automation-and-the-future-of-work-understanding-the-numbers/

Osgood, C.E. (1963) Part four, psychological approaches, semantic differential technique in the comparative study of cultures. *American Anthropologist* 66 (3), 171–200.

Osgood, C.E., Suci, G.J. and Tannenbaum, P.H. (1957) *The Measurement of Meaning*. Urbana, Chicago and London: University of Illinois press.

Otoo, F.E., Kim, S. and Choi, Y. (2020) Understanding senior tourists' preferences and characteristics based on their overseas travel motivation clusters. *Journal of Travel & Tourism Marketing* 37 (2), 246–257.

Ouyang, Z., Gong, X. and Yan, J. (2020) Spill-over effects of a hotel scam: How public perception influence communicative actions in social media in China. *Current Issues in Tourism* 23 (23), 2986–3000.

Owens, K. and Walker, A. (2020) Those designing healthcare algorithms must become actively anti-racist. *Nature Medicine* 26 (9), 1327–1328.

Packard, V. (1957) *The Hidden Persuaders*. New York: David McKay Books.

Packard, V. (1964) *The Naked Society*. New York: David McKay Books.

Page, S.J., Bentley, T. and Walker, L. (2005) Tourist safety in New Zealand and Scotland. *Annals of Tourism Research* 32 (1), 150–166.

Pan, Y., Wang, X. and Ryan, C. (2021) Chinese seniors holidaying, elderly care, rural tourism and rural poverty alleviation programmes. *Journal of Hospitality and Tourism Management* 46 (March), 134–143.

Panchal, J.H. (2013) Tourists "Me Time" in Asian Spas. In P. Mandal (ed.) *Proceedings of the International Conference on Managing the Asian Century: ICMAC 2013* (pp. 567–573). Singapore: Springer Science & Business Media.

Panksepp, J. (2010) Affective neuroscience of the emotional Brain Mind: Evolutionary perspectives and implications for understanding depression. *Dialogues in Clinical Neuroscience* 12 (4), 533–545.

Panksepp, J., Herman, B., Conner, R., Bishop, P. and Scott, J.P. (1978) The biology of social attachments: Opiates alleviate separation distress. *Biological Psychiatry* 13 (5), 607–618.

Parasuraman, A., Berry, L.L. and Zeithaml, V.A. (1991) Refinement and reassessment of the SERVQUAL scale. *Journal of Retailing* 67 (4), 420–450.

Parasuraman, A., Berry, L. and Zeithaml, V. (2002) Refinement and reassessment of the SERVQUAL scale. *Journal of Retailing* 67 (4), 114.

Parasuraman, A., Zeithaml, V.A. and Berry, L.L. (1985) A conceptual model of service quality and its implications for future research. *Journal of Marketing* 49 (4), 41–50.

Parasuraman, A., Zeithaml, V.A. and Berry, L. (1988) SERVQUAL: A multi-item scale for measuring customer perceptions of service. *Journal of Retailing* 64 (1), 12–40.

Parasuraman, A., Zeithaml, V.A. and Berry, L. (1994a) Reassessment of expectations as a comparison standard in measuring service quality: Implications for further research. *Journal of Marketing* 58 (1), 111–124.

Parasuraman, A., Zeithaml, V.A. and Berry, L. (1994b) Alternative scales for measuring service quality: A comparative assessment based on psychometric and diagnostic criteria. *Journal of Retailing* 70 (3), 201–230.

Paris, C.M. and Teye, V. (2010) Backpacker motivations: A travel career approach. *Journal of Hospitality Marketing & Management* 19 (3), 244–259.

Park, D. and Noland, M. (2013) *Developing the Service Sector as an Engine of Growth for Asia*. Manila: Asian Development Bank.

Parker, J.G. and Seal, J. (1996) Forming, losing, renewing, and replacing friendships: Applying temporal parameters to the assessment of children's friendship experiences. *Child Development* 67 (5), 2248–2268.

Parliamentary Press Release (NZ) (2001) *Wearable Arts and Tourism*. Retrieved on October 17, 2022, from https://www.beehive.govt.nz/release/wearable-arts-and-tourism-partnership

Parviainen, J. and Coeckelbergh, M. (2021) The political choreography of the Sophia robot: Beyond robot rights and citizenship to political performances for the social robotics market. *AI & Society* 36 (3), 715–724.

Pearce, P.L. (1981) 'Environment shock': A study of tourists' reactions to two tropical islands. *Journal of Applied Social Psychology* 11 (3), 268–280.

Pearce, P.L. (1982) *The Social Psychology of Tourist Behaviour*. Oxford: Pergamon.

Pearce, P.L. (1985) A systematic comparison of travel-related roles. *Human Relations* 38 (11), 1001–1011.

Pearce, P.L. (1988) *The Ulysses Factor: Evaluating Visitors in Tourist Settings*. New York: Springer-Verlag.

Pearce, P.L. (2005) *Tourist Behaviour: Themes and Conceptual Schemes*. Clevedon: Channel View Publications.

Pearce, P.L. (2012) *The Ulysses Factor: Evaluating Visitors in Tourist Settings*. Singapore: Springer Science & Business Media.

Pearce, P.L. (2013) *The Social Psychology of Tourist Behaviour: International Series in Experimental Social Psychology* (Vol. 3). Oxford: Elsevier.

Pearce, P.L. (2014) *Tourist Motivations and Decision-Making*. Melbourne: Wiley.

Pearce, P.L. (2019) Behaving badly. In P.L. Pearce (ed.) *Tourist Behaviour: The Essential Companion* (pp. 283–303). Cheltenham: Edward Elgar Publishing.

Pearce, P.L. (2020) Tourists' perception of time: Directions for design. *Annals of Tourism Research* 83, 102932.

Pearce, P.L. (2021) The Ulysses Factor Revisited. Consolidating the travel career motivation pattern approach to tourist motivation. In R. Sharpley (ed.) *The Routledge Handbook of the Tourist Experience* (pp. 169–179). Abingdon: Routledge.

Pearce, P.L. and Moscardo, G.M. (1986) The concept of authenticity in tourist experiences. *The Australian and New Zealand Journal of Sociology* 22 (1), 121–132.

Pearce, P.L. and Lee, U. (2005) Developing the travel career approach to tourist motivation. *Journal of Travel Research* 43 (3), 226–237.

Pearce, P.L. and Moscardo, G. (2007) An action research appraisal of visitor center interpretation and change. *Journal of Interpretation Research* 12 (1), 29–50.

Pearce, P.L. and Gretzel, U. (2012) Tourism in technology dead zones: Documenting experiential dimensions. *International Journal of Tourism Sciences* 12 (2), 1–20.

Pearce, P.L. and Packer, J. (2013) Minds on the move: New links from psychology to tourism. *Annals of Tourism Research* 40, 386–411.

Pearl, J. and Mackenzie, D. (2018) *The Book of Why: The New Science of Cause and Effect*. New York: Basic Books.

Pechorro, P., Castro, A., Hoyle, R.H. and Simões, M.R. (2018) The brief sensation-seeking scale: Latent structure, reliability, and validity from a sample of youths at-risk for delinquency. *Journal of Forensic Psychology Research and Practice* 18 (2), 99–113.

Peralta, R.L. (2019) How vlogging promotes a destination image: A narrative analysis of popular travel vlogs about the Philippines. *Place Branding and Public Diplomacy* 15 (4), 244–256.

Petrick, J.F., Tonner, C. and Quinn, C. (2006) The utilization of critical incident technique to examine cruise passengers repurchase intentions. *Journal of Travel Research* 44 (3), 273–280.

Phillipson, J., Gorton, M., Turner, R., Shucksmith, M., Aitken-McDermott, K., Areal, F., Cowie, P., Hubbard, C., Maioli, S., McAreavey, R., Souza-Monterio, D., Newbery, R., Panzone, L., Rowe, F. and Shortall, S. (2020) The COVID-19 pandemic and its implications for rural economies. *Sustainability* 12 (10), 3973, 1–9.

Phung, M.T., Ly, P.T.M. and Nguyen, T.T. (2019) The effect of authenticity perceptions and brand equity on brand choice intention. *Journal of Business Research* 101, 726–736.

Pickens, J. (2005) Attitudes and perceptions. *Organizational Behavior in Health Care* 4 (7), 43–76.

Piketty, T. (2014) *Capital in the Twenty-First Century*. (trans A. Goldhammer). Cambridge, MA: The Belknap Press of the University of Harvard.

Piketty, T. (2020) *Capital and Ideology*. Cambridge, MA: Harvard University Press.

Pine, B.J. and Gilmore, J.H. (1999) *The Experience Economy: Work Is Theatre & Every Business a Stage*. Boston: Harvard Business Press.

Pinillos, R., Marcos, S., Feliz, R., Zalama, E. and Gomez-García-Bermejo, J. (2016) Long-term assessment of a service robot in a hotel environment. *Robotics and Autonomous Systems* 79, 40–57.

Pinto, I. and Castro, C. (2019) Online travel agencies: Factors influencing tourists' purchase decisions. *Tourism & Management Studies* 15 (2), 7–20.

Pizam, A., Reichel, A. and Uriely, N. (2001) Sensation seeking and tourist behavior. *Journal of Hospitality & Leisure Marketing* 9 (3–4), 17–33.

Plog, S.C. (1974) Why destination areas rise and fall in popularity. *Cornell Hotel and Restaurant Administration Quarterly* 14 (4), 55–58.

Plog, S.C. (1977) Why destination areas rise and fall in popularity. In E.M. Kelly (ed.) *Domestic and International Tourism* (pp. 26–28). Wellesley, MA: Institute of Certified Travel Agents.

Plog, S.C. (2002) The power of psychographics and the concept of venturesomeness. *Journal of Travel Research* 40 (3), 244–251.

Plog, S.C. (2006) 'One more time': A commentary on the Litvin paper on the Plog psychographic system. *Cornell Hotel and Restaurant Administration Quarterly* 47 (3), 254–259.

Pocock, D. (1992) Catherine Cookson country: Tourist expectation and experience. *Geography* 77 (3), 236–243.

Podilchak, W. (1991) Distinctions of fun, enjoyment and leisure. *Leisure Studies* 10 (2), 133–148.

Polansky, N.A. (1986) There is nothing so practical as a good theory. *Child Welfare* 65 (1), 3–15.

Pope, D. (1983) *The Making of Modern Advertising*. New York: Basic Books.

Portal, S., Abratt, R. and Bendixen, M. (2019) The role of brand authenticity in developing brand trust. *Journal of Strategic Marketing* 27 (8), 714–729.

Prayag, G. and Ryan, C. (2011) The relationship between the 'push' and 'pull' factors of a tourist destination: The role of nationality – An analytical qualitative research approach. *Current Issues in Tourism* 14 (2), 121–143.

Prentice, R. (2004) Tourist familiarity and imagery. *Annals of Tourism Research* 31 (4), 923–945.

Priest, S. and Bunting, C. (1993) Changes in perceived risk and competence during white-water canoeing. *Journal of Applied Recreation Research* 18 (4), 265–280.

Pritchard, M.P. and Havitz, M.E. (2006) Destination appraisal an analysis of critical incidents. *Annals of Tourism Research* 33 (1), 25–46.

Pung, J.M., Yung, R., Khoo-Lattimore, C. and Del Chiappa, G. (2020) Transformative travel experiences and gender: A double duoethnography approach. *Current Issues in Tourism* 23 (5), 538–558.

Qiao, Q. (2019) An Investigation of Chinese Business Event Experience: A Third Place Perspective. Unpublished Thesis. BUU China-New Zealand Tourism Research Unit, University of Waikato Management School.

Qu, Y., Xu, F. and Lyu, X. (2019) Motivational place attachment dimensions and the pro-environmental behaviour intention of mass tourists: A moderated mediation model. *Current Issues in Tourism* 22 (2), 197–217.

Raines, S.S. (2019) *Conflict Management for Managers: Resolving Workplace, Client, and Policy Disputes.* Lanham, MD: Rowman & Littlefield.

Ramkissoon, H. (2023) Perceived social impacts of tourism and quality-of-life: A new conceptual model. *Journal of Sustainable Tourism* 31 (2), 442–459.

Ramkissoon, H., Smith, L.D.G. and Weiler, B. (2013) Testing the dimensionality of place attachment and its relationships with place satisfaction and pro-environmental behaviours: A structural equation modelling approach. *Tourism Management* 36, 552–566.

Rashbrooke, M. (2021) *Too Much Money: How Wealth Disparities Are Unbalancing Aotearoa New Zealand.* Wellington: Bridget Williams Books Ltd.

Rašovská, I., Kubickova, M. and Ryglová, K. (2021) Importance–performance analysis approach to destination management. *Tourism Economics* 27 (4), 777–794.

Raworth, K. (2017) *Doughnut Economics: Seven Ways to Think Like a 21st-Century Economist.* Chelsea: Chelsea Green Publishing.

Relph, E. (1976) *Place and Placelessness.* London: Pion Limited.

Richard, L., Lockshin, L., Cohen, J. and Corsi, A. (2019) A latent growth model of destination image's halo effect. *Annals of Tourism Research* 79, 102767.

Richard, L., Khan, H. and Bellman S. (2021) Mere association of product image and travel destination. *Annals of Tourism Research* 86, 103062.

Richard, M.D. and Allaway, A.W. (1993) Service quality attributes and choice behaviour. *Journal of Services Marketing* 7 (1), 59–86.

Richards, G. and Wilson, J. (2004) *The Global Nomad: Backpacker Travel in Theory and Practice.* Clevedon: Channel View Publications.

Rickly, J.M. (2022) A review of authenticity research in tourism: Launching the annals of tourism research curated collection on authenticity. *Annals of Tourism Research* 92, 103349.

Ritzer, G. (1993) *The McDonaldization of Society.* Thousand Oaks: Pine Forge Press.

Riva, E.F.M., Riva, G., Talo, C., Boffi, M., Rainisio, N., Pola, L., Diana, B., Villani, D., Argenton, L. and Inghilleri, P. (2017) Measuring dispositional flow: Validity and reliability of the dispositional flow state scale 2, Italian version. *PLoS One* 12 (9), 1–15.

Roberts, B.W., Chernyshenko, O.S., Stark, S. and Goldberg, L.R. (2005) The structure of conscientiousness: An empirical investigation based on seven major personality questionnaires. *Personnel Psychology* 58 (1), 103–139.

Robson, D. (2019) *The Intelligence Trap: Why Smart People Make Dumb Mistakes.* New York: WW Norton & Company.

Robson, D. (2022) *The Expectation Trap.* London: Cannongate.

Rocha, C.M. and Cao, G. (2022) Impacts of urban regeneration on small business in preparation to host the Beijing 2022 winter Olympic games. *Sport in Society* 1–18. https://doi.org/10.1080/17430437.2022.2088357

Rogers, R. (ed.) (2019) *Understanding Esports: An Introduction to the Global Phenomenon.* Lanham, MD: Lexington Books.

Rorty, R. (2016) *Philosophy as Poetry.* Charlottesville, VA: University of Virginia.

Rotfeld, H.J. (2014) The pragmatic importance of theory for marketing practice. *Journal of Consumer Marketing* 31 (4), 322–327.

Routledge, C., Arndt, J., Sedikides, C. and Wildschut, T. (2008) A blast from the past: The terror management function of nostalgia. *Journal of Experimental Social Psychology* 44 (1), 132–140.

Runco, M.A. (2009) Parsimonious creativity and its measurement. In E. Villalba (ed.) *Can Creativity be Measured. Proceedings from the Conference Measuring Creativity* (pp. 393–405). Brussels May 28th–29th. Luxembourg: Publications Office of the European Union.

Runco, M.A. and Albert, R.S. (1990) *Theories of Creativity.* Thousand Oaks, CA: Sage Publications, Inc.

Rooney, D. (2021) *About Time: A History of Civilization in Twelve Clocks.* Harmondsworth: Penguin.

Rubin, D.C. (2005) A Basic-systems approach to autobiographical memory. *Current Directions in Psychological Science* 14 (2), 79–83.

Rubin, D.C. and Siegler, I.C. (2004) Facets of personality and the phenomenology of autobiographical memory. *Applied Cognitive Psychology* 18 (7), 913–930.

Rubin, D.C., Schrauf, R.W. and Greenberg, D.L. (2003) Belief and recollection of autobiographical memories. *Memory and Cognition* 31 (6), 887–901.

Russell, J.A. and Mehrabian, A. (1974) Distinguishing anger and anxiety in terms of emotional response factors. *Journal of Consulting and Clinical Psychology* 42 (1), 79.

Russell, J.A. and Mehrabian, A. (1977) Evidence for a three-factor theory of emotions. *Journal of Research in Personality* 11 (3), 273–294.

Ryan, C. (1991) *Recreational Tourism: A Social Science Perspective.* London: Routledge.

Ryan, C. (1994) *Researching Tourist Satisfaction: Issues, Concepts, Problems.* London: Routledge.

Ryan, C. (1995) Tourism and Leisure - the application of leisure concepts to tourist behaviour -a proposed model. In A. Seaton (ed.) *Tourism, The State of the Art* (pp. 294–307) London: John Wiley and Sons.

Ryan, C. (1997a) Rafting in the Rangitikei, New Zealand - an example of adventure holidays. In D. Getz and S.J. Page (eds) *The Business of Rural Tourism - International Perspectives* (pp. 162–190). Chichester: Wiley.

Ryan, C. (1997b) *The Tourist Experience - A New Approach.* London: Cassell.

Ryan, C. (1998) The travel career ladder an appraisal. *Annals of Tourism Research* 25 (4), 936–957.

Ryan, C. (1999) From the psychometrics of SERVQUAL to sex - measurements of tourist satisfaction. In A. Pizam and Y. Mansfeld (eds) *Consumer Behavior in Travel & Tourism* (pp. 267–286). Binghamton, NY: Haworth Press.

Ryan, C. (2002a) Equity, power sharing and sustainability - Issues of the "new tourism." *Tourism Management* 23 (1), 17–26.

Ryan, C. (2002b) "The time of our lives" or "Time for our lives": An examination of time in holidaying. In C. Ryan (ed.) *The Tourist Experience* (2nd edn). London: Continuum.

Ryan, C. (2003a) Risk acceptance in adventure tourism – Paradox and context. In J. Wilks and S.J. Page (eds) *Managing Tourist Health and Safety in the New Millennium* (pp. 55–66). Oxford: Pergamon.

Ryan, C. (2003b) *Recreational Tourism: Demand and Impacts.* Clevedon: Channel View Publications.

Ryan, C. (2007a) Re-enacting the Battle of Aiken: Honour redeemed. In C. Ryan (ed.) *Battlefield Tourism: History, Place, and Interpretation* (pp. 193–206). Oxford: Pergamon.

Ryan, C. (2007b) Yorktown and patriot's point, Charleston, South Carolina: Interpretation and personal perspectives. In C. Ryan (ed.) *Battlefield Tourism: History, Place, and Interpretation* (pp. 211–220). Oxford: Pergamon.

Ryan, C. (ed.) (2007c) *Battlefield Tourism: History, Place and Interpretation.* Oxford: Pergamon

Ryan, C. (2013) Review of "The Tourist Gaze 3.0". *Tourism Management* 36, 234–236.

Ryan, C. (2020a) *An Advanced Introduction to Tourism Destination Management*. Cheltenham: Edward Elgar Publishing.

Ryan, C. (2020b) Refereeing articles including SEM – what should referees look for? *Tourism Critiques: Practice and Theory* 1 (1), 47–61,

Ryan, C. and Cessford, G. (2003) Developing a visitor satisfaction monitoring methodology: Quality gaps, crowding and some results. *Current Issues in Tourism* 6 (6), 457–507.

Ryan, C. and Cliff, A. (1996) Users and non-users on the expectation items of the Servqual scale. *Annals of Tourism Research* 23 (4), 931–934.

Ryan, C. and Cliff, A. (1997) Do travel agencies measure up to customer expectation? An empirical investigation of travel agencies' service quality as measured by SERVQUAL. *Journal of Travel and Tourism Marketing* 6 (2), 1–32.

Ryan, C. and Glendon, I. (1998) Application of leisure motivation scale to tourism. *Annals of Tourism Research* 25 (1), 169–184.

Ryan, C. and Gu, H. (2007) Bodies, carnival and honey days: The example of Coney Island. In A. Pritchard, N. Morgan, I. Ateljevic and C. Harris (eds) *Tourism and Gender: Embodiment, Sensuality and Experience* (pp. 126–137). Wallingford: CABI.

Ryan, C. and Gu, H. (2010) Constructionism and culture in research: Understandings of the fourth Buddhist Festival, Wutaishan, China. *Tourism Management* 31 (2), 167–178.

Ryan, C. and Huang, S. (2013) *Tourism in China: Destinations, Planning and Experiences*. Bristol: Channel View Publications.

Ryan, C. and Lutz, J. (1993) Attitudes of Businesswomen to Hotel Service – An analysis of businesswomen hotel programmes. *Tourism Management* 14 (5), 349–356.

Ryan, C. and Ma, L. (2021) Social consequences of Airbnb – a New Zealand case study of cause and effect. *Journal of Sustainable Tourism* 29 (10), 1565–1585.

Ryan, C., Trauer, B., Cave, J., Sharma, A. and Sharma, S. (2003) Backpackers – what is the peak experience? *Tourism Recreation Research* 28 (3), 93–96.

Saaty, T.L. (2000) *Fundamentals of Decision Making and Priority Theory with the Analytic Hierarchy Process*. Pittsburgh: RWS Publications.

Sachdev, S.B. and Verma, H.V. (2002) Customer expectations and service quality dimensions consistency. *Journal of Management Research* 2 (1), 43–52.

Saleh, F. and Ryan, C. (1991a) Service quality in the hospitality industry – An application of the Servqual model. *Service Industries Journal* 11 (3), 324–345.

Saleh, F. and Ryan C. (1991b) Service quality in the hospitality industry. In B. Thomas and P. Johnson (eds) *Choice and Supply in Tourism Products* (pp. 107–122). London: Mansell.

Sato, T. and Valsiner, J. (2010) Time in life and life in time: Between experiencing and accounting. *Ritsumeikan Journal of Human Sciences* 20 (1), 79–92.

Sartre, J.P. and Mairet, P. (1960) *Existentialism and Humanism*. London: Methuen.

Savin, G.D., Fleșeriu, C. and Batrancea, L. (2022) Eye tracking and tourism research: A systematic literature review. *Journal of Vacation Marketing* 28 (3), 285–302.

Schachter, S. and Singer, J. (1962) Cognitive, social, and physiological determinants of emotional state. *Psychological Review* 69 (5), 379–399.

Scannell, L. and Gifford, R. (2010) Defining place attachment: A tripartite organizing framework. *Journal of Environmental Psychology* 30 (1), 1–10.

Schachter, S. and Singer, J. (1962) Cognitive, social, and physiological determinants of emotional state. *Psychological Review* 69 (5), 379.

Schneider, P.P. and Vogt, C.A. (2012) Applying the 3M model of personality and motivation to adventure travelers. *Journal of Travel Research* 51 (6), 704–716.

Schroeder, J. (2002) *Visual Consumption*. London: Routledge.

Scott, D., Hall, C.M. and Gössling, S. (2019) Global tourism vulnerability to climate change. *Annals of Tourism Research* 77, 49–61.

Scott, N. (2020) Cognitive psychology and tourism–surfing the "cognitive wave": A perspective article. *Tourism Review* 75 (1), 49–51.

Scott, N., Zhang, R., Le, D. and Moyle, B. (2019) A review of eye-tracking research in tourism. *Current Issues in Tourism* 22 (10), 1244–1261.

Scott, N., Le, D., Becken, S. and Connolly, R.M. (2020) Measuring perceived beauty of the Great Barrier Reef using eye-tracking technology. *Current Issues in Tourism* 23 (20), 2492–2502.

Selwood, J. (2006) The evolution, characteristics and spatial organization of cottages and cottagers in Manitoba, Canada. In N. McIntyre, D.R. Williams and K.E. McHugh (eds) *Multiple Dwelling and Tourism: Negotiating Place, Home and Identity* (pp. 207–218). Wallingford: CABI.

Sever, I. (2015) Importance-performance analysis: A valid management tool? *Tourism Management* 48, 43–53.

Shaheer, I., Lee, C. and Carr, N. (2021) Factors motivating working holiday travel: The case of Latin American visitors to New Zealand. *Tourism and Hospitality Research* 21 (3), 330–343.

Sharma, R.K. (2020) Who is lonely in lockdown? This cross-cohort analysis suggests students may be at risk. *Public Health* 189, 5.

Sheldon, P.J. (2020) Designing tourism experiences for inner transformation. *Annals of Tourism Research* 83, 102935.

Sherman, E., Mathur, A. and Smith, R.B. (1997) Store environment and consumer purchase behavior: Mediating role of consumer emotions. *Psychology & Marketing* 14 (4), 361–378.

Shi, H., Liu, Y., Kumail, T. and Pan, L. (2022) Tourism destination brand equity, brand authenticity and revisit intention: The mediating role of tourist satisfaction and the moderating role of destination familiarity. *Tourism Review* 77 (3), 751–779.

Shi, S., Gursoy, D. and Chen, L. (2019) Conceptualizing home-sharing lodging experience and its impact on destination image perception: A mixed method approach. *Tourism Management* 75, 245–256.

Sihvonen, J. and Turunen, L.L.M. (2022, January) Multisensory experiences at travel fairs: What evokes feelings of pleasure, arousal and dominance among visitors? *Journal of Convention & Event Tourism* 23 (1), 63–85.

Sirgy, M.J. (2010) Toward a quality-of-life theory of leisure travel satisfaction. *Journal of Travel Research* 49 (2), 246–260.

Skavronskaya, L., Moyle, B., Scott, N. and Kralj, A. (2020) The psychology of novelty in memorable tourism experiences. *Current Issues in Tourism* 23 (21), 2683–2698.

Skinner, B.F. (1933) "Resistance to extinction" in the process of conditioning. *Journal of General Psychology* 9 (2), 420–429.

Skinner, B.F. (1953) *Science and Human Behavior*. New York: Macmillan.

Smith, A. (2012) *Events and Urban Regeneration: The Strategic Use of Events to Revitalise Cities*. Abingdon: Routledge.

Smith, K.U. (1962) *Delayed Sensory Feedback and Behavior*. Philadelphia: Saunders.

Smith, J.C. (2007) The psychology of relaxation. In R.L. Woolfolk and P.M. Lehrer (eds) *Principles and Practice of Stress Management* (3rd edn, pp. 38–52). New York: Guilford Publications.

Smith, M.K. and Puczkó, L. (2016) *The Routledge Handbook of Health Tourism*. Abingdon: Routledge.

Smith, S.L.J. (1990a) A test of Plog's allocentric/psychocentric model: Evidence from seven nations. *Journal of Travel Research* 28 (4), 40–43.

Smith, S.L.J. (1990b) Another look at the carpenter's tools: A reply to Plog. *Journal of Travel Research* 29 (2), 50–51.

Smith, T.J. (2022) Experiencing time—A commentary on recent perspectives on the perception of time. *Ergonomics in Design*. https://doi.org/10.1177/10648046.

Smith, T.J., Henning, R.A. and Li, Q. (1998) *Teleoperation in Space-Modeling Effects of Displaced Feedback and Microgravity on Tracking Performance (SAE Technical Report Number 981701)*. Society of Automotive Engineers International.

Smith, T.J., Wade, M.G., Henning, R. and Fisher, T. (2015) *Variability in Human Performance*. Boca Raton, Florida: CRC Press.

Smith, V. (2012) *Hosts and Guests: The Anthropology of Tourism*. Philadelphia: University of Pennsylvania Press.

Solomon, R.C. (2001) *Phenomenology and Existentialism* (2nd edn). Lanham, MD: Rowman & Littlefield.

Song, H. and Bae, S.Y. (2018) Understanding the travel motivation and patterns of international students in Korea: Using the theory of travel career pattern. *Asia Pacific Journal of Tourism Research* 23 (2), 133–145.

Song, Y. and Yan, L. (2020, August) "Who is Buddha? I am Buddha."—The motivations and experiences of Chinese young adults attending a Zen meditation camp in Taiwan. *Journal of Convention & Event Tourism* 21 (4), 263–282.

Sonnentag, S. and Fritz, C. (2007) The recovery experience questionnaire: Development and validation of a measure for assessing recuperation and unwinding from work. *Journal of Occupational Health Psychology* 12 (3), 204–221.

Spalding, M., Burke, L. and Fyall, A. (2021) Covid-19: Implications for nature and tourism. *Anatolia* 32 (1), 126–127.

Stein, H. (1998) *Coney Island*. London: W.W. Norton.

Stigliani, I. (2020) Navigating an academic maze: Experiences of an international female scholar. *Journal of Management Inquiry* 29 (3), 360–363.

Stebbins, R.A. (1992) *Amateurs, Professionals, and Serious Leisure*. Montréal: McGill-Queen's University Press.

Stebbins, R.A. (1997) Casual leisure: A conceptual statement. *Leisure Studies* 16 (1), 17–25.

Stebbins, R.A. (2001) *New Directions in the Theory and Research of Serious Leisure*. Lewiston, NY: Edwin Mellen Press.

Steen Jacobsen, J.J., Farstad, E., Higham, J., Hopkins, D. and Landa-Mata, I. (2021) Travel discontinuities enforced holidaying-at-home and alternative leisure travel futures after COVID-19. *Tourism Geographies*, 1–19.

Stors, N., Stoltenberg, L., Sommer, C. and Frisch, T. (2019) Tourism and everyday life in the contemporary city. In N. Stors, L. Stoltenberg, C. Sommer and T. Frisch (eds) *Tourism and Everyday Life in the Contemporary City* (pp. 1–23). New York: Routledge.

Strong, E.K. (1925) *The Psychology of Selling and Advertising*. New York: Mcgraw-Hill.

Strzelecka, M., Boley, B.B. and Woosnam, K.M. (2017) Place attachment and empowerment: Do residents need to be attached to be empowered? *Annals of Tourism Research* 66, 61–73.

Stronza, A.L., Hunt, C.A. and Fitzgerald, L.A. (2019) Ecotourism for conservation? *Annual Review of Environment and Resources* 44, 229–253.

Stylidis, D. (2018a) Place attachment, perception of place and residents' support for tourism development. *Tourism Planning & Development* 15 (2), 188–210.

Stylidis, D. (2018b) Residents' place image: A cluster analysis and its links to place attachment and support for tourism. *Journal of Sustainable Tourism* 26 (6), 1007–1026.

Su, C.P. and Wu, T.C. (2022) The dark side of solo female travel: Negative encounters with male strangers. In L. Berdychevsky and N. Carr (eds) *Innovation and Impact of Sex as Leisure in Research and Practice* (pp. 121–138). New York: Routledge.

Su, L., Stepchenkova, S. and Dai, X. (2020) The core-periphery image of South Korea on the Chinese tourist market in the times of conflict over THAAD. *Journal of Destination Marketing & Management* 17, 100457.

Suess, C., Woosnam, K.M. and Erul, E. (2020) Stranger-danger? Understanding the moderating effects of children in the household on non-hosting residents' emotional solidarity with Airbnb visitors, feeling safe, and support for Airbnb. *Tourism Management* 77 (4), 1–14.

Suess, C., Woosnam, K., Mody, M., Dogru, T. and Turk, E.S. (2020) Understanding how residents' emotional solidarity with Airbnb visitors influences perceptions of their impact on a community: The moderating role of prior experience staying at an Airbnb. *Journal of Travel Research* 60 (5), 1039–1060.

Sundaram, D.S. and Webster, C. (2000) The role of nonverbal communication in service encounters. *Journal of Services Marketing* 14 (5), 378–391.

Svenson, S. (2004) The cottage and the city: An interpretation of the Canadian second home experience. In C.M. Hall and D.K. Müller (eds) *Tourism, Mobility and Second Homes: Between Elite Landscape and Common Ground* (pp. 55–74). Clevedon: Channel View Publications.

Taggart, S.M., Girard, O., Landers, G.L., Ecker, U.K.H. and. Wallman, K.E., (2023) Seasonal influence on cognitive and psycho-physiological responses to a single 11-h day of work in outdoor mine industry workers, *Temperature*. https://doi.org/10.1080/23328940.2023.2208516

Taecharungroj, V. and Mathayomchan, B. (2019) Analysing TripAdvisor reviews of tourist attractions in Phuket, Thailand. *Tourism Management* 75, 550–568.

Talbert, R.J. (2017) *Roman Portable Sundials: The Empire in Your Hand*. Oxford: Oxford University Press.

Tan, P.Y., Ismail, H.N. and Syed Jaafar, S.M.R. (2022) A comparative review: Distance decay in urban and rural tourism. *Anatolia*, 1–18. https://doi.org/10.1080/13032917.2022.2051057.

Tasci, A.D., Gartner, W.C. and Tamer Cavusgil, S. (2007) Conceptualization and operationalization of destination image. *Journal of Hospitality & Tourism Research* 31 (2), 194–223.

Tassinary, L.G., Cacioppo, J.T. and Vanman, E.J. (2000) The skeletomotor system: Surface electromyography. In J.T. Cacioppo, L.G. Tassinary and G.G. Berntson (eds) *Handbook of Psychophysiology* (2nd edn, pp. 267–299). Cambridge: Cambridge University Press.

Taylor, J.S. (2001) Dollars are a girl's best friend? Female tourists' sexual behaviour in the Caribbean. *Sociology* 35 (3), 749–764.

Taylor, S.A. and Cronin Jr, J.J. (1994) An empirical assessment of the SERVPERF scale. *Journal of Marketing Theory and Practice* 2 (4), 52–69.

Teas, R.K. (1993) Expectations, performance evaluation, and consumers' perceptions of quality. *Journal of Marketing* 57 (4), 18–34.

Teas, R.K. (1994) Expectations as a comparison standard in measuring service quality: An assessment of a reassessment. *Journal of Marketing* 58 (1), 132–139.

Tetzlaff-Deas, B. (2022, September 13) Supermarket giant Morrisons turns down checkout beeps and bans music after Queen's death. *Daily Mirror*. Retrieved from https://www.mirror.co.uk/news/uk-news/supermarket-giant-morrisons-turns-down-27975959

Thomas, S., White, G.R. and Samuel, A. (2018) To pray and to play: Post-postmodern pilgrimage at Lourdes. *Tourism Management* 68, 412–422.

Thurstone, L.L. (1928) Attitudes can be measured. *American Journal of Sociology* 33 (4), 529–554.

Tikkanen, I. (2007) Maslow's hierarchy and food tourism in Finland: Five cases. *British Food Journal* 109 (9), 721–734.

Tinsley, H.E.A. and Tinsley, D.J. (1986) A theory of the attributes, benefits and causes of leisure experience. *Leisure Sciences* 8 (1), 1–45.

Tinsley, H.E.A. and Tinsley, D.J. (1987) Use of factor analysis in counseling psychology research. *Journal of Counseling Psychology* 34: 414–424.

Toffler, A. (1970) *Future Shock*. New York: Random House.

Tracey, J.B., Sturman, M.C. and Tews, M.J. (2007) Ability versus personality: Factors that predict employee job performance. *Cornell Hotel and Restaurant Administration Quarterly* 48 (3), 313–322.

Tran, X. and Ralston, L. (2006) Tourist preferences influence of unconscious needs. *Annals of Tourism Research* 33 (2), 424–441.

Tribe, J. and Snaith, T. (1998) From SERVQUAL to HOLSAT: Holiday satisfaction in Varadero, Cuba. *Tourism Management* 19 (1), 25–34.

Trinh, T.T. and Ryan, C. (2016) Heritage and cultural tourism: The role of the aesthetic when visiting Mỹ Sơn and Cham Museum, Vietnam. *Current Issues in Tourism* 19 (6), 564–589.

Tripathy, M. (2018) Role of creative thinking as an imperative tool in communication at workplace. *Journal of Organizational Culture, Communications and Conflict* 22 (2), 1–7.

Trunfio, M. and Campana, S. (2020) A visitors' experience model for mixed reality in the museum. *Current Issues in Tourism* 23 (9), 1053–1058.

Truong, T.H. (2005) Assessing holiday satisfaction of Australian travellers in Vietnam: An application of the HOLSAT model. *Asia Pacific Journal of Tourism Research* 10 (3), 227–246.

Tse, D.C., Nakamura, J. and Csikszentmihalyi, M. (2020) Beyond challenge-seeking and skill-building: Toward the lifespan developmental perspective on flow theory. *The Journal of Positive Psychology* 15 (2), 171–182.

Tuan, Y.F. (1975) Place: An experiential perspective. *Geographical Review* 65 (2), 151–165.

Tuan, Y.F. (1977) *Space and Place: The Perspective of Experience*. Minneapolis: University of Minnesota Press.

Turner, C. and Manning, P. (1988) Placing authenticity—On being a tourist: A reply to Pearce and Moscardo. *The Australian and New Zealand Journal of Sociology* 24 (1), 136–139.

Tuten, T.L. and Neidermeyer, P.E. (2004) Performance, satisfaction and turnover in call centers: The effects of stress and optimism. *Journal of Business Research* 57 (1), 26–34.

Twigger-Ross, C.L. and Uzzell, D.L. (1996) Place and identity processes. *Journal of Environmental Psychology* 16 (3), 205–220.

Uddin, L.Q., Rayman, J. and Zaidel, E. (2005) Split-brain reveals separate but equal self-recognition in the two cerebral hemispheres. *Consciousness and Cognition* 14 (3), 633–640.

Urquhart, E. (2019) Technological mediation in the future of experiential tourism. *Journal of Tourism Futures* 5 (2), 120–126.

Urry, J. (1990) *The Tourist Gaze*. London: Sage Publications

Urry, J. (2000) *Sociology Beyond Societies: Mobilities for the Twenty-First Century*. London & New York: Routledge.

Urry, J. (2002) *The Tourist Gaze: Second Edition*. London: Sage Publications.

Urry, J. (2016) *Mobilities: New Perspectives on Transport and Society*. New York: Routledge.

Urry, J. and Larsen, J. (2011) *The Tourist Gaze 3.0*. London: Sage Publications.

Valentine, G. (1989) The geography of women's fear. *Area* 21 (4), 385–390.

Vallerand, R.J., Blais, M.R., Briere, N.M. and Pelletier, L.G. (1989) Development of the French form of the academic motivation scale. *Canadian Journal of Behavioural Science* 21, 323–349.

van Gennep, A. (1960) *The Rites of Passage*. London: Routledge & Kegan Paul.

Vega-Vázquez, M., Rodríguez-Serrano, M.Á., Castellanos-Verdugo, M. and Oviedo-García, M.Á. (2021) The impact of tourism on active and healthy ageing: Health-related quality of life. *Journal of Policy Research in Tourism, Leisure and Events* 13 (3), 349–373.

Villacé-Molinero, T., Fernández-Muñoz, J.J., Orea-Giner, A. and Fuentes-Moraleda, L. (2021) Understanding the new post-COVID-19 risk scenario: Outlooks and challenges for a new era of tourism. *Tourism Management* 86, 104324.

Vince, G. (2020) Timekeepers. *Natural History (April)* 128 (4), 34–39.

Vitterso, G. (2007) Norwegian Cabin Life in Transition. *Scandinavian Journal of Hospitality and Tourism* 7 (3), 266–280.

Von, W.L. (1933) Ueber Erholungsfursorge. *Mitteilungen des Volksgesundheitsamts* 7, 193–197. Retrieved on October 8, 2022, from https://www.cabdirect.org/cabdirect/abstract/19332701432

Vroom, V.H. (1964) *Work and Motivation.* New York: Wiley.

Walmsley, D.J. and Jenkins, J.M. (1992) Tourism cognitive mapping of unfamiliar environments. *Annals of Tourism Research* 19 (2), 268–286.

Walmsley, D.J. and Young, M. (1998) Evaluative images and tourism: The use of personal constructs to describe the structure of destination images. *Journal of Travel Research* 36 (3), 65–69.

Walsh, P.R. (2011) Creating a "values" chain for sustainable development in developing nations: Where Maslow meets Porter. *Environment, Development and Sustainability* 13 (4), 789–805.

Walters, T. (2011) Beach, Bach and beyond: The luxury of leisure and second home ownership in New Zealand. In *Biennial Australia and New Zealand Association of Leisure Studies (ANZALS): Challenging Leisure.* University of Otago.

Walters, T. (2019) Caves to castles: The development of second home practices in New Zealand. *Journal of Policy Research in Tourism, Leisure and Events* 11 (1), 1–15.

Walton, J.K. (1983) *The English Seaside Resort. A Social History 1750–1914.* Leicester: Leicester University Press.

Wang, K.-C., Hsieh, A.-T. and Huan, T.-C. (2000) Critical service features in group package tour: An exploratory research. *Tourism Management* 21 (2), 177–189.

Wang, N. (1999) Rethinking authenticity in tourism experience. *Annals of Tourism Research* 26 (2), 349–370.

Wang, N. (2017) Rethinking authenticity in tourism experience. In D. Timothy (ed.) *The Political Nature of Cultural Heritage and Tourism: Critical Essays* (pp. 469–490). London & New York. Routledge.

Wang, Y. (2007) Customized authenticity begins at home. *Annals of Tourism Research* 34 (3), 789–804.

Wang, S., Berbekova, A., Uysal, M. and Wang, J. (2022) Emotional solidarity and co-creation of experience as determinants of environmentally responsible behavior: A Stimulus-Organism-Response Theory Perspective. *Journal of Travel Research*, 00472875221146786.

Wearden, J.H. (1988) Some neglected problems in the analysis of human operant behaviour. In G. Davey and C. Cullen (eds) *Human Operant Conditioning and Behaviour Modification* (pp. 197–224). Chichester: John Wiley & Sons.

Wellings, K., Macdowall, W., Catchpole, M. and Goodrich, J. (1999) Seasonal variations in sexual activity and their implications for sexual health promotion. *Journal of the Royal Society of Medicine* 92 (2), 60–64.

Weng, L., Huang, Z. and Bao, J. (2021) A model of tourism advertising effects. *Tourism Management* 85, 104278.

Wheeller, B. (1993) Sustaining the ego. *Journal of Sustainable Tourism* 1 (2), 121–129.

Wheeller, B. (2007) Sustainable mass tourism: More smudge than nudge – the canard continues. *Tourism Recreation Research* 32 (3), 73–75.

White, C.J. (2005) Culture, emotions and behavioural intentions: Implications for tourism research and practice. *Current Issues in Tourism* 8 (6), 510–531.

Whittaker, E. (2012) Seeking the Existential Moment. In D. Picard and M. Robinson (eds) *Emotion in Motion: Tourism, Affect and Transformation* (pp. 73–84). Farnham: Ashgate.

Wickens, E. (2000) Rethinking tourists' experiences. In M. Robinson (ed.) *Motivations, Behaviour and Tourist Types: Reflections on International Tourism* (pp. 455–472). Sunderland: Centre for Travel and Tourism in association with Business Education Press.

Wickens, E. (2002) The sacred and the profane: A tourist typology. *Annals of Tourism Research* 29 (3), 834–851.

Wickens, E. (2006) Tourists, motivations and experiences: A theoretical and methodological critique. In A. Aktas, M. Kesgin, E. Cengiz and E. Yenialp (eds) *Turk–Kazakh International Tourism Conference 2006.* Proceedings Book 1, (pp. 66–76). Antalya, Turkey 20–26 November. Akdeniz University Antalya Faculty of Business. Ankara: Detay.

Wickens, E. and Harrison, A. (1996) Staging modernity: The consumption of hybrid playful experiences in Chalkidiki, Northern Greece. In M. Robinson, N. Evans and P. Callaghan (eds) *Tourism and Culture, Towards the 21st Century: Culture as the Tourist Product* (pp. 437–44). Newcastle: Athenaeum Press.

Wickens, E. and Sönmez, S. (2007) Casual sex in the sun makes the holiday: Young tourists' perspectives. In Y. Apostolopoulos and S. Sönmez (eds) *Population Mobility and Infections Disease* (pp. 199–214). Boston: Springer.

Wight, A.C. (2020) Visitor perceptions of European Holocaust Heritage: A social media analysis. *Tourism Management* 81, 104142.

Wight, P.A. (1996) North American ecotourists: Market profile and trip characteristics. *Journal of Travel Research* 34 (4), 2–10.

Wildish, B. and Spierings, B. (2019) Living like a local: Amsterdam Airbnb users and the blurring of boundaries between 'tourists' and 'residents' in residential neighbourhoods. In N. Stors, L. Stoltenberg, C. Sommer and T. Frisch (eds) *Tourism and Everyday Life in the Contemporary City* (pp. 139–164). New York: Routledge.

Williams, A.M., King, R., Warnes, A. and Patterson, G. (2000) Tourism and international retirement migration: New forms of an old relationship in southern Europe. *Tourism Geographies* 2 (1), 28–49.

Williams, D.R. and Miller, B.A. (2020) Metatheoretical moments in place attachment research: Seeking clarity in diversity. In L.C. Manzo and P. Devine-Wright (eds) *Place Attachment: Advances in Theory, Methods and Application* (pp. 12–28). New York: Routledge.

William, J.N. (2005) Learning without awareness. *Studies in Second Language Acquisition* 27, 269–304.

Williams, R. (2011) Cognitive Theory. In K.L. Smith, S. Moriarty, K. Kenney and G. Barbatsis (eds) *Handbook of Visual Communication: Theory, Methods and Media* (2nd edn, pp. 193–210). Abingdon: Routledge.

Wilson, E. and Little, D.E. (2008) The solo female travel experience: Exploring the 'geography of women's fear.' *Current Issues in Tourism* 11 (2), 167–186.

Witt, S.F. and Witt, C.A. (1995) Forecasting tourism demand: A review of empirical research. *International Journal of Forecasting* 11 (3), 447–475.

Witt, C.A. and Wright, P.L. (1992) Tourist motivation: Life after Maslow. In P. Johnson and B. Thomas (eds) *Choice and Demand in Tourism* (pp. 33–35). London: Mansell Publishing.

Wójcik, M. (2017) Holograms in libraries-the potential for education, promotion and services. *Library Hi Tech* 36 (1), 18–28.

World Bank (2022) *Poverty and Shared Prosperity 2022: Correcting Course.* Washington DC: The World Bank.

World Economic Forum (2021) *Global Issue – Inequality.* Briefing based on views from the World Economic Forum's Expert Network curated in partnership with Professor Henrietta L. Moore, Founder and Director, Hannah Collins, Research Associate, and researchers including Rayhaan Lorgat and Farah Khokhar at the Institute for Global Prosperity, University College London. Retrieved on October 3, 2022 from https://intelligence.weforum.org/topics/a1G0X000006NwUZUA0?tab=publications

World Economic Forum (2022) *Travel & Tourism Development Index 2021 Rebuilding for a Sustainable and Resilient Future.* Geneva: World Economic Forum.

World Tourism Organization's Global Code of Ethics for Tourism (1999) *Global Code of Ethics for Tourism for Responsible Tourism.* adopted by resolution A/RES/406(XIII) at the thirteenth WTO General Assembly (Santiago, Chile, 27 September - 1 October 1999).

Wright, C. (2019) Putting foucault to work in tourism research. *International Journal of Tourism Research* 21 (1), 122–133.

Wright, C. (2022) Tourism, the tourist experience and post modernity: Theory, application and research. In R. Sharpley (ed.) *The Routledge Handbook of The Tourism Experience* (pp. 9–23). Abingdon: Routledge.

Wu, C.H.J. and Liang, R.D. (2011) The relationship between white-water rafting experience formation and customer reaction: A flow theory perspective. *Tourism Management* 32 (2), 317–325.

Wu, J., Law, R., Fong, D.K.C. and Liu, J. (2019) Rethinking travel life cycle with travel career patterns. *Tourism Recreation Research* 44 (2), 272–277.

Wu, M.Y. and Pearce, P.L. (2014) Chinese recreational vehicle users in Australia: A netnographic study of tourist motivation. *Tourism Management* 43, 22–35.

Xie, H., Costa, C.A. and Morais, D.B. (2008) Gender differences in rural tourists' motivation and activity participation. *Journal of Hospitality & Leisure Marketing* 16 (4), 368–384.

Xie, K.L., Zhang, Z. and Zhang, Z. (2014) The business value of online consumer reviews and management response to hotel performance. *International Journal of Hospitality Management* 43, 1–12.

Xie, K.L., Zhang, Z., Zhang, Z., Singh, A. and Lee, S.K. (2016) Effects of managerial response on consumer eWOM and hotel performance: Evidence from TripAdvisor. *International Journal of Contemporary Hospitality Management* 28 (9), 2013–2034.

Xu, S., Stienmetz, J. and Ashton, M. (2020) How will service robots redefine leadership in hotel management? A Delphi approach. *International Journal of Contemporary Hospitality Management* 32 (6), 2217–2237.

Xu, X. (2023) Visitor Experience and Emotion in Six Types of Theme Parks. Doctoral degree thesis, The University of Waikato Management School, New Zealand.

Xu, X. and Schrier, T. (2019) Hierarchical effects of website aesthetics on customers' intention to book on hospitality sharing economy platforms. *Electronic Commerce Research and Applications* 35, 100856.

Xu, X., Liu, W. and Gursoy, D. (2019) The impacts of service failure and recovery efforts on airline customers' emotions and satisfaction. *Journal of Travel Research* 58 (6), 1034–1051.

Xu, Y., Zhang, Z., Law, R. and Zhang, Z. (2020) Effects of online reviews and managerial responses from a review manipulation perspective. *Current Issues in Tourism* 23 (17), 2207–2222.

Xu, Z., Zhang, Y. and Ryan, C. (2022, June) Visitor Experience and Emotion at Six Types of Theme Parks. Paper presented at the 2022 TTRA International Conference, Victoria, British Columbia. Retrieved from https://scholarworks.umass.edu/ttra/2022/researchabstract/16/

Xu, Z., Zhang, Y. and Ryan, C. (2023, June) Do Visitors' Expressed Experiences and Emotions Vary Between Scales and Reviews? Paper presented at the *TTRA Annual International Conference, St. louis, Missouri, USA*. Retrieved from https://scholar-works.umass.edu/ttra/2023/virtual/4/

Yang, J., Ryan, C. and Zhang, L. (2013) Ethnic minority tourism in China-Han perspectives of Tuva figures in a landscape. *Tourism Management* 36, 45–56.

Yang, J., Ryan, C. and Zhang, L. (2014) Sustaining culture and seeking a Just Destination: Governments, power and tension – a life-cycle approach to analysing tourism development in an ethnic-inhabited scenic area in Xinjiang, China. *Journal of Sustainable Tourism* 22 (8), 1151–1174.

Yee, T.P. and Ismail, H.N. (2020) A review of distance decay research trends in tourism from 2000–2020. *Environment-Behaviour Proceedings Journal* 5 (14), 137–145.

Yen, H.R., Gwinner, K.P. and Su, W. (2004) The impact of customer participation and service expectation on Locus attributions following service failure. *International Journal of Service Industry Management* 15 (1), 7–16.

Yeoman, I. and Mars, M. (2012) Robots, men and sex tourism. *Futures* 44 (4), 365–371.

Yeoman, I., McMahon-Beattie, U. and Sigala, M. (eds) (2022) *Science Fiction, Disruption and Tourism*. Bristol: Channel View Publications.

Yerkes, R.M. and Dodson, J.D. (1908) The relation of strength of stimulus to rapidity of habit-formation. *Journal of Comparative Neurology and Psychology* 18, 459–482. https://doi.org/10.1002/cne.9201805037

Yiannakis, A. and Gibson, H. (1988, June 29th to July 3rd) Tourist Role Preference and Need Satisfaction: Some Continuities and Discontinuities Over the Life Course. Paper presented at the International Conference of Leisure Studies Association, Brighton, England.

Yiannakis, A. and Gibson, H. (1992) Roles tourists play. *Annals of Tourism Research* 19 (2), 287–303.

Yıldırım, O. and Çakici, A. (2020) The effect of sensation seeking on holiday preference: A comparison among domestic tourists according to their level of change seeking. *Tourism: An International Interdisciplinary Journal* 68 (1), 100–111.

Yoon, Y. and Uysal, M. (2005) An examination of effects of motivation and satisfaction on destination loyalty: A structural model. *Tourism Management* 26 (1), 45–56.

Young, B. (1983) Touristization of traditional Maltese fishing-farming villages: A general model. *Tourism Management* 4 (1), 35–41.

Zamora, N. (2022) Some People Know "Game of Thrones" Better Than Real-Life History, New Survey Shows. *Mental Floss*. April 25. Retrieved from https://www.mentalfloss.com/article/653100/game-of-thrones-vs-real-life-history-survey

Zhang, Y., Ramsey, J.R. and Lorenz, M.P. (2021) A conservation of resources schema for exploring the influential forces for air-travel stress. *Tourism Management* 83, 104240.

Zhang, X., Ryan, C., Fu, S.J. and Chen, W.B. (2021) Visitors' understanding of a film and cultural site, and reflections on contemporary China. *Tourism Management Perspectives* 40, 100909. https://doi.org/10.1016/j.tmp.2021.100909.

Zhang, X.Y., Ryan, C. and Cave, J. (2016) Residents, their use of a tourist facility and contribution to tourist ambience: Narratives from a film tourism site in Beijing. *Tourism Management* 52, 416–429.

Zhang, X., Ryan, C., Zhang, G. and Wan, Y., (2022) The Fuxi Taihao Mausoleum: Sustaining cultural tradition. *Tourism Recreation Research*, 1–18.

Zhang, X.Y., Li, P. and Ryan, C. (2023) Chinese females and vacation time.

Zikas, P., Bachlitzanakis, V., Papaefthymiou, M., Kateros, S., Georgiou, S., Lydatakis, N. and Papagiannakis, G. (2016, October) Mixed Reality Serious Games and Gamification for smart education. Paper presented at the *European Conference on Games Based Learning, England*. Retrieved from https://www.proquest.com/docview/1859715075/fulltextPDF/A59D96E818EF49E2PQ/1?accountid=17287

Zimbardo, P.G. and Boyd, J.N. (1999) Putting time in perspective: A valid, reliable individual-difference metric. *Journal of Personality and Social Psychology* 77 (6), 1271–1288.

Zoğal, V., Domènech, A. and Emekli, G. (2020) Stay at (which) home: Second homes during and after the COVID-19 pandemic. *Journal of Tourism Futures* 8 (1), 125–133.

Zou, J. and Schiebinger, L. (2018) AI can be sexist and racist—it's time to make it fair. *Nature* 559, 324–326.

Zuckerman, M. and Kuhlman, D.M. (2000) Personality and risk-taking: Common biosocial factors. *Journal of Personality* 68 (6), 999–1029.

Zuckerman, M., Eysenck, S. and Eysenck, H.J. (1978) Sensation seeking in England and America: Cross cultural and sex comparisons. *Journal of Consulting and Clinical Psychology* 46 (1), 139–149.

Zuckerman, M., Kolin, E.A., Price, L. and Zoob, I. (1964) Development of a sensation-seeking scale. *Journal of Consulting Psychology* 28 (6), 477–482.

Zurn, P. and Bassett, D.S. (2018) On curiosity: A fundamental aspect of personality, a practice of network growth. *Personality Neuroscience* 1 (e13), 1–10.

Author Index

Subject Index

201 (Also see place attachment and holiday homes)
Fast Moving Consumer Goods 4, 179
Flow Theory xiii, xiv, 19, 33, 89-107, 113, 174, 201, 209, 210

Hedonic 17-18, 42, 58, 151, 156
Hedonism/hedonist 11, 12, 58, 115, 134, 151, 187, 211
Heritage 28, 34, 57, 78, 87, 118, 121, 134, 138, 224
Hierarchy of Needs (also see Maslow), xiv, 107, 108-110, 116-117, 130, 133
Holiday homes xv, 4, 5, 19, 38, 182-194, 206-207
HOLSAT xiv, 77-79, 80
Hoteliers Dilemma 5-6

Images (of place, destinations) xiii, xiv, 3,6-7, 9, 10, 13, 35, 37, 38, 39, 50, 55-56, 58, 59, 129, 149
Images in marketing xiii, xiv, 15, 23, 24, 53, 60, 170
Images (commercialised) 181
Images (and time) 216
Interpretation 21, 24, 34, 48, 78, 83, 84, 106, 112, 117, 121, 155, 170, (Interpretation of time 205- 201)

Leisure Motivation Scale xiv, 21, 28, 126, 132, 133, 139-142, 159, 164, 210
Liminal/liminality 174, 214

Marketing 3, 4, 5, 10, 13, 15, 22, 23, 36, 37-39, 45, 50-51, 57-58, 61-62, 68-69, 71, 75, 79, 82, 87, 97-98, 109, 129, 173, 179, 192, 197-198, 202, 219
Mobility/mobilities 172, 188, 190, 198-200
Motivations xiii, 1, 3, 6, 9, 10, 11, 14, 15, 19, 20-21, 26-54, 76, 89, 90, 97, 100, 103-105, 108, 110-114, 123-131, 132-133, 137, 139-143, 145, 152, 159, 162, 164, 168, 173, 185, 191, 210

Neuroscience research 41, 47-51, 165, 166, 175, 219, 220-221, 224

New York 38, 94, 110, 150, 218

Philosophies xii, 15, 89, 94, 109, 112, 114, 115, 118, 119, 123, 152, 169, 172, 175, 180, 218, 221-224
Pilgrimage 69, 107, 174, 177, 180, 196
Place attachment xv, 4, 5, 63, 122, 146, 167-168, 182-185, 189-190, 194-198, 201
Placelessness 167
Polin Museum 171-172
Psychocentrics 30

Quality of Life 45, 101, 104, 105-107, 122, 138, 153, 160, 175, 179, 194, 221
Push and Pull Motivation xiii, 10, 26-53, 142, 164, 199

Roles of Tourists xiv, 10, 11, 19, 24, 32, 108, 132-139, 143-148

Second homes (see holiday homes)
Self-actualisation 8, 90, 106, 108, 110-117, 118, 124-126, 128, 130, 148, 152, 218
Self-determination theory 162-164
Self-image/identity 8, 11, 24, 28, 34, 37, 38, 68, 127, 173, 175, 177, 178, 180, 189, 193, 201, 210
Sensation Seeking 29, 30, 31, 32, 56, 166
ServPerf 78, 80
Servqual xiv, 57, 61-63, 71-76, 77, 78, 81, 87, 154
Stimulus 20, 30, 41-42, 44-45, 47, 49, 50-51, 56, 80, 90, 93, 97, 114, 125, 128, 132, 140, 141, 142, 144, 145, 154-157, 164, 166, 210, 213, 220
Stimulus-Organism-Response (S-O-R) theory 44-45, 51, 154, 220
Sundials 207-208

Time (perception of) xiv, 3, 23, 29, 39, 54, 56, 64, 65, 66, 71, 73, 74, 82-83, 111, 180, 209, 211, 215, 222
The Language of Tourism: A Sociolinguistic Perspective 10

Printed in the USA
CPSIA information can be obtained
at www.ICGtesting.com
JSHW061944140324
59250JS00006B/85

9 781845 419233